Solving the
Reemployment Puzzle

D0875118

DATE DUE

Solving the Reemployment Puzzle

From Research to Policy

Stephen A. Wandner

2010

W.E. Upjohn Institute for Employment Research
Kalamazoo, Michigan

Library of Congress Cataloging-in-Publication Data

Wandner, Stephen A.
  Solving the reemployment puzzle : from research to policy / Stephen A. Wandner.
  p. cm.
  Includes bibliographical references and index.
  ISBN-13: 978-0-88099-364-7 (pbk. : alk. paper)
  ISBN-10: 0-88099-364-2 (pbk. : alk. paper)
  ISBN-13: 978-0-88099-365-4 (hardcover : alk. paper)
  ISBN-10: 0-88099-365-0 (hardcover : alk. paper)
  1. Unemployed—Services for—United States. 2. Occupational training—
Government policy—United States. 3. Unemployment insurance—United States.
4. Displaced workers—United States. I. Title.
  HD5724.W265 2010
  331.13'770973—dc22
                                        2010036014

The facts presented in this study and the observations and viewpoints expressed are the sole responsibility of the author. They do not necessarily represent positions of the W.E. Upjohn Institute for Employment Research.

Cover design by Alcorn Publication Design.
Cover photo courtesy of Franklin D. Roosevelt Library.
Index prepared by Diane Worden.
Printed in the United States of America.
Printed on recycled paper.

For Leo and Joseph Grossinger

In memory of Paul Wandner

Contents

Tables

Acknowledgments

The experiments discussed in this book would not have taken place without the efforts of the many people who made them happen. The experiments had to be designed, operated, and evaluated. They involved three groups of people. First, staff within the U.S. Department of Labor initiated the projects, selected the research contractors and participating states, and then monitored the projects and their evaluations. Participants included federal government staff and contractors, who worked side by side. At the department the key participants included Bill Coyne, Wayne Gordon, Norm Harvey, Jon Messenger, Doug Scott, and Wayne Zajac. Many computer contract staff members participated in the project, including Lynn Cao, John Chang, Jun Chen, and Shu Lin-Tung.

Only a small number of research organizations in the United States have the capability to design, operate, and evaluate large social science experiments. For the Unemployment Insurance (UI) Experiments we used several of them: Abt Associates, Battelle Institute, Mathematica Policy Research, and the W.E. Upjohn Institute for Employment Research. Some of the senior researchers from these organizations who participated in the experiments were Jacob M. Benus, Walter Corson, Paul Decker, Terry R. Johnson, Stuart Kerachsky, Christopher O'Leary, Larry Orr, and Robert Spiegelman.

Finally, the experiments would not have been successful without the active support and participation of the state and local workforce agencies. The local agency staff actually ran the demonstrations. The state staff worked on their design, implementation, and management. Some of the key state staff members who worked on the projects include Bonnie Dallinger in Massachusetts; Roger Emig and Nancy Snyder in New Jersey; Howard Flot, Richard Puerzer, Larry Punch, and Jack Rudy in Pennsylvania; and Gary Bodeutsch, Kathy Countryman, Judy Johnson, Pat Remy, and Graeme Sacrison in Washington.

After the demonstration projects were completed, interventions from two of the demonstrations became policy initiatives of the department and subsequently became legislation. Passing the legislation involved large numbers of people throughout the department and in Congress. Once the programs were enacted into law, a great number of people in the department's national and regional offices, as well as in the states and localities, worked to design and implement the programs and assure that they worked the way they were supposed to work. Worker Profiling and Reemployment Services (WPRS) had to be implemented as a cooperative program involving three workforce development organizations. David Balducchi, Brian Deaton, and Jon Messenger cooperatively developed the operational design for how the Employment Service and the Job Training Partnership Act program would operate with the Unemployment Insurance Program at the state and local level to make it work.

Implementation of the WPRS system and the Self-Employment Assistance (SEA) program was accomplished by thousands of state workforce agency staff at the state and local level. They are responsible for transforming a design and some operating procedures into a living program that has helped millions of workers return to work.

At the department, the UI Experiments team made these experiments happen. Project management was divided up among members of the team. Wayne Zajac and Jon Messenger worked on the design of the New Jersey Experiment and made sure the experiment and then its evaluation worked as planned. Jon Messenger managed the Self-Employment Assistance experiments, and he played an important role in designing and implementing an active program from the federal legislation. Bill Coyne and Wayne Gordon managed the reemployment bonus experiments.

In writing this book, I owe a special debt to three colleagues. Walt Corson was coprincipal investigator for the New Jersey experiment for Mathematica Policy Research. In 1995, he and I developed a draft paper on the New Jersey Experiment and the enactment of federal legislation. We never completed the paper, but much of it survives in Chapter 2. Jon Messenger and I wrote a draft paper on the SEA program in 1997. Parts of the paper survive as Section II of Chapter 8. Finally, David Balducchi and I have talked about employment issues for many years. Of special interest to both of us has been work sharing, and we finally sat down and wrote a work sharing paper that was published in the winter 2008 issue of *Publius*. Modified parts of that paper can be found in the middle of Chapter 9. David also made important contributions to Chapter 6 on reemployment services policy, an area that he knows very well.

I also owe a debt of gratitude to the many people who have patiently answered my questions when I interviewed them. Tom Stengle provided data on the Work Sharing, Worker Profiling and Reemployment Services, and Self-Employment Assistance programs. Ralph Smith and Paul Cullinan reviewed Chapter 3. Markus Franz, counselor for labor and social affairs for the Embassy of the Federal Republic of Germany in Washington, D.C., arranged for German government officials to write a description of the German self-employment assistance and work sharing programs. He then had the description translated into English. Frank Wiessner of the Institute for Employment Research also took pity on my inability to read German and wrote an English description of the German self-employment assistance program for me.

David Balducchi did an extraordinary job of reviewing Chapters 4 through 7, Chapter 9, and the final chapter. He did more than review the chapters; he taught me a great deal about how the workforce development system works and how it has evolved over time. I received excellent comments on Chapter 8 from Jon Messenger. Two anonymous referees read the book and provided cogent comments. One of the referees, Ernie Stromsdorfer, emerged from anonymity, many years after he had served on my PhD dissertation committee. Finally, my wife, Marleigh Dover, read every chapter, and her edits enormously improved the book. I appreciate the patience of my family during the last months of writing this book, when I was consumed with finishing it.

Despite my indebtedness to a great number of people whom I have had the pleasure to work with and who have provided input to this book, I am responsible for whatever errors or shortcomings exist in the final product.

Preface

This book is about the interrelationships between research, policy, and programs that have dealt with the problems faced by experienced, unemployed workers over the past 25 years. Much of its focus is on a series of social science experiments that were conducted during the late 1980s and early 1990s. It particularly concentrates on the Unemployment Insurance (UI) Experiments, which all sought to develop cost-effective ways to help dislocated workers by speeding their return to work or by improving their earnings. These experiments are examined with respect to their evaluation results and with respect to the policy, legislative initiatives, and programs that flowed from them. The book also looks at related research and policy during this period. The major theme explored is how rigorous research has been used to effectively guide, support, and implement policy initiatives. It also tells what has happened when the research results have been ignored.

The UI Experiments examined five different ways to help UI claimants return to work: 1) comprehensive job search assistance, 2) reemployment bonuses, 3) short-term training, 4) relocation assistance, and 5) self-employment assistance (SEA). Other approaches—short-time compensation and wage supplements—have been proposed as experiments, but those experiments were never conducted.

The UI Experiments have had a substantial impact on employment and training policy. Two interventions—comprehensive job search assistance and self-employment assistance—were shown to be cost-effective and were enacted as permanent federal programs in the 1990s. A third intervention—reemployment bonuses—has been proposed as a federal program by the Clinton and Bush II administrations but has not been enacted into law. Short-time compensation became a permanent part of the UI programs, and wage supplements were made part of the current Trade Adjustment Assistance program, both despite the lack of rigorous evaluations.

I played a role in events recounted in this book because of my association with the experiments and the public policy and programs that flowed from them. In 1985, it was I who proposed conducting the experiments to Secretary of Labor William Brock and who requested funding for them from him. Funding was provided, and I oversaw the design, operation, and evaluation of the experiments between 1985 and 1996. Finally, I worked on two pieces of legislation that were enacted in 1993, as well as on the design and implementation of the two resulting programs over the next several years.

The book proceeds as follows. The first chapter provides an overview of the UI Experiments. The second chapter reviews the origins of the UI Experiments and reviews the New Jersey and Job Search Assistance (JSA) Experiments. The third chapter looks at the 1993 enactment of the Worker Profiling and Reemployment Services (WPRS) program. The fourth chapter reviews the WPRS program's implementation and operations. The fifth and sixth chapters deal with reemployment services research findings and public policy as they relate to the WPRS and other employment programs. The seventh chapter covers training research and evaluation and recent training policy. The eighth chapter reviews the SEA experiments, legislation, and program operation. Short-time compensation research and policy is discussed in the ninth chapter, followed by an analysis in the tenth chapter of the reemployment bonus experiments and unsuccessful policy initiatives. The book ends with the eleventh chapter, which summarizes the lessons learned from the research and policy of the last two and a half decades.

This book reflects the opinions of the author and not necessarily the opinions or positions of the U.S. Department of Labor.

Stephen Wandner
September 2010

1
Introduction

This book examines how research and evaluation have been conducted, and what public policy use has been made of research with respect to employment and training programs over the past 25 years. It focuses particularly on a series of social science experiments that were conducted in the 1980s and 1990s and their relationship to public policy, legislation, and programs. The book also looks more broadly at the effect of a larger body of research on public policy regarding reemployment services and training. Mostly it focuses on the research and programs designed to help dislocated workers become reemployed. The theme throughout the book is that rigorous research can have, and has had, a strong and positive impact on public policy.

But this book also examines instances in which the research findings have been ignored, contravened, or suppressed. A summary conclusion of this book is that federal policymakers made good use of sound research findings in the mid-1980s and again in the mid-1990s, but frequently misused research findings in the 2000s. To a significant extent, the book follows the story of the employment and training social science experiments that identified three cost-effective, targeted interventions: 1) comprehensive job search assistance, 2) self-employment assistance, and 3) reemployment bonuses. All three were pursued as policy options, and two were enacted into federal law.

Much of this book deals with issues with which I have been closely associated during my tenure at the U.S. Department of Labor (USDOL). I was in charge of unemployment insurance (UI) research during the 1980s and 1990s, when I developed and managed the UI Experiments.[1] As deputy director of the office that conducted research, actuarial analysis, and legislative activities, I sought to have the results of applied research guide policy and legislation. I later directed research for the department's Employment and Training Administration (ETA). As a result, this book follows the flow of policy development from research to legislation and on to program operations.

1

BACKGROUND

Worker dislocation emerged as a problem in the 1970s. At first, the problem was largely experienced by blue-collar workers as the United States deindustrialized. Later, worker dislocation became more widespread, affecting a broad spectrum of workers. Today, most layoffs are permanent, and there are relatively fewer temporary layoffs even during recessionary periods.

The Federal-State Unemployment Insurance Program is the first line of defense for dislocated workers—i.e., experienced workers who permanently lose their jobs. Because of dislocated workers' strong attachment to the labor force, they are nearly all eligible for UI, and if they are unemployed for any length of time, nearly all of them collect UI.

As a result, UI policymakers began to explore ways that UI, together with other workforce development programs, could adapt and facilitate the transition of dislocated workers into new jobs. Researchers and policymakers explored numerous ways to accomplish this goal. This book examines a wide variety of reemployment services research, but it focuses mainly on reemployment services that researchers have tested using experimental methods. Specifically, the UI Experiments examined five different ways to help UI claimants return to work: 1) comprehensive job search assistance, 2) reemployment bonuses, 3) short-term training, 4) relocation assistance, and 5) self-employment assistance. Each of these approaches was tested one or more times during the life of the UI Experiments.

The experiments received guidance from two secretaries of labor— Bill Brock and Robert Reich. Brock became secretary of labor in April 1985. That September, he approved the New Jersey Experiment and provided it with funding. He also secured funding for other experiments through a new initiative in the fiscal year 1987 federal budget. While he was secretary, he gave speeches in which he emphasized the potential importance of these experiments in developing policies to assist dislocated workers, even though he would no longer be secretary at their completion.

In early 1993, Reich became secretary of labor. He and his staff examined the results of the experiments that had been authorized by Secretary Brock and transformed them into legislative proposals. In his first year as labor secretary, Reich supported two legislative provisions, one that provided comprehensive job search assistance to dislocated workers and another that made self-employment assistance available to these workers if they wanted to start their own microenterprises. Congress enacted legislation including these initiatives before the end of Reich's first year in office.

The UI Experiments generated a number of policy initiatives. In 1993, Congress enacted Worker Profiling and Reemployment Services (WPRS) legislation, which authorizes the provision of comprehensive job search assistance services that were tested in the New Jersey Experiment. Congress also made Self-Employment Assistance (SEA) a temporary UI program in 1993 based on the Massachusetts self-employment experiment. The program was made permanent in 1998 (Table 1.1).

Table 1.1 The Unemployment Insurance Experiments: Evaluations and Legislative Activity

Intervention	Experiment site	Evaluation	Legislation
Job search assistance	New Jersey	1989—final report 1991—four-year follow-up 1995—six-year follow-up	1993—Worker Profiling and Reemployment Services (enacted)
Self-employment assistance	Massachusetts	1991—interim report	1993—Self-Employment Assistance (enacted for five years)
		1995—final report	1998—Self-Employment Assistance (permanently enacted)
Reemployment bonuses	Illinois New Jersey Pennsylvania Washington	1987—final report 1989—final report 2002—final report 2002—final report	1994—Reemployment Act (not enacted)
			2003 and 2005—Personal Reemployment Accounts (not enacted)
Individual Training Accounts	Multiple locations	2006—first "final" report	2006—Career Advancement Accounts (not enacted)
		2009—second final report	

Although four reemployment bonus experiments and subsequent analyses made the case for enacting reemployment bonuses as part of the Unemployment Insurance Program as an incentive to speed reemployment, no reemployment bonus provision was ever enacted. The Clinton administration proposed reemployment bonuses as part of the Reemployment Act of 1994—a legislative proposal that was an unsuccessful attempt to replace the Job Training Partnership Act (JTPA). Reemployment bonus policy was reborn in George W. Bush's administration, which twice proposed Personal Reemployment Accounts (PRAs), once as a free-standing bill and again as part of a bill reauthorizing the Workforce Investment Act (WIA). Neither proposal was enacted.

The Individual Training Account (ITA) Experiment tested three approaches to training, including a "free choice" model that the Bush administration used to justify its 2006 Career Advancement Accounts (CAA) proposal as the centerpiece for WIA reauthorization. But because there was little prior research or usage of the model, the justification was weak, and the legislative proposal went nowhere.

A work sharing experiment was planned, but it was never carried out. Nevertheless, work sharing was enacted as a temporary federal program in 1982 and as a permanent program in 1992. Wage supplement experiments were proposed twice, but they were never conducted. Despite the lack of testing, wage supplements became part of the Trade Adjustment Assistance (TAA) program in 2002.

Other policy initiatives were made that flew in the face of research findings. Despite findings that reemployment services are cost-effective, funding for the Reemployment Services Grants to states—used to provide services under the WPRS program—were eliminated in June 2006. Although the Employment Service's (ES) provision of job matching and other employment services had been found to be cost-effective, the Bush administration repeatedly proposed eliminating the ES and rolling its funds into block grants to the states. Similarly, the national automated labor exchange system—America's Job Bank—was evaluated and found to be cost-effective. Nevertheless, it was eliminated in June 2007.

The umbrella term "Unemployment Insurance Experiments"— described below—is used for several reasons. The experiments all involved dislocated workers who applied for and were eligible for UI.

The experiments mostly were administered by staff in the Unemployment Insurance Service rather than elsewhere in the Department of Labor.[2] The policy recommendations that have stemmed from evaluations of the experiments generally have involved amendments to federal UI legislation. The demonstration designs of two UI Experiments have been translated into programs and have been enacted as permanent provisions of UI law—the WPRS and the SEA programs.

This book reviews a wide spectrum of research—experimental and nonexperimental—that sheds light on the effectiveness of reemployment services and reemployment incentives that have implications for public policy. Research other than the UI Experiments that is relevant to public policy also is included. Going beyond the research itself, this book examines the public policy response to these experiments and other related research. In general, this book considers both the effects on public policy when research results are considered, and the effects on public policy when research results are ignored.

OVERVIEW OF THE EXPERIMENTS

The UI Experiments represented an enormous effort by the USDOL. The experiments all used rigorous evaluation methods to try to develop practical, cost-effective policies. They involved a substantial commitment of the department's research funds and staff. They were based on close and cooperative relationships between departmental staff, computer contractors, research contractors, and state and local staff from state workforce agencies.

Random Assignment

From a federal policy perspective, random assignment experiments offer the best hope of determining what works and what does not work. Once researchers agree that an approach works, it becomes easier to forge a consensus among policymakers on whether to implement interventions.

There is broad consensus among researchers that random assignment experiments are a valuable tool for developing public policy.

There is, however, disagreement about when and where to use experiments, what the balance should be between the use of experimental and quasiexperimental (comparison group) methods, and which econometric methods to use (Berlin 2007; Burtless 1995; Heckman, LaLonde, and Smith 1999; Nathan and Hollister 2008). The department has used a mixed approach to its program evaluations—a combination of experimental, quasiexperimental, and econometric methods to evaluate programs, depending on a number of different factors (Balducchi and Wandner 2009).

The UI Experiments were conducted at a time when employing experimental methods was highly desirable if legislative change was going to be accomplished. Sustaining old programs or developing new programs required convincing policymakers in the executive branch and Congress, as well as stakeholders in the programs, that policy changes were justified. During most of the period in which the experiments were conducted, the executive branch and Congress were controlled by different political parties. Divided government made it particularly difficult to obtain consensus on new policy directions. Random assignment experiments facilitated gaining agreement on the policy options that were tested.

Overview of the Demonstration Projects

The UI Experiments tested a number of different interventions that were designed to help displaced UI claimants. The interventions included comprehensive job search assistance (JSA), reemployment bonuses, training and training vouchers, and self-employment assistance. The experiments stemmed from a desire to both improve existing interventions (such as JSA and training) and test new interventions (such as reemployment bonuses, self-employment assistance, and training vouchers). In addition, the Department of Labor sought to use random assignment methods to test work sharing and wage supplements, but neither of those experiments came to fruition.

The UI Experiments were expensive to conduct and represented a significant but minority portion of the department's research budget for employment and training programs. The cost of the UI Experiments can be broken down into operational costs and research costs. The operational costs were paid directly to the state workforce agencies or Workforce Investment Boards (WIBs) that participated in the demonstration projects. These agencies agreed to carry out the interventions that were proposed. Research funds were provided to private research firms that were selected to design, monitor, and evaluate the projects. Operational costs were approximately $24 million for the 11 demonstrations, for an average of approximately $2.2 million per demonstration, and varied from no cost to nearly $6 million (Table 1.2). Those costs included the treatments themselves as well as administrative funds for the states or localities that operated the demonstrations.

In addition to the operational costs, total research costs for the 11 experiments amounted to more than $18 million, or an average cost per experiment of less than $1.7 million. However, the last three demonstration projects cost much more than those that were operated in the late 1980s and early 1990s. Funding for the experiments initially came largely from JTPA funds and later from WIA appropriations for research and evaluations. The UI Experiments staff obtained USDOL research and demonstration funding. In two cases, however, the funding for the experiments came from the federal portion of the Unemployment Trust Fund (UTF). Federal legislation mandated UTF funding both for the JSA Demonstration in Florida and Washington, DC, and for the Massachusetts SEA Demonstration. The UTF was available as a funding source because the demonstrations provided reemployment services to UI beneficiaries.

The responsibilities of the research contractors consisted of designing, implementing, monitoring, and evaluating costs. To facilitate project monitoring and evaluation by the research contractors and departmental staff, project tracking systems were developed; they were used for operational purposes, for random assignment of individuals into the treatment and control groups, and for gathering administrative data for project evaluation. Because the data was entered in real time, the tracking system allowed constant monitoring of the quality of the operations. Moreover, in the case of the reemployment bonus demonstrations, tracking was used to determine when to stop project enrollment to ensure that the project did not go over budget. Evaluation costs included the collection of project and administrative data, the administration of telephone surveys, and the conducting of implementation, net impact, and cost-benefit analyses.

Table 1.2 U.S. Department of Labor Experiments, 1986 to Present: Descriptive Information

Experiment	Dates	Number of treatments	Sample size[a]	Number of sites	Partners	Funding (millions $)
UI Experiments						
New Jersey Experiment	1986–87	3	T = 8,675; C = 2,385	10	State	3.4[b]
Pennsylvania Reemployment Bonus Experiment	1988–89	4	T = 11,410; C = 3,595	12	State	2.2
Washington Reemployment Bonus Experiment	1988–90	6	N = 17,000	21	State	1.1[c]
Massachusetts SEA Experiment	1990–93	1	T = 755; C = 752	7	State	UTF[d]
Washington SEA Experiment	1989–91	1	T = 614; C = 608	6	State	ca. 5.0
D.C. JSA Experiment	1995–96	3	N = 8,071	1[e]	State	UTF = 1.3[d,f]
Florida JSA Experiment	1995–96	3	N = 12,042	10	State	UTF = 1.4[d,f]
Maryland Work Search Experiment	1994–95	4	N = 27,000+	6	State	ca. 0.25[g]
Other Related Experiments						
Lifelong Learning Experiment	1995–97	1	T = 104,668	12[h]	Educational	0.0[i]
ITA Experiment, original	2000–04	3	T = 7,922; C = 0	8	Local boards	4.3
Project GATE	2003–04	1	T = 2,097; C = 2,104	5	3 states	4.0

[a] T = treatment group; C = control group; N = sample.
[b] Mathematica Policy Research was funded by the New Jersey Department of Labor from an overall grant to conduct the New Jersey Experiment. The total cost of $4.7 million was split between research costs of $1.3 million and operational costs of $3.4 million.
[c] The Washington Reemployment Bonus Experiment was originally funded from USDOL research funds in the amount of $1.0 million. The Upjohn Institute conducted the design, monitoring, and evaluation of the experiment with its own funds, but it received supplemental research funding in the amount of $90,000 from the Alfred P. Sloan Foundation.
[d] UTF = Unemployment Trust Fund. For the Massachusetts SEA and the Florida and District of Columbia JSA experiments, the states were able to draw funds from their state UTF accounts to pay for self-employment allowances and for job search assistance. In both cases, the states participating in these experiments were given this authority through federal legislation.

[e] JSA services were provided by one site, but participants were selected based on their UI claims at all local UI offices, including those in suburban Maryland and Virginia, where D.C. claimants could file D.C. claims for D.C. benefits.

[f] For the JSA Experiment, the funding source was the Unemployment Trust Fund. Decker et al. (2000, p. 68) put the total UTF-funded demonstration costs at $1,301,267 for D.C. and $1,356,659 for Florida. Greenberg and Shroder (2004) put the combined cost of the two demonstration projects at $2.68 million.

[g] For the Maryland Work Search Experiment, Greenberg and Shroder (2004) put the cost at $250,000. But in an e-mail message to me on November 16, 2007, Michelle Wood said that all funding went to Abt, in the amount of $248,000. There is no indication of funding provided to Maryland to conduct the demonstration. This figure was confirmed by a February 25, 2008, telephone interview with Tom Wendell, Maryland UI director.

[h] Twelve Baltimore-area institutions participated, including community colleges, private career colleges, and four-year colleges and universities.

[i] A portion of the funding provided to Abt for the Lifelong Learning Demonstration was used to operate the project, but no funding was given directly to the state of Maryland or to the educational institutions, so the amount is shown as 0.

SOURCE: Greenberg and Shroder (2004); UI Experiment evaluation reports; USDOL grant and contract files; research contractor files.

The UI Experiments generally tested a single intervention, but they frequently included multiple treatment groups to test design features such as the method of providing the treatment or the payment level for a reemployment bonus. The New Jersey Experiment, however, was more ambitious and tested three different treatments: 1) comprehensive job search assistance, 2) training (and relocation allowances), and 3) reemployment bonuses.

Most of the UI Experiments offered reemployment services or incentives to a large group of individuals. Sample sizes of the treatment and control groups had to be sufficiently large to allow for evaluation of treatment impact both in the aggregate and with respect to important subgroups. Workers were randomly assigned to treatment or control groups in all experiments except the training voucher experiment. In that case, training vouchers had already been mandated by the WIA, so three different approaches to providing training vouchers were compared to one another rather than to a control group.

The Players and the Process: The Executive Branch and Congress

The UI Experiments would not have been carried out without the support of departmental policymakers, Congress, and state and local workforce agencies. The department took the lead in initiating the experiments, administering them, proposing policy initiatives, and implementing the two new programs that flowed from them. In 1985, I had proposed the experiments for consideration by the incoming secretary of labor, William Brock.[3] Secretary Brock previously had been United States Trade Representative, the country's chief trade negotiator; in that capacity, he had been concerned about the plight of American workers dislocated by the effects of international trade. He quickly supported the experiments as a new departmental initiative. Indeed, he went to the Office of Management and Budget and gained support for a special appropriation to begin the experiments. A number of assistant secretaries for Employment and Training and many other policymakers and staff also supported the experiments.

The final evaluation of the New Jersey Experiment was completed in 1989, and an interim evaluation of the SEA experiments was completed in 1992. In 1993, Secretary Reich used these findings to propose two new pieces of legislation: 1) WPRS, which was based on the job search assistance component of the New Jersey Experiment, and 2) SEA, based on the Massachusetts SEA Demonstration. The Clinton administration supported these two initiatives, and administration staff members were able to gain bipartisan congressional support for both initiatives. General confidence in the integrity of the evaluations of these two interventions helped them to garner widespread support.

Congress supported the UI Experiments at their inception in 1985 and appropriated $5.0 million to fund some of the experiments in 1986. Later, Congress relied on evaluations of the JSA and the Massachusetts SEA experiments, and the project designs were the basis for the federal legislative proposals. Congress supported the proposals for JSA and SEA programs and enacted them into law in 1993. The SEA program was enacted with a five-year sunset provision. In 1998, Congress made the program permanent. In contrast, Congress considered reemployment bonuses in 1994 and 2003 but did not authorize states to offer them as a means of encouraging the unemployed to return to work.

Cooperative Effort

Setting up and operating the UI Experiments was a cooperative effort between state, federal, and contractor staff. Labor Department staff generally selected the participating state workforce agencies and the research contractor with the concurrence of the assistant secretary for Employment and Training. State workforce agencies and local offices were recruited, although in cases where many states were interested in participating, competitive selection processes were established. The research contractor and USDOL staff secured the interest and support of states for random assignment methods and the experimental design of the project. Participating state and local staff were trained so that they could carry out the experimental design. State and local staff then operated the demonstration project.

Close monitoring of the experiments by USDOL staff and the research contractors helped ensure that they were carried out as they had been designed. In many cases, state work agency staff from the state central office also participated in the monitoring.

The evaluations of the experiments were conducted by research contractors but with the close cooperation of Labor Department staff. Evaluations required the gathering of high-quality project and administrative data from the states. Expensive surveys conducted by the evaluators provided input to the evaluation. The survey data were needed when the project evaluation required more than UI wage records—employment, earnings, and retention data—to measure project outcomes. When the evaluations were completed, the department reviewed and commented on the evaluation reports before accepting them.

The Players and the Process, Part 2: The State Workforce Agencies

State workforce agencies and the local offices that run their programs often do not like random assignment projects. Random assignment is a rigorous process that is very different from the way individuals are normally selected to participate in reemployment services in ongoing programs. The idea of random assignment is sometimes seen as inequitable, whereas describing this approach as a "lottery" is more easily understood and supported.[4]

The UI Experiments were carefully designed to test the treatments while not interfering with the regular operations of the UI, the ES, or training programs. State program administrators would not support demonstration projects that interfered with the daily operations of their programs or with the state computer systems that are critical for their operation.

The state workforce agencies played a crucial role: they volunteered to participate in the experiments, participated in developing the demonstration designs, implemented the demonstrations, provided administrative data, made participating staff available for interviews, and facilitated the conducting of the evaluations by the researchers. State workforce agencies were involved in all of the projects, although for the Lifelong Learning Demonstration the participating organizations were a number of Maryland community colleges and universities, and for the Individual Training Account Experiment the participating agencies were local WIBs.

When two of the experiments resulted in changes to federal legislation, the entire state workforce system was affected. Since participation in the WPRS initiative became mandatory for state UI programs, all state and local offices have participated in WPRS. By contrast, participation in the SEA program is voluntary, and fewer than a dozen states have been involved in program implementation and operation.

The Research Contractors That Conducted the UI Experiments

The UI Experiments were conducted by a relatively small number of research contractors because few research firms in the United States have experience in running social science experiments for workforce programs. In each experiment, a single research group designed, monitored, and evaluated the project. Although consideration was given to using different contractors—one to design the project and another to evaluate it—that approach was ultimately considered impractical.

For all of the experiments except the Washington Reemployment Bonus Experiment, the contract to design, conduct, and evaluate the demonstration project was competitively bid. In the case of the Washington experiment, the W.E. Upjohn Institute for Employment Research offered to conduct the experiment without a fee, so its arrangements with the USDOL were contained in a nonfinancial agreement.

The research contractors used in the experiments were Abt Associates, Battelle Memorial Institute, IMPAQ International, Mathematica Policy Research (MPR), Social Policy Research Associates, and the Upjohn Institute. Of the 11 experiment evaluations listed in Table 1.1, the principal evaluators of these projects were tightly concentrated: MPR evaluated five, Abt three, and Battelle, the Upjohn Institute, and IMPAQ International one each (Table 1.3).

The concentration of evaluators for UI Experiments followed a similar pattern for social experiments in general. A review of 70 U.S. social science experiments conducted between 1983 and 1996—when most of the UI Experiments were initiated—found that 47 percent of experiments were evaluated by the "Big Three": Abt, MDRC, and MPR. Of the rest, 19 percent were evaluated by academics, 10 percent by government employees, and the remaining 24 percent by a diverse group of think tanks and private sector firms. Academics generally evaluated smaller experiments, and government employees were generally the evaluators of state-sponsored experiments (Greenberg and Shroder 2004, p. 466). Since the UI Experiments were large in size, the dominance of the Big Three is not surprising. Because MDRC works almost exclusively with disadvantaged or low-wage worker popula-

Table 1.3 U.S. Department of Labor Experiments, 1986 to Present: Research Contractors and Funding Levels

Experiment	Contractor	Contractor funding (millions $)
UI Experiments		
New Jersey Experiment	MPR	1.23[a]
Pennsylvania Reemployment Bonus Experiment	MPR	1.00
Washington Reemployment Bonus Experiment	Upjohn Institute	Nonfinancial agreement[b]
Massachusetts and Washington SEA Experiments	Abt/Battelle	1.65
D.C. and Florida JSA Demos	MPR/Battelle	1.50
Maryland Work Search Demo	Abt/Battelle	0.25
Other Experiments		
Lifelong Learning Experiment	Abt	2.88[c]
ITA Experiment, original	MPR/SPRA	3.53[d]
Second Survey	MPR/SPRA	1.30
Project GATE	IMPAQ/MPR	6.40[e]

[a] Mathematica Policy Research was funded by the New Jersey Department of Labor from the overall grant that it was awarded to conduct the New Jersey Experiment. The total cost of $4.7 million was split between the research cost of 1.3 million and the operational cost of $3.4 million (Greenberg and Shroder 2004). In an e-mail message to the author on December 10, 2007, Paul Decker, president of Mathematica Policy Research, indicated that, according to Mathematica contract files, the research cost was $1.23 million.

[b] Self-financed by the W.E. Upjohn Institute for Employment Research, with additional research funding provided to the Upjohn Institute by the Alfred P. Sloan Foundation. USDOL had a nonfinancial agreement with Upjohn to conduct the evaluation. Greenberg and Shroder (2004) incorrectly indicate that the cost was $450,000.

[c] Some of the funding provided to Abt was used for project operations.

[d] The contract for $2.2 million was supplemented with $0.7 million in 1998. Greenberg and Shroder (2004) put the total at $2.2 million.

[e] In a telephone conversation with the author on June 9, 2007, Janet Javar gave the following figures: the MPR contract was for $4,027,990. About $500,000 of that was used for the ITA/ETP (Eligible Training Provider) Demonstration, and the balance of $3,528,000 was used for the ITA Experiment.

SOURCE: Greenberg and Shroder (2004); USDOL grant and contract files; research contractor files.

tions rather than with dislocated workers, it did not bid on any of the UI Experiments.

The USDOL contracted directly with all of the contractors except in three cases. For the New Jersey Experiment, the state of New Jersey contracted with Mathematica Policy Research. For the Maryland Work Search Demonstration, the state of Maryland contracted with Abt Associates. For the Washington Reemployment Bonus project, the USDOL signed a nonfinancial agreement with the Upjohn Institute.

U.S. Department of Labor Staff

Within the department, all eight of the UI Experiments were conducted by the Unemployment Insurance Demonstration Group within the Unemployment Insurance Service. This group was formed in response to the high level of effort required to conduct the experiments. The purpose of the group was to conduct the series of demonstration projects to determine whether new approaches could be found to help dislocated workers—most of whom were also UI claimants—return to work. The group formed in 1985 to work on the New Jersey Experiment and continued in existence for over a decade, until the last of the eight projects had been completed. Three related projects were conducted by the staff in the ETA's Office of Policy Development and Research.[5]

Contract computer staff worked along with departmental staff in designing, developing, maintaining, and overseeing the data systems. They developed an operational and research database that allowed the USDOL and the research contractor to monitor and manage the experiments with data that was available in real time. The project data systems could be used both to manage the projects and to accumulate the data that would be needed to evaluate the demonstrations.[6]

THE UNEMPLOYMENT INSURANCE PROGRAM

The UI Experiments were conducted within the national UI program. They were all designed to transform the UI program into a reemployment program, while maintaining its essential role as an income maintenance program.

The UI program was established by the Social Security Act of 1935, and it has operated for more than seven decades. It pays unemployment insurance benefits to workers who are unemployed through no fault of their own. UI benefits replace about half of lost wages up to a maximum amount that is set by each state. The average weekly payment was $300 in 2008. In almost all states, workers can receive up to 26 weeks of regular benefits. Thus, in normal economic times the average unemployed worker can receive up to approximately $7,500 while unemployed during a year.

Workers drawing UI must show that they are able, available, and actively searching for work. Indeed, they must certify that they are searching for work each time they request another UI payment. Workers who are permanently separated from their previous jobs must register for work with the local Wagner-Peyser Act agency—i.e., the Employment Service. They must accept a job to which they are referred if that job is determined to be suitable. The suitability determination includes consideration of whether the job to which the unemployed worker is referred pays a wage similar to the worker's previous job.

Wagner-Peyser agencies provide a wide variety of reemployment services to workers permanently separated from their jobs who receive benefits. However, these workers are not assured that they will actually receive all of the options in the wide spectrum of assistance when searching for a new job. Wagner-Peyser agencies target reemployment services to individual workers based on a determination of which services are likely to work for which individuals. Because of limited funding, ES staff also have to make allocation decisions among a broad group of workers who could benefit from the various possible services.

Unemployed workers can receive UI benefits whether they are on temporary or permanent layoffs, but it is the permanently displaced workers who need assistance in finding new jobs. This book therefore concentrates on displaced workers and the ways of providing reemployment services—or reemployment incentives—to them.

The UI Experiments were established to determine which reemployment services and incentives were most effective in returning permanently separated UI beneficiaries to work. It is important to know what interventions work so that workers can receive those services that will speed their return to work or increase their human capital.

In addition, because of limited resources, not all workers can be provided all services, even among those services that were determined to be effective for a wide variety of unemployed workers. Thus, a system of targeting had to be developed. The system of targeting treatments to workers who are most likely to exhaust their entitlement to UI benefits is called worker profiling.

DISLOCATED WORKERS AND THE NEED FOR REEMPLOYMENT SERVICES

The UI Experiments focused on UI beneficiaries who were permanently separated from their jobs both because of the increase in worker displacement over the preceding decade and because most dislocated workers who are unemployed for more than a few weeks collect UI benefits. Thus the UI system searched for ways to help these UI beneficiaries speed their return to work or assist them in improving their skills through education and training. In addition, at the time the experiments commenced, prior research had concentrated more on disadvantaged than on dislocated workers, and more was known about the effectiveness of workforce programs for disadvantaged workers than for dislocated ones because policymakers were more concerned with this population (LaLonde 1995, p. 161). The time was ripe to devote federal resources to conducting large-scale experiments to determine what worked to help reemploy dislocated workers.

The targeting of dislocated workers by the UI Experiments was atypical: a study of 193 social science experiments that were undertaken between 1962 and 1996 found that most of them targeted a population of disadvantaged individuals or families. Taken together, these experiments served welfare recipients (35 percent), low-income families (14 percent), the unemployed (13 percent), and youth (12 percent) (Greenberg and Shroder 2004, p. 461). The UI Experiments were a subset of the 13 percent of experiments serving the unemployed; they served the less disadvantaged portion of that population, since they dealt with unemployed workers who had had a strong enough attachment to the labor force to qualify for unemployment insurance but were nevertheless permanently separated from their previous jobs. Average UI recipients had prior annual earnings that placed them and their families at about double the poverty line, and when these workers become reemployed they are not likely to join the poor. For example, the average weekly wage for all workers in UI-covered employment was $854 in 2007, and the average annual wage in covered employment was over $43,000.

The Problem of Worker Dislocation

Worker dislocation has been a significant problem in the United States over the past three decades. By 1984, the problem was widely recognized, and the Bureau of Labor Statistics (BLS) responded by initiating a biennial series of special dislocated worker surveys as supplements to the Current Population Survey (CPS), in order to estimate the magnitude of the problem and to discern any trends in worker dislocation. These surveys showed that in the 1980s approximately 2 million long-tenured workers were dislocated each year. While the numbers increased during periods of recession, they remained high in all years, even years with relatively low unemployment. In the 1980s, worker dislocation was concentrated in the goods-producing sector of the economy, but there also was significant dislocation among workers in the service sector and among white-collar workers (CBO 1993).

The nature of worker dislocation has changed since the 1980s, however, and the problem has become more pervasive. In the 1990s, the share of worker dislocation among service-sector and white-collar workers increased, narrowing the gap relative to goods-producing industries (Hipple 1999). While the rate of worker dislocation remained higher in manufacturing and construction than in other industries, in 2002 the actual number of dislocated white-collar workers (1.2 million) was almost twice the number of dislocated blue-collar workers (0.65 million) and nearly 10 times the number of those in service occupations. The total number of long-tenured dislocated workers in 2002 was 2.0 million (Helwig 2004).

The BLS definition of "dislocated workers" is a narrow one, restricted to unemployed workers who lost jobs they had held for three years or longer because 1) their plant closed, 2) their employer went out of business, or 3) their employer laid them off and they were not recalled. Many UI claimants do not meet this definition, even if they are permanently separated from their previous jobs by their employers. A study of UI recipients by Corson and Dynarski (1990) shows that while more than half of unemployed workers had no expectation of recall, only about 36 percent of them met the BLS definition of worker dislocation.[7]

In the seven fiscal years from 2000–2001 to 2006–2007, the number of unemployed workers collecting a UI first payment varied between 7.4 million and 10.4 million. In February 2008, the department projected the number to remain steady at approximately 8 million over the next six years (USDOL 2008a). At least half of these UI recipients, or approximately 4 million of them, are likely to be permanently separated from their jobs and likely will benefit from receiving reemployment services. In addition, reemployment services may be needed by workers who do not collect UI, including reentrants to the labor force.

What has changed in the past two decades is that laid-off workers are decreasingly on temporary layoff. For many decades now, the permanent layoff rate has been much greater than the temporary layoff rate. In addition, the permanent layoff rate always has been, and continues to be, highly cyclical, increasing sharply in recessionary periods. In contrast, while the proportion of workers on temporary layoffs formerly was highly cyclical—spiking during recessions—the temporary layoff rate is now steady and low over the cycle. Since the mid-1980s, in fact, the temporary layoff rate has been relatively flat and has remained well below 2 percent. Groshen and Potter (2003, p. 3) find a structural change in the U.S. economy with respect to temporary layoffs. "In the four recessions before 1990," they write, "unemployment from temporary layoffs rose throughout the downturn and fell sharply after the trough, adding substantially to the run-up and then the decline in total unemployment. In the 1990–91 and 2001 recessions, by contrast, temporary layoffs contributed little to the path of unemployment. These layoffs barely increased in the 1990–91 recession and figured even less importantly in the 2001 recession."

With permanent layoffs becoming predominant, more unemployed workers need assistance in returning to work. Studies show that dislocated workers experience substantial earnings loss when they return to work (Kletzer 1998). Based on BLS survey data comparing their wages before and after unemployment, Farber (1997) estimates that, between 1985 and 1995, dislocated workers experienced wage losses of

13 percent. Those dislocated also have a tough time finding work: in the 2001–2003 BLS survey, 35 percent of job losers remained unemployed at the survey date, and 13 percent of those who had lost full-time jobs were only employed part time (Farber 2005). Dislocated workers also experienced longer durations of unemployment before they returned to work.

For those dislocated workers served by the WIA and ES systems, there are an array of available services consisting of core, intensive, and training services. Because of funding limitations, however, training services cannot be made available to all dislocated workers. Since 2002, approximately 200,000 WIA Adult and Dislocated Worker program participants have received training annually.[8] Under the 2006 Bush administration proposal that would have replaced much of the employment and training system with a CAA training voucher, the number of workers receiving public training would have increased to between 500,000 and 600,000 per year.

Even if CAAs had been implemented, training would have been offered to only a small portion of the approximately 2 million workers that become dislocated each year and an even smaller portion of all UI recipients who are permanently separated. For the vast majority of workers, when they come to the department-funded One-Stop Career Centers, they can expect to receive no more than the core and intensive services available under the WIA and ES programs. As a result, we need to look at what is known about the effectiveness of the delivery and targeting of comprehensive job search assistance and other reemployment services.

Dislocated worker studies reveal that dislocated workers have labor force characteristics that can be used for statistical targeting by applying worker profiling methods. While not all dislocated workers have difficulty becoming reemployed, a large portion of those having long job tenure are likely to need some type of reemployment assistance. Workers who accumulated three years' tenure or more with their previous employer have been found to experience longer spells of unemployment and to be more likely to experience a reduction in earnings of 20 percent or greater than workers with less than three years of tenure (CBO 1993). Thus, tenure at job separation may be an important indicator of the risk of becoming unemployed over a long period and experiencing an earnings loss. This and related findings were considered in designing a worker profiling methodology.

Reemploying Dislocated Workers: The Role of the Unemployment Insurance Program

The traditional role of the unemployment insurance program is to pay temporary income support to unemployed workers. UI's underlying premise is that unemployed workers' skills will match job vacancies in local labor markets, and that vacancies can be discovered with a combination of reasonable search efforts and watchful waiting. This premise has determined the states' basic approach to administering their UI programs. State UI programs test whether unemployed workers are able, available, and actively seeking work. In most states, program administration stresses monitoring workers' continuing attachment to the labor force for those to whom it pays UI benefits, to make sure they are searching for work. Providing reemployment services to help them return to work has received less emphasis.

The UI system began paying benefits in 1938, but the UI program soon became insignificant with the advent of World War II, a period of relatively full employment. From the end of that war through the early 1970s, workers displaced from their jobs tended to represent a sufficiently small number of all UI claimants that the UI program's limited emphasis on reemployment services appeared warranted. It was only with the emergence of worker dislocation as a major phenomenon in the late 1970s and the 1980s that the need to provide UI claimants with reemployment services emerged.[9]

Even today, dislocated workers with long tenure make up only a minority of all UI claimants—perhaps one-quarter of the claimants served in a year. These workers, however, have needs beyond income support, and they frequently have great difficulty returning to work without the receipt of reemployment services from the ES or from WIA's Adult and Dislocated Worker programs.

In recent years, worker dislocation has become an area of increasing concern to the UI program. Overall, the UI program serves just half of all dislocated workers. However, the UI system serves nearly all dislocated workers likely to experience long-term unemployment, the group most in need of reemployment assistance. Many dislocated workers return to work quickly, even if they have been permanently separated, and many of these early returnees never file for UI benefits (Vroman 1991, 2008; Wandner and Stengle 1997).[10] Thus, over a year, UI serves fewer than one-third of the dislocated workers who have been unemployed for less than five weeks, but it serves 80 to 90 percent of those unemployed for 15 weeks or longer (O'Leary and Wandner 1997). This latter group represents the great majority of all dislocated workers who need reemployment assistance to obtain new jobs. Because the UI program serves these workers when they first become unemployed, it is well-positioned to act as a gateway for early referral to reemployment services.

TREATMENTS TESTED AND METHODS OF EVALUATION

The treatments provided in the UI Experiments are typical of those provided by most social experiments. In a study of the 193 experiments started between 1962 and 1996, 293 different treatments were tested. Only 26 of these treatments focused on areas outside of employment. The 267 employment treatments provided education and training (92), job placement and job search assistance (94), information and counseling (57), and income transfers (24). Thus, the concentration of experimental treatments on employment is common across all organizations sponsoring experiments and across all populations served (Greenberg and Shroder 2004, p. 461).

More specifically, the UI Experiments tested the following treatments in the following states or other sites: comprehensive job search assistance (Washington, New Jersey, the District of Columbia, Florida, and Pennsylvania); training and education (New Jersey, Lifelong Learning, and ITA experiment sites); reemployment bonuses (New Jersey, Pennsylvania, and Washington state experiments); and self-employment assistance (Massachusetts and Washington). The fact that there were multiple tests of the same treatment generally served three functions: 1) to verify earlier results (i.e., comprehensive job search assistance and reemployment bonuses); 2) to search for more cost-effective approaches (i.e., training and education); and 3) to test new reemployment approaches (i.e., self-employment assistance).

Because over 90 percent of the 293 treatments studied by Greenberg and Shroder concentrated on employment and work, the evaluations of these treatments have tended to concentrate on the same outcomes. Four-fifths of the studies begun between 1983 and 1996 examined the effect of the treatments on employment and earnings (Greenberg and Shroder 2004, p. 461). Similarly, all of the UI Experiments examined the treatments' effects on employment and earnings.

The 193 social experiments frequently included process analyses and benefit-cost analyses. For the completed studies that Greenberg and Shroder examine, benefit-cost analyses were conducted in just under half of the evaluations. Benefit-cost analysis has become increasingly prevalent.

In general, Greenberg and Shroder find that social experiments have become simpler, more streamlined, and cheaper over time. Experiments have increasingly tested incremental changes in existing programs, rather than testing new programs. Between 1962 and 1974, over four-fifths of experiments tested new programs, whereas since 1983 only one-quarter of experiments completed have tested new programs. This change may stem from declining public funds to conduct more ambitious experiments and a perception that incremental changes to existing programs are more likely to be implemented.

The way experiments have been operated also has been streamlined. The cost of administering the treatments tested has declined because of at least six factors: 1) increased use of administrative data rather than the use of more expensive surveys, 2) reduced sample attrition, 3) administration of experiments by agencies already serving the target population, 4) shorter follow-up tracking periods, 5) a declining number of treatment groups, and 6) more rapid evaluation, completion, and release of results. As a result both of less expensive treatments and project administration and of simpler project designs, sample sizes for treatments have increased (Table 1.1). The median sample size for experiments has increased from 401 in the period 1962–1974 to 870 during 1975–1982 and to 2,312 during 1983–1996 (Greenberg and Shroder 2004, pp. 462–465). Because the UI Experiments were looking for treatments that worked, they tested both new programs (self-employment assistance, reemployment bonuses, and training vouchers) and programs with incremental changes (enhanced training, education, and job search assistance).

Social experiments are highly concentrated in certain areas of the United States. Although Greenberg and Shroder find that experiments have been run in every state except Alaska and Idaho, they also find that the same states have participated repeatedly. The nine states that participated most frequently in completed experiments were New York (27); California (26); Illinois (19); Pennsylvania (19); Ohio (16); and Florida, Massachusetts, Texas, and Washington, all with 13 each (Greenberg and Shroder 2004, p. 469). It is thus not surprising that the UI Experiments were run in five of these nine states (Illinois, Pennsylvania, Florida, Massachusetts, and Washington). In addition, Texas unsuccessfully applied to participate in the reemployment bonus demonstrations, and California would have been one of the work sharing experimental sites if the experiment had not been canceled.

The funding source for social experiments has changed over time. The federal government has been the dominant funder of experiments, but its role has declined: it went from funding 80 percent of experiments during 1962–1982 to funding 64 percent during 1983–1996. Over that same period, state funding increased from 18 to 40 percent, but most of that increase was due to the evaluations of welfare reform under state waivers that took place before the enactment of the Temporary Assistance for Needy Families (TANF) program in 1996 (Greenberg and Shroder 2004, p. 465).

The UI Experiments ended without testing other promising treatments for dislocated workers. For example, they did not test the effects of providing wage supplements to dislocated workers. A wage supplement experiment for trade-affected workers who found new jobs paying less than their old ones was required by federal law in the late 1980s, but the requirement was dropped because states were unwilling to participate. A more recent legislative proposal—this one for a wage supplement experiment for TAA-eligible workers—instead became an entitlement program in 2002.

Some treatments that have already been tested experimentally have not been revisited. Although classroom training has been closely studied, a number of additional training experiments could be tested. For example, researchers could compare alternative training methods (e.g., on-the-job training versus classroom training), could vary training by duration or intensity, could focus more on incumbent training, could compare training by fields of study, and could compare types of training providers (e.g., nonprofit versus for-profit). A number of comprehensive reemployment services also need to be tested or retested using experimental methods.

TARGETING

The UI Experiments tested various ES and WIA reemployment services and incentives that might help displaced claimants return to work more quickly and in some cases increase their earnings.

The experiments were designed with two types of targeting in mind. First, since the goal of the experiments was to find cost-effective treatments, the treatments had to be targeted to the workers for whom they would be most cost-effective. Second, even if cost-effective treatments could be identified, the limited availability of funding meant that an objective targeting mechanism was needed to select and limit the claimants who would be referred to services.

Targeting thus was an integral part of the UI Experiments. Later chapters will show that the experiments' design included both built-in targeting and the use of subgroup analysis in project evaluation to determine for whom the treatments would be most cost-effective.

When federal legislation was enacted in the form of WPRS and SEA, the legislation mandated targeting, and the Department of Labor developed a worker profiling method that was adopted by the participating state workforce agencies. Worker profiling also would have been mandated by reemployment bonus programs that were unsuccessfully proposed by both the Clinton and Bush II administrations.

More recently, new targeting methods have been developed and used for TANF, welfare-to-work, and training and education programs (Eberts, O'Leary, and Wandner 2002). The Frontline Decision Support System (FDSS), which operated in Georgia, incorporated a comprehensive approach to targeting reemployment services for workforce development programs at local One-Stops. The FDSS project systematically helped dislocated workers return to work by matching them with job openings, helping them search for work, and referring them to targeted, cost-effective reemployment services (Eberts and O'Leary 2004).

The United States was an innovator in the development of worker profiling methods. Similar approaches have been studied and adopted elsewhere, first in Australia and Canada and then in other industrial nations (OECD 1998; Rudolph and Konle-Seidl 2005).

Targeting is recognized as an important component of active labor market policies throughout the industrialized world. An International Labour Organization review of the provision of reemployment services in industrialized countries finds that "carefully targeted measures can achieve better results than broad measures applying to everyone or larger groups" (Auer, Efendioğlu, and Leschke 2005).

BUDGET NEUTRALITY

The design of the UI Experiments and the eventual enactment of both WPRS and SEA in 1993 were greatly influenced by federal budget rules initiated in the 1980s. These rules were designed to reduce the budget deficit, and they constrained the development of all new federally sponsored programs that might eventually be enacted into law, including any new approaches to reemployment services.

The congressional budget process was established by the Congressional Budget Act of 1974. Because of persistent federal budget deficits in the early 1980s, Congress enacted the Balanced Budget and Emergency Deficit Control Act of 1985 (also known by the name of its sponsors as the Gramm-Rudman-Hollings [GRH] Act) to impose additional discipline on the federal budget. Under the temporary GRH Act, federal deficit targets were set to decline each year until they reached the final target of a zero deficit by fiscal year 2000. While deficits did shrink somewhat under GRH, the budget targets were not met, in large part because of economic and other factors that were beyond the control of the budget process.

When GRH did not succeed in bringing the deficit to zero, Congress tried a new approach, enacting the Budget Enforcement Act (BEA) of 1990. The BEA had a two-part approach to enforcing budget discipline: it established separate constraints on discretionary and mandatory ("direct") spending, but for both types of spending it only attempted to make Congress responsible for actions within its control. The BEA rules were in effect for fiscal years 1991 through 2002. During that period, discretionary spending—which annual appropriation acts controlled and provided the funds for—was constrained by statutory limits. Violations of those limits were subject to a process of sequestration, which corrected such violations with automatic, across-the-board spending reductions for all discretionary spending. For mandatory spending, a "pay as you go" (PAYGO) rule placed limits on new legislation that was estimated to result in either increased expenditures or decreased revenues. Congress could not enact new legislation that would increase the cost of entitlement programs, such as the UI program, without providing simultaneous offsetting reductions in expenditures or increases in revenue. If Congress did not adhere to these PAYGO rules, mandatory expenditures could also be subject to sequestration (Holtz-Eakin 2004; Keith 2007).

By the time the first UI Experiment was being designed, GRH had already taken effect. Thus, all of these experiments operated within the strictures of these budget limits, and any policy and legislative proposals developed were also subject to these limits. New proposals could avoid the GRH constraints only by fully paying for themselves within the federal government sector. As a result, the UI Experiments were designed with the goal of being cost-effective, not just to society as a whole, but, more restrictively, to the federal government. The evaluations of the UI Experiments therefore also examined the cost-effectiveness of these interventions, both from the perspective of the federal government as a whole and from the perspective of the Department of Labor budget. The goal was to have an intervention be at least budget-neutral, in the sense that the cost of the intervention and its administration would be offset by the benefits to the government, which included reduced UI payments and increased tax payments to the U.S. Treasury.

CONCLUSIONS

The UI Experiments were designed to enable workforce development systems to find new or improved ways to help unemployed workers. The experiments showed that some approaches were cost-effective and held great promise. In two cases, the experiments led directly to the enactment of federal legislation establishing new programs. In other cases, completed experiments led to legislative initiatives that were not enacted. In still other cases, failed attempts at launching experiments were nonetheless followed by program enactment. And in yet other cases, completed experiments have validated findings that had not been tested previously through experimentally evaluated demonstration projects.

This book examines the UI Experiments and other research, the policy proposals to implement research results, and the programs that have been implemented. It examines these experiments in the political and economic environment in which they were considered and operated. That environment included three factors: 1) concerns about worker dislocation, 2) a restrictive federal budgetary environment, and 3) the need for careful targeting to achieve cost-effective results.

The UI Experiments were targeted at dislocated workers, most of whom are eligible for UI benefits. The goal of these demonstrations was to assist UI claimants in returning to work by developing or enhancing reemployment assistance approaches likely to be cost-effective. The demonstrations operated in an environment of budget austerity in the 1980s, which guided their design. Their budget-neutral design was helpful in getting two treatments enacted into law: 1) enhanced comprehensive job search assistance and 2) self-employment assistance. Budget neutrality also helped to gain bipartisan support for another treatment option—targeted reemployment bonuses, which were recommended for legislative implementation by both the Clinton and the Bush administrations. As the UI demonstrations proceeded, it became clear that effective targeting of reemployment services was critical for developing cost-effective approaches to providing reemployment services and for allocating scarce program resources in an environment of declining funding.

This book demonstrates that rigorous research can have an impact on employment policy, and indeed, that such research has had that effect, especially in the mid-1990s. Conversely, the book also describes how employment research can be ignored in developing public policy, and how this was done throughout most of the 2000s.

Notes

1. In this work I have chosen to capitalize the term "UI Experiments," since that is the term used by USDOL staff and researchers to bring together the work they did in running experiments serving UI claimants and dealing with job search assistance, training, reemployment bonuses, and relocation allowances.
2. The Unemployment Insurance Service is now called the Office of Workforce Security.
3. At that time, I directed unemployment insurance research and developed the proposal to conduct a multitreatment experiment as an enhancement to the fiscal year (FY) 1987 federal budget.
4. The Pennsylvania Reemployment Bonus Demonstration was approved by the secretary of labor and industry for the state. He was replaced by a new secretary early in the operation of the experiment. I attended a conference of state workforce administrators at the Mayflower Hotel in Washington, D.C., and was walking in through the lobby when I heard the new secretary call out loudly to me, "Hello, Mr. Random Assignment!" Needless to say, the secretary was not a strong supporter of the experiment.
5. The key staff who worked on most of the UI Experiment projects were Wayne Gordon, Jon Messenger, and Wayne Zajac. Other staff members who worked on one or more of the projects included Bill Coyne, Norm Harvey, and Doug Scott. Many individuals within the Unemployment Insurance Service worked on actuarial, budget, legislative, and program implementation issues. For the projects that operated in the Office of Policy Development and Research, the key staff were Gordon, Messenger, Janet Javar, and Jonathan Simonetta.
6. Among the computer staff working on the experiments were Jun Chen, Lynn Cao, and John Chang.
7. Because of the decline in temporary layoffs in the past two decades, the percentage of UI claimants who have no recall expectation would be much higher now.
8. In program year (PY) 2007, the WIA Adult and Dislocated Worker programs provided training to 176,000 individuals who exited the program.
9. In 1992, the Unemployment Insurance Service developed its first "Mission, Vision, Values, Goals" statement. It stated, "The program's mission is to provide unemployed workers with temporary income support and facilitate reemployment." I was a member of the work group that came up with that language, and even in the early 1990s my suggestion to include the words "and facilitate reemployment" met with initial resistance (O'Leary and Wandner 1997, pp. 702–703).
10. A substantial number of American workers never file for UI benefits when they become unemployed. Only about one-third of all unemployed workers appear to apply for UI benefits. Even among job losers, who are the prime potential UI recipient population, only a little over one-half apply (Vroman 1991, pp. 22–24).

2

The Unemployment
Insurance Experiments Begin

The New Jersey and Job
Search Assistance Experiments

with Walter Corson

SEARCHING FOR COST-EFFECTIVE SOLUTIONS: THE
DECISION TO BEGIN THE NEW JERSEY EXPERIMENT

The New Jersey Experiment was the first of eight UI Experiments undertaken by the U.S. Department of Labor between 1985 and 1996. The economic and political environment of the time made these experiments possible and shaped their design. Three key aspects of this environment were 1) the need to create efficiently operating employment and training systems, 2) the impact of the federal budget on the initiation of new policy, and 3) concern about worker dislocation in the United States.

U.S. employment and training programs continued to operate in the 1980s, but their staffing and funding was reduced at the federal, state, and local level.[1] As a result, attention was focused on ways to make employment and training programs administratively more efficient by making greater use of interprogram coordination, linkages, and consolidation. At the same time, an effort was made to determine the most effective methods for delivery of services to participants.

Underlying the UI Experiments was the belief that the UI program could improve the coordination and linkages of reemployment services for dislocated workers by becoming a part of the reemployment service delivery system. Thus, it was expected that the UI program would join the Employment Service (ES) and Job Training Partnership Act (JTPA) programs in assisting in the reemployment process. The UI program was posited as a potential gateway for directing unemployed workers to reemployment service providers. UI staff were expected to be able to identify unemployed workers in need of reemployment services when they first became unemployed and filed for benefits. However, from the UI program's perspective, it was recognized that while many permanently separated UI claimants needed services, effective reemployment services had to be targeted at those claimants for whom reemployment services would be most cost-effective. The resulting service delivery system would provide quicker, more effective, and more efficient reemployment services.

The experiments were rooted in the reality of the 1980s federal budgetary process, which made it exceedingly difficult to initiate a new federal program. Experimental methods were expected to make any positive finding of cost-effectiveness more widely accepted and more difficult to refute. To use these experiments to initiate public policy, their evaluation results would have to be sufficiently positive that they would be cost-effective not only to society as a whole but to the government sector as well. Furthermore, given the nature of the federal budget process, which divides the budget into separate cabinet-level appropriations, it also was desirable to have new program proposals be cost-effective to the USDOL to ease the enactment of federal legislation.

The UI Experiments were rooted in the growing concern about economic dislocation that stemmed from the large number of mass layoffs and plant closings, including those resulting from international trade competition. Economic dislocation thus emerged as a policy issue. Recognizing the importance of this issue, the USDOL in 1984 initiated biennial surveys of worker dislocation. At that time, worker dislocation resulted in long durations of unemployment for workers: more of the unemployed were remaining unemployed for 27 weeks or more. For the UI program, this meant that more workers were exhausting their 26 weeks of UI benefits, even after the 1980–1982 recession came to an end. Changing labor markets and increased numbers of long-term unemployed workers forced the UI program to adapt. Its traditional role of providing income maintenance was expanded to incorporate helping the long-term unemployed return to productive employment. At the same time, the worker dislocation surveys showed that the UI program served the majority of displaced workers who remained unemployed for more than a few weeks. Thus, UI was indeed an appropriate gateway to dislocated worker programs.

As the numbers of dislocated workers grew, the federal government took note of the problem. In the late 1970s and early 1980s, the Department of Labor conducted an experiment in the downriver area of southeastern Michigan (Kulik, Smith, and Stromsdorfer 1984). Similar experiments were run at several sites, including Buffalo, New York; Delaware; and Texas (Corson, Long, and Maynard 1985). These experiments concentrated on providing training and other comprehensive reemployment services to dislocated workers. They were local in nature and tended to focus on blue-collar dislocated workers. What emerged during the 1980s, however, was a broader form of displacement that spread to other occupations, including the white-collar occupations. Within the department, the UI program began to offer a more promising possibility—that of serving as a gateway for a diverse set of dislocated workers. The idea was that when these workers first became unemployed and filed their initial claims for UI benefits, they might be identified as being in need of reemployment services and referred to reemployment service providers. What was needed, however, was a champion for a new approach to serving dislocated workers with department-funded programs.

As the U.S. trade representative in the Reagan administration, William Brock worked to protect free trade, which both he and President Reagan believed in. Political pressure, however, was growing in the early 1980s to protect the United States against foreign goods and services. Brock thought that the United States could do a better job of adapting to global competition. Critical to making that adaptation was improving education, training, and methods of rapid transition to new jobs for American workers, such as comprehensive job search assistance. He was concerned that no one was talking about the critical issues of human development and job transition, and he started to speak out on this issue, as he would do for many years to come.[2]

On April 29, 1985, Brock was appointed the sixteenth secretary of labor. He replaced Raymond Donovan, who had resigned under a cloud of larceny and fraud charges. Under the circumstances, the Reagan administration wanted a clean and distinguished replacement for Donovan. Brock initially resisted taking the Labor job; when President

Reagan's chief of staff, Donald Regan, offered it to him, he refused. He was happy as U.S. trade representative and believed that he was better suited for that job. If he were going to take a cabinet position, he wanted to be secretary of state or the treasury. He ultimately accepted the Labor job, but only after being asked personally by President Reagan (Buhl 1989, pp. 111–118).

In his years as chair of the Republican National Committee and as U.S. trade representative, Brock was considered by many to be a transformational leader, and was known to be supportive of new ideas and policies. At the Labor Department, Brock wanted to generate a sense of mission among the staff. He wanted to improve the quality of life on the job by creating excitement, trying new things, and making programs work better. He wanted to show that things were changing. He opened the doors to his office suite, which had been closed during Secretary Donovan's tenure. Believing training to be crucial for staff, he founded the DOL Academy in 1987. He sent a memorandum to the Office of Management and Budget (OMB) saying that *he* was in charge of the department, and that as such he was not going to follow an OMB directive to close three regional offices (Buhl 1989).

Brock's tenure at the Labor Department was short. He left in 1987 to join Senator Robert Dole's presidential campaign. His efforts to innovate and transform the department were concentrated in the first year of his two-year tenure. He tried to transform the department by communicating his policy vision to his top managers at a conference attended by more than 200 career and political managers. In a 1987 publication, *Workforce 2000: Work and Workers for the Twenty-First Century* (Johnston and Packer 1987), he also sought to give a sense of direction to the USDOL as a whole by communicating a vision of where the department and the American workforce were headed as well as the institutional transformations that would be required to get there (Buhl 1989).

Through his work as U.S. trade representative, Secretary Brock had become interested in worker dislocation, in part as a result of its origins in international competition. He wanted to know the impact of this phenomenon on American workers so he could make the U.S. economy more competitive. He believed strongly in free international trade, but he also knew that he had to do something for workers who paid the price of free trade by becoming displaced from their jobs.

Anticipating Brock's interest in the worker dislocation issue, I proposed in the spring of 1985 to conduct a series of dislocated worker experiments that would test alternative approaches to returning these workers to employment. The proposal was developed as a request for new funding in the Labor Department's proposed budget for fiscal year 1987. This proposal was the beginning of a long and uncertain funding process. The various components of the department were developing proposals for submission by the secretary to the OMB in September 1985. These proposals then would be considered for inclusion in President Reagan's budget proposal to be announced in February 1986. The budget would have to be approved by Congress and would not become effective until October 1, 1986. In an administration that was trying to cut government spending, the prospects for the proposal seemed dim at best.

My proposal was reviewed by the Unemployment Insurance Service administrator, Carolyn Golding. Golding enjoyed being the UI administrator. She believed that the UI program was underrated as a component of macroeconomic stimulus. Golding welcomed the idea of UI becoming more active in helping workers to become reemployed. Supportive of research, she saw research as the "seed corn" to develop the UI program in the years ahead. She believed that future improvements of the UI programs would require evidence in order to cause a slow and conservative political process to support an expanded reemployment role for employment and training programs. Golding thought that Bill Brock would be interested in my proposal. She approved it and forwarded it to her boss, Assistant Secretary Roberts T. Jones, whom she believed was an "excellent reader of the political tea leaves" and would pass the proposal on to Secretary Brock.[3]

In the spring of 1985, Jones approved the proposal on behalf of the Employment and Training Administration (ETA). He sent the proposal forward to the department's budget office to be considered for incorporation into the department's overall budget submission to the White House. This proposal, if approved, would result in a $10 million increase in the department's budget for fiscal year 1987. Secretary Brock reviewed the proposed FY 1987 budget in late August 1985 and asked for a briefing by Jones. Jones briefed Brock about this demonstration project in a meeting attended by a number of Brock's political colleagues. Brock's colleagues were perplexed by the discussion, but

Brock understood the demonstration project's content and implications, and he and Jones discussed them in detail. Brock liked what he heard, and at the end of the meeting Brock quickly made up his mind, saying, "Let's do it." The matter was settled, and Jones was surprised by how quickly and decisively the issue had been resolved.[4]

Brock thought that the proposal to start the UI Experiments made "perfect sense." He had been concerned about human capital development and job transition in a competitive world economy, and the UI Experiments showed ways to "make it work" with respect to job training and comprehensive job search assistance. He hoped that some of the tested reemployment services would be shown to be effective as methods of improving the employment adaptability of American workers, making them more competitive in the world market. These cost-effective services could then "spread out," becoming well-funded, national programs that could make a difference.[5]

At the department, Brock's concern about promoting human development for American workers was first expressed in his support of the UI Experiments. He wanted to get the word out that the United States had been "coasting" in the 1960s, 1970s, and early 1980s instead of coming to grips with the education, training, and job transition issues it faced. He did so by jointly sponsoring a Youth 2000 conference with the secretaries of education and health and human services. The conference found that America was not doing enough to develop human resources nor to adapt to technological and other challenges. Brock was concerned that no one was talking about these issues. He got out the word by publishing *Workforce 2000*, which grew out of the conference.[6]

Brock approved the proposed budget increase for the UI Experiments. He was highly supportive of the experiments, but he did not want to wait over a year—from his approval in August 1985 to the beginning of FY 1987 on October 1, 1986—for project funding to become available. He therefore directed Assistant Secretary Jones to have the ETA initiate a demonstration project with unobligated FY 1984 funds over the next five weeks—before the fiscal year ended on September 30, 1985. Assistant Secretary Jones called me into his office on the day following Labor Day, told me what Brock wanted to do, and made available the remaining ETA discretionary funds for the fiscal year. He told the ETA's contracting office to be ready to complete the contracting process before the end of the month.

With one month remaining in the fiscal year, there was a mad dash to accomplish two things: 1) complete a preliminary design for an experiment that would test three alternative packages of reemployment services and 2) find a state that was both willing to participate and able to negotiate and sign a cooperative agreement with the department in under a month. In less than a week, Ray Uhalde from the Office of the Assistant Secretary for Policy, Evaluation, and Research and I developed a design for a three-treatment demonstration project, determined its approximate sample size, and estimated the cost of operating and evaluating it. I was interested in a range of treatments and in assuring that they could be compared to each other to determine which worked best. Uhalde was working on an evaluation of the JTPA training programs, so he was particularly interested in having a targeted training treatment that was linked to the UI program. He hoped that such targeting could increase the effectiveness of dislocated worker training programs.[7]

The department decided that the state of New Jersey would be a good site for the demonstration. As a Republican, that state's governor, Thomas Kean, was compatible with the Reagan administration. Assistant Secretary Jones knew the assistant commissioner of the New Jersey Department of Labor and Industry, and so did UI administrator Golding. One of Golding's office directors, Robert Schaerfl, was dispatched to Trenton to talk to the assistant commissioner. The goal of the meeting was to convince New Jersey to participate. The assistant commissioner was concerned about whether the project would be fully funded, whether he could convince the New Jersey agency leaders to participate in a random assignment experiment, and whether the results would shed a favorable light on New Jersey. The lunch ended with a promise that New Jersey would seriously consider participating.[8]

New Jersey agreed to be the demonstration site, and a cooperative agreement was signed on September 30 providing New Jersey with funding in the amount of $4.7 million for operating the demonstration and evaluating the demonstration results.[9] Mathematica Policy Research was competitively selected to conduct the research and evaluation.

Brock also took action to assure that there would be additional UI experiments. Fiscal year 1987 was a very tight budget year. The department proposed a number of budget increases that were sent to OMB, but they all were rejected. Brock personally appealed to OMB director

James Miller for only one proposed budget increase—the one to fund additional UI Experiments.[10] Brock won the appeal, and the UI Experiments were incorporated into the president's budget request to Congress. The House of Representatives accepted the proposal at the proposed $10 million level, but the Senate reduced it to $5 million. In conference committee negotiations to reconcile the differences between the two budgets passed by the two houses of Congress, the House acceded to the Senate's $5 million funding level.

Once the $5 million was appropriated by Congress, USDOL staff developed a plan to test two additional types of interventions for dislocated workers: 1) reemployment bonuses and 2) self-employment assistance.[11] The $5 million was used to fund two reemployment bonus demonstrations—one in Pennsylvania and the other in Washington State.

The department continued to support the UI Experiments as the experiments examined alternative new employment interventions; USDOL funded a total of eight experiments. In early 1987, the department also funded a Washington State self-employment assistance (SEA) experiment. In December 1987, Congress mandated three additional self-employment experiments, only one of which was implemented— in Massachusetts.[12] The Massachusetts demonstration was the first to be authorized to use state accounts in the Unemployment Trust Fund to fund the experimental operations, while the USDOL paid for the project evaluation. Congress mandated a Job Search Assistance Demonstration in 1991, once again authorizing use of Unemployment Trust Fund resources for this purpose. Two such demonstrations were conducted, one in Washington, D.C., and another in Florida. Finally, the department funded a Maryland work search experiment, also in 1991.

THE NEW JERSEY EXPERIMENT

Overview

The New Jersey UI Reemployment Demonstration Project (the "New Jersey Experiment") tested whether the UI system could identify dislocated workers early in their spells of unemployment.[13] The project also tested alternative early intervention strategies to accelerate these individuals' return to work. Three packages of services, or treatments, were tested: 1) job search assistance (JSA) only, 2) JSA combined with training or relocation assistance, and 3) JSA combined with a cash bonus for early reemployment. A key component of the demonstration was that eligible claimants were identified and provided services through the coordinated efforts of the UI, ES, and JTPA systems. Another key component was that the UI program required claimants to report for services; failure to report could lead to the denial of benefits.

The demonstration began operations in July 1986. By the end of June 1987, 8,675 UI claimants had been offered one of these three packages. Another 2,385 claimants who received services currently being provided were randomly selected to provide a control group. Services to eligible claimants continued into Fall 1987 to ensure that all eligibles, if they wished, were able to receive a full set of demonstration services. During the demonstration period, the New Jersey economy experienced worker dislocation, generated by a long-term secular decline in manufacturing, while substantial growth occurred in other sectors. Overall, the state economy was quite strong, and the unemployment rate was about 5 percent.

The initial evaluation of the demonstration (Corson et al. 1989), combined with two follow-up studies that extended the analysis for approximately six years after the initial UI claim (Anderson, Corson, and Decker 1991; Corson and Haimson 1996), found that each treatment reduced UI benefit payments for the current UI benefit year—and for one or more additional years—and increased employment and earnings for at least the initial year. Although the initial evaluation found no evidence that the training component of the second treatment increased earnings in the year after the initial claim, the follow-up studies suggested that each component of the treatments—JSA, training, and the reemployment bonus—contributed to the impacts on reduced UI receipt and increases in earnings and that the treatments helped workers find more stable jobs than those found by control group members. The evaluation also indicated that the demonstration succeeded in targeting claimants who, in the absence of the demonstration treatments, would have experienced more severe long-run reemployment difficulties. Finally, the evaluation found that all three treatments offered net benefits to claimants and to society, when compared with existing services. The JSA-only and JSA-plus-reemployment-bonus treatments also led to net gains for the federal government. Whether the policy proposal is cost-effective to the government sector has important public policy implications when federal budget constraints make new program implementation impractical if its impact is less than budget-neutral.

These findings of net benefits to claimants and to the government suggested that the demonstration treatments represented useful reemployment tools that could be directed toward UI claimants. However, several other evaluation findings had to be considered if the treatments were to be implemented as full-scale programs. First, with respect to reemployment services, two aspects of the treatments significantly contributed to their success—the mandatory participation requirements and the high degree of interagency coordination in service provision. These aspects could not be ignored in future applications. Second, analyses of the treatments by population subgroup suggested that the treatments were most successful in promoting the reemployment of individuals who already had marketable skills. Finally, benefit-cost analyses of the individual treatments provided the strongest support for the JSA-only treatment. Indeed, these findings suggested that the mandatory comprehensive JSA-services emphasized in the New Jersey demonstration are cost-effective for a broad range of permanently displaced UI claimants.

Demonstration Design

The New Jersey demonstration addressed three objectives:

1) It examined the extent to which UI claimants who could benefit from reemployment services could be identified early in their unemployment spells.

2) It assessed effective policies and adjustment strategies for helping such workers become reemployed.

3) It examined how such a UI reemployment plan could best be implemented.

To achieve these objectives, the design called for identifying demonstration-eligible individuals in the week after their first UI payment, and then assigning them randomly to one of three treatment groups offered alternative packages of reemployment services or to a control group receiving existing services. The demonstration sites were 10 state UI offices. The sites were chosen randomly, with the probability of their selection proportional to the size of the UI population in each office.

Definition of eligibility

The demonstration plan incorporated specific screens to identify experienced workers who were likely to be permanently dislocated from their jobs. The following eligibility screens were chosen:

First payment. The demonstration excluded claimants who did not receive a first UI payment. To promote early intervention, it also excluded claimants who did not receive a first payment within five weeks of an initial claim. Individuals who were working and, consequently, received a partial first payment also were excluded, because their job attachment meant that they had not necessarily been dislocated. Finally, special claims (e.g., unemployment compensation for ex–service members or federal civilian employees, interstate claims, and combined wage claims) were excluded.

Age. An age screen of age 25 or older was applied to eliminate the broad category of young workers, who have traditionally shown limited attachment to the labor market, and whose employment problems may be quite different from those of older, experienced workers.

Tenure. Demonstration-eligible claimants had to exhibit a substantial attachment to a job, so that the job loss was likely to be associated with one or more reemployment difficulties. Each claimant was required to have worked for his or her last employer for three years prior to applying for UI benefits and could not have worked full time for any other employer during the three-year period. The department's Bureau of Labor Statistics used the three-year requirement to define dislocated workers (Helwig 2004).

Temporary layoffs. Because the demonstration treatments were not intended for workers who were temporarily laid off, it was desirable to exclude claimants on temporary layoff. However, previous research and experience showed that some claimants say they expect to be recalled even when their chances of actual recall are slim. To ensure that these individuals were not excluded from the demonstration, only individuals who both expected to be recalled and had a specific recall date were excluded.

Union hiring hall arrangements. Individuals who are typically hired through union hiring halls exhibit a unique attachment to a specific labor market and were thus excluded from the demonstration.

The treatments

The demonstration tested three treatment packages designed to enhance the likelihood of reemployment. Eligible claimants were randomly assigned to a control group that received existing services or to one of the three treatment groups: 1) job search assistance only, 2) JSA plus training or relocation, or 3) JSA plus a reemployment bonus.

The initial components of all three treatments were the same: notification, orientation, testing, a job search workshop, and an assessment/counseling interview. These services were delivered sequentially, early in claimants' unemployment spells. First, a notification letter was sent to claimants approximately four weeks after they filed their initial claims. Claimants usually began to receive services during their fifth week of unemployment. Services were provided when claimants reported to a demonstration office (usually an ES office). They received orientation and testing during a one-week period. In the following week, they attended a job search workshop, consisting of five half-day sessions, and a follow-up, one-on-one counseling/assessment session in the subsequent week. These initial treatment components were mandatory; failure to report could lead to the denial of all UI benefits.

The job search workshop was conducted from Monday through Friday for approximately three hours per day, for a total of approximately 18 hours. The workshop followed a standard curriculum that included sessions on topics such as the following: adjusting to the job loss, conducting an effective self-assessment, developing realistic job goals, organizing an effective job search strategy, developing resumes and job applications, and practicing interview techniques. The curriculum included both individual activities and group discussions.

Beginning with the counseling/assessment interview, the nature of the three treatments differed. In the JSA-only group, claimants were told that, as long as they continued to collect UI, they were expected to maintain periodic contact with the demonstration office, whether directly with staff to discuss their job search activities or by engaging in search-related activities at a resource center in the office. The resource center offered job search materials and equipment, such as job listings, telephones, and occupational and training literature. Claimants were encouraged to use the center actively and were told that, if they did not come to the office periodically, ES staff would contact them and ask them to do so. These periodic follow-up contacts were to occur 2, 4, 8, 12, and 16 weeks following the assessment interview. Local ES staff were expected to notify UI when the claimant did not report for services.

Claimants in the JSA-plus-training group also were informed about the resource center and their obligation to maintain contact during their job search. They were told about the availability of classroom and on-the-job training and were encouraged to pursue training if interested. Staff from the local JTPA service delivery area worked directly with these claimants to develop training options. These claimants also were advised about the availability of relocation assistance, which those who elected not to pursue training could use for out-of-area job searches and moving expenses.

Claimants in the JSA-plus-reemployment-bonus group were offered the same set of JSA services as the first group (JSA only), in addition to a bonus for rapid reemployment. The maximum bonus equaled one-half of the claimant's remaining UI entitlement at the time of the assessment interview. This amount would be paid if the claimant started working either during the assessment week or within the next two weeks. Thereafter, the potential bonus declined at a rate of 10 percent of the original amount per week, until it was no longer available. Claimants recalled by their former employer could not receive a bonus; neither could those who were employed by a relative or in temporary, seasonal, or part-time jobs. Claimants who collected a bonus received 60 percent of the bonus if they remained employed for four weeks, and the remainder if they stayed employed for 12 weeks.

Each treatment tested a different aspect of the employment problems dislocated workers faced. The JSA-only treatment was based on the assumption that many dislocated workers have marketable skills but do not have enough job search experience to identify these skills and sell them in the job market. In contrast, the training treatment was based on the assumption that some workers' skills are outmoded and must be upgraded. Finally, the reemployment bonus treatment was based on the assumption that JSA alone is an insufficient incentive for claimants to seek to obtain employment rapidly, and that an additional incentive will help them recognize the realities of the job market and accept a suitable job more quickly.

With the exception of the reemployment bonus and relocation assistance, the demonstration services were similar to those available under existing ES and JTPA systems in New Jersey. However, there were important differences. The likelihood that a claimant would be offered and would receive demonstration services was considerably greater than under the existing system. The timing of the receipt of services also differed: demonstration services generally were provided earlier in the spell of unemployment. In addition, the mandatory nature of the initial services differed. Under the existing system, non-job-attached claimants were expected to register with the ES, but registration was sometimes delayed during peak load periods, and subsequent services were generally not mandatory. In the demonstration, claimants were expected to report for initial services, and this requirement was enforced.

Findings

Effectiveness of the eligibility definition

The eligibility requirements targeted demonstration services to about one-quarter of the claimants who received a first UI payment. The first round of exclusions (for delayed first payments, partial first payments, special claims, and under 25 years of age) was made on the basis of routinely collected UI agency data and an examination of the records of all claimants who received a first payment. This process excluded about 28 percent of the claimants, with the largest number being excluded because of the age restriction.

The rest of the eligibility requirements (consisting of screening out workers based on job tenure of less than three years, temporary layoffs, and union hiring-hall arrangements) were applied with data collected specifically for the demonstration by UI staff. The most restrictive screening device applied at this point was the tenure requirement, which excluded individuals who had not worked for their pre-UI employer for three years. This requirement excluded about half of the claimants who passed the initial eligibility screens.

The other important eligibility requirement was the temporary lay-off screen, which excluded claimants with a definite recall date. This screen excluded about 13 percent of the claimants who survived the initial examination. In devising this screen, the demonstration designers decided it was important to establish that the layoff was indeed temporary, rather than relying solely on the claimant's expectation of recall to his or her prior job. Having a defined recall date was used for this purpose. As expected, the percentage of claimants who said that their layoff was temporary was substantially larger than the number who actually had a recall date. Only half of the claimants who expected to be recalled, but who had no recall date, did return to their pre-UI job.

The New Jersey Experiment findings indicate that the eligibility screens directed demonstration services to a population that faced reemployment difficulties. An examination of the characteristics of the eligible population showed that it contained a substantial percentage of individuals whose age, industry of employment, and other characteristics are usually associated with a dislocated worker population and with difficulties in becoming reemployed. Moreover, compared with a sample of individuals who were not eligible for the demonstration, the eligible population experienced considerably longer periods of UI collection and longer unemployment spells, on average, during the initial benefit year. During the full six years of follow-up, the group targeted in the New Jersey demonstration continued to experience large reductions in earnings relative to group members' base-year earnings. These earning reductions were considerably larger than those realized by noneligibles, indicating that a dislocated worker population had indeed been identified. The long-term UI receipt of demonstration eligibles was significantly shorter than that of noneligibles, a finding that can be attributed, in part, to the fact that workers in seasonal industries were among the noneligible population.

However, it is unlikely that all demonstration eligibles actually required services. Some were in the prime of their working lives, and some were individuals from industries (e.g., service industries) that were strong and growing in New Jersey. Moreover, some claimants were recalled by their pre-UI employers.

Receipt of initial services

All claimants who were selected to participate in the demonstration treatment group were offered a common set of reemployment services early in their UI claim period. These services occurred in sequence and consisted of orientation, testing, a job search workshop, and an assessment/counseling interview.

Data on the receipt of these initial services show that 77 percent of the selected claimants attended orientations as requested. Most attended their scheduled session, but some attended a later session, generally after a follow-up contact by the UI claims examiner. Three-quarters of the claimants who attended orientations continued in the program through the assessment/counseling interview. However, not all such individuals received career testing or attended a job search workshop. Some were excused from participation, generally because their recall expectations could be substantiated. In addition, a large number were excused from testing and the job search workshop because of their language or reading comprehension difficulties, which precluded testing.

Most claimants attended orientation during the fifth week after their UI claim, and most completed assessment during the next three-to-four-week period. Thus, the goal of early intervention generally was achieved as planned.

The level at which treatment group members received the initial services—testing, job search workshops, and counseling—substantially exceeded the level at which control group members received such services from the ES and JTPA through existing referral mechanisms. Thus, the demonstration achieved its objective of increasing the level of services delivered.

Receipt of additional services

The additional services that were offered to claimants at the assessment/counseling interview included the periodic JSA activities, training and relocation assistance, and the reemployment bonus.

JSA follow-up. The objective of the follow-up activities was to encourage all claimants, except those engaged in training, to pursue an ongoing, intensive job search. This intensive job search was promoted by disseminating job search materials at the resource centers and by requiring claimants to maintain periodic contact with demonstration staff, either through the resource centers or in person.

Data on claimants who were collecting UI at the five follow-up points (2, 4, 8, 12, and 16 weeks after assessment) showed that 92 percent satisfied the first follow-up requirement (that is, the two-week contact) and that 80 percent had a contact at 16 weeks. Although the rate of contact declined, the degree of contact was high relative to other employment and training programs, which typically do not have systematic follow-up procedures. However, these periodic contacts did not always follow the strict schedule that had been laid out in the design, nor were all contacts made in person as desired. In addition, only a few of the resource centers appear to have been extensively used; consequently, the use of these centers probably had a minor impact on demonstration outcomes.

Training and relocation assistance. Classroom and on-the-job training opportunities were offered to claimants in the second treatment to test the efficacy of a service package that, early in the unemployment spell, attempted to alter or upgrade skills no longer in demand.[14] About 15 percent of the claimants who were offered training took advantage of it. Most of this training was classroom-based. Much of the classroom training was geared toward business and office services or computer and information services, while the on-the-job training tended to be in technical, clerical, and sales occupations. It appears that the training offered was in fact directed toward occupations with strong employment prospects in New Jersey.

The rate of training received through the demonstration project was higher than the rate observed for comparable groups of claimants who were offered training opportunities through referrals from the regular New Jersey JTPA program. Thus the offer of training under the demonstration achieved the objective of increasing the receipt of training, even though the overall rate of training was lower than initially expected.

Two general reasons appear to explain the lower-than-expected increase in training participation. First, the nature of the training intervention differed from that offered by other programs. The offer occurred early in the layoff period, which may have been before many individuals were ready to accept the fact that an occupational change was necessary. Moreover, not all individuals who were offered training were interested in or needed reemployment services, let alone training. However, they were offered services because of the mandatory nature of the initial services.

The second reason that training participation was less than might have been expected pertains to the manner of the demonstration implementation. The training treatment relied on existing JTPA program operators to provide training placement, and some operators were considerably more successful than others at placing claimants in training.[15] Their success stemmed from a number of factors, including an early and enthusiastic presentation of the training option and the capability to offer a wide range of individual training slots.

Reemployment bonus. The third treatment package included a reemployment bonus that was offered at the assessment/counseling interview. The purpose was to provide a direct financial incentive for claimants to seek work actively and become reemployed. The full bonus offer averaged $1,644 and was paid for jobs that started by the end of the second full week following the interview. After that, it declined by 10 percent of the initial amount each week, falling to zero by the end of the eleventh full week of the offer.

Nineteen percent of claimants who were offered the bonus received a first bonus payment, which was paid to individuals who held a bonus-eligible job for at least four weeks. Eighty-four percent of this group also received the final bonus payment, which was paid after 12 weeks of work. Overall, the total of the two bonus payments averaged close to $1,300.

Thirty-one percent of the claimants who were offered a bonus began a job within the bonus period, compared with 19 percent who were offered and then received a bonus. The remaining 12 percent appeared to be largely ineligible for the bonus, primarily because they obtained a job with their pre-UI employer.

Impacts of the demonstration on unemployment insurance receipt

The demonstration treatments were expected to affect the receipt of UI benefits by eligible claimants. The JSA-only and JSA-plus-reemployment-bonus treatments were expected to help eligible claimants become reemployed rapidly, thereby reducing the amount of UI benefits received by treatment group members relative to the amount received by control group members. Further, the JSA-plus-reemployment-bonus treatment was expected to have a larger impact on UI receipt because of the reemployment incentives created by the bonus. Expectations about the effect of JSA plus training or the relocation treatment on short-run UI receipt were less clear. Individuals who received this treatment offer but did not participate in training were expected to experience a reduction in UI receipt, but those who entered training would experience an increase in receipt, since individuals who accepted training continued to collect UI while being trained.

Estimates of the treatment impact on the receipt of regular UI benefits show that all three treatments reduced the number of weeks claimants collected benefits over the benefit year: by a half-week for the JSA-only and JSA-plus-training treatments and by one week for the JSA-plus-reemployment-bonus treatment (Table 2.1). As expected, these reductions were largest for JSA-plus-reemployment-bonus. These impacts were mirrored in the amount of benefits collected.

Longer-run reductions in UI receipt were also observed. Significant reductions occurred in the second year for the JSA-only and JSA-plus-reemployment-bonus treatments. In addition, there was a significant reduction in extended benefit program payments for the JSA-plus-training-or-relocation-assistance treatment group.[16] During the six-year follow-up period, the treatments reduced the receipt of UI benefits by about three-quarters of a week for the JSA-only treatment group, by one-and-a-half weeks for the JSA-plus-training-or-relocation-assistance treatment group, and by nearly two weeks for the JSA-plus-reemployment-bonus treatment group. These findings suggest that each of the treatment components—job search assistance, training, and the reemployment bonus—contributed to the longer-term impacts and that the treatments led to employment that was more stable than the employment of control group members.

Employment and earnings impact

The treatments were expected to promote quicker reemployment of claimants. Short-run impacts were expected to be greater for the JSA-only and JSA-plus-reemployment-bonus treatments than for the JSA-

Table 2.1 New Jersey Unemployment Insurance Reemployment Demonstration Project: Estimated Treatment Impacts on UI Receipt

	JSA only	JSA plus training/ relocation	JSA plus reemployment bonus	Control group mean
Regular UI				
Weeks paid in benefit year	−0.47**	−0.48**	−0.97***	17.90
Weeks paid in second year	−0.53***	−0.02	−0.44**	31.99
Weeks paid over six years	−0.76	−0.93	−1.72	31.99
Dollars paid in benefit year	−87**	−81**	−170***	3,228
Dollars paid in second year	−94***	−39	−78**	600
Dollars paid over six years	−181	−165	−333*	6,031
All UI programs				
Weeks paid over six years	−0.78	−1.47	−1.92	35.70
Dollars paid over six years	−222	−293	−375	6,852

NOTE: The category "All UI programs" includes regular UI, Emergency Unemployment Compensation (EUC), and two special state extended benefit programs. JSA = job search assistance. * statistically significant at the 90 percent confidence level for a two-tailed test; ** statistically significant at the 95 percent confidence level for a two-tailed test; *** statistically significant at the 99 percent confidence level for a two-tailed test.

SOURCE: Corson and Haimson (1996), pp. 23–42.

plus-training treatment, since individuals who entered training were expected to sacrifice short-run earnings for longer-run earnings gains.

Estimates of the short-run impacts of the treatments on employment and earnings suggest that JSA-only and JSA-plus-reemployment-bonus increased the claimants' short-run earnings. For these two treatments, the estimated earnings impact based on interview data was positive and statistically significant for the first two quarters in the year after the initial UI claim. The earnings impact estimates based on wage records for the JSA-plus-reemployment-bonus treatment also were positive and significant for the first calendar quarter after the initial UI claim (Table 2.2). In addition, employment impact estimates (not reported in the table) were also positive and significant for the same period. The timing of these impacts indicates that the treatments promoted early reemployment.

Another short-run employment and earnings issue was investigated—the impact of the treatments on the characteristics of the claimants' first job after receiving UI benefits. This is important because, by promoting rapid reemployment, the treatments might have prompted claimants to accept jobs that were less appropriate than those obtained by claimants who were not offered special services. An examination of this issue indicates that the early reemployment promoted by the treatments did not entail any sacrifice in hourly wages or hours worked. In fact, the treatments appeared to have led to modest increases in hourly wage rates in post-UI jobs (Table 2.2).

The evaluation also looked at long-run employment and earnings impacts. These estimates, based on wage record data, showed no statistically significant treatment impacts over the six-year follow-up period (beyond those observed in the initial quarters following the UI claim). Also, a relatively small number of claimants participated in training, so the impacts of training would have to have been quite large to have been detected through treatment-control comparisons.

For this reason, the evaluation examined the earnings experiences of trainees to determine whether the pattern of earnings suggested that training might have had an impact not detected in the treatment-control comparisons. This analysis showed that trainees who participated in classroom-based occupational skills training had relatively low earnings while they participated in training, but that compared with similar claimants not offered training they had relatively higher earnings

Table 2.2 New Jersey Unemployment Insurance Reemployment Demonstration Project: Estimated Treatment Impacts on Earnings and Post-UI Wages

Earnings	JSA only	JSA plus training/ relocation	JSA plus reemployment bonus	Control group mean
Interview data ($)				
Claim quarter 1	125**	82	160**	687
Claim quarter 2	263**	103	278***	1,945
Claim quarter 3	171	83	131	2,701
Claim quarter 4	49	77	22	3,012
Wage records data ($)				
Calendar quarter 1	28	58	176**	1,638
Calendar quarter 2	75	−23	79	2,174
Calendar quarter 3	101	47	46	2,507
Calendar quarter 4	31	28	79	2,517
Post-UI wages				
% change in post-UI relative to pre-UI hourly wage	0.041**	0.030**	0.041**	

NOTE: For percentage change in post-UI wages relative to pre-UI hourly wage, data came from the demonstration project interview. Quarters for the interview data are defined relative to the data of the UI claim. That is, Quarter 1 is the first three months following the date of claim, Quarter 2 is the next three months, and so on. Quarters for wage record data are calendar quarters beginning with the first full quarter after the date of UI claim. ** statistically significant at the 95 percent confidence level for a two-tailed test; *** statistically significant at the 99 percent confidence level for a two-tailed test.

SOURCE: Corson and Haimson (1996).

in later periods (relative to their base period earnings). Claimants who participated in on-the-job training had substantially higher earnings throughout the six-year follow-up period. Although these impact estimates could be biased, because the analysis could not completely control for unobserved factors that affect self-selection of training participants, the analysis suggests that both classroom (occupational skills) and on-the-job training did enhance trainees' earnings.

Benefit-cost analysis

An important question with respect to any program or policy is whether the benefits obtained from offering the services exceed their costs. This question was examined for the three treatments in the demonstration by examining the benefits and costs from the perspective of claimants, the government, and society as a whole. For example, reductions in UI benefit receipt represent a cost to claimants, a benefit to the government, and neither a benefit nor a cost to society, since UI payments are a transfer payment. The analysis for the government sector considered net benefits (including gains in earnings and taxes paid) and net costs, relative to the existing service system.

In terms of costs, the costs of providing the three treatments were estimated at $169 per claimant for the JSA-only treatment, $491 per claimant for the JSA-plus-training-or-relocation treatment, and $299 per claimant for the JSA-plus-reemployment-bonus treatment. Because some reemployment services were already provided to UI claimants under the existing service system, the net cost of providing these treatments was lower: $155 for the first treatment, $377 for the second, and $276 for the third.

The results of the benefit-cost analysis indicated that each of the treatments offered net benefits to society as a whole as well as to claimants, when compared with existing services (Table 2.3).[17] The JSA-only and JSA-plus-reemployment-bonus treatments also led to net gains for the government sector as a whole and for the USDOL subagencies that actually offer the services, since the reductions in UI benefits outweighed the net cost of providing additional services to claimants. Overall, net benefits were similar for these two treatments, and the JSA-plus-training/relocation treatment was more expensive than the other two from all perspectives.

Table 2.3 New Jersey Unemployment Insurance Reemployment Demonstration Project: Benefit-Cost Comparison with Existing Services ($ per claimant)

Perspective	JSA only	JSA plus training/relocation	JSA plus reemployment bonus
Society	581	41	565
Claimants	407	200	400
Government	175	−159	165
Labor Department	52	−219	45
Other government	123	60	120

NOTE: Entries are net benefits (the sum of benefits minus costs) relative to existing services.
SOURCE: Corson and Haimson (1996).

Policy Implications of the New Jersey Experiment

Of the three treatments, job search assistance was the most cost-effective. Based on the strength of these findings, the job search assistance component quickly had an impact on workforce policy. The final evaluation report was published in 1989. Six years later the WPRS system was enacted into law, taking the lessons learned about the effectiveness of job search assistance for dislocated workers from the New Jersey Experiment and using them to launch a nationwide program.

The lessons learned from the job search assistance treatment went beyond the effectiveness of JSA. The requirement for claimants to participate in initial JSA demonstration services also played a role in the treatment's success. Failure to report to the orientation session was reported to UI local office staff, and UI staff members were expected to follow up with a fact-finding interview with the claimant. A formal determination of eligibility (a nonmonetary determination) was to be conducted if the interview raised a potential eligibility issue.[18] This issue could result in the denial of benefits (a nonmonetary denial). In accordance with the project design, the evaluation found that mandatory participation was enforced, resulting in increased nonmonetary determinations and denials for the treatment groups compared to the control group. Nonmonetary determinations were made for 40 percent of the treatment group compared to 27 percent of the control group, and most of the issues raised were related to reporting for demonstration services. Denials for treatment group members exceeded those for control group members, 19 percent to 15, with denials being higher for those not reporting for the orientation than for those who did. The evaluators found that enforcing mandatory participation in initial demonstration services contributed significantly to the reduction in duration of UI receipt, not only directly through the increase in benefit denials but also indirectly through the establishment of a rigorous compliance process (Corson et al. 1989, pp. 273–277). These findings, in combination with the findings from the other experiments that are reviewed below, argue for rigorous enforcement of the UI work test.

The lessons learned about the other two treatments—JSA plus training and JSA plus reemployment bonuses—had no immediate impact. As discussed below, reemployment bonuses were revisited as a policy initiative in 1994 and again in 2003. For training, there has been a continuing search for what kind of training works. Researchers have continued to review the evidence, and the department began an Individual Training Allowance (ITA) Experiment in 2001, a new experiment to determine what kind of training voucher is most effective.

JOB SEARCH ASSISTANCE DEMONSTRATIONS IN THE DISTRICT OF COLUMBIA AND FLORIDA

Overview

The efficacy of job search assistance for UI claimants that was found in New Jersey created interest in determining whether these results could be expanded and generalized to other states. This interest led to enactment of federal legislation in the early 1990s that authorized additional demonstration projects, requiring the department to conduct a new job search assistance demonstration to replicate the New Jersey Experiment. This requirement was contained in the initial 1991 law authorizing the Emergency Unemployment Compensation (EUC) program, which extended benefits during the recession of the early 1990s.[19] Operational funds for the JSA Demonstration were provided from the Unemployment Trust Fund, following the precedent of the Massachusetts SEA Demonstration. The JSA Demonstration provisions were incorporated into the 1991 EUC extension in the expectation that further research work would be needed before a permanent JSA program for dislocated workers could be enacted. However, such a job search assistance program was enacted in 1993 as the Worker Profiling and Reemployment Services, before the new demonstration project even began (see Chapter 3).

The legislation authorizing the JSA Demonstration, Title II of the Emergency Unemployment Compensation Act of 1991, required the department to implement and evaluate a demonstration to provide job search assistance to UI claimants. The act's provisions defining the JSA program were modeled on those of the New Jersey demonstration. The provisions were as follows:

Eligibility. Eligible individuals would be those who were receiving unemployment insurance benefits and who had at least 126 weeks of work with their last base-period employer in the three years prior to the end of the base year. Individuals were not eligible if they had definite recall dates or if they were seeking employment through union hiring halls.

Comprehensive job search program. Eligible individuals would be provided with a comprehensive job search program that included orientation, testing, a job search workshop, an individual assessment and counseling interview plus ongoing contact with program staff, follow-up assistance, resource centers, and job search materials and equipment. These were the same service components and the same support services that were provided in the New Jersey Experiment. This basic job search assistance package was to be tested by using a design similar to that previously tested in New Jersey but also by testing alternative treatments building on the basic treatment.

Mandatory participation. Eligible individuals were required to participate in services, with failure to participate leading to benefit disqualification of up to 10 weeks. The state could waive the participation requirement for good cause or if the state determined that participation was not appropriate for the individual.

The legislation specified that the demonstration should use an experimental design, with random assignment of eligible claimants to each of the treatments. A control group would receive nondemonstration services. Thus, experimental methods would be used to measure the effectiveness of the treatments in promoting reemployment. This approach assured that the demonstration project could be rigorously evaluated, yielding results that Congress could use in its future decision-making.

Following a precedent from a 1987 congressionally authorized SEA demonstration sponsored by Congressman Ron Wyden of Oregon, the Unemployment Trust Fund was directed to fund the demonstration. For participating states, trust fund dollars equal to the state average weekly benefit amount per individual were authorized to fund demonstration services. This funding meant that the department could proceed with the demonstration project without seeking new appropriations to fund it, but that the department would still have to pay for the design, oversight, and evaluation of the project from its research budget.

The USDOL proceeded to implement the demonstration project as soon as authorizing legislation was enacted in 1991. In early 1992, the department announced a competition to participate in the project, and states applied to participate. In September 1992, three sites—the District of Columbia, Florida, and Wisconsin—were selected to participate in the demonstration.[20] As a result of the enactment of the WPRS initiative in 1993, implementation of the demonstration was delayed and did not begin until 1995. That April, just as implementation was about to begin, Wisconsin withdrew as a participant, leaving only two demonstration sites.

In 1993, a competition was conducted to select a research firm to design, oversee, and evaluate the project. Mathematica Policy Research was selected as the research contractor. The cost of the contract with Mathematica was $1.4 million. The demonstration project operated in one local office in the District of Columbia. Based on statistical analysis, the demonstration targeted a sample of UI claimants from the entire population of claimants, selecting 8,071 of them to participate between June 1995 and June 1996. The Florida demonstration operated in 10 local offices and assigned 12,042 claimants to the project between March 1995 and March 1996.

Job Service Assistance Demonstration Design

In accordance with the authorizing legislation, the JSA Demonstration tested three packages of reemployment services designed to promote rapid reemployment among UI claimants expected to experience long spells of unemployment. Eligible claimants were identified early in their claim periods—in fact, as soon as their first UI payments were made—using a profiling model similar to the one developed by the department for the WPRS system. These claimants were then randomly assigned either to a control group that received regular services or to one of the three treatments: 1) structured job search assistance, 2) individualized job search assistance, or 3) individualized job search assistance with training.

Structured Job Search Assistance (SJSA). This treatment replicated the basic JSA treatment tested in New Jersey. Claimants who were assigned to this treatment were sent a letter telling them to report to an ES orientation session. This letter was sent during approximately the fourth week of unemployment, assuming claimants applied for UI as soon as they were laid off. Claimants reported for orientation during approximately the sixth week of unemployment. At the orientation, claimants were told generally about the reemployment services available to them and specifically about the demonstration services. They were tested the same week and scheduled for a one-week job search workshop lasting approximately three hours per day, to be conducted the following week. After the workshop, they were scheduled for a one-on-one assessment/counseling interview to discuss their reemployment plans. Attendance at this initial set of services was mandatory, unless the claimant was explicitly excused from services. Individuals who continued collecting UI benefits had a minimum of two additional contacts with local office staff. In addition, each office established a job search resource center for participants.

Individualized Job Search Assistance (IJSA). This treatment was similar to the job search assistance treatment, except that a decision was made on an individual basis about the services a claimant should receive. Eligible claimants were sent a letter telling them to report for a group orientation session held during approximately their fifth or sixth week of unemployment. At that session, they were given an overview of the services available to them and scheduled for an individual assessment interview later that week or the next week. An individual service plan was developed during the assessment interview. This plan varied by individuals, but the services agreed to—such as testing, the job search workshop, or additional assessment/counseling interviews—were mandatory. Additional ongoing contacts could also be required. Claimants in this treatment could also receive any other services, such as placement assistance, from the local Employment Service office.

Individualized Job Search Assistance with Training (TJSA). This treatment was identical to the preceding one, except that a special effort was made to enroll interested claimants in training. In all treatments, the availability of JTPA dislocated worker training was mentioned during the orientation session. Referrals to JTPA were made for claimants who expressed interest in training. However, in this treatment, the discussion of training opportunities during the orientation was more extensive. (When possible, a JTPA staff member made the presentation.) In addition, the possibility of training was explicitly discussed during the individual assessment interview. Any claimant who expressed interest was scheduled to talk to a JTPA staff member. To the extent possible, this discussion took place in the Employment Service office immediately following the assessment interview. This one-stop approach to service delivery was facilitated by having the assessment interviews for this treatment scheduled on a day in which a JTPA staff member could be stationed at the Employment Service office. To ensure that training was available, the states participating in the demonstration were asked, as indicated in their agreements with the department, to designate a portion of their JTPA dislocated worker funds to provide training to members of this group (Decker et al. 2000, pp. 10–13).

Eligibility criteria for the demonstration

Before the JSA Demonstration could be implemented, a national WPRS program was enacted in 1993, and all states began to prepare to implement this JSA program. As a result, it made no sense to have the demonstration eligibility criteria—as specified in legislation—differ from those for WPRS, since the WPRS provisions were being implemented in all states. Using the WPRS provisions would allow the department to test the new legislative design experimentally and would allow the department and the research contractor to provide technical assistance to Florida and the District of Columbia in setting up their state WPRS programs. This issue was solved by having staff from the USDOL and the House Ways and Means Committee meet and agree to allow the demonstration to follow the WPRS eligibility provisions.

As a result, demonstration-eligible claimants were identified using the worker profiling statistical model approach developed by the department during 1993. This model (discussed in Chapter 4) uses a two-step process to identify claimants who are expected to experience long spells of unemployment. The research contractor and the states agreed that the contractor would estimate the model for each of the states for their use not only during the demonstration but also for the WPRS program (Decker et al. 2000, pp. 7–9).

Delay of WPRS implementation

The enactment and upcoming implementation of WPRS also would have adversely affected the current services environment of the demonstration project if members of the control groups had been required to participate in WPRS and receive program services that were similar to demonstration JSA services. Once again there was agreement between USDOL and House Ways and Means staff that the demonstration was an adequate substitute for WPRS, and hence WPRS implementation could be delayed in the District of Columbia (since the entire District participated in the demonstration) and in the 10 participating Florida local offices until the project was completed (Decker et al. 2000, pp. 7–9).

Findings of the Job Search Assistance Demonstration

The JSA Demonstration, conducted in the District of Columbia and Florida, replicated the New Jersey Experiment. Participation rates in the JSA Demonstration varied from those of the New Jersey Experiment. More treatment group members participated in reemployment services in New Jersey than in D.C. and Florida. The orientation attendance rate of 79 percent in New Jersey was similar to that in D.C. (77 percent) but was higher than that for Florida (62 percent). Attendance rates for services beyond orientation tended to be higher in D.C. than in New Jersey, while the Florida rates tended to be lower. For example, job search workshop attendance was 60 percent in D.C., while the New Jersey rate was 50 percent and the Florida rate was only 44 (Decker et al. 2000, p. 42).

Impact on UI receipt

The impact on UI receipt was measured in four ways: 1) the effect of the demonstration treatment on the number of weeks claimants drew benefits, 2) the rate at which UI benefits were exhausted, 3) the percentage of beneficiaries with at least one nonmonetary determination, and 4) the percentage of beneficiaries with at least one nonmonetary benefit denial. The four measures reflected the intent of speeding the return to work. The measures also recognized that calling UI claimants into a local UI office to offer them job search assistance would raise eligibility issues for some claimants, and those issues could relate either to whether they reported to receive demonstration services or whether they continued to be eligible for UI benefits.

For both D.C. and Florida, each treatment had a significant impact on all four measures of UI receipt during the initial benefit year (Table 2.4). Job search assistance treatments were expected to have short-term impacts rather than long-term impacts. In accordance with those expectations, none of the treatments had a significant impact after the initial benefit year. This result, however, is inconsistent with the New Jersey Experiment, which found that participants who received job search assistance had reduced receipt of UI in the second benefit year.

The structured job search assistance (SJSA) treatment in D.C. experienced a reduction of 1.1 weeks in UI receipt, far greater than the experience for all of the other treatments in D.C. and Florida, which varied between reductions of 0.4 and 0.6 weeks and were more in line with the New Jersey results. The rate of exhaustion of benefits decreased in all cases, declining between 2 and 5 percent. Examining the week-to-week exit rates from UI benefit receipt, the evaluators found that most of the effect of the JSA treatments was felt soon after the offer of services, indicating that exiting from UI benefit receipt was caused more by the requirement to report for services than by the job search skills learned from the receipt of reemployment services.

Table 2.4 Job Search Assistance Demonstration: Estimated Impact of the JSA Treatments on UI Receipt in Year 1

	District of Columbia			Florida		
Outcome	SJSA	IJSA	TJSA	SJSA	IJSA	TJSA
Weeks of benefits received in benefit year	−1.13***	−0.47**	−0.61**	−0.41**	−0.59	−0.52**
Dollars of UI benefits received in benefit year	−182***	−56	−37	−39	−100**	−73*

NOTE: SJSA = structured job search assistance; IJSA = individualized job search assistance; TJSA = individualized job search assistance with training. * statistically significant at the 90 percent confidence level for a two-tailed test; ** statistically significant at the 95 percent confidence level for a two-tailed test; *** statistically significant at the 99 percent confidence level for a two-tailed test.
SOURCE: Decker et al. (2000).

The evaluation did not yield a definite conclusion about which treatment was most successful at reducing UI receipt because of differences in outcomes between D.C. and Florida. These differences seemed to be primarily due to stricter enforcement of participation in the mandatory services under the SJSA treatment. Also contributing to the disparity was a substantial difference in economic conditions—spells of unemployment were longer in D.C. than in Florida. However, it appears that with strict enforcement, the mandatory participation approach of the SJSA is the most effective approach in reducing UI receipt.

As in the New Jersey Experiment, participation in the Job Search Assistance Demonstration was mandatory. If claimants did not report, UI staff conducted fact-finding interviews that could result in nonmonetary determinations and denial of benefits. In both D.C. and Florida, this process resulted in a significant increase in the rate of nonmonetary determinations conducted and denials of UI benefits based on those determinations—for all treatment groups. Because of stronger enforcement by the District of Columbia, these effects were much greater there than in Florida: they increased from 29 percent to 37 for the rate of nonmonetary determinations and from 7 percent to 11 for the denial rate. More specifically, for the structured JSA treatment there was a fourfold increase in denials stemming from determinations that claimants were "not unemployed." The evaluators found that the effect of conducting determinations went beyond enforcement of mandatory participation in the demonstration project: local office staff also used information gathered during enforcement of demonstration participation to increase the enforcement of UI continuing eligibility requirements. Much of the decline in UI receipt was related to that enforcement (Decker et al. 2000, pp. 122–135).

Impact on earnings

The JSA treatments had very different earnings impacts between the locations, with some statistically significant impacts in D.C. but none in Florida (Table 2.5). In D.C., the structured JSA treatment yielded positive earnings impacts throughout the 10-quarter period of follow-up, whereas for the other treatments there were positive and significant results only for some quarters during the first six quarters. In Florida, the earnings results were not significant. Thus, no apparent impact on earnings occurred in Florida.

In designing the Job Search Assistance Demonstration, one concern was whether the provision of JSA could result in workers taking lower-quality jobs. However, the results showed that the treatment groups found jobs paying as well as or better than those taken by the control group (Decker et al. 2000, pp. 137–164).

Impact on job search

Another purpose of the JSA Demonstration was to provide UI claimants with job search skills, and to have them make intensive use of these skills. Participants were expected to search for work more and receive more referrals to job openings from Employment Service staff. The impact of the treatments on claimants' ability to successfully search for jobs was measured by the following three factors: 1) the number of employer contacts claimants had per week, 2) the hours of job search per week, and 3) the percentage of claimants receiving a job referral from the Employment Service. The results showed a positive impact on the number of employer contacts and receipt of job referrals, but no effect on the hours of job search per week (Table 2.6).

Even though treatment members were more likely to receive job referrals from the Employment Service, there was no indication that these referrals had any impact on their likelihood of obtaining job offers

Table 2.5 Job Search Assistance Demonstration: Estimated Impact of the JSA Treatments on Earnings ($)

	District of Columbia			Florida		
Quarter	SJSA	IJSA	TJSA	SJSA	IJSA	TJSA
1	30	22	22	53	−48	−24
2	172***	102	147***	−4	−6	20
3	152**	111	176**	−53	−18	14
4	281**	161**	83	−2	112	50
5	280**	913**	180	−92	−36	−12
6	241**	183**	106	−66	−36	5
7	177**	96	−23	−57	−5	63
8	263**	129	38	−98	−41	−20
9	185*	76	10	−98	−41	−49
10	224**	100	50	123	−30	−44

NOTE: SJSA = structured job search assistance; IJSA = individualized job search assistance; TJSA = individualized job search assistance with training. * statistically significant at the 90 percent confidence level for a two-tailed test; ** statistically significant at the 95 percent confidence level for a two-tailed test; *** statistically significant at the 99 percent confidence level for a two-tailed test.
SOURCE: Decker et al. (2000).

from these referrals. Nonetheless, the learning process of seeking jobs from job referrals may have had a positive impact on claimants' ability to search for work on their own (Decker et al. 2000, pp. 165–176).

Cost-effectiveness of the treatments

The benefit-cost analysis for the JSA Demonstration was examined from three perspectives: that of the U.S. Department of Labor, that of the federal government as a whole, and that of society in general (Table 2.7). Thus the government sector was considered both from the narrower perspective of the agency administering the UI programs and from the broader perspective of the entire federal government. During the budgetary stringency period of the 1980s and early 1990s, the interventions being tested were expected to be more policy-relevant if they were cost-effective from one or both government perspectives.

The evaluators measured the cost and benefits of each of the treatments in both D.C. and Florida. In all cases the cost of the treatments

Table 2.6 Job Search Assistance Demonstration: Estimated Impact on Job Search

Outcome	District of Columbia			Florida		
	SJSA	IJSA	TJSA	SJSA	IJSA	TJSA
Employers contacted per week	1.6*	1.9*	3.0*	1.4*	1.5*	2.1*
Hours of search per week	0.2	0.6	0.9	0.4	0.7	1.7***
% receiving a job referral from the Job Service	8.7***	2.9	8.7***	3.4*	3.8*	10.3***

NOTE: SJSA = structured job search assistance; IJSA = individualized job search assistance; TJSA = individualized job search assistance with training. * statistically significant at the 90 percent confidence level for a two-tailed test; *** statistically significant at the 99 percent confidence level for a two-tailed test.
SOURCE: Decker et al. (2000).

was low, varying between $100 and $300, while the cost of the structured JSA was between $200 and $300. The benefit-cost results showed that none of the treatments produced net benefits in Florida. In D.C., each of the treatments resulted in net benefits to the government sector as a whole and to society at large, but did not produce net benefits from the perspective of the Department of Labor (Decker et al. 2000, pp. 177–193).

Summary

The findings for the structured JSA treatment in the District of Columbia confirmed those from the New Jersey Experiment. The structured approach in both experiments led to net benefits to society and to the government as a whole. The findings for Florida, with its weaker enforcement of participation, were less favorable because of the lack of positive earnings outcomes.

The positive findings regarding a structured approach to the provision of job search assistance services suggest that the states' offer of these services at the One-Stop centers—whether through the WPRS system or some other mechanism—will be more effective if participation is mandatory, either through the provision of a single set of services

Table 2.7 Job Search Assistance Demonstration: Cost-Effectiveness of Treatments ($ per claimant)

Benefits and costs	Claimant	USDOL	Other gov't	Gov't total	Society
District of Columbia					
SJSA					
Net benefits ($)	1,930	−126	557	431	2,361
Rate of return (%)	—	−44	—	151	826
IJSA					
Net benefits ($)	1,136	−110	327	217	1,353
Rate of return (%)	—	−55	—	109	680
TJSA					
Net benefits ($)	806	−186	223	37	844
Rate of return (%)	—	−86	—	17	391
Florida					
SJSA					
Net benefits ($)	−653	−224	−127	−351	−1,004
Rate of return (%)	—	−93	—	−146	−416
IJSA					
Net benefits ($)	−196	0	−20	−20	−215
Rate of return (%)	—	0	—	−20	−222
TJSA					
Net benefits ($)	−12	−55	7	−48	−61
Rate of return (%)	—	−54	—	−47	−59

NOTE: — = data not available. SJSA = structured job search assistance; IJSA = individualized job search assistance; TJSA = individualized job search assistance with training.
SOURCE: Decker et al. (2000).

for all participating claimants or through individual service plans that are customized for each claimant.

Beyond the provision of job search assistance services themselves, the JSA Demonstration had an effect on state workforce agency local offices. These offices used the information gathered as part of the JSA Demonstration in their administration of regular services to UI claimants. In the process, they increased the enforcement of the UI work test.

Enforcement of the UI work test yielded an increase in the identification of issues relating to continuing eligibility for UI benefits (e.g., nonseparation, nonmonetary determinations) and, in some cases, denial of benefits to claimants who were found to be collecting benefits but should not have been. Thus, making JSA participation mandatory was critical to identifying issues of continuing eligibility for UI benefits. The result was a more rigorous enforcement of the UI work test, both to determine whether UI claimants are unemployed and to determine whether they are searching for work. The evaluation showed that, if the provision of job search assistance is done rigorously, as it was in the District of Columbia, it is likely that eligibility issues will be identified and benefit denials will substantially increase (Decker et al. 2000, pp. 128–130, 195–207).

PROFILING THE NEW JERSEY EXPERIMENT RESULTS

The New Jersey Experiment's evaluation results were used to justify the WPRS system. The targeting of treatment group members (and control group members), however, did not use the worker profiling mechanism that is part of the ongoing program. Rather, unemployed workers were selected for participation in the project based on several screens. While the purpose of the screens was to identify dislocated workers, they did so in a very different way from the WPRS system.

The New Jersey Experiment included two follow-up studies which took place after the 1989 final evaluation report. The main purpose of the follow-ups was to measure the long-term impacts of training. The four-year follow-up did not find positive training results, and neither did the six-year follow-up.

The six-year follow-up study also tested the new worker profiling mechanism that was put into effect in 1994. The study included a simulation analysis that was applied to the original New Jersey Experiment microdata. Corson and Haimson (1996) conducted the simulation and found that, indeed, profiling both treatments and controls increased the cost-effectiveness of the job search assistance treatment.

LESSONS LEARNED FROM THE JOB SEARCH
ASSISTANCE EXPERIMENTS

Much was learned from the evaluation results of the New Jersey and JSA demonstrations:

- Workers who are permanently separated from their jobs and who are likely to have difficulty becoming reemployed can benefit from receiving help as they seek to return to work. That help can come from a range of reemployment services, including job referrals, if a job is available, and job search training that provides tools for self-search for jobs. At the same time, stronger enforcement of the UI work test can also reduce the compensated duration of unemployment and speed claimants' return to work.

- Providing a comprehensive package of job search assistance (e.g., orientation, assessment, testing, counseling, job search workshop, and follow-up services) can reduce the duration of unemployment. The cost of these services is low, and savings from reduced UI benefit payments and increased tax payments can make the provision of these services cost-effective (Corson et al. 1989; Decker et al. 2000; USDOL 1990).

- For job search assistance to be cost-effective, participation must be mandatory. Otherwise, most workers who are offered the services will not participate, and the overall impacts on workers will be small (Corson et al. 1989; Decker et al. 2000).

- Required participation in job search assistance can be tied to either a standardized, comprehensive package of services or a customized package of services based on the development of an individual employability plan. A standardized, comprehensive package has a greater impact on reducing the duration of unemployment, but a customized package can also have a substantial impact if participation is carefully monitored and enforced. Without claimants' participation in a number of substantive services, JSA will not be effective (Corson et al. 1989; Decker et al. 2000).

- There is a synergy that results from calling dislocated UI claimants into the One-Stop center for JSA services. In addition to offering JSA services, local office staff can provide immediate referrals to jobs from available job openings. Also, if UI claimants do not report or participate in JSA services, UI staff can use this information to enforce the UI work test (Decker et al. 2000).

• Cooperation between UI and ES staff can contribute to the effectiveness of providing reemployment services to UI claimants (Corson et al. 1989; Decker et al. 2000; USDOL 1990). Interagency cooperation and coordination is particularly needed in an era of remote claims-taking, in which UI staff generally are not available in the One-Stop Career Centers.

• Local office staff can refer these UI claimants and others to job openings. When claimants are provided with job search assistance services, referrals to job openings can result in significantly higher placement rates than normally result from such referrals (Corson, Long, and Maynard 1985; Decker et al. 2000).

• Stronger enforcement of the UI work test can reduce the duration of compensated unemployment, whether enforcement is done separately or in conjunction with job search assistance services. An enhanced UI work test can take the form of requiring claimants to report to the One-Stop center and demonstrate that they are able, available for work, and actively searching for work. It can also take the form of requiring a more intensive job search (Corson, Long, and Maynard 1985: Decker et al. 2000; Johnson and Klepinger 1991, 1994).

• Conducting eligibility reviews is an effective method of enforcing the UI work test and can be performed separately either by One-Stop Career Center staff or by UI staff. However, joint efforts by both One-Stop center and UI staff have been found to be more effective (Almandsmith, Adams, and Bos 2006; Corson et al. 1989; Decker et al. 2000; USDOL 1990).

• An effective way to increase the enforcement of the UI work test is to enhance the work search requirement by increasing the number of job search contacts. Verifying a sample of those contacts can also reduce duration (Johnson and Klepinger 1994; Klepinger et al. 1998).

- The implication for a program such as Worker Profiling and Re-employment Services is that, whereas providing reemployment services separately can be cost-effective, bringing together the three separate components of reemployment services can be even more cost-effective. [The three components are 1) a comprehensive job search assistance package of services, 2) referral to job openings, and 3) an enhanced UI work test.] A program that provides all three sets of services to UI claimants can reduce costs and create synergy.

- Simulations of the worker profiling mechanism used by the WPRS system starting in 1994 were shown to make the New Jersey Experiment more cost-effective (Corson and Haimson 1996). While the job search assistance treatment of the New Jersey Experiment was cost-effective for the government sector in the Corson et al. (1989) analysis, the result improved significantly when more focused targeting was achieved by applying the worker profiling mechanism.

Notes

1. For example, full-time-equivalent staff of the Employment and Training Administration peaked in Program Year 1971, numbering 4,283, but had declined to 3,185 by 1980. After two reductions in force in the early 1980s, the number of staff has been less than 2,000 since 1983, and has been less than 1,400 since 1996 (O'Leary, Straits, and Wandner 2004, p. 316). By 2008 the staffing level was less than 1,000.
2. William Brock, telephone conversation with the author, October 24, 2008.
3. Carolyn Golding, telephone conversation with the author, December 5, 2008.
4. Roberts T. Jones, telephone conversation with the author, July 15, 2008.
5. Brock, conversation.
6. Ibid.
7. Ray Uhalde, in-person interview with the author, August 12, 2008.
8. Robert Schaerfl, telephone conversation with the author, July 15, 2008.
9. Normally the department signed financial agreements either as contracts or grants, and with a state the department typically would have signed a grant agreement. However, in order to have more leverage on how the New Jersey Experiment was conducted, the department signed its first cooperative agreement to provide the department with more authority over the operation of the experiment.
10. Because of his stature in the Reagan administration, Brock had easy access to the president and to other senior officials, and, according to Assistant Secretary Jones, he took advantage of this access.

11. I developed the plan for the Department of Labor to conduct a series of UI experiments for testing interventions to assist dislocated workers to return to work.

12. The department selected three states to participate—Massachusetts, Minnesota, and Oregon—but the last two states dropped out of the project before operations began.

13. Unless otherwise indicated, this section is based on Corson et al. (1989), Anderson, Corson, and Decker (1991), and Corson and Haimson (1996). Walter Corson wrote most of this section for an article on the New Jersey Experiment that we never completed.

14. Individuals in this treatment group were also offered relocation assistance. As previous experience had suggested, few individuals were interested in relocation, and fewer than 1 percent of those who were offered relocation assistance received it.

15. The participation rate in training varied widely among the 10 demonstration sites, from 8 to 27 percent (Corson et al. 1989, p. 108).

16. Specifically, the reduction was in Emergency Unemployment Compensation (EUC) benefits.

17. The net benefits to society occur largely because it is assumed that claimants' increased employment and earnings represent a net increase in output; that is, the more rapid reemployment of claimants does not displace the employment of other individuals. This no-displacement assumption was reasonable given the strength of the New Jersey economy at the time of the study.

18. A nonmonetary determination is a determination of UI eligibility made at an initial level by state UI staff based on facts related to issues detected about either the conditions under which UI claimants were first separated from their jobs or about their continuing eligibility for benefits.

19. The JSA Demonstration provision was included in the EUC bill following discussion about the New Jersey demonstration and the usefulness of its replication for future policy purposes between Rich Hobbie (then senior majority staffer for the Human Resources Subcommittee of the House Ways and Means Committee) and me. At the time of this discussion, he and I did not anticipate the enactment of the JSA program in the form of the WPRS system without further experimental replication of the New Jersey demonstration results.

20. The District of Columbia—along with Puerto Rico and the Virgin Islands—is considered a "state" for purposes of federal UI legislation.

3

Enacting Worker Profiling and Reemployment Services

FROM RESEARCH TO POLICY TO LEGISLATION

For research to have a direct impact on public policy, a number of planets have to align, as they did for the enactment of Worker Profiling and Reemployment Services (WPRS) in 1993. The New Jersey Experiment and related research about job search assistance (JSA) had been completed, and their evaluations had been published and widely disseminated. The research findings used a methodology that all researchers and policymakers could agree upon—random assignment methods. The research had been widely read by researchers and policymakers.

The new Clinton administration selected a number of political appointees for posts at the U.S. Department of Labor who knew and understood the research findings. Discussion between the political appointees and key career staff at the department revealed agreement about the effectiveness of providing comprehensive job search assistance through the employment and training system. The department proposed enacting WPRS to the White House, and key political appointees in the White House, along with career staff at the Office of Management and Budget (OMB), supported the initiative. WPRS could not have been enacted unless the budget gatekeepers at OMB and at the Congressional Budget Office (CBO) accepted the budget savings derived from JSA recipients' returning to work sooner. The budget assessments of both agencies accepted the New Jersey Experiment's findings. Finally, Congress needed to enact legislation that included WPRS provisions. All of these things happened in March and again in November of 1993. The planets were aligned.

THE NEW JERSEY EXPERIMENT

It took four years after the New Jersey Experiment results were published before the WPRS system was enacted. Although three secretaries of labor—Ann McLaughlin, Elizabeth Dole, and Lynn Martin—had supported the ongoing UI experiments during their tenures between 1988 and 1992, no political leaders in the executive branch advocated any legislative initiatives based on the results of the New Jersey Experiment. Nonetheless, staff interest as well as congressional and executive branch activity continued to focus on the New Jersey Experiment's evaluation findings.

Between 1989 and 1993, the USDOL, OMB, and members of Congress expressed convictions about the need to provide dislocated workers with reemployment services and additional UI benefits. High unemployment lingered after the 1990–1991 recession. The continuing dislocated worker problem was spreading from manufacturing into white collar and service occupations. The interest in reemployment services was due, in part, to briefings and reviews of the New Jersey Experiment's evaluation results. Staff from all of these organizations had received both the design report for the experiment and its evaluation reports. Many from both the legislative and the executive branches of government had attended meetings at the department on the demonstration, including on its evaluation designs and the draft of the final evaluation report. Early on, they were given a chance to make recommendations about the project and evaluation designs and later for the final evaluation report. The published final evaluation report (Corson et al. 1989) was widely distributed. In 1991, a four-year follow-up report was published on the employment experiences of the treatment and control groups, as well as reestimates of the net impacts and benefit-cost results.

Acting Chairman Thomas Downey (D-NY) of the House Ways and Means Committee's Subcommittee on Human Resources, which has legislative authority over the UI program, called a hearing in February 1991 to focus on the reemployment of dislocated UI claimants. Much of the questioning of witnesses was done by Rich Hobbie, then a committee staffer. He had formerly worked on employment and training issues for the Congressional Research Service and had followed the New Jersey

Experiment closely. The hearing featured the New Jersey Experiment and its findings. As part of the research panel, staff members from Mathematica Policy Research, the research contractor that had conducted the experiment, were asked to testify. While no permanent legislative proposal flowed from the hearing, in November 1991 Congressman Downey successfully proposed adding a Job Search Assistance Demonstration to the bill (the Emergency Unemployment Compensation Act of 1991, or P.L. 102-164) that initially enacted Emergency Unemployment Compensation (EUC), a program that provided additional UI benefits to long-term unemployed workers during and after the 1990–1991 recession.[1] The Job Search Assistance Demonstration replicated the New Jersey Experiment, and its goal was to prepare the way for later legislation.

In 1990, Rep. Sander Levin (D-MI), a member of Congressman Downey's subcommittee, requested a briefing by Mary Ann Wyrsch, administrator of the Unemployment Insurance (UI) Service, about the permanent extended benefit program and the New Jersey Experiment. Wyrsch and I jointly conducted the briefing in her office. Levin was concerned about his state's high unemployment during the 1990–1991 recession. He wanted to understand why the triggering process for permanent extended benefits was not working and what could be done to improve the process. He knew of the efforts to reemploy workers in New Jersey, and he was interested in doing the same for Michigan's workers. Levin later would support EUC legislation in 1991, as well as WPRS when it was proposed as a section of the March and November 1993 extensions of EUC. At the briefing, Levin was accompanied by his legislative director, Kitty Higgins, who had interned in the ETA's research and policy office in 1969 and knew a great deal about employment and training programs. She would support WPRS legislation when she returned to the department in 1993 as Secretary of Labor Robert Reich's chief of staff.[2]

In the spring of 1992, the Subcommittee on Human Resources asked the USDOL to brief its majority and minority staff members on the UI Experiments.[3] I conducted the briefing, which reviewed the outcomes of the New Jersey and other department-sponsored experiments, including interventions relating to job search assistance, training, reemployment bonuses, and self-employment assistance. The attendees disagreed about the effectiveness of other workforce development interventions, but they all agreed that comprehensive job search assistance was a cost-effective public policy. The stage was set for staff-level support of a bipartisan policy initiative, but an advocate within the executive branch was still needed.

FINDING WHAT WORKS

Secretary Reich became the champion of a series of public policy initiatives that were based on the UI Experiments. While he was interested in a wide variety of public investment issues, "workforce-development programs . . . were closest to the hearts of Reich and his inner circle" (Donahue 2008). Before he could guide employment policy as secretary, however, he first had to bring policymakers with him to the department who were familiar with the lessons learned from the UI Experiments.

When Reich had worked on the Clinton campaign in 1992, he had searched for policy options that past research had shown to be cost-effective. Reich was a consumer rather than a creator of research: he relied on others to bring him a synthesis of the findings about which programs or program initiatives worked. During 1992, he worked regularly with Larry Katz of the Harvard Department of Economics and Jack Donahue of Harvard's Kennedy School of Government.[4]

Robert Reich was an old friend of Bill Clinton's. They had met in 1968 on their way to Oxford University, where they both were Rhodes Scholars. They later went to Yale Law School together. They remained friends and became political allies. In 1992, Reich was teaching at the Kennedy School and developing domestic economic policy for Clinton's presidential campaign. He worked on the public investment plan to devote $50 billion a year to education, job training, preschooling, mass transit, and other issues (Reich 1997).

Reich believed that the answer to global competition and technological change was education and job training, so when Clinton asked him in late November 1992 what office he wanted, he said secretary of labor or chair of the Council of Economic Advisers. He was nominated to be secretary of labor on December 11 and had his confirmation hearing in early January 1993. During 1992 he had been looking for new policy options, especially those dealing with employment issues (Reich 1997).

Larry Katz became active in the Clinton campaign after the July 1992 Democratic convention. At first he worked more broadly on economic stimulus and microeconomic issues for the Clinton team headed by Gene Sperling and Robert Rubin. He began concentrating more narrowly on labor issues and working more closely with Reich after Reich was named secretary of labor. He had read a great deal of the labor research literature and had taught advanced seminars that examined which labor policies worked and which did not—a matter on which Katz consulted with other economists, especially Bruce Meyer, a labor economist at Northwestern University. Katz's goal was to identify those policies that might be the basis for Reich's policy agenda as secretary.[5]

Jack Donahue's interests were complementary to those of Katz: he had less of a background in labor issues and was more concerned with the delivery models for government. At USDOL he dealt with governance issues for proposed employment and training programs, designing the relationships between local, state, and federal government. He also was in the middle of the debate about the choice of public versus private provision of traditionally publicly provided services. And he worked on tax issues, including the Targeted Jobs Tax Credit.[6]

Like Clinton, Donahue had a long relationship with Reich. He had gotten his PhD from the Kennedy School, where he had been a research assistant to Reich, who later became his thesis adviser. He joined the Kennedy School faculty and continued to work with Reich; they wrote a book together (Reich and Donahue 1985).

The USDOL's policy agenda had to fit within the policy framework of the Clinton-Gore campaign. That framework was set forth in their campaign book, *Putting People First* (Clinton and Gore 1992). The country was coming out of a recession, and unemployment was still high. In this sluggish economic climate, James Carville coined the campaign's unofficial motto: "It's the economy, stupid." The Clinton/Gore proposal was a national economic strategy that, as noted above, would invest $50 billion a year to put America back to work. The emphasis of the strategy, which promised to fight for the "forgotten middle class," was definitely populist. Investments would be paid for by "making the rich pay their fair share" and by policies encouraging "corporate responsibility." The department's role in this strategy would be to help "make sure American workers can get training and retraining throughout their careers so that America can achieve a high-skill, high wage economy" (4President.org 1992).

The Clinton-Gore agenda included numerous labor and employment policy recommendations. Employers would be required to spend 1.5 percent of their payrolls to provide continuing education and training to all of their workers. An apprentice-style training program would be developed for non-college-bound youth. The minimum wage would be increased to keep pace with inflation. The prevailing wage provisions of the Davis-Bacon Act would be enforced (Clinton and Gore 1992). Reich would bring many of these themes and policy proposals with him to the Labor Department. He was comfortable with the ideas in *Putting People First*—as he should have been, since many of the themes and proposals in the book had come from his own book, *The Work of Nations* (Reich 1992).[7]

Reich and Katz came up with a workforce development agenda that they believed should be pursued. Their list included five items: 1) a school-to-work program, 2) expanding the Job Corps, 3) changing youth employment programs to make them more effective, 4) creating One-Stop Career Centers to better integrate employment and training programs, and 5) implementing the effective interventions of the UI Experiments. Reich championed new One-Stop centers, while Katz and Meyer touted UI Experiment implementation.[8]

Meyer was the academic expert on the UI Experiments. He had started by reading the evaluation reports about the Illinois Reemployment Bonus Experiment. In 1988, he received the microdata of the Illinois experiment's evaluators from the W.E. Upjohn Institute for Employment Research and reanalyzed the data, writing a number of working papers dealing with the Illinois experiment (Meyer 1988, 1991, 1992). After a comprehensive review of the available literature on the reemployment bonus and job search assistance experiments, he completed an early version of his review article on the UI Experiments by early 1992 and submitted it to the *Journal of Economic Literature.* He had shared drafts of the paper with Katz and other academics and with the department, and he received 11 pages of written comments from me and other departmental staff working on the UI Experiments.[9] Meyer continued to add to his UI Experiments paper through 1993 as new evaluation results were published. When his article was finally published (Meyer 1995), he had reviewed two of the three reports on the New Jersey Experiment. While Meyer did not leave Northwestern University to join the Clinton administration, both Katz and Donahue would work for Reich, bringing with them the policy ideas they and Meyer had developed during the campaign.

Meyer and Katz had gone to graduate school together at MIT. They had discussed the UI Experiments since 1988. Katz liked the idea of targeting reemployment services to workers on permanent layoff because it fit with his own research, which had shown great differences in behavior between workers on temporary layoffs and those on permanent layoffs. It made sense to him to have special programs targeted at permanently separated workers (Katz 1985; Katz and Meyer 1990).[10] Katz had even assigned a portion of the 1989 New Jersey Experiment evaluation report as a reading in his graduate labor economics seminar.[11]

From the evaluations of the UI Experiments, Katz was convinced that the three approaches of 1) job search assistance, 2) self-employment assistance, and 3) reemployment bonuses were cost-effective, worked, and should be pursued as public policy. Katz was shocked that nothing was being done to implement these powerful findings. However, he thought that of these three, the area that presented the most compelling case for new policy was that of comprehensive job search assistance. He also believed that the case for funding self-employment assistance was stronger than that for funding reemployment bonuses. Nonetheless, all three policy options looked promising when combined with worker profiling, and he assumed that this targeting mechanism would be used for all of them.[12] He knew that Secretary Reich would be ready to champion all three of the interventions derived from these successful UI Experiments.

Reich had known about the UI Experiments before he became secretary of labor. Katz initially had briefed him about them, and Reich had appreciated the analysis's strength and rigor. Reich also knew that a Clinton White House would be receptive to new ideas, would want to introduce new policy, and would want to know about facts that justified any new policy proposal.[13]

Katz became the department's first chief economist in January 1993 and served as a key research and policy leader, playing a major role in the enactment of both the WPRS and the SEA programs. Katz asked two economists in his office, Marcus Stanley and Isaac Schapiro, to synthesize the lessons learned during 1992 in a monograph called *What's Working (and what's not)*. The monograph's conclusion about the job search assistance experiments stated, "Job search assistance . . . clients found a new job more quickly, and the need for UI benefits was reduced . . . The program was cost-effective for the government . . . Shorter job searches did not lead to jobs that paid less" (USDOL 1995b). Meyer (1995) published his careful review of the UI Experiments as "Lessons from the U.S. Unemployment Insurance Experiments."

REDUCING THE DEFICIT VERSUS INVESTING IN PEOPLE

Reich expected to have wide latitude in implementing new labor programs that would stimulate the economy and improve the conditions for workers. However, he lost the battle for implementation of this package of wide-ranging labor legislation before he even took office.

After the election, Clinton asked Reich to coordinate the economic transition team. Members of the team included Roger Altman, Ira Magaziner, Robert Rubin, Gene Sperling, Larry Summers, and Laura Tyson (Reich 1997). The economic transition team began meeting in November 1992; its goal was to develop a plan to fulfill Clinton's promise to "get the country moving again." The team met frequently to develop this plan, and Clinton presided over many of these meetings (Stephanopoulos 1999).

As Inauguration Day approached, the economic team expanded and split into two opposing groups. Reich led the faction that sought to make a series of new public investments and to create new programs as the main economic thrust of the new administration. Reich's camp wanted to follow through on a number of campaign promises, including a middle-class tax cut and human capital investments. This faction included Sperling, deputy director of the National Economic Council; and George Stephanopoulos, senior political adviser to the president. On the other side were the deficit hawks, who wanted to reduce the budget deficit using macroeconomic policy. This faction was led by Rubin, director of the National Economic Council, and included Lloyd Bentsen, secretary of the treasury; Leon Panetta, OMB director; and Vice President Al Gore (Stephanopoulos 1999).

The conflict among administration economic policy officials was ideological, but it also became personal. In 1993, this confrontation between the center and the left of the Democratic Party was known to policy and budget staff as the "Battle of the Bobs." Some 15 years later, during the 2008 presidential campaign, Bob Reich and Bob Rubin were still active in economic policy, and the economic struggle still had the same name among staffers (Leonhardt 2008).

The deficit hawks were stronger and more influential, but they also were aided by new information obtained after the November 1992 election. The OMB had revised its budget assessment in December 1992, and the results revealed that the deficit was larger than had previously been estimated. Any room for increasing federal expenditures and reducing taxes that might previously have existed was now greatly diminished. In early January 1993, the president's economic team met to establish a policy framework for the new administration. Reich did not attend. The team decided to implement a macroeconomic approach aimed at reducing the deficit. This approach severely limited the possibility of developing expensive new federal programs, and so it sharply diminished Reich's hope of developing new training programs and other major reemployment initiatives (Clinton 2004; Stephanopoulos 1999). Reich thus was faced with identifying new initiatives that did not result in large new expenditures.

Reich realized the deficit had grown substantially—to about $350 billion—when he met with outgoing OMB director Richard Darman in early December 1992, but it took him a while to realize how the deficit would circumscribe his ability to affect public policy. He wanted to "focus like a laser beam on jobs and incomes," but he saw his public investment plan cut back in January, and in mid-February Clinton's State of the Union address made it clear that the main message was deficit reduction, with public investment secondary (Reich 1997).

MARCH 1993 WORKER PROFILING AND REEMPLOYMENT SERVICES LEGISLATION

Jack Donahue came to Washington during the Clinton transition in late 2002, and he walked in the door of the department with Bob Reich on January 21, 1993. He studied the inventiveness of the department during Reich's years as secretary.[14] Donahue found an unusually high level of innovation during that period, which he attributes in part to "Reich's motives, background, and character," describing him as a "thick-skinned, softhearted, risk-tolerant, camera-loving intellectual." Reich created a culture that was "emphatically and explicitly supportive of innovation," and he was "convinced that a wealth of untapped inventiveness lay dormant within the career workforce." As evidence of the success of this unleashed inventiveness, Donahue cited the enactment of WPRS as "the single most elegant policy innovation of the Reich years" (Donahue 2008).

Reich continued to focus on "jobs and incomes"; his goal was to reemploy American workers in the context of an American labor market suffering from lingering unemployment initiated by the 1990–1991 recession. He explored options that might still be available to him within the deficit reduction policy on which the Clinton economic policy was focused.

Another budget constraint would affect the ability of the department to enact new legislation: the federal budget enforcement provisions installed in the mid-1980s were still in effect. Congress had imposed them to try to reduce the large budget deficit. If Reich was going to seek funds for USDOL programs, and especially if he wanted money for new initiatives, he would have to better understand how to work within the federal budget process. He found an expert in the process, Darla Letourneau, a careerist who had recently moved from the ETA to the Office of Congressional and Intergovernmental Affairs within the Labor Department. Letourneau would help to ensure that department policy options fit within the budget process. Not only did she have extensive budget experience in Congress, she had also served as the budget officer in the UI Service, where she had worked closely with me and had followed the progress of the UI Experiments.

Meetings about policy options at Labor began as soon as Reich arrived. Reich's method was to run policy meetings that operated like Harvard seminars, but the goal was always to quickly develop policy options. Reich was searching for new ideas that could further his goal of getting Americans back to work. One of the first issues that had to be dealt with was the extension of the EUC program, which was expiring in early March.

Secretary Reich convened a number of meetings in late January about employment and training issues. Regular attendees included both political staff—Deputy Secretary Tom Glynn, Chief of Staff Higgins, Chief Economist Katz, and Assistant Secretary for Policy Donahue—as well as careerists such as Carolyn Golding, acting assistant secretary for Employment and Training, and Letourneau and Gerri Fiala of the Office of Congressional and Intergovernmental Affairs. They engaged in freewheeling discussions about new policy options. Reich's theme was reemployment services that might get workers back to work. One-Stop Career Centers—an expansion of the local employment security agencies to encompass multiple agencies, including those outside of the department's funding realm—were one concept identified; One-Stops would be implemented in 1994. Other options were considered, including providing comprehensive job search assistance to dislocated workers based on the experience of the New Jersey Experiment. Job search assistance for dislocated workers fit into Reich's goal of capturing the public imagination by restarting and regenerating the U.S. labor market.[15]

At these early meetings, Reich was gathering information. Golding was promoting two issues—the findings of the UI Experiments and the need to expand youth programs. She believed there was a unique opportunity to promote reemployment services approaches based on the hard evidence of the UI Experiments, and she was advocating for the group's taking advantage of the narrow window she saw for the administration to adopt new programs and provide new funding.[16]

At one meeting, Katz reviewed the findings of the New Jersey Experiment and related rigorous research dealing with the provision of comprehensive job search assistance. He presented the arguments for implementing this cost-effective approach to returning workers to productive employment. Around the room heads were nodding in support; Reich, Higgins, and Glynn all "loved it." At the end of the meeting, Glynn gave the attendees a chance to poke holes in the proposal, asking if anyone saw "any traps" in a job search assistance initiative. No one spoke up.[17]

Comprehensive job search assistance was half of WPRS; the other half was targeting workers through the worker profiling mechanism. At a smaller meeting Katz excited Reich and others by presenting an argument for how powerful—i.e., efficient and effective—targeting could be, using worker profiling.[18] The wheels were set in motion for WPRS.

Reich responded positively to the worker profiling proposal. He appreciated the concept of cost-effectively getting workers back to work. He also realized that although the administration was focused on deficit reduction, Bill Clinton was still interested in new ideas if their cost was low. This idea, he thought, would be "gobbled up."[19]

Katz wrote a memorandum about implementing WPRS as part of the effort to extend EUC. Reich revised the memo and sent it to Clinton, bypassing the National Economic Council. Clinton approved the proposal, but the council admonished Reich to go through proper channels in the future.[20]

Katz was known as a brilliant young labor economist, but it was not clear how he would do in his first foray into Washington politics. He adapted quickly and took charge of the WPRS initiative. He would play a key role in many other issues—among them the labor issues relating to the North American Free Trade Agreement (NAFTA), which involved the Self-Employment Assistance initiative.[21]

In early 1993, the temporary EUC program was being administered by the ETA. Golding, a senior career official, was serving as acting assistant secretary for Employment and Training until a political appointee could be named. Reich told her he wanted to do more than just reauthorize EUC; he wanted to introduce a new initiative at the same time. The two discussed introducing a comprehensive job search assistance program modeled after the New Jersey Experiment. Golding was familiar with the New Jersey Experiment and its evaluation results, since the experiment had been conducted in the UI Service while she was administrator of that agency. She was highly supportive of the new initiative.[22]

Golding thought it essential to provide reemployment services to dislocated UI recipients, and she was convinced that the New Jersey Experiment demonstrated the effectiveness of such services. Although she had believed in their effectiveness even before the New Jersey Experiment, she found that experiment to be innovative because it showed that early intervention was the key to making early reemployment happen. The early intervention aspect was what made her most supportive of this policy effort.[23]

Reich was pleased with the department's career staff—they were better than he had expected. He was hungry for evidence, and the UI Experiments had the evidence. Golding considered early 1993 to be a "happy moment" when information met opportunity. She spoke to Reich about my role as director of research for the UI program, explaining that since I had been in charge of the experiments, I was the best person to work on preparing the legislative and policy material to implement such a comprehensive initiative.[24]

Reich heard more about the UI Experiments at a huge, all-employee meeting held in late January, shortly after his taking charge. He spoke of his vision for the department and asked employees for new policy ideas. A scribe took down the names of the employees who spoke, where they worked, and their recommendations for policy innovations. Steve Marler raised his hand, identified himself, and said that he had worked for me on the UI Experiments. He described the New Jersey Experiment and suggested that Reich make use of its policy findings. A month later, he and I were summoned to the White House and attended President Clinton's March 4 signing of the EUC extension legislation, which also enacted WPRS provisions. At the ceremony, Marler and I were given credit for the idea behind the WPRS legislation.[25]

In May 1993, an issue of *The Labor Exchange*, a new departmental publication distributed to all employees, carried the lead article "Idea Packs a Punch: ETA Employees Plant Seed That Sprouts into Law," which again credited Marler and me with initiating the WPRS legislation (USDOL 1993). No mention was made of the significant role Katz and Golding had played. Reich was making a point. He wanted to demonstrate to the career workforce at the department that he was listening to them.

When Marler had mentioned the UI Experiments at the January all-employee meeting, Reich loved it. It fit with his hope that ideas could and should bubble up from the department's career staff, and it gave him the opportunity to provide recognition for a specific instance where that had occurred.[26]

I met with Reich in late January to discuss an initiative to incorporate comprehensive job search assistance as part of the EUC reauthorization. Reich had recruited me to work with other department staff to quickly develop a concrete proposal and supporting materials. Within a week we had prepared the material that would allow Clinton and Reich to announce the new initiative.

Reich and Katz conducted discussions with White House Chief of Staff Thomas "Mac" McLarty about incorporating WPRS into the EUC

extension. Agreement was quickly reached to include the WPRS initiative.[27] On February 8, 1993—only three weeks after taking office—Clinton announced a new policy to help dislocated workers: "No short-term
solution to their problem is adequate; many, many of those unemployed
workers are what we call permanently displaced—and they need much
better access to reemployment services that will provide them with the
information and changing skills necessary to compete in a changing
world" (Clinton 1993).

The initiative would include "reforms to the unemployment insurance programs that will dramatically improve the reemployment services available to structurally unemployed workers," Clinton said. "A
number of demonstration projects, particularly the New Jersey reemployment demonstration, showed that this kind of profiling and referral
can significantly reduce the time these workers spend unemployed."

Reich (1993) said when the announcement was made, "With this
initiative, we plan to go beyond business as usual in our efforts to spur
job creation and assist the unemployed."

The WPRS bill created a program for states to profile new UI claimants "to determine which claimants may be likely to exhaust regular
unemployment compensation and may need reemployment assistance
services to make a successful transition to new employment" (P.L. 103-6,
Sec. 4[a]). Such workers would be offered reemployment services.
States' participation in WPRS would be voluntary, and UI claimants'
participation in services they were referred to would also be voluntary.
States would bear the cost of providing the reemployment services,
using state funds or federal Wagner-Peyser Act ES or JTPA funds.

The bill was only the sixth that President Clinton had signed into
law. Senators and House members stood behind Clinton; Reich, Marler, and I stood to the right; and out of the sight of the cameras stood
McLarty. At the signing ceremony in the Roosevelt Room, Clinton
joked to the attendees and the press that he was still learning how to
sign his name with 20 different pens so that he could give each attendee
one of the signing pens.

The bill's WPRS provisions were tentative. They announced that
the Clinton administration thought that comprehensive job search assistance was a good idea, but that participation in the profiling system
was voluntary on the part of both the states and the UI claimants. The
secretary was to encourage participation, but he could not compel it.

Reich had been able to act quickly to incorporate something new into the EUC extension because of the nature of WPRS and the manner in which it had been enacted. Any amendment added to the EUC extension had to be noncontroversial so it wouldn't provoke a congressional hearing. WPRS was less controversial because of the rigor with which comprehensive job search assistance treatments had been evaluated using random assignment methods. WPRS was even less controversial because it was adopted as a voluntary program. The WPRS provision was also enacted because it had been administratively easier and less time consuming to add an amendment to the extension of existing legislation than it would have been to adopt the measure through the regular legislative process. Finally, the imminent expiration date of the EUC program gave Reich additional leverage, because delay would have meant a gap in the payment of extended UI payments.[28]

Thus, WPRS was enacted quickly and painlessly. However, department policymakers knew they would have to revisit WPRS and make participation in the program mandatory. The opportunity arose in November.

NOVEMBER 1993 LEGISLATION

Six months after enactment of voluntary WPRS, in November 1993, unemployment levels remained high, and the temporary EUC program was expiring again. The administration proposed a fourth and final extension of the program. Under congressional budget rules, the cost of Emergency Unemployment Compensation would have to be offset either by an increase in taxes or a cut in expenditures by the amount of the extension's cost.

At the same time, while the USDOL had been enthusiastic about enactment of the new profiling provisions and had begun to encourage and support state implementation, a number of departmental policymakers wanted to ensure that the system would be applied nationally and that participation by UI claimants would be mandatory. The New Jersey Experiment's findings and other research evidence had shown that providing comprehensive job search assistance was more cost-effective when UI claimant participation was mandatory: the cost of providing comprehensive JSA had been found to be less than the combined savings from reduced UI benefit payments and increased tax payments by workers who returned to work more rapidly.

Paying for another EUC extension and making WPRS mandatory became linked when the idea of using the cost savings from WPRS to fund the EUC extension was born. If the budget estimators at the OMB and the CBO would accept the New Jersey evaluation results, making WPRS mandatory could "pay" for the EUC extension. Taxes would not have to be raised nor expenditures cut. The expected change in behavior of UI beneficiaries who were offered reemployment services might thus be used to pay for EUC under the federal budget rules.

Whose idea was it to fund the extension by making participation in WPRS mandatory? Reich (1997) claims Higgins originated the idea of changing WPRS to require state and individual participation. She understood that the participation requirement was the key to the success of the New Jersey Experiment and could contribute to the success of the WPRS system. She also understood that, under budget rules, the extension of EUC had to be paid for by offsetting reduction in expenditures somewhere else. The potential cost reductions in UI benefits, which would be derived from UI claimants going back to work sooner if WPRS were made mandatory, might be used to pay for the EUC extension. The department estimated these budgetary savings using the savings in UI benefits indicated in the evaluation of the New Jersey Experiment. These savings were projected forward to yield a five-year savings figure that was used to fund the EUC extension. A few members of Congress questioned both the projected savings and the appropriateness of making the program required, but the bill passed easily with bipartisan support (Reich 1997).

Although Reich credited her with the approach, Higgins makes no claim that she originated the idea.[29] In fact, both Katz and Meyer knew that the key to the success of the job search assistance intervention in the New Jersey Experiment had been mandatory participation, without which it would not have been cost-effective. When the EUC came up for renewal in November, since neither tax increases nor expenditure cuts were palatable, Katz recommended using the savings that would accrue from reducing the duration of UI compensation.[30]

Finding a noncontroversial method of funding EUC was important for another reason. While the administration wanted to extend EUC, it did not want EUC renewal to imperil the enactment of NAFTA, which Clinton had made a priority and which Congress would be considering at the same time as EUC (both were enacted in November 1993).[31]

Reich knew it was critical to have Congress accept the savings projections from implementing WPRS to fund the renewal of the EUC program. He spoke to OMB director Panetta to convince him to support the budget scoring of the new legislation. Traveling on Air Force One with President Clinton, Reich spoke to Rep. Dan Rostenkowski (D-IL), chairman of the House Ways and Means Committee, to urge him to support the legislation and its budget scoring method.[32]

The arbiters determining the costs and savings of proposed legislation at the OMB (for the executive branch) and at the CBO (for Congress) would have to accept the projected budget savings from enacting a mandatory WPRS program. While department leadership anticipated that the OMB would accept the use of WPRS to finance EUC, convincing the CBO about this financing approach was considered to be a problem.[33]

At the OMB, Panetta, although initially skeptical, was ready to be convinced. His concern about avoiding controversy in funding the EUC extension and enhancing NAFTA's chances made seizing on the WPRS budget savings irresistible.[34]

However, before embracing the EUC legislative proposal, Panetta called a meeting with the USDOL. Department political leaders Reich, Higgins, and Glynn were accompanied by senior career staff including Letourneau, Golding, and Wyrsch. OMB senior staff were skeptical about the estimated budget savings derived from WPRS and had to be convinced by USDOL staff members, who were knowledgeable about the proposal and the research. While the subject of the meeting was the EUC extension legislation, Secretary Reich pressed for the message to be about reemployment services. Reich inflated the role of WPRS in the extension of UI benefits; it otherwise would have been treated as a side issue.[35]

The OMB career budget examiners estimated the impact of the EUC extension on the budget. They were concerned that they had to assume a behavioral response by UI claimants without any new funding for the WPRS system. At the same time, OMB staff had to assume that the Employment Service would commit existing funding to provide reemployment services. The cost estimators would have been more comfortable with the process if new funds had been appropriated and had a realistic chance of generating the savings: it appeared to them to be an unfunded mandate. The pressure put on the OMB was part of a larger issue—that of the Clinton administration trying to bypass the pay-as-you-go (PAYGO) process during a period of high unemployment. Neither the OMB nor the CBO was happy with the proposed funding process for EUC. Nevertheless, the estimators concluded that the cost of implementing WPRS—the cost of providing comprehensive job search assistance to profiled workers—was more than offset by the cost reduction.

Katz worked to gain support for the bill. After he received concurrence from Higgins and White House staff about using WPRS savings to offset EUC extension costs, he went to the CBO to discuss the budget scoring of WPRS under the federal budgetary PAYGO rules. Since enacting mandatory WPRS could be shown to result in a likely reduction in the compensated duration of unemployment, logically that would reduce the level of unemployment. The problem was that, under the budget rules, the expected unemployment rate could not be changed. Hence, Katz developed the theory that the behavioral response to WPRS would not reduce the unemployment rate but would change the mix of the unemployment rate between insured unemployment and all other unemployment. Thus, only the mix of unemployment would change, not the level.[36] The CBO accepted Katz's approach and incorporated it into its cost estimates.[37]

Within the ETA, Golding supported the effort to make participation in WPRS mandatory. She understood that budget scoring is a political process, but she thought that this effort made a good deal of sense. She believed in the WPRS system, and she knew that the money to provide the reemployment services was already available within the Unemployment Trust Fund—if Congress would appropriate it.[38]

The actuarial division of the UI Service also made budget estimates of the WPRS proposal. The actuaries believed in the results of the New Jersey Experiment. They believed that WPRS—implemented as in the New Jersey Experiment—would result in a decline in the duration of insured unemployment which would reduce compensated duration of unemployment and increase payment of taxes. However, the UI actuaries doubted the magnitude of the estimated savings and thought that WPRS might result in some displacement of workers who did not receive reemployment services.[39]

Thus, the CBO, the OMB, and the USDOL all estimated the net budget costs of the WPRS initiative. In estimating budgetary impacts, they all used the data from the New Jersey Experiment evaluation and consulted with departmental research staff. Not surprisingly, their estimates were fairly close to one another. The closeness of their estimates made them more believable and made it easier to enact the WPRS provisions: it was difficult to dispute the budget savings if the budget gurus of two branches of government embraced the same savings estimates.[40]

Enactment of the WPRS provision depended on congressional support. The congressional leaders also had to be educated about the savings that could be derived from mandatory WPRS. The White House and USDOL lobbyists were enlisted to talk to members of Congress and their staffs. Ultimately, WPRS received wide support, although Rep. John Boehner (R-OH), now House minority leader, was a lone but strong opponent of the program.[41]

The Unemployment Compensation Amendments of 1993 (P.L. 103-152), enacted on November 24, 1993, made participation in WPRS mandatory both for states and for UI claimants who are identified and referred to reemployment services. Section 4(a) reads as follows:

> The state agency charged with the administration of the State [unemployment compensation] law shall establish and utilize a system of profiling all new claimants for regular compensation that . . . identifies which claimants will be likely to exhaust regular compensation and will need job search assistance services to make a successful transition to new employment . . . [and] refers claimants identified . . . to reemployment services, such as job search assistance services, available under any State or Federal law.

Reemployment services provided by state employment security agencies could be broader than job search assistance, but the main focus would be on comprehensive job search assistance (JSA). However, the legislation still did not provide any new sources of funding for these services. Rather, states had to make use of whatever funds were available under current law. The lack of funding would be a problem for the future of the WPRS system.

FUNDING OF WORKER PROFILING AND
REEMPLOYMENT SERVICES

WPRS started on weak financial footing: it was enacted without Congress's authorizing additional funding for the reemployment services. As enacted, the initiative assumed that sufficient funds would be provided from existing employment and training programs. The Employment Service was assumed to be the primary provider of the additional reemployment services, but the ES national funding level was about to decline sharply, and JTPA/WIA funding would drop as well. ES grants to states peaked in 1995 at $839 million and steadily declined to $703 million by 2008. (See Table 6.1.)

Budget increases were critical to funding WPRS and Reich's other policy initiatives. These policy proposals required and assumed increases in the department's budget. In fact, Reich was able to propose and get budget increases for the first two years of the Clinton administration: in 1993 and 1994, federal funding increased for many of the employment and training programs, including Dislocated Workers and the Job Corps. When the Republicans took control of Congress after the 1994 midterm elections, budget increases ended.[42]

The WPRS system was weakened not only by the lack of a new funding source but by an actual decline in employment and training funding available to states after 1995. New programs would inevitably falter if they could not be adequately funded. Departmental staff later recognized the WPRS funding weakness and proposed new funding for it, and Congress approved approximately $35 million a year between 2001 and 2005.

SUMMARY AND CONCLUSIONS

The enactment of the Worker Profiling and Reemployment Services provisions in 1993 was a classic case of research informing and guiding policy and legislation. The WPRS legislation flowed directly from the New Jersey Experiment and related, rigorous research.

The New Jersey Experiment used random assignment methods and was rigorously evaluated. It found that comprehensive job search assistance provides net benefits to the government sector. The evaluation was widely disseminated and read. The findings were consistent with those from other rigorous evaluations of job search assistance.

Specifically, the research cited by the department to justify WPRS included the New Jersey Experiment, the Charleston Claimant Placement and Work Test Demonstration, and three state-funded experiments operated in Minnesota, Nevada, and Washington.[43]

Larry Katz, the USDOL's chief economist, brought the research findings to the attention of the department's political leadership in January 1993. Katz based his conclusions on his review of the job search assistance experiments and on Bruce Meyer's analysis of the UI Experiments.

Robert Reich was receptive to new policy approaches based on research evidence. Katz recommended the WPRS approach to him, and he responded positively. Because of his outreach to career staff, he received the same recommendation from Acting Assistant Secretary Carolyn Golding and from a staff member on the UI Experiments team, Steve Marler.

The WPRS initiative benefited from the support of other senior officials at the USDOL, including Deputy Secretary Tom Glynn, Chief of Staff Kitty Higgins, Assistant Secretary for Policy Jack Donahue, and Darla Letourneau of the Office of Congressional Affairs. It also had support from staff at the House Ways and Means Committee, the Office of Management and Budget, and the Congressional Budget Office. Just as importantly, virtually no one opposed the initiative, in either the executive branch or the legislative branch.

The WPRS initiative provided no new funding for the provision of reemployment services. Reich assumed that new funding would be provided from increased funding of employment and training programs. In fact, grants to states for employment and training programs declined after 1995. WPRS did receive limited funding in the form of Reemployment Services Grants between 2001 and 2005, but there was no further funding through 2008.

Notes

1. During the fall of 1991, Rich Hobbie and I met to develop specifications for a multistate Job Search Assistance Demonstration as a follow-up to confirm the New Jersey Experiment's results. These specifications were incorporated into the Emergency Unemployment Compensation Act of 1991. The demonstration was conducted in the District of Columbia and Florida.
2. Katherine Higgins, interview with the author, July 17, 2008; Mary Ann Wyrsch, interview with the author, July 29, 2008.
3. The majority staff members were Wendell Primus and Rich Hobbie. The minority staffers were Ron Haskins and Andrew Bush.
4. Lawrence Katz, interviews with the author, August 21 and September 25, 2008; John D. Donahue, interview with the author, September 24, 2008.
5. Katz, interviews.
6. Donahue, interview.
7. Ibid.
8. Katz, interviews.
9. Bruce D. Meyer, interview with the author, August 25, 2008.
10. Ibid.
11. Lawrence Katz, discussion with the author, 1993.
12. Katz, interviews, 2008.
13. Robert B. Reich, interview with the author, November 21, 2008.
14. Donahue, interview.
15. Darla Letourneau, interview with the author, August 11, 2008.
16. Carolyn Golding, interview with the author, December 5, 2008.
17. Donahue, interview.
18. Ibid.
19. Reich, interview.
20. Katz, interviews.
21. Donahue, interview.
22. Golding, interview.
23. Ibid.
24. Ibid.
25. Steve Marler, interview with the author, September 25, 2008.
26. Golding, interview.
27. Katz, interviews.
28. Letourneau, interview.
29. Higgins, interview.
30. Katz, interviews.
31. Ibid.
32. Reich, interview.
33. Katz, interviews.
34. Ibid.
35. Letourneau, interview.

36. Katz, interviews.
37. When one estimates the budget impact of a program change, the budget rules constrain the cost and revenue estimates, so that the level of nominal GDP must stay constant—i.e., there cannot be a change in the level of economic activity. However, if the level of unemployment had decreased in the estimate for the November 1993 WPRS legislation, the estimate would have been associated with an increase in nominal GDP. This information comes from an interview the author conducted with Ralph Smith of the Congressional Budget Office on August 25, 2008.
38. Golding, interview.
39. Michael Miller, interview with the author, October 7, 2008.
40. Letourneau, interview.
41. Katz, interviews.
42. Ibid.
43. These experiments are cited in the discussion of worker profiling and job search assistance in the paper *What's Working (and what's not)* (USDOL 1995b). The experiments other than the New Jersey Experiment are discussed in Chapter 5.

4
Worker Profiling and Reemployment Services

Implementation and Operations

This chapter reviews the implementation of the Worker Profiling and Reemployment Services (WPRS) program and the results of the first decade and a half of its operation. The first section of this chapter reviews the WPRS legislation; the second discusses the development of the WPRS program. The worker profiling mechanism is discussed in the third section. The fourth section describes the delivery of reemployment services from 1994 to the present; it also discusses the use of worker profiling in other industrial nations. The chapter ends with a summary and conclusions.

FEDERAL LEGISLATION

The Unemployment Compensation Amendments of 1993, which became Public Law 103-152 on November 24, 1993, are the basis of the WPRS initiative. This statute amended the Social Security Act by adding a new subsection, 303(j), which requires each state agency charged with the administration of the state unemployment compensation law to establish and utilize a worker profiling system for all new claimants for regular compensation.

Worker profiling is a system that

1) identifies which claimants will be likely to exhaust regular compensation and will need job search assistance services to make a successful transition to new employment;

2) refers such claimants to reemployment services, such as job search assistance services available under state or federal law;

97

3) collects follow-up information relating to the services received by such claimants and the employment outcomes of such claimants subsequent to receiving such services and utilizes this information in making identifications (Step 1, above); and

4) meets such other requirements as the secretary of labor determines appropriate.[1]

In addition, the conference report for P.L. 103-152 defined the reemployment services that should be provided to profiled and referred claimants: "Reemployment services will include job search assistance and job placement services, such as counseling, testing, and providing occupational and labor market information, assessment, job search workshops, job clubs and referrals to employers, and other similar services."

Thus, the system's emphasis is on speeding the return to work of job-ready dislocated workers.

The WPRS legislation is part of federal unemployment insurance (UI) law and requires that state workforce agencies establish WPRS systems and make participation in reemployment services mandatory for claimants referred through profiling.[2] It does not, however, provide any new or additional funding for the provision of these reemployment services: state agencies must provide reemployment services from existing state and federal funding sources. If the funds for reemployment services are not available, states are not required to supply them. The ultimate size and adequacy of the WPRS system thus has been constrained by the existing funding for reemployment services. In every state, WPRS funding has generally fallen well short of the potential demand that can be identified by profiling methods. The identification and referral process under WPRS must adjust the number of referrals to the available capacity of state and local service providers, and that capacity has been quite limited.

In March 1993, WPRS was enacted as a national program, but state participation in reemployment services was voluntary. Before the program became operational, however, the law was changed in November 1993 to make state participation mandatory (Table 4.1).

Table 4.1 Chronology of Worker Profiling and Reemployment Services

Period	Development
1986–1987	New Jersey Experiment is conducted.
1989	New Jersey Experiment final report published.
March 1993	WPRS enacted as a national program with voluntary participation in reemployment services.
Summer 1993	National worker profiling model developed.
September 1993	UI Program Letter 45-93 broadly describes the WPRS profiling model and the design of the WPRS system.
Fall 1993	Maryland is first state to implement WPRS.
November 1993	New WPRS legislation makes individual WPRS participation mandatory.
December 1993	ETA Basic Understanding Team makes recommendation on the WPRS process to ETA executive staff.
Winter 1994	State WPRS profiling model completed and implemented by Maryland.
March 1994	Field Memorandum 35-94 provides detailed description of WPRS.
Late 1994	WPRS guidance compiled and released in "Green Book."
Spring 1996	All states implement WPRS.
June 1996	National WPRS Colloquium.
1994–1999	WPRS evaluation conducted.
October 1997	Employment Service Program Letter 1-98 published.
1998–1999	Federal-State WPRS Policy Workgroup meets and makes recommendations.
February 1999	WPRS Policy Workgroup issues its final report and recommendations.
1999	Significant Improvement Demonstration Grants awarded to 11 states to improve WPRS reemployment services.
1999	Funding for WPRS services ($35 million) requested by USDOL.
2000	WPRS reemployment services funded.
July 2001	WPRS reemployment services funding of $35 million per year begins.
2002	*Targeting Employment Services* (Eberts, O'Leary, and Wandner 2002) published.

Table 4.1 (continued)

Period	Development
2004	USDOL budget request excludes WPRS reemployment services funding.
2005	USDOL budget enacted without WPRS reemployment services funding.
June 2006	WPRS reemployment services funding terminates after five years of funding at an annual level of approximately $35 million.
2007	Study of worker profiling models completed.
June 2007	Government Accountability Office report on WPRS published.
February 2009	Reemployment Services Grants appropriated in amount of $250 million as part of the American Recovery and Reinvestment Act.

DEVELOPMENT AND IMPLEMENTATION OF THE WORKER PROFILING PROCESS

Overview

Under the permanent WPRS system, each state program has two components: 1) a worker profiling mechanism to identify dislocated unemployment insurance claimants who are likely to exhaust their UI, and 2) provision of available reemployment services during the early weeks of unemployment for these workers. There was no precedent for the WPRS initiative; state workforce programs had never before developed a statistical model as the targeting mechanism. Similarly, a large-scale, coordinated system of providing reemployment services to UI claimants had never existed. Ultimately, it would prove far easier to develop and implement worker profiling models than to provide eligible claimants with reemployment services. It has also proven difficult to maintain and fund the WPRS system.

How the Profiling Mechanism Works

Following their initial development between 1993 and 1995, worker profiling mechanisms for state UI programs are now operating throughout the United States. Generally the profiling mechanisms were developed by state workforce agency staff. In some cases, state agencies had assistance from state universities and private research organizations. Most state models reflect the technical guidance given by the department. Many models also reflect individual state policy or state technical innovations and adaptations.

A worker profiling model predicts the likelihood that given claimants will exhaust their total UI entitlement. States have considered two approaches to developing worker profiling mechanisms: statistical models and "characteristic screening." Nationally, 45 states use a statistical model (Sullivan et al. 2007). Under this approach, profiling is a two-step process to identify permanently separated workers who have difficulty finding reemployment. First, permanently separated workers are identified by screening out two groups of unemployed workers who are considered job-attached: workers subject to recall and workers subject to a union hiring hall agreement.[3] Claimants must also be eligible to receive UI benefits. They must pass these profiling screens before moving to the second step.

Second, reemployment difficulty is predicted statistically by using a logit regression analysis applied to historical data. The measure of reemployment difficulty is the dependent variable. It is generally a binary variable (i.e., a zero or a one, depicting whether or not the worker is likely to exhaust all entitlement to UI benefits).[4] This variable facilitates creation of a profiling model where the outcome measure is the predicted probability that claimants will remain unemployed for about six months.

The worker profiling model estimates the probability of exhaustion for individuals based on their demographic characteristics as well as current state labor market conditions (i.e., the independent variables). These variables are evaluated for their impact on exhaustion. The impacts produce state-specific weights for the independent variables. The weights are incorporated into computer programs that apply the profiling model to identify and refer selected claimants to receive reemployment services. This profiling process is generally run weekly.

In addition to the two variables used to identify permanent separation (i.e., recall status and union hiring hall agreement), the USDOL recommended that states use five additional variables in designing and estimating their worker profiling statistical models. The variables are

1) education,

2) job tenure,

3) change in employment in previous industry,

4) change in employment in previous occupation, and

5) local unemployment rate.

States have generally adopted this modeling approach, but some states have incorporated substantial variations from the department's approach. These variations include three broad types: 1) introducing additional variables, 2) changing the specifications of some of the department-recommended variables, and 3) delaying introduction of one or more variables for which states did not have sufficient data when they implemented their WPRS systems.[5] Despite the aging of state profiling models, many states have neglected updating their models. Nevertheless, the department encourages states to make continuing improvements to their profiling mechanisms and to update them every year or two to address changes in demographic and economic conditions.

In 1993, staff from the Department of Justice's Civil Rights Division advised the department that federal civil rights legislation prohibits states from using certain variables as part of their worker profiling mechanisms, including age, race or ethnic group, and gender. As a result, these variables are excluded from the statistical models. An analysis comparing the results of worker profiling selection when these variables are included or omitted indicates that the effect of omission is very small.[6]

In those few states that use characteristic screening, the process relies on a small number of characteristics, each of which has a preset cutoff value or criterion. Individuals are selected if they meet the criterion for each screen used, without any weighting mechanism. A number of states that initially used characteristic screening converted to statistical models because models have proven to be a more flexible and accurate targeting device for making referrals to reemployment services. For example, the model can rank referrals by probability of exhaustion, which characteristic screens cannot do. Thus, the model more precisely scales inflows to available services. After reviewing the two approaches, the department recommended that states use statistical models instead of characteristic screening.

Development of Early Intervention/Profiling Models

The New Jersey Experiment did not develop a worker profiling mechanism. While it targeted a dislocated worker population, it used a series of screens to select the treatment and control group members rather than a statistical model (Corson et al. 1989).[7] Once WPRS was enacted, state employment security agencies needed an administratively simple mechanism that would allow them to target reemployment services. The mechanism would both select individuals in need of these services and allow limiting the provision of services in a rational and defensible manner.

No mechanism for conducting worker profiling existed, and the development of such a mechanism became a priority after the enactment of WPRS in March 1993. I was responsible for developing such a system during the summer of 1993. Kelleen Worden Kaye, who previously had worked on UI research projects as a researcher at the Urban Institute, developed a national worker profiling model, using a data set from the Current Population Survey (CPS) that was provided by Ralph Smith of the Congressional Budget Office (CBO). Kaye documented the approach, and a worker profiling approach was ready for adoption and use by states by the end of the summer (USDOL 1994b, pp. 121–163).

This national model was designed to be a prototype for state use in developing state-specific worker profiling models. It was based on past research regarding the nature and characteristics of dislocated workers. It was designed to provide a flexible, accurate, and defensible mechanism for selecting unemployed workers to participate in reemployment services.[8] In 1994, the department began providing technical assistance to the states, helping some of them to develop and test their own worker profiling models using their own state data (USDOL 1994b).[9] The department had a small technical assistance staff, consisting of federal employees and contractors, who provided technical assistance to all states requesting such help. Technical assistance to update and improve worker profiling models has been ongoing: every few years, a worker profiling seminar is conducted to provide assistance to the states.[10]

In the fall of 1993, Maryland became the first state to implement WPRS. It did so without a statistical worker profiling model. Late that year, concerned about the inflexibility of its characteristic screening model, Maryland volunteered to be the first pilot state to implement the new worker profiling model.[11] The state model was developed by the department profiling modeling team that had been brought together to assist the states (USDOL 1994b, pp. 164–272).

Since WPRS implementation was mandatory for all state workforce agencies, states reviewed the national worker profiling model as adapted for use by Maryland. Initially, most states adopted this model, generally without changes. A small number of states developed a characteristic screening system for UI claimants, selecting WPRS participants who met the screens and excluding those who did not.

While the worker profiling model is a relatively crude tool for identifying dislocated workers who require reemployment services, it has worked reasonably well. A long-term follow-up study to the New Jersey Experiment simulated what would have happened if the New Jersey worker profiling model of the mid-1990s had been used to select participants for the 1986–1987 experiment. The simulation measured how accurately the worker profiling model would have identified UI program exhaustees if it had been used as part of the experiment. The report provides additional support for the WPRS approach, stating that "using a profiling model to target reemployment services on workers with high probabilities of UI benefit exhaustion directs reemployment services to a group of workers who are likely to benefit from the services . . . thereby generating relatively large savings in UI receipt for the given level of expenditures on services" (Corson and Haimson 1996).

The department sponsored an evaluation of profiling models in order to better understand how the models are working and to determine how they might be improved (Sullivan et al. 2007). In 2005, the researchers conducted a survey of all 50 states and the other three jurisdictions that have UI and WPRS programs (Table 4.2). With respect to the operation of the WPRS models, the study found that most states use statistical models and update their models with new data but have never revised the structure of their models (Sullivan et al. 2007).

Table 4.2 State WPRS Profiling Model Characteristics, 2005

State	Model type	Functional style	Date of last update	Model revision
Alabama	statistical	logit	never	2000
Alaska	statistical	logit	1/06	1/05
Arizona	statistical	—	7/03	7/03
Arkansas	statistical	linear regression	never	none
California	statistical	logit	12/01	none
Colorado	statistical	logit	never	none
Connecticut	statistical	neural network	never	none
Delaware	characteristic		never	none
D.C.	statistical	logit	1/04	10/04
Florida	no scoring		never	1/02
Georgia	statistical	logit	1/98	none
Hawaii	statistical	logit	1/95	1/02
Idaho	characteristic		5/05	5/05
Illinois	statistical	logit	1997	none
Indiana	statistical	linear regression	never	none
Iowa	statistical	logit	never	none
Kansas	statistical	logit	never	none
Kentucky	statistical	tobit	1/97	none
Louisiana	statistical	logit	6/03	6/03
Maine	statistical	logit	9/04	1/00
Maryland	statistical	logit	1/00	none
Massachusetts	characteristic		never	5/05
Michigan	statistical	linear regression	6/03	6/03
Minnesota	statistical	logit	5/05	5/05
Mississippi	statistical	—	never	none
Missouri	statistical	logit	12/04	12/04
Montana	statistical	logit	never	none
Nebraska	statistical	logit	2000	2000
Nevada	statistical	logit	never	none
New Hampshire	statistical	logit	4/05	none
New Jersey	statistical	logit	1/04	1/04
New Mexico	statistical	logit	1/04	none
New York	characteristic		6/05	1/03
North Carolina	statistical	logit	never	none

Table 4.2 (continued)

State	Model type	Functional style	Date of last update	Model revision
North Dakota	statistical	logit	9/05	1/03
Ohio	characteristic		1/00	none
Oklahoma	statistical	linear regression	8/06	none
Oregon	statistical	logit	7/03	none
Pennsylvania	statistical	logit	1/05	1/03
Puerto Rico	characteristic		never	none
Rhode Island	statistical	linear regression	1/00	none
South Carolina	statistical	logit	3/05	none
South Dakota	statistical	logit	never	none
Tennessee	statistical	logit	8/03	none
Texas	statistical	logit	9/03	7/03
Utah	statistical	logit	never	none
Vermont	statistical	logit	3/05	3/05
Virginia	statistical	logit	never	none
Virgin Islands	characteristic		never	none
Washington	statistical	logit	never	7/04
West Virginia	statistical	logit	8/01	8/01
Wisconsin	statistical	logit	1994	none
Wyoming	statistical	discriminate analysis	7/05	5/05

NOTE: Blank = not applicable; — = information not available.
SOURCE: Sullivan et al. (2007), pp. 98–102.

By 2007, of the 50 states and three other jurisdictions, the overwhelming majority—45—used statistical WPRS models. Seven states use characteristic screening models, and one state—Florida—uses no variables at all. Florida provides local One-Stop Career Centers with a list of all UI claimants who are eligible to participate in WPRS services, and the centers determine the number and type of claimants to be called in for services regardless of their worker profiling scores. Thus, despite urging by the department to adopt statistical models, eight states use less objective methods, and Florida uses a totally subjective method.

Although it is important to update the data in statistical models, 13 states have never updated their WPRS models. As a result, those models reflect the characteristics of unemployed workers of more than a decade ago. These models do not reflect either the current state of the economy or the characteristics of workers who are currently searching for work. For the states that have updated their models, many model changes reflect data collection modifications, particularly the conversion of occupational and industrial coding.

Of the 45 states with statistical models, 26 have never revised the structure of their models. Twenty-three states have revised their models since 2000. As a result, the structure of most state models is in need of updating.

Having reviewed and analyzed state profiling models, Sullivan et al. (2007) recommend a number of technical modifications to state WPRS profiling models. They recommend use of logistical regression models and adoption of an expanded number of independent variables, including continuous variables, second-order, and cross-term variables.

Identification and Referral

Most states use the following general process to identify and refer workers to reemployment services. All unemployed workers who file for UI benefits and receive a first UI check are required to be profiled. However, state agencies may profile workers prior to UI benefit receipt. When claimants file for UI benefits, data are collected for use in the worker profiling model. Identification and referral are conducted on a weekly basis. If claimants are determined to be permanently separated and not job-attached, they are run through the state profiling model and assigned a probability of benefit exhaustion. For each local employment security office, UI claimants are arrayed by their exhaustion probability—from high to low—which is the basis for their referral to reemployment service providers. The number of claimants referred to receive reemployment services can be adjusted weekly. States are encouraged to establish flexible referral procedures that can adjust the number of UI claimants referred according to the availability of reemployment services.[12]

Under WPRS, identification and referral to services can only be done using the worker profiling mechanism. State workforce agency staff are not authorized to use their own subjective judgment as a factor in the process. On the other hand, provision of reemployment services (e.g., job finding and placement services) is not restricted to WPRS participants. As a result, WPRS participants often participate in services alongside nonparticipants.[13] These nonparticipants in WPRS can be selected by any method consistent with federal requirements that the state or locality chooses.

Participation in reemployment services is a UI program requirement for workers who are identified and referred to reemployment services through worker profiling. Claimants who refuse to participate can be denied UI benefits.

The purpose of WPRS is to provide reemployment services as soon as possible after the onset of unemployment, so states select and refer claimants to services within five weeks of claimants' filing their UI claims (USDOL 1994b). Unemployed workers can only be profiled once during a period of unemployment, and if reemployment services are not available to them within five weeks, they are generally not enrolled in WPRS. States' agencies have referred claimants to services in a timely manner. At least two states—Georgia and Illinois—have accelerated the process to assure early identification and referral to services by completing the profiling process in local offices at the time the initial claim is filed.

Once participants have been referred to reemployment services, they report to a designated reemployment service provider, generally the local Wagner-Peyser Act/Employment Service agency. The service providers develop an individual service plan for participation in WPRS-required reemployment services, which must be approved by their state agency counselor and is subject to the availability of services. There is wide variation among states regarding the extent to which counselors participate in plan development and in the degree of individualization of plans. Participants are required to complete all the services included in their plans in a timely manner—usually within one to three weeks. Upon completion, there is no further participation requirement, even if workers remain unemployed. The WPRS system does not affect the continuing entitlement to UI benefits, unless referred workers refuse to participate in reemployment services.

Unemployed workers can request additional services beyond those available through WPRS, including training. However, these additional services are provided separately from the WPRS program, usually through the Employment Service (ES) or through the Workforce Investment Act's (WIA) Dislocated Worker program, and thus participation is not guaranteed. Program slots must be available and program eligibility criteria must be met.

The WPRS system has succeeded in drawing attention and providing reemployment services to UI recipients who are permanently displaced. Virtually all initial claimants were profiled in the early years of WPRS—over 90 percent were profiled through 2002—however, that percentage has declined to between 80 and 85 percent.

The interim WPRS evaluation report funded by the department found that states were successful in implementing their profiling models, and that the models successfully identified those UI claimants most likely to exhaust their UI benefits. States appeared to be successfully determining service capacity for providing reemployment services. In some states this determination was done by the state, while in others it was conducted locally. The study found two common obstacles to the provision of services in many states: a shortage of employment counselors to provide services, and a lack of space in many local offices to provide orientations, workshops, and other group services (Hawkins et al. 1996).

IMPLEMENTING AND OPERATING REEMPLOYMENT SERVICES

Background

The 1993 WPRS legislation required that reemployment services be provided in a manner that necessitated close cooperation at the state and local level between staff working for the UI, ES, and JTPA/WIA programs. The cooperative effort would be much greater than was usual at that time. Many department staff members developed new working relationships as they came together to design the new system. They had to create the reemployment services component of the WPRS system from scratch. The worker profiling model had to be developed. The model was implemented as a prototype in one or more states and then had to be tailored to individual states. The states implemented an approach that involved statistical methods that are not normally part of the operation of workforce development programs.

Mary Ann Wyrsch was the administrator of the UI Service when WPRS was enacted. A history major in college, she had studied the annals of the employment security system. She also had worked in employment security in Washington State. WPRS made sense to her: WPRS went back to the roots of the employment security system under which the ES had always provided reemployment services to UI claimants and administered the UI work test. WPRS also fit with her understanding that job search assistance was more cost-effective than training, and that WPRS would be beneficial to UI claimants. She was ready to support the implementation of WPRS.[14]

Enacted as an amendment to federal UI legislation, WPRS was considered by many to be the primary responsibility of the federal UI staff. Staff in the national UI office oversee the development of the worker profiling model, and state and local UI staff refer UI claimants to reemployment services. The provision of reemployment services, however, cannot be done by the UI program; it has to be done by state Wagner-Peyser Act and JTPA/WIA programs, which provide reemployment and training services. At the federal level, a complex system was developed quickly, involving a number of partners. Each program agency had to agree to the design of the system, determine how to implement it, provide guidance to the state and local workforce development partners who would carry out the program, and provide support for implementation and devotion of resources to carry it out.[15]

Thus, implementation of a WPRS system in every state represented a significant effort by the federal employment security agency community, especially the UI, ES, and JTPA dislocated worker programs.[16] Implementation required the establishment of operational linkages between employment and training programs at the state and local levels. It also required cooperation between local, state, and federal government entities.

Federal planning for the WPRS program was based on a broad legislative interpretation of what it meant and how it would work. This interpretation of the WPRS legislation was provided to the states in three UI program letters during 1994 (USDOL 1994b, pp. 22–50).

During the spring of 1993, WPRS system design began with the development of the WPRS components and the claimant flows through the new voluntary system. The design included four aspects: 1) the process and timing of worker profiling, 2) the referral process to reemployment service providers, 3) the content and design of the reemployment services, and 4) the responsibilities among agencies for providing these services. The basic design was reduced to a simple flow diagram that was distributed in September 1993 in UI Program Letter 45-93.

Shortly before the November enactment of the mandatory WPRS program, the Employment and Training Administration (ETA) formed a team consisting of ES, JTPA Dislocated Worker, and UI Service staff, representing the three major ETA programs. It was referred to as the Basic Understandings Workgroup, and its mission was to design the operational features of the WPRS system at the national, state, and local workforce area levels.[17] At the time, the ETA recognized that WPRS was the first component of the emerging One-Stop delivery system, and the manner in which it was implemented reflected upon the potential success of the department's entire workforce reform initiative. The work group met daily for several months to hammer out a process that would foster cooperation between key state workforce agency partners.[18]

The Basic Understandings Workgroup reached an agreement in mid-December 1993 that was the basis of all subsequent ETA field guidance to the states.[19] The agreement included a description of the delivery of reemployment services and training, a standard menu of reemployment services, requirements for individual service plans, a refined flow diagram of state and local operational responsibilities, and other state agency requirements. Subsequently, ETA program offices began work on developing specific operational guidance.[20]

The overall WPRS design was summarized as a flow diagram, which evolved when program participation became mandatory. The design also was a summary of the efforts of the Basic Understandings Workgroup to develop the individual parts of the system, determine responsibilities for carrying them out, and ensure that the parts fit together well. This cooperative effort culminated in a final detailed design—including a new flow diagram—that was issued as Field Memorandum 35-94 and distributed directly to the states in March 1994 (USDOL 1994b, pp. 57–103).[21]

Federal Guidance

Field Memorandum 35-94 encompassed a broad view of WPRS. It emphasized the department's commitment to proactively support the goals of WPRS and serve the needs of its dislocated-worker customers. It attempted to encourage the development and implementation of comprehensive state WPRS systems, coordination and linkages between individual state employment and training organizations (i.e., UI, ES, and JTPA/WIA programs), and provision of the most effective possible services for dislocated workers (USDOL 1994a, pp. 57–103).[22] The department tried to ensure that states understood the purpose of a WPRS system and how the profiling mechanism worked. The department also developed prototype designs for the provision of customized but comprehensive reemployment services, particularly comprehensive job search assistance.

In August 1994, the department provided comprehensive instructions to state UI programs as field guidance that described minimum requirements states had to meet to conform to federal law. These requirements encompassed such matters as the nature and process of identification and referral, the relation of the UI system to reemployment service providers, the definition of reemployment services, and a number of UI program administration issues, such as notification of claimants, what mandatory participation means for UI claimants, and due process considerations (USDOL 1994b, pp. 35–50).[23]

By mid-1994, the department had issued four UI program letters, three field memorandums, and four UI Service information bulletins about the WPRS system. After discussion with state employment security agency staff who were concerned that they did not have all of the information they needed to implement the WPRS program, I assembled, edited, and wrote an introduction to all the material the department had produced about the program (USDOL 1994b). For the remaining two years of WPRS implementation, this "Green Book"—the color of its cover—was used by the states to implement their WPRS programs. The ETA issued three supplements to Field Memorandum 35-94 containing a total of 47 answers to questions posed by the state agencies. Furthermore, the ETA developed a WPRS implementation guide that was used by federal staff to conduct on-site reviews of each state's WPRS system as input to develop a statutorily mandated report to the Congress.[24]

The ES took a strong and active role in implementing WPRS. It examined the early experience of WPRS implementation and provided guidance to states in late 1997 in ES Program Letter No. 1-98. The program letter emphasized the "long-standing" relationship between UI and ES programs and the "need to provide improved reemployment services to UI claimants." To provide "quality reemployment services," states were urged to consider a number of recommendations based on knowledge gained from past studies about how to best speed the return to work. UI claimants should receive job search assistance early, including "immediate job referrals" if they had suitable skills and experience. Reemployment services should be individualized to increase the likelihood of rapid reemployment. Specifically, it was recognized that many WPRS participants were only receiving a group orientation and a group job search assistance (JSA) workshop, rather than a more robust set of personalized services. Finally, states were encouraged to provide an "expansion of the variety, length, and number of services provided to claimants," which had been shown to increase customer satisfaction. Specific examples of types of counseling, workshops, and technological procedures were recommended.

Implementation Process and Funding

The implementation of WPRS required new techniques and procedures. It was implemented in such a manner that the states could learn from one another. Five states (Delaware, Florida, Kentucky, New Jersey, and Oregon) were selected early in 1994 to develop prototype systems. They were followed by "first wave" states, which began implementing their systems later in 1994; a second and final wave of states began in 1995.

Because worker profiling is technically complex and represented a departure from prior methods of identifying program participants, the department provided extensive technical assistance to individual states to initially develop their profiling mechanisms. This assistance was provided by a small team skilled in econometrics and UI data systems. The team began by assisting a single state (Maryland) in developing and testing its profiling mechanism in early 1994. Gradually, it expanded the scope of assistance to other states, and it served a large number of states during the 1990s.

In addition to providing technical assistance to individual states, the department conducted a series of seminars for state technicians to help them develop and update their profiling models. These seminars included computer laboratory sessions during which state staff could work on developing state profiling models using their own state's data.

Beginning in 1994, the Department of Labor provided the states with start-up funding to initially establish their individual WPRS systems and to build capacity to provide reemployment services to claimants referred by WPRS. The UI national office provided over $20 million in funding to assist states in building their own state profiling mechanisms as well as to develop other infrastructure for their WPRS systems. In addition, the JTPA Dislocated Worker Program provided states with nearly $20 million in funds held in a national reserve account to expand their capacity to provide reemployment services to claimants through WPRS. In both cases, this funding was for one-time, capacity-building activities; the states were not provided with ongoing funding for WPRS reemployment services (Wandner 2008).

Worker Profiling and Reemployment Services Reporting

Since WPRS is a client-based system that involves the entire U.S. employment and training system, its analysis requires data that indicate how unemployed workers move through the system and what impact the system has on them. Two WPRS state reports were developed in 1996. The ETA-9048 Report is a quarterly report of the flow of UI claimants into and through the system. It follows claimants through the identification and referral process and counts participation in and completion of reemployment services.[25] In addition, the ETA-9049 Report is a quarterly report on program outcomes. It gathers data on employment and wage outcomes of program participants. It was hoped that the ETA-9049 Report could be used for evaluation purposes, but it has never been used for that purpose.

Worker Profiling and Reemployment Services Evaluation

The department funded an evaluation of WPRS in 1994, shortly after the program was enacted. The goal of the evaluation, conducted by Social Policy Research Associates (SPRA), was to provide an analysis of the operations and effectiveness of state WPRS systems, so state and national policymakers could learn how to improve WPRS. The evaluation included an implementation and process analysis, based on case study site visits and a customer satisfaction survey. It also included an analysis of program impacts and effectiveness, using a comparison group methodology.

Two interim reports preceded the SPRA's 1999 final report. The first was based on the implementation and process analysis and the second (which went to Congress) on the program impact analysis, both for six early participating states (Dickinson, Kreutzer, and Decker 1997; Hawkins et al. 1996). The final report included program impact analysis for the six participating states, as well as a national survey of all states.

The evaluation was hampered by significant problems. First, unlike the New Jersey Experiment and the JSA Demonstration, which were run as random assignment experiments, SPRA evaluated an ongoing program. Second, much of the data needed to conduct the demonstration were not available because states did not retain WPRS data after the data were used to conduct the program. For example, without data on profiling scores for UI claimants, comparison groups were difficult to construct for an ongoing program. Finally, impacts were expected to be much lower than for the experiments because state WPRS-provided reemployment services were found to be quite limited because of the lack of direct funding for the program.

The second interim report's impact study determined the net impact of providing WPRS services on program outcomes. The study found that WPRS significantly reduced UI receipt. Evidence was insufficient regarding the expected increased employment and earnings under WPRS, although there was strong positive evidence in one of six states.

The study found that WPRS claimants received substantially more reemployment services than comparison group claimants. In particular, they were much more likely to receive an orientation and assessment, which are key initial components of the WPRS service package. Receipt of other services varied, as individual states had their own strategies for achieving reemployment. The study also found that under WPRS the states successfully accelerated the provision of services (Dickinson, Kreutzer, and Decker 1997).

The final report (Dickinson et al. 1999) presented the WPRS net impact analysis across six states. It found that in four of the six states

WPRS significantly reduced the receipt of UI. The two states for which there was little or no impact on UI receipt—Kentucky and South Carolina—were the states providing the least number of hours of services.[26] Participating states, however, generally appeared to provide fewer services and considerably fewer hours of reemployment services than in the New Jersey and JSA experiments. In comparing participating claimants, those with higher profiling scores (that is, scores indicating greater difficulty in securing new employment) were found to experience greater reductions in receipt of UI. Reduction in UI receipt also was greater in states with greater enforcement of WPRS participation, as measured by UI administrative determinations and denials of benefits. These results generally were consistent with the findings of the New Jersey Experiment and indicate that the WPRS system is more effective in states that both provided comprehensive services and enforced program participation.

The study's 1997 survey of all states found that many were providing relatively few hours of reemployment services through their WPRS systems. Forty-five percent of the states provided between one and nine hours of services (Table 4.3). Unlike the New Jersey and JSA experiments, the majority of claimants did not receive the most time-intensive

Table 4.3 Percentage of Profiled and Referred Workers Receiving Worker Profiling and Reemployment Services (WPRS) and Length of Required Services, 1997

Receipt of WPRS services	% of claimants
Assessment	60.4
Counseling	20.9
Job placement	58.4
Job search workshop/job club	37.2
Referral to education or training	16.6
Duration of required services	% of states
1 to 4 hours	16
5 to 9 hours	29
10 to 19 hours	18
20 or more hours	9
Claimants required to participate until UI benefits stop	22

SOURCE: Dickinson et al. (1999).

services: counseling and job search workshops/job clubs (Dickinson et al. 1999).

When the WPRS initiative was proposed, some interest groups expressed concern about possible negative effects flowing from its requirement of participation in reemployment services. Specifically, they were concerned that the enforcement of participation in reemployment services would be used to increase UI disqualification rates. These fears have not been realized. As is consistent with its policy goals, program operations appear to be directed toward helping unemployed workers find jobs; the program is not pushing claimants off the UI rolls. Program participants appear to be willing to participate, and UI local staff have rarely found reason to deny benefits because of refusal to participate. In fact, early results showed that less than 2 percent of claimants referred to services were denied any benefits for nonparticipation (Dickinson, Kreutzer, and Decker 1997).

The final report (Dickinson et al. 1999, II-14, II-15) found that ES programs were the major providers of WPRS services in over two-thirds of the states, while JTPA programs took the lead in the other states. Since the study found that the ES also was an active partner in the states where JTPA programs had the lead, I estimate that ES provides over four-fifths of reemployment services nationwide.

Funding of Services

Since its inception in November 1993 as a mandatory program, WPRS largely has been an unfunded mandate. That is, states are required to conduct work profiling and provide reemployment services to targeted dislocated workers within their existing budgets. No new funds were appropriated for this initiative in the early years of the program. States had to decide how much of their ES and JTPA (and later WIA) funds to commit to providing WPRS reemployment services. It quickly became clear to some federal policy officials that if the provision of job search assistance to UI claimants was going to become more widespread, dedicated funding would be needed to provide these and other reemployment services under WPRS.

One solution was to build reemployment services into the design of a new dislocated worker program. That was the proposal contained in a bill—the Reemployment Act (REA) of 1994—that was introduced by the Clinton administration shortly after the enactment of WPRS. REA envisioned a workforce program built from the bottom up. The cost analysis for the bill estimated the mix of services based on historical data and the expected take-up rates for job search assistance, other employment services, and training. Department staff estimated that the combined participants served by both Rapid Response teams and WPRS would be 1.6 million in 2000, when the program would reach a steady state. Funding to serve these participants was estimated to be $652 million per year. Thus, the WPRS funding per participant would have been approximately $400—enough to provide comprehensive services similar to those provided in the New Jersey Experiment. If appropriations had been forthcoming, WPRS reemployment services would have been fully funded by the new REA program (Reed and Uhalde 1994). However, REA was not enacted. It was introduced in the year that the Republicans won control of the Congress. The Clinton administration would have to negotiate a compromise approach to replace JTPA.

New employment and training legislation was not enacted until four years later, as the Workforce Investment Act (WIA) of 1998. However, the WIA dislocated worker provisions did not address the provision of WPRS reemployment services. WIA authorized core and intensive services that might include reemployment services for WPRS participants, but provision of reemployment services to WPRS participants was not addressed directly by the legislation.

At the time, section 3(c)(3) of the Wagner-Peyser Act was amended to specifically authorize the provision of reemployment services. However, the authorization to provide reemployment services to UI claimants required to participate in reemployment services was not accompanied by any increase in federal funding for ES grants to the states.

From its enactment, provision of reemployment services by the ES under section 3(c)(3) would have been facilitated by dedicated funding for reemployment services. Increased funding was needed if these services were going to reach a reasonable scale and intensity. As a result, in 1997 the ES requested additional funds to provide reemployment services. For FY 1998, 1999, and 2000, the ES unsuccessfully proposed special formula funding from the Wagner-Peyser Act annual grants to provide reemployment services to UI claimants. These requests were rejected either by the department's policymakers or by the OMB. For

FY 2001, the Reemployment Services Grants were proposed again, and this time they became part of President Clinton's budget request. Congress provided funding for these Reemployment Services Grants in the amount of $35 million for FY 2001 and then again in approximately the same amount for the next four years—through FY 2005.[27] The funds were provided to the state ES agencies based upon the number of state UI first payments and other factors. They were targeted for use in providing reemployment services to individuals referred to the Wagner-Peyser Act programs through the WPRS process, and they partially supplemented other ES funds.

These Reemployment Services Grants provided only a small portion of the funds needed to provide WPRS services. For example, in 2005 approximately 850,000 UI recipients reported to the One-Stop centers to receive reemployment services under WPRS. Assuming that 80 percent of these workers were served by Employment Services and that comprehensive provision of these reemployment services cost $400 per worker, the total cost of providing comprehensive WPRS services by the ES would have been approximately $270 million. This means that 2005 Reemployment Services Grants paid for about 13 percent of comprehensive reemployment services. Because the underfunding was so great, the reemployment services provided by the states were far less comprehensive than they should have been, and funding for WPRS reemployment services in excess of the $35 million came from the basic state Wagner-Peyser Act allocations.

Funds for Reemployment Services Grants were terminated in June 2006 at the end of program year 2005. The Bush administration did not request funding for FY 2006 or any succeeding year. In the FY 2006 appropriation, Congress did not include funds for the Reemployment Services Grants. The grants also were not included in the FY 2007 through 2010 budgets (Balducchi, Johnson, and Gritz 1997, p. 497; Balducchi and Pasternak 2004, pp. 42, 43, 62).[28]

Worker Profiling and Reemployment Services Policy Workgroup

In 1998, USDOL policymakers reviewed how the fully implemented WPRS program was working and what could be done to improve it. They established a WPRS policy work group and asked me to chair the group. It consisted of USDOL national and regional office staff as well as representatives of state employment security agencies. The group members came to a broad consensus about what needed to be done to improve the WPRS system, and their recommendations were comprehensive.

The work group made seven recommendations:

1) The worker profiling model should be updated regularly by states. The department should provide technical assistance to states and information on best practices.

2) States should profile all new initial claimants.

3) States should accelerate their profiling and referral process to ensure that WPRS is an early intervention system. States should ensure that workers referred to reemployment services are the workers most likely to exhaust their benefits.

4) Reemployment services provided should be greater in number and be comprehensive because provision of greater numbers of reemployment services yields greater customer satisfaction and is cost-effective.

5) For WPRS purposes, operational linkages between Wagner-Peyser Act, JTPA Title III (now WIA), and UI programs should be further strengthened.

6) Additional resources should be devoted to WPRS reemployment services through increased appropriations and reallocation of resources between employment and training fund sources.

7) The states and the department should work to improve WPRS communications, feedback systems, and reporting.

The work group's recommendations represented a consensus and were reasonable and balanced. They were consistent with prior federal guidance. These recommendations represented the views of practitioners and policy staff about what ought to be done to improve the WPRS program. The members also understood the mutual responsibilities that had to be exercised at all levels of government and by all employment and training programs. Beyond commitment to make WPRS work, the work group recognized that a key issue was the need for direct funding of reemployment services. While it was clear to the members that such funding was required, the provision of such funding was the responsibility of the president and Congress, and in 1999 it did not appear that such funding would be forthcoming (Wandner and Messenger 1999).

Significant Improvement Demonstration Grants

By 1999, the WPRS system had been operating nationally for three years. Two evaluations of the program had been conducted—an external evaluation by SPRA and an internal evaluation by the WPRS policy work group. They both made recommendations for improving the program. The department provided more than $5 million to 11 states to develop and demonstrate improvements in WPRS operations. The states receiving these Significant Improvement Demonstration Grants (SIG) conducted three types of demonstration activities: 1) making changes in the worker profiling mechanism and process to better target workers most in need of reemployment services, 2) improving reemployment services, and 3) improving the coordination and communication between agencies participating in the WPRS process.

An evaluation of the SIG grants was conducted by a third-party evaluator. The evaluation identified a number of ways to improve the WPRS program from the demonstration results. These recommended improvements in the WPRS system derived from best practices observed while conducting an implementation analysis for the demonstration states. The recommendations dealt with changing the worker profiling process, improving reemployment services, and enhancing communications between programs and agencies (Needels, Corson, and Van Noy 2002). The SIG grant recommendations were ignored. The Bush II administration marginalized the WPRS program and the provision of reemployment services in general. Despite research results to the contrary, Bush administration policy recommendations placed nearly all of the administration's emphasis on expanding short-term training.

Government Accountability Office 2007 Report

The Government Accountability Office (GAO) conducted a review of the WPRS program for the House Ways and Means Committee in June 2007. The study addressed three questions:

1) How do states identify UI claimants who are likely to exhaust their benefits?

2) To what extent do states provide reemployment services in the manner recommended by the department?

3) What is known about the extent to which WPRS speeds the return to employment?

The study used the USDOL-sponsored study of the worker profiling mechanism (Sullivan et al. 2007) to reiterate that 45 states use statistical models to identify and select individuals to participate in WPRS but that these models are not regularly updated. The GAO recommended that the department take a more active role in ensuring the accuracy of the worker profiling models.

The GAO found that states tended not to provide the recommended comprehensive reemployment services. The office examined seven states and found that six of them provided a weak service package: they referred individuals to services and made participation mandatory but then provided only one or more group sessions that included an orientation and job search skills. Only one state conducted an in-depth assessment and developed individual service plans for participants. The GAO recommended that the department take an active role in encouraging states to provide a more comprehensive package of reemployment services.

The GAO further concluded that little was known about the current effectiveness of WPRS because no evaluation had been conducted since the Dickinson, Kreutzer, and Decker (1997) study, and that study had made use of early WPRS data from the period 1994 through 1996. The department had no plans to conduct a new evaluation of WPRS, but the GAO recommended that it do so (GAO 2007).

While the GAO recognized state agency claims that the termination of the Reemployment Services Grants in June 2006 was a key reason for the decline in provision of WPRS reemployment services, the GAO did not deal with the key issue of inadequate funding for the WIA and ES programs, which made it unrealistic to expect these programs to provide comprehensive WPRS reemployment services.

Worker Profiling and Reemployment Services under the Bush Administration

The Bush administration took no interest in the WPRS program. As will be discussed in later chapters, the public policy initiatives of the administration were at variance with the WPRS goal of providing reemployment services to dislocated workers.

In 2003, the Workforce Investment Act expired and required reauthorization. The key component of the Bush WIA reauthorization legislative proposal was the consolidation of the ES and all WIA components into a block grant. Consolidation meant eliminating the ES program, which is the principal provider of WPRS reemployment services. The elimination of the ES would likely result in a precipitous decline in the provision of WPRS reemployment services. Similar Bush administration bills were proposed in 2005 and 2007.

In his 2006 State of the Union address, President Bush announced the American Competitiveness Agenda. It was a many-faceted proposal, but one without new funding. One component of the proposal was Career Advancement Accounts (CAAs), training vouchers designed to provide maximum individual choice. Under a new Bush administration WIA reauthorization proposal that incorporated CAAs, funding for CAAs would consume nearly four-fifths of all employment and training funding. With no new funding, almost no funds would remain to provide WIA core and intensive services or to keep open the more than 3,000 One-Stops, located in almost every county across the United States. The likely effect of this proposal would have been to shutter the employment and training system and to eliminate virtually all funding for reemployment services for WPRS participants and other individuals in need of services.

When Congress rejected the Bush proposals for WIA reauthorization, the USDOL acted administratively to eliminate the U.S. Employment Service within the department. The organization that had provided leadership to provide WPRS reemployment services through Wagner-Peyser Act programs was thus silenced.

In an effort to justify the destruction of the ES, the creation of an employment and training block grant program, and the moving of nearly all funding into training vouchers, Bush administration spokespeople disparaged as wasteful the overhead costs to provide core and intensive services to more than 10 million individuals. WPRS was neglected, and no guidance or technical assistance was provided to the states with respect to the program requirements or the provision of reemployment services. Strangely, however, continuing technical assistance was provided to states to update and evaluate their worker profiling models.

The result was an effort to maintain good worker profiling models, while disparaging the reemployment services that were to be provided to likely UI exhaustees based on these profiling models. It was not clear what the worker profiling models would be used for if not to provide reemployment services.

Thus, there were two phases of WPRS from 1993 to 2008. In the first phase, WPRS was developed and encouraged. In the second phase, it was ignored and reemployment services were impugned. An examination of the provision of reemployment services under the WPRS program reveals that these two phases corresponded to a rise and decline in the provision of reemployment services.

THE SCOPE OF REFERRAL TO AND PROVISION OF REEMPLOYMENT SERVICES

WPRS Operations Begin

WPRS makes early provision of reemployment services to UI claimants practical. In the past, serving UI recipients soon after they became unemployed was a daunting task: UI recipients are too numerous to all be referred to service providers, and many of them do not need assistance. There was no rapid and systematic way to sort through all UI claimants to make appropriate referrals. WPRS allows referral of just those claimants who most appear to need services—and then, only of those claimants for whom services are actually available.

The USDOL recommended that the states provide a systematic and structured set of reemployment services that would provide customized assistance to dislocated claimants referred through worker profiling. Under this approach, a comprehensive set of reemployment services would be offered, but all participants would not receive the same set of services. Rather, the policy focus was on the development of an individual service plan for each referred worker, to meet the needs of the individual customer and to avoid the approach of "one size fits all."

Although the WPRS process makes early provision of reemployment services practical, the states and their reemployment service providers must make the WPRS system work. They must determine who delivers the services, what kinds of services are provided, and how many workers are served.

Reemployment services are generally funded by the ES and the WIA programs. Although WIA programs are a major service provider in a number of states, states have generally used the ES rather than the WIA programs to provide most reemployment services. This choice is related to the U.S. institutional history. The public Employment Service and Unemployment Insurance were created as two interdependent programs in the 1930s, and they have been closely associated at both the state and the local level. Organizationally, they are located in the same state workforce agency, and the Wagner-Peyser Act, in Section 7(a)(3)(F), has long required that the ES provide UI claimants with job finding and placement services and administer the UI work test. Before state UI staff began moving out of local offices in the mid-1990s in response to the introduction of telephone and Internet claims-taking, 9 out of 10 local employment security offices around the country were colocated, housing both the ES and UI units. It is this close working relationship between the two programs that explains why the great majority of WPRS reemployment services have been provided through ES programs.

By contrast, the WIA program and its predecessors have more recent origins. They were established as an alternative program delivery system, with operational authority that was locally rather than state-based, and they rarely have been colocated with the UI program. Program linkages with UI seldom developed prior to the implementation of the WPRS system. In addition, WIA's main focus was on the provision of training and intensive services rather than on job search assistance or labor exchange services. As a result, WPRS operational linkages with WIA remain limited. In most states, WIA has been the recipient of WPRS referrals to training by local WPRS service providers, rather than the provider of WPRS job search services.

The WPRS evaluation report politely found that "coordination linkages between the UI and ES programs were working relatively well, but in most sites, the linkages between UI and ES with EDWAA [JTPA Dislocated Worker] were less well established" (Hawkins et al. 1996). The report recommended improving linkages with the JTPA Dislocated Worker (now the WIA Dislocated Worker) program to take advantage of its expertise in serving dislocated workers.

The capacity to provide reemployment services varies widely by state. This capacity depends on factors such as which agencies provide the reemployment services, their resource availability, and their commitment to the system. There also are wide variations in capacity between localities within states.

From its inception, the nationwide WPRS system had a substantial effect on the behavior of reemployment service providers. For example, the ES has experienced a dramatic increase in the services it has provided to UI claimants. Of the 8 to 9 million UI claimants served by the ES in the three program years ending on June 30, 1996, the percentage of claimants receiving some "reportable services" increased during these three years from 46 to 52 and then to 54 percent. More specifically, from the perspective of the WPRS program, the percentage of UI claimants receiving job search assistance during this period increased from 17 to 23 to 29 percent. The ES expended a great deal more effort helping return UI claimants to work during this period of WPRS implementation than it did before.

An early analysis of WPRS national reporting on program participation showed the types of reemployment services that WPRS participants received (Johnson 1996). For the early period of October 1995 through June 1996, 87 percent of all workers receiving UI first payments were profiled, and 11 percent of those profiled were referred to services. The number of referrals reflects only those dislocated workers for whom reemployment services were available. The larger population of UI claimants in need of reemployment services was not measured, but it was likely to number between 1 and 2 million claimants annually. The percentages of referred claimants reporting to individual services were as follows:[29]

- orientation, 62 percent
- assessment, 61 percent
- counseling, 27 percent
- placement assistance, 70 percent
- job search workshops, 42 percent

Thus, the largest number of referred workers who received services between October 1995 and June 1996 were provided with an orientation, an assessment, and placement services. Fewer workers participated in job search workshops and still fewer received individual counseling. It was the more costly and time-intensive services that had lower participation.

In looking at the level and mix of services provided by individual states, Johnson (1996) observed wide variation in service provision by state. The six WPRS service components that were reported consisted of orientation, assessment, counseling, placement, job search workshops, and referral to education and training. Levels of services were measured in terms of the percentage of referred claimants who reported to services. "High" and "low" participation rates were set at rates 25 percent higher or lower than the national average, respectively:

- *Comprehensive Services*: One-fifth of the states provided a high level of services in three or more services. Two-fifths of the states provided a high level in two or more services.

- *Limited Services*: Nearly one-fifth of the states provided a low level of services in three or more services. Twenty-nine states provided low levels of services in two or more services. Of these 29 states, 16 did not provide high levels of services in any service.

Thus, early in the operation of WPRS, state systems provided widely different levels of services to participating dislocated workers. Perhaps two-fifths of the states provided reasonably comprehensive services, while nearly one-third of the states provided minimal levels of services. The remaining states fell in between.

Individual participation in training is not a part of WPRS. Rather, if other reemployment services are not adequate to help unemployed workers return to work because they lack transferable skills, service providers are encouraged to refer workers to training. As part of the WPRS assessment process, participants may be referred to training on a voluntary basis. Early in its program operations, WPRS linked nearly one-fifth of referred workers with training and educational services.

The 1996 WPRS interim evaluation report found that the states were, in many cases, providing services that were neither comprehensive nor intensive. A major reason for the limited nature of the services provided was that many WPRS staff members were reluctant to refer claimants to an increased number of services because claimants might be denied benefits for nonparticipation in even one of the services contained in their service plans. To guard against this possible outcome, staff members instead might offer claimants only what was minimally required. The staff's concern, however, was at odds with the results of the WPRS evaluation's customer satisfaction survey, which found that customers' satisfaction increased substantially as the number of services provided increased. As a result, the evaluation recommended that states "develop more comprehensive and intensive services, including a wider array of services and longer-term services appropriate for WPRS claimants" (Hawkins et al. 1996).

To achieve the WPRS system's goals, states must offer reasonably comprehensive reemployment services to WPRS participants. The effectiveness of the WPRS system depends on dislocated workers' receiving enough reemployment assistance to enhance their search for work, resulting in a more rapid return to work. In the mid-1990s, the WPRS system had not yet reached a steady state, and it was hoped that the delivery of reemployment services would increase. In fact, because of funding limitations, the provision of reemployment services declined as the state WPRS systems matured. Thus, the WPRS system as described below is but a shell of what it was supposed to be, referring fewer WPRS-profiled workers to reemployment services and then having participants receive a weaker mix of services.

Operations of the WPRS Program, 1994–2008

While some states began implementation of WPRS in 1994, all states did not have operational programs until mid-1996. Thus, we must also look at the evolution of the program from 1996 to the present. Table 4.4 summarizes the state WPRS reports to the USDOL on the provision of WPRS reemployment services. The table demonstrates the nature of the WPRS program and how it has evolved over time. The table reveals the scope of the program, the effectiveness of WPRS at identifying and referring workers to reemployment services, and the number and type of reemployment services that UI beneficiaries can receive.

The data show that first payments in the UI program have numbered between 7 and 10 million since 1994. Since WPRS became operational nationally in 1996, the great majority of UI beneficiaries have been profiled. Of the beneficiaries profiled, over 1 million have been referred to reemployment services each year since 2001. Most of the referred

Table 4.4 Worker Profiling and Reemployment Services (WPRS) Data and Unemployment Insurance Program First Payments, 1994–2009

Year	First pays	Profiled	Referral	Reported	Orientation
1994	7,959,281	122,065	23,087	17,184	14,126
1995	8,035,229	4,061,731	456,533	453,005	283,508
1996	7,995,135	7,208,694	821,443	1,036,806	512,045
1997	7,325,093	6,985,048	745,870	990,041	474,891
1998	7,341,903	6,882,571	783,779	1,033,482	477,913
1999	6,967,840	6,483,514	803,401	990,737	447,032
2000	7,035,783	6,475,605	977,440	1,229,352	557,250
2001	9,868,193	8,952,312	1,154,743	1,499,364	666,610
2002	10,092,569	9,178,024	1,220,466	986,719	619,917
2003	9,935,108	8,238,485	1,147,448	919,450	595,564
2004	8,386,623	7,037,337	1,106,776	880,263	602,833
2005	7,917,301	6,441,561	1,128,710	845,789	607,905
2006	7,350,734	6,340,253	1,170,126	856,587	627,668
2007	7,652,634	6,586,553	1,230,093	911,055	644,797
2008	10,052,694	8,539,918	1,262,651	935,378	665,376
2009	14,182,053	12,165,239	2,304,519	1,392,985	1,061,971

Year	Assessment	Counseling	Placement	JSW	Training
1994	9,876	5,883	5,671	11,042	4,492
1995	246,655	140,301	267,281	213,512	74,292
1996	507,824	214,528	613,544	338,508	166,456
1997	455,914	194,818	630,760	336,959	160,741
1998	416,027	191,315	676,284	296,681	156,462
1999	403,195	198,571	668,492	253,451	141,398
2000	471,712	146,917	645,170	342,856	113,879
2001	531,020	129,136	506,172	452,439	120,093
2002	462,643	125,103	376,757	369,756	76,448
2003	423,977	114,142	378,180	400,245	70,295
2004	343,903	93,215	378,181	379,735	73,508
2005	350,443	109,697	376,342	355,843	77,915
2006	406,158	134,837	405,558	369,564	92,200
2007	425,711	149,101	437,744	390,454	100,780
2008	479,230	141,806	402,902	382,888	122,234
2009	650,383	212,432	533,153	551,037	195,955

Table 4.4 (continued)

NOTE: Data is from the Unemployment Insurance Data Base as of July 2009. For WPRS data, Puerto Rico, the Virgin Islands, and New Mexico are missing in the 2004 and 2005 data; Puerto Rico and the Virgin Islands are missing in the 2006 data; and Puerto Rico is missing in the 2007 and 2008 data. Data for 2009 is from the Unemployment Insurance Data Base as of June 2010.

The column headings are defined as follows:

Concept	Definition
UI first pays	Number of first UI payments for new benefit years established.
Profiled	Number of UI claimants profiled by state WPRS systems.
Referred	Number of profiled claimants referred to reemployment services.
Reported	Number of profiled and referred claimants who report for WPRS services.
Orientation	Number of profiled and referred claimants who report to an orientation.
Assessment	Number of profiled and referred claimants who report to an individual assessment.
Counseling	Number of profiled and referred claimants who report to job counseling.
Placement	Number of profiled and referred claimants who report to placement services.
JSW	Number of profiled and referred claimants who complete a job search workshop.
Training	Number of profiled and referred workers who are referred to government-funded education or training.

SOURCE: Summary of monthly state reports to the ETA. UI first payment data from ETA Report 5159. Other WPRS data from ETA Report 9048.

workers have reported for services, but, strangely, substantially more beneficiaries reported for services than were referred for the years 1996 through 2001. A state-by-state analysis indicates that this anomaly was caused by the misreporting of a small number of states.[30]

Most, although not all, claimants who reported to reemployment services received an orientation. However, a group orientation is not a true reemployment service; it only provides information about the WPRS process and requirements. After receiving an orientation, reportees can receive five true reemployment services: 1) assessment, 2) counseling, 3) placement services, 4) a job search workshop, and 5) referral to training.[31] Recently, the most prevalent service is placement assistance, while referral to training and counseling are least prevalent. Assessment and job search workshops are in an intermediate position.

Assessment, counseling, and placement assistance are types of employment services that are less staff intensive and costly than skill and occupational training. Since 1994, as a result of technological innovations in job matching and decreased ES and WIA funding, there has been greater reliance on self-administered services and facilitated self-help and less on staff-assisted (i.e., person-to-person) reemployment services. Thus, it is not surprising that the decline in program funding has resulted in the provision of fewer staff-assisted WPRS reemployment services and that services are being provided as cheaply as possible: only job search workshops have not experienced a steady decline. This decline is not cyclical but occurred generally through the years of the Bush administration. By contrast, counseling has been declining ever since the establishment of the WPRS national program in 1996.

A countercyclical component also can be seen in the WPRS system. With the program having reached a steady state before the onset of the 2001 recession, WPRS activity peaked by some measures during the recession. The number of beneficiaries profiled and referred to reemployment services peaked in 2002, while the number reporting and receiving an orientation peaked in 2001. UI program beneficiaries reached a cyclical maximum of 10.1 million in 2002. The number of UI beneficiaries profiled (9.2 million) and referred (1.2 million) to the WPRS system also reached a maximum in 2002. The number of beneficiaries reporting for services peaked at 1.5 million in 2001.

The recession that began in December 2007 again created greater demand for WPRS. In 2008, worker profiling and referral to reemployment services increased sharply. Without new funding, however, the receipt of reemployment services did not keep pace. Orientations and assessment increased, but counseling, placement services, and job search workshops declined. Only referrals to training increased sharply, as WPRS referrals became an increasingly important source of trainees for the WIA system.[32]

While the increase in unemployment during the 2001 recession resulted in a proportional increase in profiling, referral and reporting for reemployment services, and receipt of orientations, the receipt of WPRS services did not similarly increase. Between 1999 and 2001, UI first payments increased by 42 percent and the number of claimants profiled, reporting for services, and receiving an orientation increased correspondingly. During the same period, however, only assessments and job search workshops increased substantially, while counseling, placement services, and referral to training declined substantially. Lack of funding significantly undermined the provision of needed services. The same was true in 2008, when the recession that had begun at the end of the previous year did not yield increased funding, and the provision of reemployment services under WPRS did not rebound.

Examining the changing percentage of UI beneficiaries who are profiled, referred, and receive reemployment services adds perspective to the provision of services (Table 4.5). The extent of the profiling and referral of UI recipients has changed over time. From 1996, when WPRS was fully operational in all states, through 2002, over 90 percent of workers receiving a first payment were profiled. Thus, nearly all UI recipients, and probably virtually all permanently separated recipients, were profiled during these years. That percentage has declined to between 81 and 86 percent in the period from 2003 through 2008. The number of UI beneficiaries who were profiled declined from 2002 through 2005, stabilized in 2006 and 2007, and increased sharply in 2008.

The number of beneficiaries who were referred to reemployment services was fairly stable at between 700,000 and 800,000 from 1996 to 1999, with a referral rate of 9 to 11 percent. That number actually increased and has remained at approximately 1 million or more from 2000 through 2008. These referrals have remained at this level because the percentage of profiled workers who were referred to reemployment services has increased to between 11 and 16 percent through 2007.

Because the state UI program only refers as many UI claimants to WPRS services as the availability of services in an individual career center permits, the referral rate approximates the capacity to serve profiled workers. This capacity has been quite steady over time. Thus, the referral of between 11 and 16 percent of all UI beneficiaries to the career centers represents the centers' ability to receive and serve them.

Because of steady decreases in ES funding, some states have curtailed the provision of WPRS service provision in recent years. This is often referred to as a WPRS "resource threshold"—the point beyond which profiled claimants who are likely to exhaust benefits are not referred to service providers, or beyond which providers do not call claimants in for services because of a lack of local workforce staff. For example, at various times in 2003, up to one-third of Wisconsin

Table 4.5 WPRS, Percentage of UI Beneficiaries Profiled and Referred to WPRS Services and of Referrals Receiving Reemployment Services and Referral to Training, 1996–2008

Year	As % of UI beneficiaries		As % of referrals					
	Profiled	Referred	Orientation	Assessment	Counseling	Placement	JSW	Training
1996	90.2	10.3	62.3	61.8	26.1	74.7	41.2	20.3
1997	95.4	10.2	63.7	61.1	26.1	84.6	45.2	21.6
1998	93.7	9.4	70.1	53.1	24.4	86.3	37.9	20.0
1999	93.0	11.5	55.6	50.2	24.7	83.2	31.5	17.6
2000	92.0	13.9	57.0	48.3	15.0	66.0	35.1	11.7
2001	90.7	11.7	57.7	46.0	11.2	43.8	39.2	10.4
2002	90.9	12.1	50.8	37.9	10.3	30.9	30.3	6.3
2003	82.9	11.5	51.9	36.9	9.9	33.0	34.9	6.1
2004	83.9	13.2	54.5	30.7	8.5	35.7	34.1	6.7
2005	81.3	14.2	53.8	31.0	9.7	33.3	31.5	6.9
2006	86.3	16.0	53.6	34.7	11.5	34.7	31.6	7.9
2007	85.6	16.1	52.4	34.7	12.1	35.6	31.8	8.2
2008	85.0	12.6	52.7	38.0	11.2	31.9	30.3	9.7

NOTE: Data is from the Unemployment Insurance Data Base as of July 2009. For the WPRS data, Puerto Rico, the Virgin Islands, and New Mexico are missing in the 2004 and 2005 data; Puerto Rico and the Virgin Islands are missing in the 2006 data; and Puerto Rico is missing in the 2007 and 2008 data.
SOURCE: USDOL, ETA Report 9048 and ETA Report 5159.

workforce areas were not providing WPRS services because of lack of reemployment service funding (Almandsmith, Adams, and Bos 2006).

Looking at individual reemployment services, a downward trend developed in the provision of almost all services. Orientations were initially given to 60 to 70 percent of UI claimants reporting for services ("reportees") from 1996 to 1998, but orientations have declined to between 50 and 60 percent since then. Assessments were given to over 50 percent of workers through 1999 but have declined sharply since then—down to between 30 and 35 percent—with a small increase in 2008. Counseling was initially provided to one-quarter of reportees but is now provided to only 1 in 10. Placement services were initially provided to over two-thirds of reportees but are now provided to only 1 in 3. Job search workshops were initially provided to over 40 percent of reportees, but subsequently have been provided to between 30 and 40 percent. Referral to training was initially provided to 20 percent of reporting workers, but is now down to between 6 and 10 percent.

As expected, the one service that is provided to most reporting workers is an orientation session. However, less than 60 percent of reportees receive an orientation, when nearly all should. Placement services—trying to match job seekers with job openings—make up the second-most-used service, yet only about one-third of reportees receive placement services. The next most frequently provided services are assessments and job search workshops. Less than one-tenth of reportees receive counseling, and referrals to counseling services have declined in the 2000s. Referrals to training have declined the most sharply of any of the services, from a high of over 160,000 in 1996 and 1997 to fewer than 80,000 between 2002 and 2005. They now represent less than one-tenth of referees. Thus, the more time-intensive and expensive reemployment services—assessment and counseling, job search workshops, and referrals to training—are the least-used services.

All UI beneficiaries who report to WPRS reemployment services receive one or more reemployment services. While state data reports do not determine the number of the WPRS-reported services each worker receives, the average number of services provided is between two and two-and-a-half services per reporting worker. For example, in 2005, the 911,648 beneficiaries reporting to the career centers received 1.9 million services, for an average of 2.1 services per reporting worker. More reemployment services would be expected to be provided if states were following the model of the New Jersey Experiment, especially since an orientation is an introduction to WPRS rather than a reemployment service.

WPRS-referred Unemployment Insurance claimants are closely related to the population of dislocated workers. The Bureau of Labor Statistics' biennial surveys of displaced workers show that between two-fifths and three-quarters of them collect UI benefits. The percentage is higher in recessionary periods, and at all times the percentage is higher still when those displaced workers who are unemployed for less than five weeks (and therefore not likely to apply for UI benefits) are excluded (Helwig 2004).

According to the Current Population Survey (CPS), the trend in the duration of unemployment has been one of increasing length, whether measured by the insured duration or the proportion of individuals who are unemployed for longer than 26 weeks. More reemployment services should be provided to dislocated workers as the difficulty of becoming reemployed increases, but the WPRS programs have not been able to respond to this need. Dislocated workers thus have been getting less reemployment assistance just when they need it more.

Role of the Employment Service in the Provision of WPRS Services

The ES has served UI claimants since the UI system began paying benefits in 1938. A statutory function of the ES is to conduct the UI work test, including work registration of UI claimants. Between 1994 and 2001, approximately 85 to 95 percent of individuals who receive a first payment from UI registered with the ES (Table 4.6). Generally all UI claimants are required to register with the ES unless they are subject to recall, and in recent years fewer of the unemployed are on temporary layoffs. The number of registrants is highly cyclical, increasing during periods of high unemployment.

In program year (PY) 2002, however, as a result of the advent of electronic self-help services and companion WIA performance requirements, new ES performance measurement and reporting requirements were established. The new requirements made it voluntary as to whether to register UI claimants who went to the state ES agency but did not receive staff-assisted services (Smole 2004, pp. 116–121). State agencies continued to be required to register UI claimants who used staff-assisted services. In PY 2002, unemployment increased, and we

**Table 4.6 Employment Service Registrants and a Percentage of UI First
Payments, 1984–2007**

Year	Eligible UI claimants	UI first payments	Registrants as a ratio of UI claimants
1984	6,776,674	7,742,547	0.88
1985	6,504,592	8,372,070	0.77
1986	7,001,207	8,360,752	0.84
1987	6,431,701	7,203,357	0.88
1988	6,256,440	6,860,662	0.91
1989	6,525,583	7,386,766	0.88
1990	7,096,457	8,628,557	0.82
1991	8,973,942	10,074,550	0.89
1992	10,436,910	9,243,338	1.13
1993	9,235,977	7,884,326	1.17
1994	7,662,050	7,959,281	0.96
1995	7,413,036	8,035,229	0.92
1996	7,254,009	7,995,135	0.91
1997	6,663,475	7,325,093	0.91
1998	6,406,794	7,341,903	0.87
1999	6,165,645	6,967,840	0.88
2000	6,600,708	7,035,783	0.97
2001	8,432,026	9,868,193	0.94
2002	6,187,161	10,092,569	0.59
2003	5,648,894	9,935,108	0.54
2004	5,655,186	8,368,623	0.68
2005	4,822,914	7,917,301	0.61
2006	4,805,817	7,350,734	0.65
2007	5,573,634	8,338,028	0.67

SOURCE: USDOL, ETA Report 9002 and ETA Report 5159.

would have expected the number of registered UI claimants to have
increased from the 2001 level of 8.4 million to somewhere in the vicin-
ity of 10 million. Instead, many states began selective registration,
resulting in a sharp decline nationally in the number of registrants,
which fell to 6.2 million in 2002. Although these 2002 registrants averaged 59 percent of UI beneficiaries nationwide, they made up only 10
to 20 percent of UI beneficiaries in Louisiana, Montana, Ohio, Utah,

and West Virginia, and less than 10 percent in the District of Columbia, Michigan, South Dakota, and Wisconsin. Additional changes to the Wagner-Peyser Act performance measures and reporting requirements were instituted in PY 2005, which eliminated the term "registered job seeker" and replaced it with "participant."

Wagner-Peyser Act programs have demonstrated their ability to handle the flow of UI claimants referred to state ES programs, both to register for employment and to receive WPRS reemployment services. In response to the enactment of WPRS, the U.S. Employment Service (USES) made clear that serving UI claimants was a priority through its policies and practices. Since full implementation of WPRS in 1996, over half of the eligible UI claimants have received "some reportable service," according to the ETA 9002 report. In addition, comparing data for WPRS and state ES programs, we see that the state ES programs provided "some reportable service" to approximately three to four times the number of workers who reported for WPRS services. Thus, the ES has adjusted its priorities to handle the flow of workers referred to reemployment services through the WPRS system.

In national ES reporting data, the best measure of the responsiveness of the ES to the introduction of WPRS is the increase in the number of UI claimants who participate in a job search activity. A "job search activity" under ES is defined as job search assistance, the primary form of reemployment service that is to be provided under WPRS. The number of individuals participating in job search activities more than doubled—from 1.6 million in 1993, before the implementation of WPRS, to a high of 3.9 million in 2001 (Table 4.7). Participation in a job search activity, as a proportion of UI claimants who received a reportable service, also more than doubled from 1993 to 2001. This indicates that the state Wagner-Peyser Act agencies took the WPRS program seriously and made great efforts to increase their provision of job search assistance.[33]

The impact of the USES policy of providing increased and improved JSA services to UI claimants is also evident in the concentration of the growth of state Wagner-Peyser Act agency provision of JSA compared to all reportable ES services. While the percentage of UI claimants receiving a reportable service increased slowly from 1992 to 2001, the percentage of claimants receiving JSA increased much more rapidly, more than doubling.

Table 4.7 Labor Exchange Activities of Eligible UI Claimants Registered for Work, 1984–2007

Program year	Eligible UI claimants (EUI)	Received some reportable service (RRS)		Activity		Entered employment	
		Number	% EUI	Participated in a job search activity Number	% RRS	Number	% RRS
1984	6,776,674	2,264,907		—		716,327	31.6
1985	6,504,592	—		—		—	—
1986	7,001,207	—		—		651,992	—
1987	6,431,701	—		—		648,064	—
1988	6,256,440	—		—		642,178	—
1989	6,525,583	—		—		647,994	—
1990	7,096,457	—		—		644,070	—
1991	8,973,942	—		—		835,251	—
1992	10,436,910	4,681,358	44.9	—		924,632	—
1993	9,235,977	4,270,711	46.2	1,588,223	37.2	890,504	20.9
1994	7,662,050	4,012,523	52.4	1,740,209	43.4	885,721	22.1
1995	7,413,036	4,004,707	54.0	2,149,171	53.7	879,562	22.0
1996	7,254,009	3,985,194	54.9	2,306,738	57.9	924,322	23.2
1997	6,663,475	3,599,511	54.0	2,262,883	62.9	918,294	25.5
1998	6,406,794	3,343,018	52.2	2,287,296	68.4	959,248	28.7
1999	6,165,645	3,417,600	55.4	2,428,242	71.1	1,116,840	32.7
2000	6,600,708	3,788,435	57.4	2,867,806	75.7	1,300,663	34.3

2001	8,432,026	4,965,528	58.9	3,911,278	78.8	1,477,455	29.8
2002	6,187,161	4,799,028	77.6	3,731,966	77.8	—	—
2003	5,648,894	4,119,382	72.9	3,126,384	75.9	2,723,057	66.1
2004	5,655,186	3,969,739	70.2	2,958,718	74.5	2,881,434	72.6
2005	4,822,914	3,599,279	74.6	1,703,166	47.3	2,575,368	71.6
2006	4,552,614	3,198,429	70.3	1,544,704	48.3	2,049,253	64.1
2007	5,573,634	3,512,898	63.0	1,863,699	53.1	3,089,304	87.9

NOTE: Eligible UI claimants are ES registrants who are monetarily eligible for UI benefits. The requirement that UI claimants register with the ES was relaxed in PY 2002. The immediate state response to the relaxing of this requirement can be seen in the decline in eligible UI claimants beginning in 2002. — = not available; blank = not applicable.

SOURCE: Program years 1984–1994, Employment Security Automated Reporting System (ESARS); 1993–1995, USDOL (1996); 1996–1999, USDOL (2001); 2000–2006, http://www.doleta.gov/performance/results/reports.cfm (accessed July 20, 2010).

In the recession year of PY 2001, the 3.9 million UI claimants who received a job search activity from state ES agencies was more than double the 1.5 million workers who reported receiving WPRS services. The ES served a substantial plurality of the 9.9 million UI beneficiaries that year.

Data for the "Great Recession" is limited, as the data for PY 2007 ends in June 2008. The data show that the percentage of eligible UI claimants receiving a reportable service declined, while the percentage of individuals receiving a reportable service and participating in a job search activity increased. The response to the recession, however, will be seen mostly in later program years.

In general, the ES has provided job search assistance to UI claimants well beyond those claimants who are required to participate in WPRS reemployment services: no more than 1.5 million workers reported for WPRS reemployment services in any year between 1996 and 2004, but the ES provided job search services to more than 2 million UI claimants in each of those nine years. In some of these years, the ES provided reemployment services to between two and four times more UI claimants than were required to participate. The ES response to WPRS can also be shown by the Wagner-Peyser Act programs' provision of job search assistance to an increasing proportion of UI recipients between 1994 and 2004. Over that 10-year span, the proportion increased from about one-fifth to more than one-third.

Beginning in 2005, the ES's support of the WPRS system declined sharply. Provision of job search activities dwindled from 3.0 million in 2004 to 1.7 million in 2005 and 1.6 million in 2006. The proportion of UI beneficiaries served with job search activities fell back to about one-fifth.

Promoting Reemployment

While all states offer job search assistance to UI claimants, a 2003 survey of state employment security agencies by the National Association of State Workforce Agencies (NASWA) provides some perspective on how these services are provided. The survey finds that the most common source of such assistance is through the WPRS process. The states cite the dissemination of labor market information, the provision of assistance in preparing resumes, and the provision of training to improve job interviewing skills (e.g., job search assistance) as the principal services they provide to UI claimants (O'Leary 2006; O'Leary and Wandner 2005).

In the same state survey, state workforce agencies report that the only two methods they used to promote reemployment were WPRS and the state Eligibility Review Programs (ERPs). Since very few states have been operating such ERP systems in recent years, the principal method of promoting reemployment is currently WPRS. UI recipients, however, are free to use WIA core and intensive services to find reemployment services without being required to do so by state UI programs, and some UI recipients do this (O'Leary 2006; O'Leary and Wandner 2005).

The conclusion to be drawn from the survey results is that the WPRS system plays a key role in the provision of reemployment services and, in some sense, in enforcing the UI work test. Unfortunately, the decline in what was formerly the robust provision of WPRS reemployment services makes the WPRS program a weak reed to lean on. If WPRS is little more than a group orientation and perhaps a brief group workshop in job search, UI beneficiaries will get little help in returning to work, and the UI system will receive little information about whether beneficiaries are actively seeking work.

OTHER USES OF TARGETING EMPLOYMENT SERVICES

While the worker profiling aspect of WPRS is a targeting mechanism to determine which workers receive the limited supply of employment services, similar mechanisms can be used to serve a variety of populations who are in need of reemployment services. The worker profiling mechanism itself is being used for the Self-Employment Assistance (SEA) program, which is also a part of the UI program. Studies have explored the potential uses of such targeting mechanisms for other employment, training, and welfare programs. Targeting mechanisms have also been researched and adopted by other countries. The status of these targeting efforts is reviewed in the book *Targeting Employment Services* (Eberts, O'Leary, and Wandner 2002).

Targeting mechanisms also can be used more systematically to help workers find jobs. The USDOL encouraged such a systematic approach by sponsoring a Frontline Decision Support System (FDSS) demonstration project to help local One-Stop office staff provide workers with the best and most appropriate services among those available. The demonstration used labor market and demographic information about workers seeking jobs and then determined how to best match them with available jobs. If the workers could not find jobs immediately, FDSS could direct them to the services that would be most effective for each individual worker. The demonstration was conducted in the offices of the city of Athens and the counties of Cobb and Cherokee in the state of Georgia, but it was never implemented statewide (Eberts, O'Leary, and Wandner 2002).

WORKER PROFILING IN OTHER COUNTRIES

The United States was an innovator in targeting reemployment services through the WPRS system. Interest in this targeting approach increased in the mid-1990s. In 1996, the Organisation for Economic Co-operation and Development (OECD) convened a meeting of experts from countries either interested in worker profiling or currently using it. At that meeting, the United States and Australia reported on programs they had made fully operational. I reported on the WPRS system. Canada reported on extensive research and developmental work it was doing to develop a sophisticated worker profiling approach (OECD 1998). Ultimately, Canada did not implement its profiling approach, in part because much of the responsibility for workforce development programs devolved from the national to the provincial governments.

The use of worker profiling spread to other industrial nations in the following decade. The European Union conducted a seminar on profiling in 2005 at which 12 countries presented what they had learned about worker profiling (Rudolph and Konle-Seidl 2005). The participating countries used profiling for three conceptual functions:

1)   As a diagnostic tool

2)   To target the scope and type of reemployment assistance provided

3)   To allocate scarce resources

Thus, a number of industrial nations, trying to get the right reemployment services to the right workers, have adopted worker profiling as a targeting mechanism (Table 4.8). Australia has changed its approach to profiling. Some countries have used variables (such as age, gender, and nationality) that are not used in the United States because of antidiscrimination statutes. The Danes, Swiss, and Germans have developed statistical tools to assign workers to reemployment services, and the Swiss have conducted an experiment to assess the acceptance and use of their model by frontline case workers (Frölich 2006; Staghoj, Svarer, and Rosholm 2007).

The common goal of the industrialized nations using targeting mechanisms to provide workforce development services is to *rationalize* the provision of services.

CONCLUSIONS AND LESSONS LEARNED

Implementation of the state WPRS systems has resulted in a cooperative and interdependent relationship between the UI, ES, and WIA programs at the state and local levels. This interdependence and cooperation first developed over the period 1994–1996 with the inception of state and local One-Stop delivery systems and provided an added foundation for One-Stop shops for dislocated workers. The UI program has become a gateway through which dislocated workers pass to receive reemployment services from the ES and WIA programs and other service providers, including community colleges.

The primary emphasis of the WPRS system initiative has been the early identification of dislocated workers and their referral to reemployment services, especially comprehensive job search assistance. But as both state and federal experiments and the early implementation of the WPRS system have shown, a small but significant portion of dislocated workers cannot find employment through reemployment services alone. Some of these workers are referred to voluntary retraining services.

The future of the WPRS system depends on what state and local practitioners do to improve the system. Improving WPRS program outcomes depends on data gathering, data analysis, and application of improved methods of operation. States can also learn from each other.

Table 4.8 Uses of Profiling in Selected Industrial Nations

Country	Approach
Australia	In 2003, an "active participation" model replaced an earlier profiling approach. Job seekers are classified as at risk of becoming long-term unemployed (receive case management) or not (receive job search workshop after 3 months of unemployment and intensive customized assistance after 12 months), using a Job Seeker Classification Instrument—a statistical diagnostic tool that assesses risk of long-term unemployment using 14 factors, including age, gender, work experience, and training.
Denmark	In 2004, Denmark introduced the "Job Barometer" for use by placement officers to standardize profiling across the country. The Barometer is a statistical model calculating the probability of one's finding employment within the next six months based on customer account information.
France	Since 2001, job seekers are assigned to one of seven groups that determine the type of services that are provided to them. A GAPP profiling tool has been used to assign job seekers to one of these groups.
Germany	A classification tool uses individual data, including gender, age, and job experience, to assign jobless workers into four categories of need for reemployment services, from none to intensive: 1) none, 2) job search assistance, 3) vocational training, and 4) special attention for long-term unemployed.
Hungary	For the PHARE project, which assesses the risk of long-term unemployment, Hungary tested a statistical model for estimating the expected duration of unemployment, using variables that included gender, age, general and vocational educational attainment, last wages earned, and place of residence.
Netherlands	Beginning in 1999, a number of different approaches to profiling were developed and used or were under development to determine job seekers' job search readiness and to classify workers to determine what reemployment services they will receive.
Switzerland	A "Statistically Assisted Program Selection" tool identifies programs and reemployment services that have proved to be the most cost-effective for job seekers based on their characteristics. It was tested as a demonstration project in 16 regional agencies, and the results were compared to a control group.
United Kingdom	For the "Job Search First" strategy, statistical models were tested to estimate the probability of rapid reemployment and to model the most efficient forms of assistance for job seekers for use in "customer segmentation" in the provision of reemployment services.

SOURCE: Rudolph and Konle-Seidl (2005).

An early information exchange took place at the National WPRS Colloquium, held in June 1996 in Atlanta, Georgia. It was an opportunity for state, local, and federal officials to gather and exchange ideas about what works and what can be done to improve state WPRS systems to better serve dislocated workers in need of assistance in returning to productive employment. Celebrating the successful implementation of state WPRS systems, Secretary Robert Reich recorded a videotaped message for the colloquium participants: "Now, the old unemployment system was fine for its time, but it often failed to quickly deliver reemployment services to workers in transition from old to new jobs," Reich said. "Our new 'reinvented' unemployment insurance system uses worker profiling and reemployment services to both identify and retrain but also place in new jobs those workers who would otherwise face long-term unemployment. Dislocated workers can now get the services they need to find the jobs they want—and it works" (Reich 1996).

The WPRS Colloquium included presentations that demonstrated the accomplishments states had made with regard to innovative design, development, and implementation of WPRS. It also offered a challenge to strengthen nascent partnerships in order for the ES, JTPA Dislocated Worker, and UI programs to better serve their common customers—dislocated workers (Balducchi 1996). Such WPRS exchanges of information should be renewed.

State worker-profiling models need be updated regularly, and states should consider whether to respecify them. The seven states with characteristic screening models should be encouraged to convert to statistical models, and Florida should be required to adopt an objective WPRS model.

The WPRS system cannot be effective without the provision of comprehensive reemployment services and without adequate funding. Yet WIA Dislocated Worker and Employment Service real funding levels declined markedly in the period after the enactment of WPRS. As a result, WPRS became "WPRS Lite": few reemployment services are made available to most participants.

WPRS cannot achieve the promise of the New Jersey and JSA experiments unless reemployment services are more comprehensive and better funded. Funding to the ES must be increased, and the Reemployment Services Grants must be resuscitated. Reemployment Services Grants would need an estimated funding level of $200–$300 million per year to provide adequate reemployment services to all of the dislocated workers who could benefit from them.[34]

Any assessment of what the WPRS system could achieve in today's economy would require a new demonstration project with strong, well-funded treatments. Without a buildup in resources, an evaluation of the current WPRS system would simply show that a weak treatment results in weak net impacts. Instead, a new WPRS demonstration should be conducted, providing reemployment services that are at least as strong as those used in the New Jersey Experiment. Such a demonstration is likely to reveal the greater effectiveness of providing comprehensive reemployment services, compared to the very modest services that were being provided through 2008.

Launching the WPRS system represented an innovative public policy approach. Implementation of the profiling component of the system reflects federal and state governments' willingness to identify and select program participants using a new and sophisticated targeting tool. Worker profiling has become a unique and highly flexible method for selecting those participants most in need of reemployment assistance and for allocating scarce government resources. WPRS also represents a willingness to implement a new system based on research results when those results reveal that a particular reemployment intervention (i.e., comprehensive job search assistance) is both effective and efficient.

The WPRS system also has broader potential than simply providing job search assistance for dislocated workers. Worker profiling is currently being used by states operating the SEA program, and it has been proposed for a reemployment bonus program. The profiling mechanism could be used for purposes other than for predicting who could make the best use of a dislocated worker program. For example, worker profiling could be used by the Job Corps to assist in selecting participants. A very different profiling mechanism could be used to identify hard-to-employ persons or former TANF recipients who also require reemployment and career advancement services (O'Leary and Kline 2008). The challenge in upcoming years is to provide states with sufficient resources to strengthen the WPRS system, expand targeting, and provide early intervention so that workers can quickly return to the labor market.

The proposed Reemployment Act of 1994 was designed to provide reemployment services to all unemployed workers who needed them, based on the research results from the New Jersey Experiment and other research about the effectiveness of reemployment services. The reauthorization of the WIA should again build from the bottom up, and appropriations should assure that sufficient resources are provided to dislocated worker programs, so that they can provide reemployment services to the workers who need them.

Notes

1. Section 4(a)(1) of Public Law 103-52.
2. To require WPRS participation, Public Law 103-152 amends section 303(a) of the Social Security Act, adding a "requirement that, as a condition of eligibility for regular compensation for any week, any claimant who has been referred to reemployment services pursuant to the profiling system . . . participate in such services."
3. The WPRS system is designed to provide reemployment services to permanently separated workers who are likely to be unemployed for long periods while they search for new jobs. Workers who find their jobs exclusively through union hiring halls, e.g., longshoremen, are considered to be job-attached and not searching for new jobs but waiting to return to their old jobs. They are not eligible to participate in WPRS reemployment services.
4. Benefit exhaustion takes place when claimants use up all of the potential duration of regular benefits to which they are entitled. In most states, potential duration varies among individuals according to their prior job attachment. The maximum potential duration is 26 weeks in all states except Massachusetts, where it may be as long as 30 weeks.
5. For initial screening, most states use recall status and union hiring hall participation. For statistical models, most also use some form of education, industry, and a measure of local economic conditions. Tenure is used to a lesser extent, in some cases because it has a negligible effect, in others because of lack of availability of data. Occupation is the least reliable of the original data elements, and it is the least used. Among the new variables used in some states are measures of five variables: 1) delay in UI filing, 2) former earnings, 3) work search requirement, 4) number of employers in the base period, and 5) potential duration of benefits.
6. Prohibited variables and the effect of their omission are discussed in USDOL (1994b), pp. 63, 151–152. Before the department completed the national worker profiling model, in the summer of 1993 I discussed the issue of prohibited variables with staff of the Civil Rights Division of the U.S. Department of Justice. Justice Department lawyers made clear that although a variable such as age might be prohibited, using a variable such as job tenure that is correlated with age would not be prohibited.
7. The screens used in the New Jersey experiment were the following five: 1) UI first payment receipt, 2) temporary layoff exclusion, 3) union hiring hall use, 4) age 25

or greater, and 5) tenure of three years or more with last employer. Most of these screens were ultimately used as variables in the WPRS profiling process.

8. The national worker profiling model was developed from a CPS data set by Kelleen Worden Kaye during the summer of 1993 in anticipation of Maryland's implementation of WPRS, which occurred during the winter of 1994.

9. Papers presenting the results of two prototype profiling mechanisms—a national model and a Maryland state-specific model—are contained in USDOL (1994b).

10. Scott Gibbons of the Office of Workforce Security, interview with the author, June 22, 2006.

11. Chuck Middlebrooks was the administrator of the Maryland employment security agency. He had previously worked on a temporary assignment at the USDOL and had observed the development of the WPRS system. He initiated the WPRS program in Maryland. When the characteristics screening model was not working well, he called the department to ask for help in developing the statistical worker profiling model.

12. Identification and referral are generally conducted subsequent to initial claims filing, on a weekly basis, in a batch mode on states' mainframe or personal computers. The profiling mechanisms can either refer a specified number of UI claimants to reemployment services, or the service provider can select WPRS participants ranked in order of probability of exhaustion. The need to vary the flow of referrals is related to those factors that may influence the resources available to provide reemployment services, including the following four: 1) statewide resource availability, both annual and seasonal; 2) local resource variability within a state; 3) business cycle variation in the demand for services; and 4) competing needs for resources by other employment and training programs and other (nondislocated worker) populations.

13. WPRS group services such as job search workshops or job clubs may have slots available for unemployed workers not participating in the WPRS system. These workers may have been selected through other methods, e.g., dislocated workers selected by rapid response efforts at the plant site prior to layoff. They may also represent other populations, e.g, walk-ins to the One-Stop centers under its open-access eligibility, or veterans who receive preferential access to some reemployment services but not under the WPRS system.

14. Mary Ann Wyrsch, interview with the author, July 29, 2008.

15. The establishment of the name of the WPRS system reflects concern that it be seen as a part of the entire employment and training system. In the postenactment period, ETA staff referred to the emerging system as "UI profiling," and early ETA field guidance uses this terminology. During the drafting of the March 1994 operating instructions, David Balducchi of the ES suggested to Jon Messenger of UI that there appeared to be staff resistance to mounting the cross-cutting effort required to implement a nationwide system. Many ETA staff believed that they were implementing another UI-type program and did not yet see how other program services fit into the overall design. Balducchi said that you don't profile UI, you profile workers; therefore, by changing the name of the emerging system, perhaps ETA staff would better see their roles. Messenger was in agreement, and he took this

proposal to me. Capitol Hill staffers provided similar feedback, not completely understanding that the UI profiling system would require coordination and support from the ES labor exchange and JTPA (Job Training Partnership Act) training service providers. At the same time Messenger suggested that ETA include the word "system" to describe the process. I agreed with both changes, and henceforth the name associated with the profiling system has been known as the Worker Profiling and Reemployment Services system. David Balducchi, interview and written materials provided to the author, July 31, 2008.

16. When WPRS was enacted, the JTPA Dislocated Worker Program was the principal dislocated worker program in the United States. Since the enactment of the Workforce Investment Act in 1998, the WIA Dislocated Worker program has taken its place. It has traditionally recruited participants through either 1) early outreach ("rapid response") to workers experiencing mass layoffs/plant shutdowns, or 2) walk-ins to local intake centers. The Employment Service serves all employed and unemployed workers, including dislocated workers. Both programs now supplement their recruitment of program participants with WPRS referral and are active participants in the overall WPRS system. For the WIA Dislocated Worker program, most but not necessarily all WPRS-referred workers are eligible for WIA Dislocated Worker services.

17. The Basic Understandings Workgroup was a subgroup of the overall Workforce Security Team, a group formed to draft legislative specifications for the administration's workforce reform bill. The U.S. Employment Service (USES) coordinated activities of the work group, and members included David Balducchi, Brian Deaton, Ingrid Evans, Eric Johnson, Wayne Zajac, and me. In the development of subsequent WPRS field guidance, ETA staff participation expanded to include Maurice Birch, Kitty Fenstermaker, Jon Messenger, and Richard Puerzer.

18. One final point of contention was how to classify "orientation." The question became, "Was an orientation a reemployment service and therefore to be counted as meeting the states' minimal provision of service requirements, or was it part of a standardized WPRS process?" By a narrow decision, it was held that an orientation would be classified as a reemployment service. In retrospect, this decision was wrong: an orientation provides basic information, but it does not provide reemployment services that help a UI claimant return to work. An orientation can count as a WPRS activity, and orientations should be provided as a standard practice, but states should subsequently provide at least one or more reemployment services. David Balducchi, interview and written materials provided to the author, July 31, 2008.

19. Wyrsch, January 4, 1994, memorandum to Jim Van Erden, Grace Kilbane, Robert Schaerfl, and Sue Schlickeisen titled "Basic Understandings, December 17, 1993."

20. David E. Balducchi, interview with the author and written materials provided to the author, July 31, 2008.

21. Issuances of field memorandums then and now were instructions to the Employment and Training Administration's regional offices. However, to expedite the dissemination of FM 35-94, Assistant Secretary Doug Ross took the unprecedented step of sending it directly from Washington, D.C., to the state employment security

agencies and the state JTPA coordinators, in addition to the regional offices. This is the single known instance of such dissemination of a field memorandum, demonstrating the importance to ETA of WPRS implementation.

22. The primary field guidance was Field Memorandum 35-94, issued in March 1994. This and other guidance discussed in this section are reproduced in USDOL (1994b).

23. In USDOL (1994b), see "Unemployment Insurance Program Requirements for the Worker Profiling and Reemployment Services System," UI Program Letter 41-94, August 16, 1994.

24. The supplements to Field Memorandum 35-94 were issued as Change 1, dated May 2, 1994; Change 2, dated June 9, 1994; and Change 3, dated July 31, 1996. Field Memorandum 50-95 contained the "Assessment/Review of State Implementation of Worker Profiling and Reemployment Services," dated July 19, 1995.

25. These early WPRS program results are for the period October 1995 through June 1996, when the WPRS system became fully operational.

26. In Connecticut, Illinois, Maine, and New Jersey, WPRS had the expected impact on UI durations, reducing the receipt of UI benefits by between one-quarter week and one full week, and reducing the receipt of UI benefits by $62, to $140. In Kentucky and South Carolina, the results for UI effects were mixed or without impact. The study found little evidence that WPRS increased employment or earnings for referred claimants; the main effect of WPRS was the reduction of duration of compensation. More recently, a single state evaluation of WPRS in the state of Kentucky has shown that WPRS reduces the duration of unemployment by more than two weeks (Black, Smith, Berger, et al. 2003).

27. Because of rescissions, the Reemployment Service Grant funding levels were reduced in their last three years. Funding levels from FY 2001 to FY 2005 were as follows:

FY 2001	$35,000,000
FY 2002	$35,000,000
FY 2003	$34,773,000
FY 2004	$34,567,000
FY 2005	$34,290,000

28. Balducchi, interview and written materials.

29. Orientation is considered to be a service under WPRS, but it consists of an introduction to WPRS and an overview of available services rather than constituting a true reemployment service. Job search assistance provides instruction in job search skills. It may consist of a variety of components including resume writing, methods of searching for jobs, and interviewing techniques.

30. An analysis of data for 1998 shows that only 12 states recorded fewer referrals than they reported, and three states—New Jersey, North Carolina, and Texas—accounted for most of the national difference. By 2007, only four states showed reporting greater than referrals, and the differences were small.

31. Referral to the Self-Employment Assistance (SEA) program is also a WPRS service, but referrals can only be made in the seven states with active SEA programs. Only four states report that they refer WPRS participants to the SEA program.

32. Reemployment services increased sharply in 2009, as state workforce agencies responded quickly to an infusion of $250 million in Reemployment Services Grants made available in early 2009.

33. "Received Some Reportable Service" is defined as "all applicants that have received some reportable service during the program year. Services include: referral to job; job placement; placement in training; obtaining employment; assessment services, including an assessment interview; testing; counseling and employability planning; case management services; vocational guidance services; job search activities, including resume assistance; job search workshops; job finding clubs; specific labor market information and job search planning; federal bonding program; job development contacts; tax credit eligibility determination; referral to other services, including skills training, educational services, and supportive services; and any other services requiring expenditure of staff time although not required to be reported. Application-taking and registration are not included as a reportable service" (ETA Handbook No. 406, ETA 9002 Data Preparation Handbook, March 1993, III-13, III-14). "Job search activities" are defined as follows: "All applicants provide services which are designed to help the job seeker plan and carry out a successful job hunt strategy. The services include resume preparation assistance, job search workshops, job-finding clubs, provision of specific labor market information, and development of a job search plan" (ETA Handbook No. 406, ETA 9002 Data Preparation Handbook, March 1993, III-11).

34. The American Recovery and Reinvestment Act (P.L. 111-5), enacted on February 17, 2009, appropriated $400 million for additional Wagner-Peyser Act services, of which $250 million was targeted exclusively for reemployment services to UI claimants. Funding could be expended over a two-and-a-half-year period ending September 30, 2011.

5
Reemployment Services Research

Job Referrals, Job Search Assistance, and the Unemployment Insurance Work Test

INTRODUCTION

A great deal of research other than the Unemployment Insurance (UI) Experiments has provided guidance for employment and training programs since the 1990s. This chapter reviews the results of a selection of research, demonstrations, and evaluations that have studied the effectiveness of job search assistance (JSA) and other forms of reemployment services provided to adult American workers by USDOL-sponsored One-Stop Career Centers. It reviews the evaluations of the services that have been provided separately and in service sets and assesses what these past studies mean for the workforce development system of today. The chapter puts particular emphasis on a number of research and evaluation projects that were completed during the Bush II administration and were suppressed for a number of years, until the Office of Management and Budget (OMB) compelled the department to release them during the summer of 2008. The overarching finding is that the major forms of reemployment services and administrative procedures—job search assistance, enhancing the UI work test, and referrals to job openings—are cost-effective separately and gain synergy when offered jointly.

Many workers need the reemployment services—core and intensive services in Workforce Investment Act (WIA) terminology—provided by the One-Stop centers. Whether workers who receive services are classified as adults or dislocated workers under the WIA programs, increasing numbers of them seek help when they become unemployed and permanently separated from their previous jobs. Demand for the services has increased for two reasons: 1) an increase in the proportion of layoffs that are permanent rather than temporary, resulting in an increase in worker dislocation (Groshen and Potter 2003); and 2) the hard-to-employ are more likely now to have been previously employed than they were in the past. Indeed, welfare reform has increased the likelihood that former welfare recipients—who make up a significant portion of WIA Adult program participants—either have previously been employed and are applying for UI benefits, or are seeking reemployment services after becoming unemployed (O'Leary and Kline 2008).

Core and intensive services provided as Wagner-Peyser Act employment services are what most customers receive when they come to a One-Stop center. The One-Stops generally serve 13 to 20 million workers each year, whereas the current and planned capacity for providing occupational and on-the-job training is a few hundred thousand per year. Yet the Bush administration's 2006 proposal to create training vouchers (Career Advancement Accounts, or CAAs) for fewer than 600,000 workers would have absorbed most of the funds available to run the One-Stop centers and to provide reemployment services. The result would have been a crippling of the ability of department-funded programs to continue to provide reemployment services to the millions of other job seekers who come to the One-Stops for help in finding jobs.

Reemployment services discussed below are divided into three categories: 1) job search assistance, 2) an enhanced work test, and 3) referrals to job openings. Helping workers return to work can be done either by providing referrals to job openings or by training those workers to use the tools to search for work themselves. Providing job search assistance can include assessment, testing, counseling, job search workshops or job clubs, and follow-up activities.

One long-standing intervention to increase the exposure of claimants to the labor market is an enhanced work test that generally includes a staff-assisted review of eligibility and efforts to search for work, as well as the referral to employment services. In the past this enhanced work test has been part of a department-funded Eligibility Review Program (ERP). Most states ceased operating these programs in the 1980s and 1990s.

In a change of policy, the department once again recognized the importance of putting more resources into the UI work test. Starting in March 2005, 21 states received grant awards for the Reemployment and Eligibility Assessment (REA) initiative,[1] and in July 2009, 16 additional states received REA grants. REAs essentially are an enhanced UI work test. The effort to strengthen the work test continued in each succeeding year under the Bush administration, despite budget reductions for employment and training services. The REA initiative is a reinvigoration of the Eligibility Review Program (ERP), which was an important tool for enforcing the UI work test while providing referrals for limited reemployment assistance.[2] From a budgetary perspective, reviewing the continuing eligibility of UI claimants can be a cost-effective treatment (Benus, Poe-Yamagata, et al. 2008). Unfortunately, however, REAs have not been provided in conjunction with reemployment services because the department deemphasized and tried to eliminate the provision of reemployment services during the Bush years.

An enhanced work test generally consists of an interview to ensure that UI claimants are able, available, and actively seeking work. In demonstration projects, it also included increasing the number of work searches that are required to be made each week or adding verification of some number of work searches. In the process of enhancing the UI work test, UI claimants frequently also receive information and reemployment assistance that aids in their search for work.

RESEARCH ABOUT REEMPLOYMENT SERVICES

Overview

Research regarding reemployment services for adult unemployed workers has been of interest to the state workforce agencies, the department, and private researchers. Most of the research conducted in this area has been funded by the department, but states and private researchers have also played an important role. This section reviews some of the more rigorous research that has been undertaken in the last three decades, with particular emphasis on more recent research.

The department has been looking at the effectiveness of reemployment services for many decades. Researchers have searched for some combination of cost-effective services that would include referral to job openings, JSA, and an enhanced UI work test. A number of demonstration projects searched for such a cost-effective service mix and will be discussed in this chapter. Some states also have had an interest in testing what is effective in helping workers become reemployed and have been willing to commit their own resources and initiate programs based on the evaluation results. Those results will also be examined.

Providing the basic components of job search assistance—orientation, testing, job search workshops, an individual assessment interview, and follow-up contacts—has been shown to be cost-effective when participation in the package of services was made mandatory. Providing services through an individual service plan—tailoring job search assistance to the individual—also can be cost-effective if it is rigorously administered.

While it did provide job search assistance, the JSA Experiment revealed that more was happening than merely the provision of the demonstration services. In addition to the provision of services, the demonstration collected information that was used by local office staff to provide the UI system with information used to enforce the UI work test. Work test enforcement resulted in nonmonetary determinations relating to claimants' continuing eligibility, some of which in turn resulted in the denial of UI benefits. The more rigorous enforcement of the UI work test thus contributed to a reduction in compensated duration of UI benefits. Finally, some UI claimants who received JSA services also received job referrals to employers with job openings, and these job referrals had a small but contributing effect of speeding the return to work of UI claimants. This section deals with other research that assesses the effectiveness of JSA, the UI work test, and efforts to place UI claimants.

Reemployment Services: Job Search Assistance, the UI Work Test, and Referral to Jobs

Previous chapters have looked at the results of evaluations of two UI Experiments that provided reemployment services—the New Jersey and JSA experiments. The analysis below divides reemployment services into three components: 1) job search assistance, 2) public labor-exchange referral of workers to jobs, and 3) administration of the UI work test (O'Leary and Wandner 2005; O'Leary 2006). Many of the studies cited deal with more than one of these components (Table 5.1).

Service-to-Claimants Projects

These projects were the first departmental effort to use social science experimental methods to demonstrate the effects of employing a more systematic UI work test and adding job search assistance to the periodic interviews that preceded the Eligibility Review Program, initiated in December 1976. A Five Cities Service-to-Claimants Project operated during 1969–1970. The Service-to-Claimants Project in St. Louis, Missouri, followed in 1971–1973. Both projects refined the approach to applying the UI work test, but they also included a program of systematic job search assistance, working through the local Wagner-Peyser Act Employment Service (ES) agency. While these projects were not able to demonstrate conclusively the effectiveness of either the UI work test or the provision of systematic job search assistance (Austermann, Crosslin, and Stevens 1975; Stevens 1974), they were pioneering studies that prompted further research in the 1980s.

Nevada Claimant Employment Projects

In the late 1970s and the 1980s, two different state-funded projects sought to find better ways to help return UI claimants to work. They were conducted under the guidance of the Nevada employment security research director, James Hanna. The project treatments—including referrals to job openings and training, eligibility reviews, and job search assistance— successfully reduced the length of workers' periods of unemployment by having a UI and ES team provide more intensive reemployment services to UI claimants.

In the second study, the Nevada employment security agency in 1987 budgeted $400,000 from its UI penalty and interest fund to institute a pilot effort, the Claimant Employment Project (CEP). The project used random assignment. During the 12 months of operation (July 1988–June 1989), 1,424 treatment group members received services early in their spells of unemployment. Of the treatment group members, 1,294 received a combination of concentrated ES and UI services. Nearly all treatment group members received ES job referrals, over half completed a UI eligibility review, and a small number participated in job search workshops. As an early intervention project, it stipulated that participating claimants could not enter the program more than four weeks into their UI benefit year, but project services were available

Table 5.1 Selected Reemployment Services Research, Demonstrations, and Evaluations

Project	Dates	Sponsor	Job search assistance	Public labor exchange	UI work test
Reemployment Service and UI work test studies					
Service to Claimants Project	1969–73	USDOL	Yes	No	Yes
Charleston Claimant Placement and Work Test Demonstration	1983	USDOL	Yes	Yes	Yes
Washington Alternative Work Search Demonstration	1986–87	WA	Yes	No	Yes
Nevada Claimant Employment Project	1988–89	NV	Yes	Yes	Yes
Reemploy Minnesota	1988–89	MN	Yes	Yes	Yes
Maryland UI Work Search Demo	1994–95	USDOL	No	No	Yes
Vroman and Woodbury	2004	USDOL	Yes	Yes	Yes
Wisconsin Reemployment Connections Project	2004–06	USDOL	Yes	Yes	Yes
Kentucky WPRS Evaluation	1994–96	KY	Yes	No	Yes
National WPRS Evaluation	1996–97	USDOL	Yes	No	Yes
Reemployment and Eligibility Assessments	2005–06	USDOL	Yes	Yes	Yes
Restart Evaluation	1986	UK	Yes	No	Yes
Restart Experiment	1996	UK	Yes	No	Yes
U.S. Employment Service Evaluations					
Public Labor Exchange (PLX) Evaluation—1983	1980–82	USDOL	No	Yes	No
PLX Evaluation—Washington and Oregon	1997–98	USDOL	No	Yes	No
National PLX Evaluation	1998–2004	USDOL	No	Yes	No

NOTE: Dates refer to the times during which demonstration projects or studies were conducted or when evaluations were completed and published.

SOURCE: Studies referred to in this chapter.

to a broad UI population and not restricted to permanently separated workers.

For the 1,294 claimants receiving these concentrated services, their compensated unemployment duration was reduced by 2.1 weeks, and savings to the Nevada UI trust fund account was estimated at $409,500. Nevada research staff estimated that the benefit-cost ratio for these claimants was 2.39, indicating a $2.39 reduction in UI expenditures for every dollar expended on this activity (USDOL 1990, pp. 150–163; USDOL 1995b).

Charleston Claimant Placement and Work Test Demonstration

This USDOL-funded study was conducted in South Carolina with approximately 6,000 UI claimants, who were randomly assigned to three treatment groups and a control group. During 1983, the services received by the treatment groups consisted of the following: a "tightened and regularized" UI work test; special employment services consisting of a placement interview, job referrals, and job development; and a job search workshop after four weeks of unemployment. Under the UI work test, treatment registration was delayed until one week after claimants had received a first payment, but then there was a computer check of UI claimants (whose records were stored in the South Carolina ES registration file) who had been called in to register for work. UI benefits were terminated for claimants who had not registered, with benefits resumption depending on the outcome of a fact-finding interview regarding continuing, nonmonetary eligibility. The treatment resulted in reductions in UI-compensated durations of between 0.55 and 0.76 weeks.

All three treatments were found to be highly cost-effective, with treatment costs of less than $20 per participant and reductions in UI benefits paid of between $40 and $60. The overall conclusion was that the most effective service was the enhancement of the UI work test, although the offer of job placement activities also substantially increased the percentage of UI claimants placed. For the treatment receiving an enhanced work test and job placement services, long-term placements increased by nearly 75 percent compared to the control group: 11.2 percent of that treatment group received long-term placements, as opposed to 6.5 percent of the control group (Corson, Long, and Nicholson 1985).

Washington Alternative Work Search Experiment

This experiment was sponsored by Washington State and conducted in Tacoma, Washington, in 1986 and 1987. Over 10,000 new UI claimants were randomly assigned to four treatment groups. The experiment tested the effects of changing the required number of employer contacts per week. The current services treatment required three employer contacts per week. The experiment's three treatments did three things: 1) eliminated the requirement to report any employer contacts, 2) varied the number of contacts by claimant characteristics and increased the number of contacts over time, and 3) retained the number of employer contacts but added reemployment services early in claimants' spells of unemployment. The first treatment was a dramatic departure from existing procedures: it eliminated the requirement to submit continued claims forms as well as to report employer contacts, and it authorized payments without claimants' needing to submit these claims forms until they reported a change of status. This treatment created a substantial moral hazard issue: workers might continue to receive UI benefits after they had returned to work or had stopped searching for work. It greatly increased the spell of compensated unemployment—by 3.34 weeks (Johnson and Klepinger 1991, 1994). This treatment dramatically showed the importance of the continued claims process and the enforcement of the UI work test for maintaining the integrity of the UI system.

The Washington Alternative Work Search Experiment also evaluated job search assistance. It found that unemployment duration was reduced for those referred to JSA. However, because in most cases UI benefit receipt ended just before JSA was scheduled, the authors concluded that the shorter durations primarily resulted from an effort to avoid the hassle of job search assistance sessions rather than as a result of the content of its services (Johnson and Klepinger 1991, 1994).

Reemploy Minnesota Project (REM)

This project tested the effectiveness of providing intensive job search assistance based substantially on the design of the job search assistance component of the New Jersey Experiment. The state employment security agency budgeted $780,000 from its UI penalty and interest fund to administer the program for the first year (1988), and it funded it again in 1989 because of the success of the first year of operation. REM assigned UI claimants to treatment and control groups, using random assignment methods. REM case managers worked one-on-one with a workload of 40 REM participants at a time. The REM participants accomplished the following: they developed a written employability plan, attended a video-based job-seeking skills seminar, were matched either with job orders from employers or with job orders that were developed for them based on their work history and requirements, and received follow-up services if they remained unemployed.

For the first 12 months of operation, Minnesota research staff calculated that average claimant duration of unemployment had been reduced by 4.08 weeks, or by about 25 percent, and that savings generated by the reduction in claimant duration had yielded a benefit-cost ratio to the state of Minnesota of nearly 2.0. These large effects appear to be related to the personalized and intensive manner in which the reemployment services were provided (USDOL 1990, pp. 68–73; USDOL 1995b, p. 49).

Pennsylvania Dislocated Worker Study

A study of dislocated workers in Pennsylvania examined the effectiveness of providing job search assistance and referrals to job openings by the public employment service. It found that JSA was most effective if it was provided early in a spell of joblessness. It also found that job referrals to employers were more likely to result in placement after job seekers had exhausted other avenues of search (Katz 1991). This study supports the early provision of JSA to dislocated workers, an approach enacted into federal law two years after the study's publication as the Worker Profiling and Reemployment Services program.

Maryland UI Work Search Demonstration

This demonstration examined alternative approaches to assisting the worker search process for UI recipients. Over 27,000 UI claimants were referred to four treatment groups and a control group. Random assignment occurred between January 1994 and January 1995. Treatments consisted of four approaches: 1) retaining the requirement of two work-search contacts per week and adding a job search workshop, 2) increasing the number of employer contacts required per week to four,

3) supplementing the normal work-search requirement with verification of 10 percent of employer contacts, and 4) not requiring claimants to document their employer contacts. The demonstration was able to show that changing the work-search requirement alone produced a significant effect, reducing the amount of UI benefits paid and the weeks compensated.

The increase in required work-search contacts from two to four per week reduced UI benefits paid by $116 and weeks paid by 0.7 weeks—a reduction in each measure of about 6 percent (Table 5.2). Retaining two contacts per week but informing claimants about the introduction of employer contact verification resulted in the reduction of UI benefits paid in the amount of $113 and weeks paid by a duration of 0.9 weeks—an 8 percent reduction for each. Requiring participation in a four-day job search workshop was also found to be effective in reducing UI outlays: relative to the normal UI work-search policy, offering the job search workshop resulted in reduced weeks paid of 0.6 weeks, and in reduced UI payments per claimant of $75 (Klepinger et al. 1998).

McVicar (2008) confirms the finding of the Maryland UI Work Search Demonstration regarding not requiring claimants to document their employer contacts. Between 2001 and 2008, local UI offices in Northern Ireland experienced interruptions in some of the usual bi-weekly "job search monitoring interviews." Because these interviews were halted for approximately eight months and resumed thereafter, they could be studied as a natural experiment. Whereas in Maryland halting monitoring of employer contacts increased UI claimant durations by 10 percent, in Northern Ireland average claimant duration

Table 5.2 Maryland Work Search Demonstration Treatment Impacts on UI Receipt, Full Benefit Year

Outcome measures	Additional contacts	No reporting of contacts	Job search workshop	Verify contacts	Control group means
Total UI benefits paid ($)	−116**	34	−75**	−113**	2,085
No. of weeks of benefits	−0.7**	0.4***	−0.6**	−0.9**	11.9
% exhausted benefits	−2.6**	1.6***	−1.1	−3.0**	28.3

NOTE: ** significantly different from control group at the 0.05 level (two-tailed test); *** significantly different from control group at the 0.01 level (two-tailed test).
SOURCE: Klepinger et al. (1998).

increased 16 percent. Agreeing with Klepinger, Johnson, and Joesch (2002), McVicar concludes that "periods of suspension of job search monitoring led to significantly lower exit rates from registered unemployment and increased average claim duration. In short . . . monitoring matters" (p. 24).

United Kingdom Restart Evaluation

In the United Kingdom (UK) in the 1980s, UI was administered by that nation's public employment service (PES) and had a uniform initial entitlement duration of 12 months. In 1987, a new program called Restart was introduced nationally. Under Restart, UI beneficiaries nearing six continuous months of benefit receipt were called in for an appointment at their local PES office and were provided an intensive package of job search assistance. A program evaluation by Dolton and O'Neill (1996) estimated the short-term effects of the UK's Restart program to be similar to those observed by Johnson and Klepinger (1994) in the Washington Alternative Work-Search Experiment. Both evaluations suggested that there was a modest shortening in the duration of compensated unemployment and that the invitation for comprehensive job search assistance acted more as a spur to leave UI than as a support for reemployment. The Restart effort led to the introduction of further programs to increase the work focus of benefits, including the New Deal for Young People, the New Deal for Long-Term Unemployed, and the New Deal for the Disabled, each of which provides enhanced reemployment interventions.

United Kingdom Restart Experiment

Dolton and O'Neill (2002) conducted a subsequent random assignment field experiment to determine what the effect would be of accelerating the offer of Restart services. In the experiment, the treatment group received the standard Restart comprehensive job search assistance services when nearing six continuous months of claiming UI, while the randomly selected control group was given the Restart services at the current services timing—when approaching 12 continuous months of receiving UI benefits. In the short run, their evaluation found that requiring participation in job search assistance spurred both groups of UI beneficiaries to go back to work. Over a longer five-year follow-up period, however, the treatment group getting job search assistance support earlier in their jobless spell had measurably higher earnings. The fact that this study—and others—found a long-term earnings effect indicates that providing job search assistance can have a positive and long-term impact for UI claimants, over and above the impact of better enforcement of the UI work test.

National Worker Profiling and Reemployment Services (WPRS) Evaluation

This evaluation (Dickinson et al. 1999) assessed the effect of the nationwide implementation of a program of reemployment services for dislocated UI claimants that was mandated in 1993 legislation. The evaluation assessed the period 1996–1997, immediately following the program implementation deadline of mid-1996 for all states. The evaluation included surveys of state agencies in both 1996 and 1997. A net impact analysis was conducted in six states: Connecticut, Illinois, Kentucky, Maine, New Jersey, and South Carolina, using a quasiexperimental approach and selecting a comparison group from claimants who filed their initial claims in the same period and who were subject to referral to WPRS but who were not referred. The evaluation of WPRS indicated shorter jobless durations for program participants, with significant duration reductions of 0.2 to 1.0 weeks in five of the six states. The research found that state WPRS implementation was uneven, and that providing reemployment services was less comprehensive than under the New Jersey and Job Search Assistance experiments. Funding for reemployment services was limited. As the New Jersey and JSA experiments showed, these modest results are not surprising for programs providing much weaker job search assistance treatments at much lower cost than the treatments provided by the two original experiments.

Kentucky Worker Profiling and Reemployment Services Evaluation

This evaluation made use of an experimental design based on random assignment methods that were built into the procedure by which UI claimants were referred to WPRS in the state of Kentucky. The evaluation examined a number of different WPRS impacts. It found that the treatment group members collected 2.2 fewer weeks of UI benefits than the control group. The treatment group members also received $143 less in UI benefits and earned an average of $1,054 more in the year after the start of their UI claim. The evaluators asserted that the larger reductions in benefit receipt in Kentucky compared to the Dickinson et al. (1999) study discussed above were due to the more comprehensive employment and training services offered in Kentucky. They also concluded that early increases in earnings by treatment group members are more closely related to the rigorous enforcement of the UI work test than to the provision of reemployment services (Black et al. 2003).

They concluded that providing reemployment services in Kentucky had little impact, which is likely attributable in large part to the fact that Kentucky provided fewer reemployment services as a part of its WPRS system than most other states during the study period of 1994–1996, and that Kentucky was providing far fewer services than were provided in the New Jersey and JSA experiments. Kentucky was one of the participating states in the national WPRS evaluation that was conducted for UI claimants filing for benefits in 1995 and 1996—the same time as the Black et al. (2003) study. The national WPRS evaluation found that Kentucky only provided five to nine hours of local services, considerably less than most of the other participating states (Dickinson et al. 1999, p. I-8).

The Kentucky evaluation carried the title, "Is the Threat of Reemployment Services More Effective than the Services Themselves?" The answer to that question is that the impact of an enhanced UI work test—i.e., the "threat of services"—indeed was probably greater than the reemployment services themselves, but this likely was due, in part, to Kentucky's providing only a minimal set of services.

Eight-State WIA Implementation Study

This study (Barnow and King 2005) was conducted by a Rockefeller Institute for Government team of researchers using field network techniques. The study found that in all eight states the state agencies responsible for Wagner-Peyser Act ES funds played a major role in the provision of core services. In addition, Barnow and King found that at most One-Stops some additional core services were provided either by the One-Stop operator or by a WIA Title I contractor. They observed that states with more "comprehensive workforce policy frameworks," such as Florida and Texas, concentrated their WIA resources more on providing intensive services and training, leaving core services to be provided by the ES and Temporary Assistance for Needy Families (TANF)-funded employment services. The more traditional program-based states, such as Maryland and Missouri, had their One-Stop centers place a greater emphasis on providing core services in the overall mix of reemployment services provided.[3]

Historical Analysis of UI and the Employment Service

Earlier studies have shown that a stronger work test can be imposed either as part of the ongoing administration of the UI program or in conjunction with the mandatory participation in job search assistance, such as provided by the WPRS system. Historically, all states operated Eligibility Review Programs as part of their determination of continued eligibility of UI claimants, but use declined over time. Claimants have reported for eligibility reviews at specified intervals for an assessment of their continuing eligibility and efforts to search for work. Some state workforce agencies, mainly in the Southern states, continue to operate ERP programs, and the substance of the eligibility review effort has been resurrected as the Reemployment and Eligibility Assessment (REA) initiative.

The impact of enforcement of the UI work test is also revealed from analyzing the aggregate UI reporting data for the individual states. In their analysis of trends and cycles in UI and ES data, Vroman and Woodbury (2004) look into the factors that contribute to the duration of UI benefits. Comparing states, they find that states with established eligibility review programs have shorter durations of compensated employment.[4] This analysis supports similar findings from experimental data that individual UI claimants subject to an enhanced work test also experience shorter UI durations than members of a control group that does not receive these services.

Workforce Development Services in Rural Areas

An important workforce development issue is the geographic availability of reemployment services throughout the United States. The emphasis of WIA policy on comprehensive One-Stops, which have many participating service providers, puts nonurban areas with low population densities at a great disadvantage for access to reemployment services. A study by Dunham et al. (2005), completed in 2005 but not released until 2008, analyzes the historical changes that have occurred in access to services, the nature of the service delivery system, and the programmatic partnerships that were forged in workforce development programs during the 25 years between 1979 and 2004. The study was based on field research in five states (Georgia, Iowa, New Mexico, Oregon, and Pennsylvania) and a quantitative geospatial analysis of the distribution of local offices in three years: 1979, 1999, and 2004. The study found that there are three types of permanent, staff-assisted access points to reemployment services under WIA and the Wagner-Peyser Act programs in rural areas: 1) comprehensive, 2) affiliates, and 3) satellite offices. Rural areas had all three types of offices, but to the extent that funds were available, rural areas concentrated more of their resources on replacing affiliate offices with comprehensive offices, both because of federal policy and because they appeared to be more efficient.

Of the five field research states, only one experienced an increase in access points to reemployment services, and that was due to the introduction of nontraditional access points in the form of libraries and churches. In the rural areas of the other four states, the number of access points declined and largely consisted of renovated Employment Service offices that served as affiliated One-Stop centers. To the extent that new One-Stop access points developed, they have tended to be comprehensive One-Stops, and they have resulted in a decline in the number of total access points. More recently, both comprehensive and affiliate One-Stop offices have declined in number as states have closed local offices in response to declining WIA and Wagner-Peyser Act program funding.

Nationally the number of access points declined from 1979 to 1999 and then increased by 2004, both for the country as a whole and in nonmetropolitan areas. The national decline between 1979 and 1999 was by almost a thousand, or by 28 percent, but the number sharply increased in the next five years, more than compensating for the prior decline (Table 5.3).

Despite the small increase in total access points between 1979 and 2004, there were large shifts in the number in almost all states, with positive or negative changes of 10 percent or more in all but three states. Twenty-six states experienced gains of 10 percent or more, while 23 experienced similar losses. The gainers were mostly in areas of popula-

Table 5.3 State Workforce Agency Access Points in 1979, 1999, 2004, and 2008—Total, and by Rural and Metro Areas

	1979	1999	2004	2008	Change in number of access points from 1979 to 2004 (%)
National	3,454	2,505	3,542	2,950	2.5
Rural	1,472	1,113	1,605		11.2
Metro	1,982	1,392	1,937		−2.3

SOURCE: Dunham et al. (2005); and America's Service Locator (www.servicelocator .org), December 31, 2008.

tion growth—the South and the Mountain West—while the losses were highly concentrated in Mid-Atlantic and Midwestern states.

The national losses between 1979 and 1999 were attributed to the sharp decline in workforce development funds available per worker between the late 1970s and today, as well as the decline in UI-only access points because of telephone and Internet UI claims-taking. The increase in access points from 1999 to 2004 is attributable to developments under the WIA program, including the development of satellite offices and computer-only, unstaffed access points. Satellite and unstaffed access points can provide limited services that would not otherwise be available in many nonurban areas. Satellite offices were found to be very small (about 400 square feet) and located in the offices of a host entity, such as the local chamber of commerce; they tended to be open part-time, staffed by one person, and offered limited services. Computer-only access points frequently consist of one computer located at a host entity. Host entities may include One-Stop partners, such as welfare (i.e., TANF) agencies, vocational rehabilitation offices, postsecondary institutions, chambers of commerce, libraries, and churches.

Rural areas experienced an increase in comprehensive One-Stops between 1999 and 2004 because of the WIA mandate that there be at least one comprehensive center in each local workforce area. Because of limited resources, each new comprehensive One-Stop has generally been offset by the closure of one or more smaller affiliate One-Stops. The affiliate One-Stops, however, perform an important function in rural areas. Affiliate access points are not stand-alone ES offices; they have either WIA Adult and Dislocated Worker staff or ES staff on-site full time, with at least one other partner program on-site part time. They provide either WIA or ES services, plus services from at least one other partner agency. In fact, since affiliates are generally ES-staffed and provide primarily ES services, access to WIA intensive and training services is generally available by referral. The Dunham et al. (2005) study finds that other partner agencies are limited in rural areas, whether hosted by public, religious, or community-based organizations. Even if partners exist, however, they usually are not colocated in the One-Stops, and they do not contribute financially to the running of the One-Stop centers.

Despite a wide variety of access points, rural access to One-Stop services is very limited. The study finds that many poor rural residents—half or more—do not own cars and cannot travel to the workforce development access points. Public transportation is scarce, transportation assistance is not effective, and alternatives to travel such as Internet and telephone services are limited and less effective than in-person services (Dunham et al. 2005, pp. III 24–32).

While the Dunham et al. (2005) study was able to observe the changes that occurred over three time periods and the situation in 2004, it missed the downward trend in access points under WIA since 2004. The number declined steadily from 3,583 on December 29, 2004, to 2,950 on December 31, 2008. Similarly, access to workforce development services appears to have declined during the operation of the WIA program, resulting in a large decline in rural access to services.

Anatomy of a One-Stop and *Anatomy of Two One-Stops*

A pair of studies, *Anatomy of a One-Stop* (Stack and Stevens 2006) and *Anatomy of Two One-Stops* (Mueser and Sharpe 2006), completed in 2006 and released in 2008, looked at the activities conducted by One-Stops around the United States, even though their field research was concentrated in three centers, in Baltimore, Maryland; Camdenton, Missouri; and Columbia, Missouri.

The studies found that the type, number, and intensity of reemployment services received by job seekers varied greatly with their demographics. Comparing two One-Stops, one in the Eastside of Baltimore and the other in Columbia, the researchers found that the services offered varied with the needs of the job seekers. In the Eastside One-Stop, the emphasis was on helping job seekers get job-ready because they had relatively lower levels of education and marketable skills. In

Columbia, clients generally were job-ready, but they still made use of a variety of staff-assisted and self-directed reemployment services.

Some job seekers must rely heavily on programs and staff assistance to negotiate entry into the labor force. Other job seekers have fewer employment barriers but still benefit from having staff coach them through skills assessment, job analysis, and job search as they seek a career change or reemployment after dislocation from previous employment. Still other job seekers quickly become self-directed after receiving instruction in use of a job search system.

The One-Stops were diverse. Eastside Baltimore served a more disadvantaged population and experienced higher unemployment rates, while Columbia served a more advantaged population in a stable economy dominated by the educational, medical, and financial industries. Eastside placed emphasis on becoming job-ready through a six-hour, two-day group event and a computer-assisted lab used to help claimants work toward a GED. Columbia's clients, by contrast, were interested in getting a job quickly. Their visits to the One-Stop were shorter, but they still needed assistance with job search and with job applications and received one-on-one assistance. The results in Table 5.4 reveal that substantial amounts of reemployment services were provided, although visits to the Columbia One-Stop lasted about one-third the time of a visit to the Eastside One-Stop.

As a result, the researchers concluded that the Bush administration's proposal for Career Advancement Accounts (CAAs) "would appear to challenge the basic approach of the One-Stop Career Centers, as it implies a reallocation of resources directly to job seekers through a voucher system" (Mueser and Sharpe 2006, p. 156; Stack and Stevens 2006, p. 90).[5]

Wisconsin Reemployment Connections Project

The advent of telephone and Internet UI claims in the 1990s has meant that most UI services are provided remotely. With little or no physical presence in the One-Stop centers, the interaction of UI and One-Stop staff has declined sharply. As a result, reemployment services to UI claimants have been reduced. At the same time, UI claimants have had less review than previously of their work search activities.

To counteract these changes, the "Strengthening Connections between Unemployment Insurance and One-Stop Delivery Systems Demonstration" operated at three sites in Wisconsin between July 2004

Table 5.4 Average Time Spent in the Eastside of Baltimore, MD, and Columbia, MO, One-Stop Career Centers, by Destination, for Tracked Job Seekers

One-Stop activities	Average number of minutes in activity
Eastside of Baltimore One-Stop center	
Attending workshops	
Early intervention workshop	337
Job readiness workshop	45
Adult education classes	69
Using labs	
Digital learning lab	84
High-tech lab	46
Meeting with staff	
Group information session	29
Meet with staff	26
Talk to staff informally	23
Assessments	40
Job search	
Job interview/application	58
Job search in career lab	45
Phone bank	36
Fax/copier	27
Information exchange	
Collect One-Stop information	15
Youth employment application	9
Pick up/drop off materials	7
Wait in reception area	50
Mean overall customer time in One-Stop	**83**
Columbia, MO, One-Stop center	
Four-week UI check	12
UI services	7
Job counseling	
WIA	55
Wagner-Peyser	15
TANF and food stamp recipients	56
Other	15
Job search	26
Job applications	23
Waiting time	2½
Mean overall customer time in One-Stop	**29**

SOURCE: Mueser and Sharpe (2006); Stack and Stevens (2006).

and March 2006 (Almandsmith, Adams, and Bos 2006). It operated as a quasiexperiment using treatment and comparison sites, with 2,151 claimants in the treatment group and 4,097 comparison group members selected using a propensity score matching process. Treatment and comparison group members were referred to reemployment services using the profiling mechanism of the WPRS system.

At the comparison group sites, claimants received services normally provided. Additional services were provided at the treatment sites, where UI and the One-Stop center staff—generally ES staff—worked together to provide enhanced services and eligibility reviews. Two treatments were provided, one more intensive and the other less so, with assignment depending on an assessment of the preparedness of UI claimants to conduct job searches, their knowledge of the local labor market, and their job search skills. Both treatment groups received enhanced reemployment services that included reemployment workshops, new job search classes (e.g., an introduction to computers), WPRS services, and at least one staff-assisted job referral (for participants who participated in the reemployment workshops). Job search workshops were much more extensive than those provided under the WPRS program in almost all sites, lasting up to four weeks. The UI work test also was enhanced through three ways: 1) increased communication between UI staff and One-Stop center staff; 2) UI staff participation in reemployment service orientations and reemployment planning sessions, both provided on-site at the One-Stops; and 3) encouragement of participants to conduct five work searches per week instead of the usual two, and monitoring of whether they do (Almandsmith, Adams, and Bos 2006).

The implementation evaluation showed that the One-Stop and UI staff established linkages and worked cooperatively according to the design of the project. The net impact evaluation was conducted for treatment group members selected in three different ways, relating to their WPRS profiling scores and whether they received services. The discussion below concentrates on Model 2's Group B, the group needing more services, whose members were assigned to services based on a profiling score of 0.47 or above, since they were WPRS participants and received reemployment services similar to those under the job search assistance treatment of the New Jersey and JSA experiments (Table 5.5). The demonstration results were significant:

- The duration of UI benefits was reduced by 0.9 of a week relative to the comparison group.

- The amount of UI benefits paid declined by $233 relative to the comparison group. (The entire demonstration at all of its sites was estimated to have saved the Wisconsin UI trust fund account about $385,000.)

- The treatment group members drew 3.4 percent less of their maximum benefit entitlement than the comparison group.

The change in average quarterly earnings was not statistically significant. The rate at which UI claimants entered into employment was not affected.

The evaluation was not able to distinguish the extent to which the reduction in the duration of UI benefits paid or the decrease in the proportion of claimants' maximum UI benefits paid was due to increased use of Reemployment Connection services as opposed to stronger enforcement of the UI work test, but the latter is likely to have been a component of these outcomes. For example, the in-person review of the reemployment plans of treatment group members enabled participating UI staff to identify continuing eligibility issues that they otherwise would not have known about.

The demonstration also showed that, despite the conversion of the

Table 5.5 Impact of the Wisconsin Demonstration Program on Participant Employment Outcomes, Model 2, with WPRS Scores of 47 Percent or Higher

	Treatment	Comparison	Difference
Sample size	1,824	3,333	
Entered employment (%)	77	77	0.3
Entered employment 1st qtr. after new claim (%)	54	52	2.3
Avg. quarterly earnings ($)	3,107	2,912	194
Avg. benefit duration (wks.)	14.8	15.7	−0.9**
% maximum benefits drawn	64	67	−3.4**
Average UI benefits drawn ($)	3,690	3,923	−233**

NOTE: ** significant at the 0.05 level (two-tailed test). Blank = not applicable.
SOURCE: Almandsmith, Adams, and Bos (2006), pp. 3–16.

UI system to remote telephone claims taken in call centers outside the One-Stop centers, UI staff can participate with One-Stop staff to speed UI claimants' return to work. Furthermore, the demonstration showed that requiring participation in extensive JSA services that are similar to the comprehensive JSA treatments of the New Jersey and JSA experiments can yield similarly strong net impacts.

Reemployment and Eligibility Assessment (REA) Evaluation

This began as a new departmental initiative in 2005 and continued throughout the Bush administration as a commitment to provide UI recipients with an enhanced work test. This test has generally included a staff-assisted review of eligibility, as well as referrals to job search assistance and job referral services. The Reemployment and Eligibility Assessment demonstrations have been evaluated, but for reasons presented below the results for REA are inconclusive.

For a number of years, an Eligibility Review Program (ERP) received separate funding from the Unemployment Trust Fund, but when the separate funding was eliminated in the 1980s, many states ceased to operate ERP programs. Today fewer than a dozen states have ERP programs (O'Leary 2006). Reemployment and Eligibility Assessments are demonstration projects that act as a revitalization of an enhanced UI work test with the restoration of separate departmental funding. In March 2005, grants totaling $18 million were given to 21 state workforce agencies. Additional funding was provided in each succeeding year during the Bush administration, culminating with a request for $40 million for REAs in President Bush's FY 2009 budget, despite austerity throughout most of the proposed budget dealing with workforce development services. An important attraction for funding eligibility reviews was their promise of reducing UI benefit payments by identifying UI beneficiaries who were not able, available, and actively searching for work. All eligibility review programs have been funded with the expectation that the reduction in UI benefits will be greater than the cost of the programs, promising net savings to the Unemployment Trust Fund.

States participating in the Reemployment and Eligibility Assessment initiative require UI claimants to report in person to a One-Stop center within a specified time as a part of an eligibility assessment. Separately from the notice to report, claimants receive a call-in notice to report to the One-Stop to receive services from the WPRS system. The state REA services include four aspects: 1) a review of ongoing claim-ant UI eligibility (including detection of eligibility issues and referral to adjudication when appropriate), 2) the provision of current labor market information, 3) the development and review of a work-search plan, and 4) referral to employment services or training when appropri-ate. Because REA funding has been provided as state UI administrative grants, REA funds can only be used to fund activities authorized under UI law. Thus, REA direct funding is restricted to paying for determina-tion of UI eligibility only, and not the other three REA services. Fund-ing for the provision of job search assistance, public employment ser-vices, or training must come from WIA, Wagner-Peyser Act, or other non-UI funds.

Staff identified to administer the REA initiative were selected from the local One-Stop offices. As REA is part of the UI work test, and in many instances UI staff are located in call centers, local administra-tion fell, in most cases, to the Employment Service. In the five states designated for analysis (Connecticut, North Dakota, Minnesota, South Carolina, and Washington), ES staff were cross-trained or had UI back-grounds (Benus et al. 2008b, p. 8).

As with most discretionary grant programs administered during the Bush administration, the Reemployment and Eligibility Assessment grants were provided without requiring states to develop a consistent and rigorous program design and without rigorous federal guidance and oversight as to how to collect program data and construct com-parison groups. An evaluation of the REA initiative was conducted in nine participating states that had the most promising programs and had collected data that might facilitate the evaluation (Benus et al. 2008b). Data collected by most of the states, however, proved to be inadequate. Ultimately, the evaluation concentrated on five states (again, Connecti-cut, North Dakota, Minnesota, South Carolina, and Washington), and implementation analyses were conducted in each of the five.

The net impact analysis was restricted to Minnesota and North Dakota—the only states amenable to evaluation because only they had constructed appropriate control groups and collected reasonably valid REA data in accordance with departmental reporting instructions. The North Dakota REA did not yield statistically significant results, and nei-ther did the Minnesota approach that consisted of a single REA inter-view. The other Minnesota approach, which used multiple interviews, did have statistically significant impacts. The first interview typically came in the third week of a UI claim and was repeated up to three times for a total of four interviews, occurring at approximately one-month intervals. The Minnesota REA initiative was implemented with a rigorous random assignment process, targeting the middle third of profiled claimants whose profiling scores were just below those of individuals selected into the WPRS program.

The Minnesota REA treatment (T2) that had multiple interviews did speed the reemployment of participating UI claimants and reduce overpayments. The number of weeks claimed was reduced by almost one week, while the number of weeks claimed and compensated for was reduced by more than one week (Table 5.6). The likelihood of exhausting UI benefits was reduced by nearly four weeks. The percentage of claimants with some overpayments in their benefit year was reduced by nearly 4 percent.

The effectiveness of the Reemployment and Eligibility Assessment initiative is uncertain. Even though state grants were provided to conduct demonstration projects, the rigor of implementation did not reach reasonable research standards. Weak program design and weak data systems make evaluations of REAs highly questionable, even in the case of the Minnesota REA. The REA initiative is more of an enhanced UI work test program than a reemployment services program. An REA

Table 5.6 Minnesota Reemployment Eligibility Assessment Net Impacts per Claimant, Treatment T2, Multivariate Analysis

Claims and payments	
Number of weeks claimed	−0.9*
Number of weeks claimed and compensated	−1.2**
Total payments ($)	100
Exhaustion	
Likelihood of exhausting UI benefits (%)	−3.7*
Overpayments	
% with some overpayment during benefit year	−3.8**
Amt. of overpayment among initial claims w/ overpayment ($)	−82
No. of overpayment wks. among initial claims w/ overpayment	−0.9

NOTE: * significant at the 0.10 level (two-tailed test); ** significant at the 0.05 level (two-tailed test).
SOURCE: Benus, Poe-Yamagata et al. (2008), p. 29.

interview that lasts for 20 minutes may be sufficient to complete a basic eligibility review process, but it cannot provide sufficient assessment and counseling to make individualized referrals to additional services, and it cannot provide a significant amount of reemployment services.[6]

THREE EVALUATIONS OF THE U.S. EMPLOYMENT SERVICE: IMPACTS OF UI CLAIMANT REFERRALS TO JOB INTERVIEWS

The review above shows that in the Charleston demonstration, supplementing a more rigorous UI work test with enhanced referrals to employer job openings can substantially increase the percentage of UI claimants who receive long-term placements in new jobs. Several other demonstrations and program evaluations included an analysis of referrals to job interviews, including Reemploy Minnesota, the Maryland UI Work Search Demonstration, and the Wisconsin Reemployment Connections Project. This section looks at three department-funded evaluations of the Employment Service that concentrated solely on the effectiveness of the referral of UI claimants to job interviews.

First National Evaluation of the U.S. Employment Service

The effect of job placement services was explored in this early study, conducted in 30 local offices in 27 states between 1980 and 1982. This nonexperimental evaluation was based on administrative records and baseline and follow-up interviews. The outcomes of a group of applicants who received job referrals were compared to those of a group who received no job referrals. The evaluation found that job referrals were effective for women: women receiving a referral went back to work 2.8 weeks sooner and earned an additional $325 over a six-month period. Job referrals were not effective for men taken as a whole, but they were effective for men over 45 years of age and men in urban areas (Johnson et al. 1983; Johnson, Dickinson, and West 1985).

The Two-State Evaluation of the Public Labor Exchange

This evaluation (Jacobson and Petta 2000) was conducted for the USDOL in Washington and Oregon. It dealt with public labor exchange services provided between 1987 and 1998 and evaluated the effect of referring UI claimants to jobs. The evaluation used a quasiexperimental approach in which a treatment group was referred to available jobs and a comparison group was referred to jobs that One-Stop staff believed to be open. When the comparison group members applied for the jobs, they did not receive interviews, because the jobs were already filled (these are called "stale job openings"). In measuring the returns to direct placement of UI claimants, the study found that the treatment had an impact on the duration of unemployment, whether referrals to jobs resulted in a placement or not. In Washington, durations declined by 7.7 weeks if referrals resulted in a placement and by 2.1 weeks if they did not. The comparable reductions for Oregon were 4.6 and 1.1 weeks, respectively. The study also found that job placements were most effective for those workers with a strong record of job attachment. The cost-effectiveness of job referrals in Washington and Oregon was examined and was measured in a number of different ways. In all cases, job referrals were found to be highly cost-effective, having benefit-cost ratios that varied between 1.2 and 4.5 (Jacobson and Petta 2000).

Second National Evaluation of the Public Labor Exchange

This Westat study (Jacobson et al. 2004) was a national evaluation covering six states—Colorado, Massachusetts, Michigan, North Carolina, Oregon, and Washington. The study goal was to evaluate the effectiveness of the public labor exchange in three traditional employment service states (i.e., states that used merit-staffed state workforce agency staff) and compare these states to three nontraditional demonstration states (i.e., states that used other public or private staff). The intent of the evaluation was to assess the overall effectiveness of the public labor exchange (PLX) and to make a determination about whether temporary privatization demonstrations in the other three states should be continued or terminated. The evaluation was started in 1998 and was completed in February 2004, but, because its findings were so contrary to Bush administration policy, it was not released or published by the Employment and Training Administration until September 2008.

According to WIA regulations (*Federal Register* 2000), despite the Wagner-Peyser Act requirement that employment services under the act must be delivered by merit staff employees of a state employment security agency, "the Department authorized demonstrations of the effective delivery of Wagner-Peyser Act services utilizing non-State agency employees in Colorado, Massachusetts, and Michigan. These three demonstrations were permitted as exceptions to the long standing policy . . . in order to assess the effectiveness of alternative delivery systems" (p. 49386).

Thus, the Westat PLX study was to determine the cost-effectiveness of alternative delivery systems. As a result, the evaluation was expected to guide the department's decision on whether to continue, expand, or eliminate the demonstrations, depending on their cost-effectiveness compared to the traditional service delivery system.

The Westat study determined, among other things, the cost-effectiveness of the public labor exchange, the effect of the PLX administrative configuration—whether traditional or nontraditional—and the impact of increased automation on the PLX. The benefit-cost analysis was conducted in only five states because Michigan did not have the administrative data necessary to conduct the analysis.

The study found a fundamental difference between the PLX services provided in One-Stop centers in which the state workforce agency took the lead and those provided in One-Stop centers in which a different entity led. In the traditional sites, the One-Stop center tended to serve all potential clients, while in the demonstration sites attention tended to be limited to a smaller population of economically disadvantaged workers, and reemployment services provided were targeted to this population.

The benefit-cost portion of the study used quasiexperimental methods. The comparison group was drawn from UI claimants who were job seekers but did not receive public labor exchange services and had strong labor force attachment. This evaluation showed that the PLX had a large and significant effect on reducing the weeks of unemployment (Table 5.7). The effect was greater for direct PLX placements to job openings, since workers received jobs shortly after referrals. The result was significant but smaller for referrals that did not result in placements—only about one-quarter as large as for placements—since workers subsequently had to find their own jobs.

Table 5.7 Public Labor Exchange Evaluation, 2004, Average Per-Claimant Effect of Placements and Referrals on Weeks of Joblessness, and Benefit-Cost Ratios

	Placement effect (wks.)	Referral effect (wks.)	Benefit-cost ratio	
			Upper bound	Lower bound
Colorado	−3.1	−0.7	4.8	2.6
Massachusetts	−8.6	−2.4	4.3	1.4
North Carolina	−7.3	2.1	8.8	6.3
Oregon	−5.7	−1.1	3.1	1.6
Washington	−7.7	−2.1	2.8	1.2

NOTE: Upper-bound estimates include the value of placements and referrals, while lower-bound estimates only include the value of placements.
SOURCE: Jacobson et al. (2004), p. 166.

Table 5.7 shows that all of the PLXs had a substantial effect on reducing the duration of unemployment. The effect of a placement on weeks of joblessness varied between −3.1 and −8.6 weeks, while the effect of a referral to placement was between +2.1 and −2.4 weeks.

Overall, the evaluation found that all six of the states had cost-effective public labor exchanges—i.e., the benefits of providing a PLX were considerably greater than its cost. While the benefit-cost ratios varied considerably, in all cases benefits exceeded cost by at least 20 percent. Specifically, the benefit-cost analysis was conducted with benefits calculated using only the value of placements (the lower-bound estimates) and with benefits calculated using both the value of placements and referrals to jobs (the upper-bound estimates). In all cases, the benefit-cost ratios were quite large, reflecting the fact that the numbers of placements and referrals were quite large, while costs were quite low per placement or per referral, generally below $350. The net benefits of the programs for UI claimants, however, varied significantly between traditional and nontraditional programs because the nontraditional programs targeted disadvantaged workers, who generally are not UI claimants. Thus, Colorado had the smallest net benefits measured in dollars because only 5 percent of placements went to UI beneficiaries, while the percentages were much higher in Washington (35), Oregon (38), and North Carolina (23).

Comparing the traditional and nontraditional One-Stops, the study found that the job-matching services were better in the traditional sites operated by state ES staff. Specifically, three of Westat's findings included 1) a much higher percentage of job vacancies were listed in the traditional states, and these listings resulted in a greater ability to make placements; 2) the job-matching systems in the traditional sites had extra features that improved job matches, provided additional information, and were easier to use; and 3) the nontraditional, devolved system resulted in lesser use of statewide job-matching systems and in greater use of job development systems that emphasized special populations, rather than a general PLX that served a wider population (Jacobson et al. 2004).

With respect to automation of public labor exchange services, the evaluation found that the increased use of automated technology resulted in increased quality of job-matching services at lower cost. The study examined the national automated PLX system that the department developed in the mid-1990s—America's Job Bank. It found that the pooling of resources among the states that was done through America's Job Bank resulted in "high quality, enormous capacity, and low cost of systems" (Jacobson et al. 2004, p. 3). The evaluation found that "America's Job Bank (AJB) provides a high-quality nationwide system for job-seekers to view job listings submitted by employers and for employers to review resumes submitted by job-seekers" (Jacobson et al. 2004, Appendix C, p. C-7).

A key finding about America's Job Bank related to how it provided job-matching to low-wage workers. The study found that "AJB's successes have engendered a degree of rivalry with state-run and private PLXs. Because AJB provides free services that encourage use by small employers and employers hiring low-wage workers, profit-making service providers would have to be subsidized in some way to serve these groups. Given the low cost and high volume of AJB, it is doubtful that . . . private firms could provide the services more efficiently" (Jacobson et al. 2004, Appendix C, p. C-8). When the department shut down America's Job Bank in June 2006, there were no subsidies offered to private providers to serve low-wage workers.

REEMPLOYMENT SERVICES RESEARCH SYNTHESES FOR THE UNITED STATES AND AROUND THE WORLD

Most studies of job search assistance and other reemployment services have found that these services are cost-effective. The findings relate to three components of reemployment services—1) job search assistance, 2) the UI work test, and 3) claimant referral to job openings—and they reveal several common findings. All of these studies of the effectiveness of these programs consistently report low cost per customer served—in the hundreds of dollars or even less. Low cost is one key to the cost-effectiveness of WIA core services and public employment service interventions.

These reemployment services do not have a large impact on the human capital of participants. Generally, they do not have long-term impacts either. However, they do provide tools: incentives or sanctions that help to reduce the compensated duration of the UI program and speed the return to work. Even services resulting in a modest reduction in the duration of joblessness show a significant return on public investment when costs are low. Interventions that improve access of UI beneficiaries to job search assistance and to job referrals as well as strengthen the operation of the UI work test (such as with Reemployment and Eligibility Assessments) have the potential to increase the efficiency of state workforce systems. These three types of interventions also seem to have a synergy that reinforces their individual effectiveness when they are provided together as a comprehensive set of reemployment services.

Many researchers have synthesized the results of studies regarding job search assistance and have generally come to positive conclusions. LaLonde (1995) examines the effectiveness of training programs—job search assistance training, on-the-job training, and classroom training for youth, adults, and dislocated workers. He finds that job search assistance is cost-effective for dislocated workers and adult women and that JSA compares very favorably to other forms of short-term training.

The department's Office of the Chief Economist summarized the research results regarding job search assistance experiments conducted in Minnesota, Nevada, New Jersey, South Carolina, and Washington. The study concluded that "job search assistance clients found a new job more quickly, and receipt of UI benefits was reduced . . . The program was cost effective for the government . . . Job search participants did not end up in lower-wage jobs than non-participants" (USDOL 1995b, p. 48). Job search assistance raised earnings because it speeded reemployment and thus increased the number of hours worked. Job search assistance did not adversely affect the workers, as was demonstrated by their not taking lower quality jobs—their new employment did not adversely affect wage rates.

A Congressional Budget Office (CBO) study (1993) also analyzed the growing importance of worker dislocation and assessed alternative methods for improving the labor market outcomes for dislocated workers. It, too, finds job search assistance to be effective: "Among the options that have been discussed for helping displaced workers . . . would be to tie eligibility for additional UI benefits to participation in some activity such as a job club or other program that helps participants find jobs faster. There is strong evidence that such assistance is effective in shortening the length of time that participants receive UI benefits."

Meyer (1995) similarly reviewed a number of state and federal experiments. He finds that "the job search experiments . . . try several different combinations of services to improve job search and increase the enforcement of work search rules. Nearly all combinations reduce UI receipt and . . . increase earnings . . . The main treatments have benefits to the UI system that exceed cost in all cases, and societal level cost benefit analyses are favorable."

Meyer recommends that job search assistance be made routinely available: "On the services side we should consider making job search assistance universal," he writes. "The exact combination of services we should include is not completely clear, but job search workshops and individual attention by the same personnel seem promising."

International reviews of active labor market policies in industrial nations have come to similar conclusions, finding that job search assistance is highly cost-effective. The International Labour Organization conducted an analysis of the use of active labor market policies (ALMP) around the world in developed and developing countries (Auer, Efendioğlu, and Leschke 2005). Examining the evidence on the effectiveness of training and JSA programs in the industrial nations from four evaluation synthesis studies, the analysis reaches the following conclusion:

These evaluation overview studies show that the effects of programmes on employment and wages are usually small and positive, but not always . . . In general ALMPs seem to be rather
effective for women and labour market re-entrants, but seldom
for youth . . . Wage subsidies to employers and employees seem
to especially serve the needs of the long-term unemployed, while
self-employment schemes and micro-enterprise development programmes often show more success among better qualified individuals and especially men. All in all, as job-search assistance is
the most cost-effective measure, it should be intensively used over
all phases of unemployment. (pp. 61–62)

In addition, "carefully targeted measures achieve better results than
broad measures applying to everyone or larger groups" but they tend
to serve fewer unemployed workers (Auer, Efendioğlu, and Leschke
2005, p. 65).

The OECD also conducted an analysis of active labor market policies, but only in the industrial member nations (Martin and Grubb
2001). The authors find the following:

Job-search assistance is usually the least costly active labour market programme . . . evaluations of social experiments from several
countries (Canada, Sweden, the United Kingdom and the United
States) show positive outcomes for this form of active measure
. . . investment in active placement efforts and raising the motivation of the unemployed, as well as taking steps to encourage
and monitor their job-search behaviour, pays dividends in terms
of getting the unemployed back to work faster. While the optimal
combination of additional job-placement services and increased
monitoring of job seekers and enforcement of work test is unclear,
the evidence suggests that both are required to produce benefits to
unemployment insurance claimants and society. (p. 27)

These research findings were strong and convincing enough to
make them an important factor in the enactment of the Unemployment
Compensation Amendments of 1993, which included the Worker Profiling and Reemployment Services provisions. (See Chapter 4.) The
effectiveness of providing job search assistance early won widespread
congressional support for WPRS on its merits. These findings also supported federal budget requirements that new legislation should not have
an adverse effect on the U.S. budget deficit. The research findings also
provided evidence of the cost-effectiveness of Reemployment Services

Grants, which were added to the Wagner-Peyser Act program budget for program years 2001 through 2005—and again in 2009 as part of the American Recovery and Reinvestment Act.

LESSONS LEARNED FROM JOB SEARCH ASSISTANCE RESEARCH

A number of lessons have been learned from the research dealing with reemployment services. A good deal of confidence exists in these lessons, as they are almost all derived from rigorous experiments that were conducted by the state workforce agencies and the department. The lessons can be summed up as follows:

- Workers who are permanently separated from their employers and who are likely to have difficulty becoming reemployed benefit from receiving help in returning to work. That help can come from a variety of reemployment services, whether it be a job referral, if a job is available, or providing separated workers (through a package of job search assistance) with the tools to search for a job on their own. At the same time, stronger enforcement of the UI work test can also reduce the compensated duration of unemployment and speed the return to work, and can be provided with or without accompanying mandatory referral to job search assistance.

- Providing a package of job search assistance (e.g., orientation, assessment, testing, counseling, job search workshops/job clubs, and follow-up services) can reduce the duration of unemployment. The cost of these services is low. Savings from reduced UI benefit payments and increased tax payments make providing these services cost-effective (Corson et al. 1989; Decker et al. 2000; USDOL 1990).

- For job search assistance to be cost-effective, participation must be mandatory. Otherwise, most workers who are offered the services will not participate, and the impacts derived from the remaining workers will be small (Corson et al. 1989; Decker et al. 2000).

- Required participation in job search assistance can be based on a standardized, comprehensive set of services or a customized set of services based on the development of an individual employability plan. A comprehensive package has a greater impact on reducing UI durations, but a customized package can also have a substantial impact if participation is carefully monitored and enforced. Without participation in a number of substantive services, job search assistance will not be effective (Corson et al. 1989; Decker et al. 2000).

- There is a synergy that results from calling dislocated UI claimants into the One-Stop center for job search assistance. In addition to offering job search assistance services, local office staff can provide immediate referrals to jobs from available job openings. Also, UI staff can use information, particularly from nonreporting or nonparticipation in JSA services, to enforce the UI work test (Decker et al. 2000).

- Cooperation between UI and One-Stop center staff can contribute to the effectiveness of providing reemployment services to UI claimants (Corson et al. 1989; Decker et al. 2000; USDOL 1990).

- Local office staff can refer worker-profiled UI claimants and others to job openings. In conjunction with job search assistance services, the referral to job openings can result in higher placement rates than are normally experienced (Corson et al. 1985; Decker et al. 2000).

- One indication of the positive longer-term effect of providing job search assistance is the fact, both in the United States and in the United Kingdom, that there have been positive effects on employment and earnings not only immediately after the services are received but in subsequent years (Corson and Haimson 1996; Dolton and O'Neill 2002).

- Two careful examinations of the details of how One-Stops operate (Mueser and Sharpe 2006; Stack and Stevens 2006) reveal that individuals benefit from lots of assessment and counseling services, whether they are hard-to-employ or more skilled workers. The nature and intensity of the assessment and counseling may vary, but One-Stop centers still find that these reemployment services are needed to assist workers in returning to work.

- Stronger enforcement of the UI work test can reduce the duration of compensated unemployment, whether done separately or in conjunction with the provision of job search assistance. An enhanced UI work test can take the form of reporting to the One-Stop center and requiring UI claimants to demonstrate that they are able, available, and actively searching for work, as well as determining that they are still unemployed. It can also take the form of requiring a more intensive job search (Corson et al. 1989; Corson, Long, and Nicholson 1985; Decker et al. 2000; Johnson and Klepinger 1991, 1994; McVicar 2008). Such past research is an indication that treatments tested in the Reemployment and Eligibility Assessment pilots could prove to be cost-effective if they are properly designed, properly implemented, and thoroughly evaluated.

- Requiring UI claimants to report to a One-Stop center can reduce the duration of compensated unemployment. Enforcing the UI work test can be performed by One-Stop center staff or by UI staff if they perform eligibility reviews. Joint efforts by both One-Stop center and UI staff appear to be highly effective (Corson et al. 1989; Decker et al. 2000; USDOL 1990).

- A specific way to effectively increase the enforcement of the UI work test is to enhance the work search requirement by increasing the required number of job search contacts. Verifying a sample of those contacts can also reduce duration (Klepinger et al. 1998).

- The implication for WPRS is that, whereas providing reemployment services (a comprehensive JSA set of services, referral to job openings, and an enhanced UI work test) separately can be cost-effective, bringing together the three separate components of reemployment services can be more cost-effective, as there can be reduced costs and synergy for a program that provides all three sets of services to UI claimants.

188

- Rural access to One-Stop services is limited and depends heavily on the availability of affiliated One-Stops, which are mostly funded and staffed by the Employment Service. Satellite and unstaffed access points provide very limited services. Rural residents also have limited access to One-Stop services because of limited access to private and public transportation and the Internet (Dunham et al. 2005).

- The Employment and Training Administration endured a period of research suppression during the Bush years. Studies whose release was delayed include Almandsmith, Adams, and Bos 2006; Dunham et al. 2005; Jacobson et al. 2004; Mueser and Sharpe 2006; Stack and Stevens 2006; and many others. These studies' findings—as will be seen later—directly contradicted major legislative initiatives of the department that were proposed but not enacted during the Bush administration.

Notes

1. Nineteen states participated in the Reemployment and Eligibility Assessment initiative in fiscal years 2006 and 2007 after Connecticut and Massachusetts dropped out of the program.
2. An Eligibility Review Program (ERP) is an interview conducted during an active claims period to explore the eligibility of the claimant, the degree of the claimant's attachment to the labor market, and the possibilities for reemployment.
3. In February 2005, the WIA study had been completed for some months. ETA approval to publish the study was suspended until after a Senate mark-up session dealing with WIA reauthorization. Both Republican and Democratic senators reacted sourly to the administration's reauthorization proposal, and they were displeased about the lack of publicly available WIA evaluations. Just prior to the session, ETA staff was directed to formally submit the study for approval to Assistant Secretary DeRocco. The morning after the mark-up, February 17, 2005, David Balducchi was tasked with contacting Richard Nathan and requesting that he promptly send the study summary to each member of the relevant House and Senate committees. Nathan did so, including a cover letter, on the same day. Soon after, the study was posted on the ETA Web site and in hard copy. If not for the congressional discomfort with the WIA reauthorization proposal, it is unlikely that the study would have received a timely release. The study findings were conveyed to Congress before ETA publication or public release, and it is the only known instance

where a third-party evaluator sent an ETA-sponsored study directly to Congress. (Richard P. Nathan, letter to Sen. Lamar Alexander [R-TN] and other congressmen, February 17, 2005; and David Balducchi, e-mail to the author, 2010.)

4. On the technical support Web site linked to the U.S. Department of Labor's ETA Web site under the heading of "Best Practices," links were provided to descriptions of Eligibility Review Programs in four states—Florida, Michigan, Tennessee, and West Virginia. Several other states also operate ERP programs. I accessed the site (http://www.itsc.org/info_tech/infotech.asp) in early 2006, but the Web page can no longer be found.

5. During the period 2005–2007, the Bush administration supported consolidation of WIA and Wagner-Peyser Act funding into a single funding stream for the state workforce agencies to provide CAAs from. The failed CAA proposal would have provided selected individuals with self-managed accounts to pay for training services—up to $6,000 per eligible worker over a two-year period.

6. The Reemployment and Eligibility Assessment interviews in Minnesota are considerably more intensive than those received by other UI claimants. While the typical REA interviews provided to WPRS-eligible claimants last 20 minutes, other WPRS participants who are not assigned to the REA program receive an average of three minutes of individual attention following group orientations (Benus et al. 2008b, p. 16).

6
Reemployment Services Policy

with David E. Balducchi

Incongruously, the demand for reemployment services across the United States grew a great deal over the decade and a half after 1993, at the same time that resources were declining. Clinton administration policies that implemented the Worker Profiling and Reemployment Services (WPRS) system and One-Stop Career Centers, automated labor-exchange services, enhanced labor-market information services, and, later, amended the Wagner-Peyser Act and enacted the Workforce Investment Act (WIA), all increased the scope of services provided. But these policies were not accompanied by a corresponding increase in the resources necessary to provide them, and the temporary funding increases for labor market information, One-Stop Career Centers, and WPRS disappeared. This chapter examines federal reemployment service policy since the early 1990s, with special attention to how research findings have informed the policy process.

OVERVIEW

Classical economic theory assumes that perfect competition governs labor markets. Perfect competition as a theory, however, assumes perfect information for the players in these labor markets: workers have to be able to find job openings, and employers similarly must be able to find workers with the skills they need. In the real world of imperfect labor market knowledge, workers and employers require considerable assistance in matching job openings with qualified workers. Since the 1930s, the Employment Service (ES) has acted as a public labor exchange to facilitate impartial job matching at no cost at the point of service to either job seekers or employers. Services are prepaid by employers through an excise tax under the Federal Unemployment Tax Act.

The primary provider of reemployment services in the United States is the U.S. Employment Service. The goals of the ES as a public labor exchange program have varied over time. It was born during the Great Depression with the enactment of the Wagner-Peyser Act of 1933 and was established to help unemployed workers find needed jobs during that time of very high unemployment. After the Unemployment Insurance (UI) Program was enacted in 1935, a policy decision was made that the ES should continue to refer the best-qualified workers to available jobs, rather than to first refer UI claimants. This policy continued after the federal UI and ES agencies were brought together within the U.S. Department of Labor (USDOL) in 1949 (Altmeyer 1966; Haber and Kruger 1964).[1]

In December 1941, the state ES programs were nationalized to support the war effort during a time of full employment and labor shortages. The goal was to ensure the full utilization of workers in the private sector for the duration of the war.[2] The ES was administered by the War Manpower Commission. In 1945, the War Manpower Commission was abolished, and federal administration returned to the U.S. Employment Service in the Department of Labor. By congressional action, states resumed administration of the programs in late 1946 (Haber and Kruger 1964). The ES returned to serving the state and local labor market needs and fulfilled the role of a universal public labor exchange that treated all workers and all areas of the country equally by referring the best applicants for jobs to job openings submitted by employers (Altmeyer 1966).

In 1961, President Kennedy redirected the Employment Service to deal with a number of special populations (e.g., older and younger workers) and special concerns (workers displaced by automation and technological change, and workers challenged by rural poverty and chronic unemployment). Provisions in the Area Redevelopment Act of 1961 emphasized serving depressed economic areas. Starting in the mid-1960s, the ES was called upon to put heavy emphasis on placing the disadvantaged, minorities, and women in jobs, in accordance with the provisions of the Economic Opportunity Act of 1964. As a result of rising job loss in the early 1970s, ES policy shifted to strengthen traditional labor exchange and employer services, which had eroded during the strong labor market of the late 1960s. At the same time, the ES expanded job placement services for welfare and food stamp recipients (USDOL 1973, pp. 2, 47).

In the 1980s, the manner of providing reemployment services began to change. The switch from staff-assisted services to self services began. The most important two factors in this switch were 1) the decline in funding, which meant that fewer staff were available to provide services, and 2) the rise of automation, which provided the computer technology to make the switch to self services. Automated job banks developed first. The department started the Interstate Job Bank in 1979, and states developed individual automated job banks by the mid-1980s. Later, both the states and the federal government would make a variety of tools available for use in resource centers and over the Internet (Ridley and Tracy 2004).

Since the early 1990s, there have been a number of major employment and training policy initiatives that have affected Wagner-Peyser Act programs. The ES was the platform for the ambitious One-Stop Career Center initiative starting in 1994 and was responsible for providing reemployment services under the WPRS initiative, which became operational in the mid-1990s. The role of the ES in the One-Stop centers was formalized with the enactment of the Workforce Investment Act of 1998. As a result, the ES became a principal component of most One-Stops, especially in areas that could not fund large comprehensive One-Stops.

Section 1 of the Wagner-Peyser Act states that "the United States Employment Service shall be established and maintained within the Department of Labor." However, in 2002, the USDOL eliminated the U.S. Employment Service as a separate organization within the department. The USDOL contended that although the agency was eliminated, its functions were maintained. Beginning in 2003, the Bush administration proposed and worked to eliminate the Wagner-Peyser Act per se and replace it and WIA with block grants to states. Meanwhile, the states have mostly ignored the Bush consolidation policy proposals. Through the federal appropriations process, the states continued to receive WIA and Wagner-Peyser Act grants, and they have continued to operate their own state Employment Services and provide reemployment services, but with little guidance from Washington, D.C.

ONE-STOP CAREER CENTERS

One-Stop Career Centers Begin

In September 1994, the Department of Labor initiated a grant program to encourage states to adopt One-Stop Career Centers. Between 1994 and 2000, every state received a grant of between $3 million and $24 million to launch its One-Stop centers (Ridley and Tracy 2004). The initiative came from the Clinton administration, arising directly from Vice President Al Gore's national performance review, an initiative that searched for more effective methods of operating the federal government. One-Stop centers were an attempt to bring many employment and social programs under one roof, providing easy access to all workers. For department-funded programs, the Job Training Partnership Act (JTPA) program, the ES, veterans' employment programs, and UI were all made mandatory partners in the One-Stop centers. There also were many voluntary partners for programs funded outside the department, such as welfare programs.

The One-Stop Career Center initiative was a large-scale effort to deliver employment and support services to the American people. The initiative was based on four principles: 1) universality, 2) customer choice, 3) integration, and 4) performance-driven/outcome-based measures. The principle of universality meant that "all population groups will have access to a wide array of jobseeking and employment development services, including the initial assessment of skills and abilities, self-help information relating to career exploration and skill requirements of various occupations, consumer report information on the performance of local education and training providers, and quality labor market information" (USDOL 1995a).

The employment and training system thus was expanded to serve all persons—employed, unemployed, or out of the labor force—who would be able to come into any One-Stop in the country and receive basic reemployment services.

While the goal of universal access might have been grand and noble, the funding of the state workforce development programs did not correspondingly increase to adequately serve the large number of people who could be expected to present themselves at a universal access facility. When Secretary Reich initiated the One-Stop movement, he recognized the need to increase funding to serve a larger, universal population, and he succeeded in increasing funding in the first years of the Clinton administration. But with the loss of Democratic control of the Congress in 1994, the budget for organizations that staffed the One-Stops began to decline.[3]

One-Stop funding continued to decrease during the Bush administration years. Appropriations to fund WIA and Wagner-Peyser Act grants to states fell sharply in the 2000s. While some voluntary partner agencies put staff in the One-Stops, they were not willing—and not required—to contribute to One-Stop administrative costs. Among the mandatory partners, most state UI programs chose not to contribute to funding the One-Stops. In the early 1990s, with the advent of telephone claims taking, the UI program began to move local claims activities to telephone call centers. This left the funding of the One-Stops to the JTPA (later the WIA) and ES programs.

Meanwhile, combined JTPA/WIA and ES program funding remained flat in nominal dollar terms from the mid-1980s to the early 2000s and declined through 2008. JTPA/WIA grants to states peaked in the early 1990s at $3.4 billion and were well below $3 billion in 2008. JTPA/WIA plus Wagner-Peyser Act state grants reached a peak at $4.2 billion in 1994 (Table 6.1). These nominal levels hide the sharp decline in real funding levels, which resulted in substantial staffing cuts. The ability to provide more (and more expensive) services declined, and self services increasingly replaced staff-assisted services.

A more complicated story emerges when we look at the individual program funding levels. Wagner-Peyser Act grants reached a peak of $839 million in 1995 and have decreased since then despite the five budget years between 2001 and 2005, when approximately $35 million in funding for WPRS was added to the state Wagner-Peyser Act appropriations. The JTPA/WIA adult state grants have declined fairly steadily ever since 1984. By contrast, in response to the problem of worker displacement that emerged in the 1970s, the JTPA/WIA dislocated worker state grants continued to increase for longer than the other programs, reaching a maximum of $1.3 billion in 2000; funding has decreased since then to $1.1 billion in program year 2008. The youth program reached a maximum of $1.5 billion in 1993 and then decreased sharply in 1995, in response to the release of an evaluation of the JTPA program

Table 6.1 Grants to States That Are Available to One-Stop Career Centers from Funding of WIA, JTPA, and Wagner-Peyser Act Programs, 1984–2008 ($000)

Program year	Wagner-Peyser Act programs	JTPA and WIA programs			JTPA/WIA total	JTPA/WIA + W-P Act
		Adult	Dislocated Worker	Youth		
1984	740,398	1,886,151	223,000	724,549	2,833,700	3,574,098
1985	777,398	1,886,151	222,500	824,549	2,933,200	3,710,598
1986	758,135	1,783,085	95,702	635,976	2,514,763	3,272,898
1987	755,200	1,840,000	200,000	750,000	2,790,000	3,545,200
1988	738,029	1,809,486	215,415	718,050	2,742,951	3,480,980
1989	763,752	1,787,772	227,018	709,433	2,724,223	3,487,975
1990	779,039	1,744,808	370,882	699,777	2,815,467	3,594,506
1991	805,107	1,778,484	421,589	1,182,880	3,382,953	4,188,060
1992	821,608	1,773,484	423,788	661,712	2,858,984	3,680,592
1993	810,960	1,015,021	413,637	1,535,056	2,963,714	3,774,674
1994	832,856	988,021	894,400	1,496,964	3,379,385	4,212,241
1995	838,912	996,813	982,840	311,460	2,291,113	3,130,025
1996	761,735	850,000	878,000	776,672	2,504,672	3,266,407
1997	761,735	895,000	1,034,400	997,672	2,927,072	3,688,807
1998	761,735	955,000	1,080,408	1,000,965	3,036,373	3,798,108
1999	761,735	954,000	1,124,408	1,000,965	3,079,373	3,841,108
2000	761,735	950,000	1,271,220	1,000,965	3,222,185	3,983,920
2001	796,735	950,000	1,162,032	1,127,965	3,239,997	4,036,732
2002	796,735	945,272	1,233,688	1,127,965	3,306,925	4,103,660

2003	791,557	894,577	1,150,149	994,459	3,039,185	3,830,742
2004	786,887	893,195	1,171,408	994,459	3,059,062	3,845,949
2005	780,591	889,498	1,184,784	986,288	3,060,570	3,841,161
2006	715,883	864,199	1,189,811	940,500	2,994,510	3,710,393
2007	715,883	864,199	1,189,811	940,500	2,994,510	3,710,393
2008	703,377	849,101	1,115,077	924,069	2,888,247	3,591,624

NOTE: All grants are adjusted for rescissions. Wagner-Peyser Act programs include Reemployment Services grants for FY 2001–2005 (in $000) as follows: FY 2001, $35,000; FY 2002, $35,000; FY 2003, $34,773; FY 2004, $34,567; FY 2005, $34,290. A variety of training programs have been in place since 1963. The Manpower Development and Training Act (MDTA) was operational from 1963 to 1972. Both MDTA and the Comprehensive Employment and Training Act (CETA) were in effect for 1973; CETA was in effect from 1974 to 1983; CETA/JTPA for 1984; JTPA from 1985 to 1998; JTPA/WIA for 1999; and WIA from 2000 to the present.

SOURCE: USDOL budget documents.

that found the youth program to be ineffective. Through congressional appropriations, youth programs gradually recovered and were funded at $900 million in 2008.

The One-Stop center initiative was ambitious but unsustainable, since funding was inadequate in 1994 and has become even more so in the years since it was initiated. The reality of inadequate funding was clear to some people in the department. In 1994, Mary Ann Wyrsch, administrator of the Unemployment Insurance Service, saw that there were insufficient resources to match the soaring ambitions of universal access. At that time, she would describe the new One-Stops as "One-Stops for a dollar ninety-eight." A dollar and ninety-eight cents did not look as if it was going to cover the bill for this new, large-scale undertaking. The JTPA and ES programs were not able to cover the cost of their new One-Stop center responsibilities. The funds for UI administration also would be needed, and even the supplementation with UI funding would not be enough.

Because UI was a required partner of the One-Stops, UI was expected to provide some of the One-Stops' administrative funding. From the 1990s to 2008, the UI program paid benefits to 7–10 million beneficiaries per year, and its administrative funding remains considerable. Basic funding for UI administration amounts to $2–3 billion per year and could have been used to supplement the declining flow of One-Stop funding as WIA and Wagner-Peyser Act grants to states declined (Table 6.1). Traditionally, the Wagner-Peyser Act programs and the UI programs were operated in the same local offices throughout the United States. The UI program and the ES jointly funded the operations of the local offices they shared, but that cooperative relationship began to fade in the mid-1990s.

If the UI program had remained in the One-Stops, it would have been a major contributor to the One-Stop funding. However, it would have been difficult or impossible to administer the UI system effectively if the program transferred large amounts of funds to the One-Stops. Not surprisingly, the UI administrator opted out of the One-Stops by supporting a policy of telephone claims-taking. The effect of opting out was to end, in large measure, the UI in-person claims-taking process in local offices and replace it with telephone claims-taking.

Endorsing telephone claims was an about-face from prior federal policy. When Colorado became the first state to introduce telephone claims-taking in April 1991, the USDOL was not supportive. It had reviewed the new procedures and questioned whether eligibility require-ments could be adequately assessed remotely. Reluctance to endorse telephone claims-taking ended in June 1995 when Wyrsch recommended that states implement telephone and other electronic claims-taking methods (O'Leary 2006; O'Leary and Wandner 2005).[4]

By 1995, Wyrsch had decided that she had been wrong not to embrace the new technology—both telephone and Internet claims-taking. She wanted to save administrative funds on claims-taking in order to devote more funding to the new Benefits Quality Control sys-tem, which was a key part of maintaining the integrity of the UI system. Wyrsch also was concerned about the quality of employment services UI claimants would receive in the One-Stops. One-Stop staffing relied on generalists who knew a little about a lot of different programs, while UI claimants needed help from specialists who could provide them with labor market information, placement services, and job search assis-tance.[5] The Unemployment Insurance Service began funding grants for state agencies to convert to telephone claims-taking in 1996 and to Internet claims-taking in 1998.

By 2005, the transition to telephone claims was nearly complete. Of the 50 states plus the District of Columbia, Puerto Rico, and the Virgin Islands, 40 states were taking initial claims over the telephone, 10 had plans for doing so, and only three had no such plans. For continuing claims, 47 states used telephone systems, five were planning to do so or were implementing a phone system, and only one state had no plans to move in that direction. The UI program had moved basic claims-taking out of the local office. UI claims-taking was often done from a "telephone on the wall" at the One-Stops—thus UI fulfilled its respon-sibility under WIA to be a partner in the One-Stops—but because it did not have a staff presence in the One-Stops, the UI program could not be assessed to cover the costs of One-Stop operations (O'Leary 2006; O'Leary and Wandner 2005).

However, even with UI financial support, the One-Stops would not have been sustainable unless they changed the way they were doing business. There would not have been enough staff to deal with the flood of job seekers. The One-Stops responded with increased automation of many core services—i.e., basic job-finding services. As part of the initiative to create the One-Stops, banks of personal computers were placed in the One-Stop resource centers that were capable of providing a wide variety of automated services, such as a spectrum of electronic labor-exchange services including testing and assessment, resumé writing, and labor-market information services. More and more workers came to the One-Stops but received few if any staff-assisted services. They went into the resource rooms and worked on their own to search for and find work (Ridley and Tracy 2004).

Reemployment Services in the One-Stop Centers

Self-service job-finding activities are available to workers directly, without their using the One-Stop staff as intermediaries. They are made available cheaply at the One-Stop centers in resource rooms with electronic job-finding services. Alternatively, workers can receive self services through the Internet on remotely accessed computers. Thus, the principle of universal access has required the One-Stops to provide core services for all who walk through their physical or virtual doors, but with most of those core services provided in a self-service rather than a staff-assisted manner.

Nonetheless, the demand for staff-assisted reemployment service has remained high. Between three and five million UI claimants registered with the Employment Service have received a reportable (i.e., staff-assisted) service each year since 1995. One-and-a-half to four million of these UI claimants have participated in a job-search activity in years since 1993, but these numbers declined sharply in 2005 and 2006 (Table 4.6). Since 2001, the WPRS system has been referring over one million UI claimants to the One-Stops, and between 800,000 and 1 million were reported to have received reemployment services between 2004 and 2008. (See Table 4.4.)

While the ES provides most of the core and intensive services to One-Stop customers, the WIA programs also provide such services. In the 1990s, under the JTPA Adult and Dislocated Worker programs, about 60 percent of program exiters participated in training, leaving about 40 percent who received reemployment services other than training. Since approximately 300,000 to 400,000 individuals exited these programs between 1993 and 1999, between 100,000 and 150,000 exiters received reemployment services but no training services each year (Table 6.2).

From 2001 through 2005, WIA exiters from the Adult and Dislocated Worker programs numbered between 300,000 and 450,000. Approximately half of these exiters received training, so between 150,000 and 200,000 received core services only or core and intensive services only. Clearly, the JTPA and WIA programs have been relatively small providers of reemployment services compared to the Employment Service.

In 2006, 2007, and 2008, the number of WIA Adult and Dislocated Worker exiters exploded. The change was due to new 2006 definitions of WIA exiters, who suddenly included ES participants who could be "coenrolled" in the WIA program, even if the WIA program provided them with no additional services. As a result, most of the increase in WIA Adult and Dislocated Worker exiters was from individuals who received core services only—i.e., Wagner-Peyser Act services—but were double-counted by the WIA programs.

Job training has been a key program service provided under the Workforce Investment Act and its predecessor organizations. However, with the decline in WIA funding and the increased demands of funding core and intensive services in the One-Stops, the provision of job training services suffered. With training costs averaging between $3,000 and $5,000 per trainee, relatively few workers served by the WIA system actually receive training services (Mikelson and Nightingale 2006). Table 6.2 shows that fewer than 300,000 JTPA exiters received training between 1993 and 1999, while under WIA's Adult and Dislocated Worker programs, trainees numbered no more than 200,000 per year.

Even with a shift from staff-assisted to self-service reemployment services and the limited availability of funding for the most expensive service—job training—the decline in WIA and ES funding has reduced the ability of the One-Stop system to maintain itself. In the 2000s, the number of One-Stops declined sharply. The decline has been seen in both the comprehensive One-Stops, which are prevalent in urban areas, and the affiliate One-Stops, which are more concentrated in areas with low population densities. (Comprehensive One-Stops must have all of the WIA-required partners operating within the One-Stop, whereas the backbone of the affiliate One-Stops is the ES.)[6] Between the end of 2003 and the end of 2008, the number of One-Stops declined steadily from nearly 3,600 to less than 3,000—a decline of 18 percent. The number of One-Stops held steady during much of the Great Recession (Table 6.3).

202

Table 6.2 JTPA Program Exiters for 1993–1999; WIA Program Exiters for 2001–2008, by Adult and Dislocated Workers

Year	Program	Job Training Partnership Act programs		
		All exiters	Training[a]	Training/all exiters
1993	Adult	180,178	126,100	
	Title III	164,826	80,800	
	Total	345,004	206,900	0.60
1994	Adult	175,647	126,500	
	Title III	187,938	94,000	
	Total	363,585	220,500	0.61
1995	Adult	162,120	118,400	
	Title III	266,401	130,500	
	Total	428,521	248,900	0.58
1996	Adult	151,155	113,400	
	Title III	283,513	147,400	
	Total	434,668	260,800	0.60
1997	Adult	147,717	110,800	
	Title III	266,112	143,700	
	Total	413,829	254,500	0.61
1998	Adult	151,580	112,200	
	Title III	240,896	134,900	
	Total	392,476	247,100	0.63
1999	Adult	113,774	83,100	
	Title III	189,794	110,100	
	Total	303,568	193,200	0.64

Workforce Investment Act programs

Year	Program	All exiters	Core services only[b]	Core & intensive services only	Training	Training/all exiters
2001	Adult	172,366	36,918	59,485	75,963	
	DW	129,969	17,777	46,000	66,192	
	Total	302,335	54,695	105,485	142,155	0.47
2002	Adult	239,252	42,533	89,048	107,671	
	DW	178,493	20,262	59,691	98,540	
	Total	417,745	62,795	148,739	206,211	0.49
2003	Adult	219,979	43,787	73,242	102,950	
	DW	187,664	23,626	61,623	102,415	
	Total	407,643	67,413	134,865	205,365	0.50
2004	Adult	225,683	48,403	68,788	109,492	
	DW	178,446	25,544	57,789	95,113	
	Total	404,129	73,947	126,577	204,605	0.51
2005	Adult	230,446	51,481	73,508	105,457	
	DW	210,117	42,402	84,016	83,699	
	Total	440,563	93,883	157,524	189,156	0.43
2006	Adult[c]	510,034	313,744	86,762	109,528	
	DW	259,564	111,235	71,169	77,160	
	Total	769,598	424,979	157,931	186,688	0.24
2007	Adult[c]	765,483	542,147	113,660	109,676	
	DW	261,354	128,783	65,909	66,662	
	Total	1,026,837	670,930	179,569	176,338	0.17
2008	Adult[c]	849,738	540,665	210,859	98,214	
	DW	293,614	154,410	84,251	54,953	
	Total	1,143,352	695,075	295,110	153,167	0.13

NOTE: No WIASRD Data Book was prepared for PY 2000. DW = Dislocated Workers. Title III was the dislocated worker section of JTPA.
[a] JTPA training includes occupational skills training and on-the-job training.
[b] WIA staff-assisted core services only.
[c] The effect of coenrollment on WIA adults and Wagner-Peyser Act registrants began to affect the WIA Adult Program statistics in 2006.
SOURCE: WIASRD and SPIR data books, various years.

Table 6.3 Number of One-Stop Career Centers in the United States, 2003–2009, and Local Offices under CETA, 1974, and JTPA, 1999

Date	Comprehensive OSCC	Affiliate OSCC	Total
1974 under CETA			3,454
1999 under JTPA			2,505
December 29, 2003	1,955	1,627	3,582
December 29, 2004	1,945	1,638	3,583
December 29, 2005	1,900	1,559	3,459
December 29, 2006	1,864	1,401	3,265
December 29, 2007	1,773	1,395	3,168
June 30, 2008	1,783	1,332	3,115
December 31, 2008	1,801	1,149	2,950
February 4, 2009	1,789	1,126	2,915
April 17, 2009	1,833	1,181	3,014
July 2, 2009	1,850	1,184	3,034
December 31, 2009	1,853	1,133	2,986

SOURCE: CareerOneStop (2010) at http://www.servicelocator.org for selected dates since 1993. Numbers for 1974 and 1999 from Dunham et al. (2005).

Mikelson and Nightingale (2006) examined the distribution of funding of employment and training programs between training and non-training services. The study's main goal was to determine the amount and percentage of funding that was spent on training for each of the department-funded programs. The study found that in 2002 "training" programs expended most of their funds for purposes other than training. Even among departmental workforce development programs in which a portion of the funds was spent on training, the training expenditures constituted an average of only 18 to 27 percent of all expenditures—between $1.1 and $1.7 billion of the $6.5 billion appropriated. (See Table 7.1.) Thus, these programs were spending three-quarters or more of all of their funds on nontraining activities.

WIA and other departmental programs are called on to fund a large number of nontraining activities as a result of the wide variety of functions performed by the One-Stops. *Anatomy of a One-Stop,* a study by Stack and Stevens (2006), describes the spectrum of reemployment services that are provided to workers, whether they are relatively unskilled or are highly skilled professional workers. While the less-skilled workers spent well over an hour at the Baltimore, Maryland, One-Stop office each time they came for assistance, the more skilled workers spent a half-hour during each visit to the Columbia, Missouri, office. (See Table 5.3.)

The department funded a study of the effectiveness of the implementation of WIA programs in eight states. The study (Barnow and King 2005) found that core services play a more prominent role in the One-Stop centers in states with traditional program-based systems than in states with more "comprehensive workforce policy" frameworks. In either case, however, core services play an important role, whether the workforce strategy is to make the provision of core services more or less central to the centers' mission.

A study of workforce services in rural areas (Dunham et al. 2005) shows that for much of the United States outside of the major metropolitan areas, affiliate One-Stops dominate the landscape, and the Wagner-Peyser Act's Employment Service is the centerpiece of these One-Stops. With reductions in funding, comprehensive One-Stops can be afforded mainly in large metropolitan areas, although the number of comprehensive One-Stops was declining through 2005. In other, less densely populated areas, affiliate One-Stops tend to have several participating agencies, but the principal agency is usually the ES; they too are declining in number.

America's Labor Market Information System (ALMIS)

Technology drives many of the recent changes in the public labor exchange system. The department developed a number of automated labor-market information tools that made use of the Internet. These tools included an expanded automated labor exchange connected to the Internet called America's Job Bank and a number of other automated labor-market information tools.

The department updated all of its labor-market information tools in the mid-1990s. America's Job Bank (AJB) was launched between 1993 and 1995. It was an updated, Internet-based, automated national labor exchange with powerful capabilities. Job seekers could create resumés and search for job openings by location, occupation, job title, and key words. Employers could search for workers' resumés by key words, occupation, or military code (Ridley and Tracy 2004). AJB played an important role in interstate job data sharing. In 2006, 39 states were submitting jobs to the site, and 33 states signed up to receive its job listings (Frauenheim 2007a). AJB was operated for over a decade by NaviSite, a for-profit firm under contract with the New York Department of Labor.

The USDOL funded an evaluation of America's Job Bank, conducted by Technical Assistance and Training Corporation (TATC 2001). The evaluation results showed that AJB was widely used. The TATC report found that 35 percent of employers who were tracked over a three-month period hired at least one person from AJB. Furthermore, the study estimated that over a one-year period approximately 345,000 workers were directly placed in jobs by AJB (Frauenheim 2007b; Woods and Frugoli 2004).

America's Job Bank was also evaluated by the six-state public labor exchange evaluation (Jacobson et al. 2004), which found that AJB was cost-effective. (See Chapter 5.)

In addition to America's Job Bank, the department developed and maintains other electronic labor-market information accessible at CareerOneStop.com (formerly America's Career Kit). This resource includes the following:

- Occupation Information Network (O*Net OnLine): contains information on the knowledge, skills, and abilities required for specific occupations.

- America's Career InfoNet: brings together state and federal data to provide information on occupations, trends in employment and wages, and state profiles.

- America's Career Locator: identifies the closest One-Stop local office for job seekers.

The department developed America's Job Bank and other labor market information tools believing that they were proper governmental functions, but this belief was challenged in the 2000s. Stiglitz, Orszag, and Orszag (2000) examined the role of government in a digital age. They viewed the role of government as being limited in this arena, but found that government has four roles: 1) determine the policies and regulatory structures, 2) deliver the programs and services of government to the citizenry, 3) use the information infrastructures to enhance the internal administrative practices, and 4) interface with citizens in the democratic process of government. They found that America's Job Bank was one of the legitimate services the government could provide to its citizens, stating that "America's Job Bank seems consistent with the principles for government action."

Privatization Demonstrations

In the process of negotiating and implementing the One-Stop Career Centers in the mid-1990s, pressures to privatize the Employment Service developed in a number of states. While Texas and Florida were unsuccessful in more broadly privatizing their Wagner-Peyser Act programs statewide, three states were able to negotiate special demonstration arrangements. In 1994, Massachusetts negotiated the ability to have its local Workforce Investment Boards deliver Wagner-Peyser Act and job training services, stipulating that both public and private agencies be permitted to deliver the services. This authority was narrowed in 1998 to be applicable to only four local boards within the state—those in Boston, Brockton, Cambridge, and Springfield. Only in these local boards could Wagner-Peyser Act services be delivered by either for-profit or nonprofit private or public agencies. Colorado was given authority in 1997 to devolve the provision of Wagner-Peyser Act services down to the county level of government as long as local office staff were protected by public merit staffing. In 1998, the department permitted Michigan to deliver Wagner-Peyser Act services by a public agency other than the state workforce agency as long as that agency used public merit staffing (Balducchi and Pasternak 2004).

In each of these three cases, the Department of Labor granted states the authority to provide Wagner-Peyser Act services by other than merit-staffed state employment security agency personnel under Section 3(a) of the act. This alternative delivery approach was authorized as a provisional demonstration project.[7] Further demonstration authority was not granted in other states, and these demonstration projects were subject to evaluation and review.

Determining the effectiveness of the demonstration sites required an evaluation of the three sites with a comparison to traditional state ES operations. In 1998, the Westat Corporation began an evaluation of Wagner-Peyser Act programs that concentrated mostly on the public labor exchange function. It evaluated three traditional programs that provide labor exchange services through state merit-staffed employment security agencies in North Carolina, Oregon, and Washington, as well as the three demonstration states. The purpose of the evaluation was to compare service delivery in the traditional states to service delivery in the demonstration states to determine whether to continue the demonstrations or to terminate them. The study was completed in February 2004 but was not released by the department until September 2008 (Jacobson et al. 2004). When the Office of Management and Budget (OMB) finally forced the release of the report on the department's Web site, it was accompanied by an unprecedented and awkward caveat impugning the findings and methodology of the study.[8]

Chapter 5 discussed the evaluation findings—that the labor exchange services offered in the demonstration states did not perform as well as the services offered in the traditional, state merit-staffed Employment Service agencies. The logical response to the evaluation results would have been to cancel the demonstrations and declare that the services provided in the traditional ES performed better than those services in the demonstration sites. If policy had followed research, the traditional approach would have been declared the only approach the department would approve, in staying consistent with the Wagner-Peyser Act.

The actual result was that the political leadership of the Employment and Training Administration suppressed the Westat study for four and a half years. In 2003, contrary to the evaluation findings, the department called for the termination of traditional public labor exchange by eliminating the Wagner-Peyser Act. The reauthorization plan for WIA called for the elimination of a 70-year-old New Deal program. The public policy recommendations were thus in direct contradiction to the research findings.

WORKER PROFILING AND REEMPLOYMENT SERVICES

The WPRS system was enacted in 1993, but the system only gradually became operational in states across the country. It was not fully operational until mid-1996, which was just as the One-Stops were becoming operational. Thus, two major changes to the workforce development system were being implemented at the same time.

Chapter 4 reviewed the implementation of the WPRS system and discussed the fact that the provision of reemployment services primarily fell to the Employment Service. The ES has been the usual provider of most core services and some intensive services in the One-Stops, and thus the ES has provided the majority of reemployment services under WPRS since it was first implemented. As a result, the ES's workload in providing reemployment services has grown sharply. In 1993, before WPRS was implemented, the ES provided UI claimants with 1.6 million reemployment services. During the 2001 recession period, the number of reemployment services provided increased to 3.9 million. With sharply declining funding and the decline in the unemployment rate, however, the number of claimants receiving reemployment services dropped sharply throughout the 2000s, hitting a low of 1.54 million in 2006. (See Table 4.7.)

In the mid-1990s, WPRS became a major focus of the ES staff. UI recipients who were profiled were sent to the One-Stops to receive reemployment services. In 1997, in two-thirds of the states, the ES was the major provider of reemployment services, delivering services to 75 percent or more of WPRS-referred claimants. The JTPA Dislocated Worker program provided only a small portion of WPRS services. In the one-third of states where the JTPA Dislocated Worker program provided WPRS services, the ES also provided services. ES provided most or some of the services in all localities in the WPRS evaluation study states (Dickinson et al. 1999).

In 2003, the National Association of State Workforce Agencies (NASWA) conducted a survey of all state UI programs that examined the job search rules and reemployment services provided to UI claimants. The study found that state UI programs used two methods to promote reemployment and carry out the UI work test: WPRS and the Eligibility Review Program. Since Eligibility Review Programs exist in fewer than a dozen states, it is WPRS that has been the main method of promoting reemployment by the UI programs in the states (O'Leary 2006; O'Leary and Wandner 2005).

The NASWA survey also found that WPRS was the most common method of providing reemployment services to UI claimants. A secondary source was WIA core services offered at the One-Stop centers. Services received by UI claimants at the One-Stops included provision of labor market information, referral of claimants to jobs, assistance with resumé preparation, and delivery of workshops to improve interviewing skills (O'Leary 2006; O'Leary and Wandner 2005). In recent years, the provision of these reemployment services, both to UI claimants and to other workers, has declined sharply, which can be attributed to the decline in Wagner-Peyser Act funding as well as the lack of federal support for the WPRS system during the Bush administration.

EMPLOYMENT SERVICES DURING THE BUSH ADMINISTRATION

Under the Bush administration, policy toward the ES and the WIA programs changed radically. The U.S. Employment Service was eliminated as an agency within the department. America's Job Bank also was eliminated. And legislative proposals to reauthorize the WIA program would have eliminated the Wagner-Peyser Act and created a single block grant to replace WIA programs and the ES. Furthermore, in its regulatory proposal published in December 2006, the department proposed to eliminate merit staffing in state employment services.

The Elimination of the United States Employment Service

The Wagner-Peyser Act requires the U.S. Department of Labor to retain the U.S. Employment Service as an identifiable organizational unit within the department to guide the state ES agencies with respect to labor exchange and related programs and policies. Section 1 of the Wagner-Peyser Act states, "the United States Employment Service shall be maintained within the Department of Labor." From its establishment in 1933 until 70 years later, the USES had always been a free-standing agency within the U.S. Department of Labor, and it had retained the name "United States Employment Service"—in accordance with the federal Wagner-Peyser statute—through the end of the Clinton administration.

The organizational status of the U.S. Employment Service changed abruptly under the Bush administration (Table 6.4): in 2002, it was downgraded from an office to a division. It temporarily disappeared as a part of the Office of Adult Services in 2003, but it later reemerged as

Table 6.4 Organization of Wagner-Peyser Programs in the USDOL for Select Years, 1977–2008[a]

Date	Name of Wagner-Peyser Act organization
Spring 1977	United States Employment Service
September 1983	United States Employment Service, Office of Employment Security
Winter 1991	United States Employment Service
Summer 1996	United States Employment Service
Fall 1998	United States Employment Service
March 2002	Division of U.S. Employment Service/America's Labor Market Information System (ALMIS), Office of Career Transition Assistance
February 2003	Office of Adult Services, Office of Workforce Investment (OWI)
February 2004	Division of Employment Service and ALMIS, Office of Adult Services, OWI
April 2005	Division of Adult, Dislocated Worker, Employment Services, and Workforce Information, OWI
April 2006	Office of Adult Services, OWI
April 2007	Division of Adult Services, OWI
April 2008	Division of Adult Services, OWI

[a] The dates given depended on the availability of USDOL telephone directories in the USDOL library when the author searched the library in 2008. The point of the table is to show that the name remained unchanged (and met the requirements of the Wagner-Peyser Act) from 1977 (and, before that, from 1933) until 2002, when the Bush administration first downgraded and then eliminated the USES.
SOURCE: USDOL telephone directory, selected years since 1977.

part of a division in 2004 and 2005. Informal and repeated renamings of the organization that housed the ES function were followed by a formal reorganization of the Employment and Training Administration (ETA) in the summer of 2005. The ETA staff was apprised of the reorganization, which was negotiated with the union representing departmental employees. The reorganization formally eliminated the U.S. Employment Service. Beginning in 2006 it became an unidentified part of an office, and then a division of Adult Services. Its function was combined with, and disappeared into, that of the WIA Adult and Dislocated Worker programs. There was no Employment Service administrator and no staff to deal solely with Wagner-Peyser Act matters. The United States Employment Service had disappeared.

Eliminating America's Job Bank

The Department of Labor shut down America's Job Bank (AJB) on June 30, 2007. AJB, however, was enormously useful to workers and employers. Both could search for work or offer job openings in states across the country or in multiple states without having to access individual state job banks. AJB served all employers and all workers at no cost, while many of the private job banks serve only niche populations at a price. Both private job banks and AJB served the high-wage, high-skilled workers. However, almost none of the private job banks were interested in serving the low-wage, relatively unskilled labor that AJB also served.

America's Job Bank was cheap to operate. Its funding had been as high as $27 million a year when it was fully operational. By early 2004, however, the department had put AJB on a "maintenance only" budget of $12 million per year, which was not sustainable and which weakened it relative to its private competitors. Before AJB was terminated, it lagged behind other commercial job boards by a substantial margin. The Web information company Alexa found that in the first five months of 2006 AJB averaged 1.9 million unique visitors per month, compared to 21 million unique visitors per month for CareerBuilder. This disparity existed despite the fact that participation in AJB was very great. AJB had 2.2 million job openings posted, far more than CareerBuilder with 1.5 million job openings. AJB also had 600,000 resumés and about 450,000 registered employers (Frauenheim 2007b).

The decision to shut down America's Job Bank was controversial, and some of the controversy was over whether or not the program was cost-effective. Former Labor Secretary Reich, who had started AJB, said that "the social benefits of efficiently and quickly matching employers and job seekers far exceed the government costs of providing this service." The department under Secretary Chao countered with a statement that "there is no evidence that AJB created an economic efficiency and quickly matched employers and job seekers. The private sector provides this service more efficiently, more effectively, and in a more customer friendly manner" (Frauenheim 2007c).

There was no way to resolve this controversy publicly because the two studies—by TATC (2001) and Jacobson et al. (2004)—that the department had commissioned were embargoed and were not made publicly available. The Bush administration had good reason to keep the studies under wraps, because those studies did not support the administration's argument. Both studies concluded that America's Job Bank was cheap and cost-effective.

The department justified the shutdown of AJB on the grounds that it duplicated the operations of job boards in the private sector. The department also asserted that AJB had outmoded computer equipment and technology. That claim was disputed by Denis Martin, executive vice president of NaviStar, the company that operated AJB for the USDOL (Frauenheim 2007c). Nonetheless, after being put on a starvation funding diet, AJB would have required substantial investment if it had been continued.

Frauenheim (2007c), in the pages of *Workforce Management,* expressed dismay at the termination of America's Job Bank: summarizing his reporting on this issue, he wrote, "Businesses liked the free government Web site. So did the states. It served a wide range of workers with many listings for low-paid jobs. During its heyday around 2000, research found the site to be a cost-effective, appropriate government service . . . America's Job Bank continued to win praise—including a 2007 honor from the respected recruiting consulting firm Weddle's."

One commentator speculated that the elimination of AJB was simply part of the Bush administration's overall privatization effort, which was proceeding in the case of AJB regardless of how well the program worked (Frauenheim 2007c).

However, the America's Job Bank concept refused to die. By April 2007, two private corporations announced that they wanted to continue the system. NaviStar announced its intention to continue AJB. It set up a new, private Internet site to continue the program, which would be called AJB2 and would be found at www.americasjobbank2.com. NaviStar, however, had competition. DirectEmployers Association, a nonprofit on-line recruiting company and an employer membership organization of large firms, also declared that it wanted to take over a successor AJB system (Electronic Recruiting News 2007).

The department had ostensibly eliminated America's Job Bank because it had no policy or financial value. Yet two private firms competed to become the successor operator of the system. Electronic Recruiting News (2007) said of the competition between the two firms that "there are major assets at stake in this transition." Something did not compute. The private firms saw value where the administration saw none.

Into this competition stepped the National Association of State Workforce Agencies (NASWA). NASWA is a nonprofit membership organization of all of the state workforce agencies. Its members are the state agencies that supplied the job openings that fed the AJB system. They also would have to feed any new system.

The individual state workforce agencies agreed that NASWA should continue to organize an America's Job Bank successor under a partnership with the private sector, taking a portion of the profits from the new operation. NASWA held a competition and selected DirectEmployers to create the new national job bank, JobCentral National Labor Exchange, which began operations in July 2007. By October 2008 all but five state workforce agencies had joined JobCentral (NASWA 2008).

A key function of AJB was that, by posting jobs to AJB, employers fulfilled Office of Federal Contract Compliance Programs (OFCCP) requirements. These requirements ensured that firms doing business with the federal government were in compliance with rules regarding nondiscrimination and affirmative action in employment. JobCentral includes a feature that also allows firms to meet their federal contact compliance obligations and veteran priority compliance requirements (NASWA 2008).

It is ironic that despite the fact that Assistant Secretary of Employment and Training Emily DeRocco ended AJB as a federal program, the states nevertheless chose to continue it. Indeed, NASWA has made money for the state workforce agencies by taking it over, and DirectEmployers pays a portion of its dues to NASWA. It is also ironic that two former ETA staff members who created AJB at the department have worked with DirectEmployers to resurrect it. James Vollman was an originator of America's Labor Market Information System while working for the department as a political appointee in the Clinton administration. David Mormon was a career department employee in charge of helping to design and implement AJB. In April 2004 Morman retired from the department, in part to protest the starvation and imminent demise of AJB (Frauenheim 2007c). Vollman and Mormon were waiting in the wings, ready to resurrect AJB in its next incarnation under another name and new ownership.

The elimination of America's Job Bank was only part of the Bush administration's attempt to eliminate funding for state labor-market information systems. During the Bush years, increasing amounts of America's Labor Market Information System funding that should have been provided to the states for state labor-market information uses were transferred to other uses, including the political initiative of the president's demand-driven workforce development system, which comprised three politically motivated programs that transmitted funding to organizations outside the workforce development system in the name of regional economic development.[9]

Finally, in 2008, as part of the president's budget request for fiscal year 2009, the Bush Administration unsuccessfully proposed ending all funding for labor market information. It proposed to incorporate labor market information into a new, more comprehensive block grant that would replace both the WIA and Wagner-Peyser Act programs.

The Employment Service under WIA Reauthorization Proposals

A steady stream of proposals to eliminate the Wagner-Peyser Act flowed out of the Bush administration during its two terms. The Workforce Investment Act of 1998 authorized the WIA program for five years. When program authorization expired in 2003, the Bush administration unsuccessfully tried to reauthorize the program three times: in 2003, 2005, and 2007, three different but related Bush administration proposals were introduced in the 108th, 109th, and 110th Congresses that would have reauthorized WIA but eliminated the Employment Service.

WIA's programs continued to operate through the federal appropriations process in the years after it expired. Through the same process, the public employment service programs also were maintained. The Bush administration's response to WIA's expiration was to propose legislation to reauthorize it in a manner that would transform it into a block grant program for various combinations of WIA programs (e.g., programs for WIA Adults, Dislocated Workers, and Youth) as well as the Wagner-Peyser Act program. The desired result of this proposal was to repeal the Wagner-Peyser Act and to eliminate both the U.S. Employment Service and the governor-controlled state employment services, with their merit-staffed state employees. But that didn't happen. The House of Representatives passed bills that were similar to the Bush administration proposals in 2003 and 2005, but the Senate refused to support the House initiatives. Instead, the Senate passed legislation, with bipartisan support, that retained the basic structure of the current WIA system (Naughton and Lordeman 2007). Most senators viewed workforce development programs from a state's perspective, and they wished to preserve statewide Wagner-Peyser Act programs.

The common theme of all of the Bush administration proposals was to consolidate the services provided by the WIA and Wagner-Peyser Act programs and replace them with block grants to states. The asserted justification for this policy was that the Wagner-Peyser Act program and administrative structure were duplicative of those of WIA and, thus, were redundant. The justification for block grant funding was that the states could replace these two programs with a single, more cost-effective program. According to the Bush administration's reasoning, increased state flexibility in the use of funds would contribute to greater program efficiency. At the release of the President's FY 2009 budget, Labor Secretary Elaine Chao denied that the block grant proposal was about spending cuts. Rather, she said, it is "a matter of effectiveness." "By eliminating the mess and maze of duplicative bureaucratic programs, we can increase the number of workers who receive training," she said. The current system, it was argued, confused clients and duplicated services. It was "overly complicated" and needed to be changed because it "shouldn't require a PhD to get help."[10] The theme throughout the Bush administration was that there was no need for employment services, not even services that made sure that the right people got the right training that could help improve employment and earnings outcomes. All that was needed was to put training vouchers on the stump and walk away.

The federal government's experience with block grants, however, did not support Chao's argument. In 1995, the General Accounting Office (GAO) reviewed the 15 block grants in place in 1989, of which nine had been established by the Reagan administration in 1981. On average the 1981 grants had experienced a funding reduction of 12 percent. Initially the states were able to maintain the programs, supplemented by state contributions and helped by streamlining the programs and increasing state flexibility in administration. But over time, pressure to increase accountability resulted in new federal constraints that had the effect of "recategorizing" the programs and reducing flexibility—making them similar to the categorical programs they were before they became block grants, but with reduced funding (GAO 1995).

As with the elimination of America's Job Bank, the principal motive for the elimination of Wagner-Peyser Act programs appeared to be a strong Bush administration penchant for privatization of government services. That preference was made explicit in December 2006 when the Bush administration claimed that, based on the results of the three-state Employment Service privatization demonstration, private employment services could be at least as cost-effective as public employment services. Interestingly, the only study of alternative ES delivery systems was conducted by Jacobson et al. (2004) at the demonstration sites in Massachusetts, Colorado, and Michigan. The conclusion by the Bush administration was at best a misreading of the Jacobson et al. study and was contrary to its findings that the public labor exchange is cost-effective. The Bush administration's claim was nevertheless used to support its proposal to eliminate traditional public employment services staffed by state employees (*Federal Register* 2006).

Attempted Stealth Elimination of the Employment Service—Federal Register Notice, December 20, 2006

The Bush administration had eliminated the U.S. Employment Service as the national office that provides guidance to the state Employment Service agencies across the country. However, starting in 2003, the administration had been unsuccessful at legislative efforts to eliminate the Wagner-Peyser Act, which authorizes the U.S. Employment Service and a system of federal-state ES offices across the country. Therefore, the Bush administration tried to accomplish the same result through federal regulation. In December 2006, after the Democrats had won a majority in both houses but before the new Congress took office in January 2007, the department made one last, desperate attempt to kill the Employment Service. A Notice of Proposed Rule Making (NPRM) was published in the *Federal Register* on December 20, 2006, pages 76558–76569, with comments due by February 20, 2007. The proposed rule would have effected a number of changes to the WIA and Wagner-

Peyser Act programs, including banning all "stand-alone" local public ES offices, known as affiliated One-Stop Career Center offices. The affiliated offices numbered approximately 1,400 in late December 2006 and represented over 40 percent of all One-Stops. The affiliated offices operate throughout the United States but are particularly heavily represented in less densely populated areas. They are distinguished from large comprehensive One-Stops, which operate primarily in large urban areas and which numbered over 1,800 in late December 2006.

Specifically, the proposed regulation would have allowed for privatization of the state Employment Service, enabled nonstate employees to administer employment services, and effectively amended without congressional authority the Wagner-Peyser Act, which mandates that merit-staffed state employees administer job placement services impartially between competing employers and job seekers. Furthermore, the regulation would have closed rural One-Stop offices by centralizing labor exchange services and would have allowed disqualifying issues surrounding labor-market availability of UI claimants under the work test to go undetected.

When the One-Stop delivery system was launched in the early 1990s, the department left the decision to state governors on the development—with Wagner-Peyser Act and WIA funds—of affiliated and comprehensive One-Stop centers. The proposed 2006 regulation would have reversed this New Federalism standard and reduced the authority of state governors by taking away much of their discretion in using Wagner-Peyser Act funds.

The department's contention that so-called stand-alone employment service offices should be created outside of the states' One-Stop delivery systems was crafted to support its policy proposals. Research has shown that affiliated One-Stop offices rarely provide only the labor exchange services funded under the Wagner-Peyser Act; more often, they provide services from two to five other workforce development programs (Dunham et al. 2005), including UI , veterans' services, WIA, and other services. In rural areas, small and medium-sized employers as well as large firms often utilize affiliated One-Stops as their recruitment centers. In every state, these affiliated One-Stops are part of the state's One-Stop delivery systems, and they are connected electronically to services and programs available in the comprehensive One-Stop centers.

The proposed regulations, which would have allowed states to terminate the Wagner-Peyser Act requirement that its employees be merit-staffed state employees, meant that states could have instead privatized all employees through contracts with local Workforce Investment Boards. Privatizing state Wagner-Peyser Act functions raises the question of whether private employees can carry out functions that are inherently governmental. If Wagner-Peyser Act functions were privatized, private employees would determine who is referred to job openings and who is not. Private employees also could assist in determining who receives or is denied UI benefits under the UI work test. To qualify for UI benefits, each year 8 to 10 million UI beneficiaries must demonstrate to the Employment Service staff that they are able to work, available for work, and actively searching for work.

The department's asserted justification for eliminating the proposed merit staff requirement was that the "three demonstrations have showed that it is possible to deliver Wagner-Peyser Act services efficiently and effectively using non–State merit staff employees . . . While a formal evaluation of the three Wagner-Peyser demonstrations has not been completed, the department believes the three demonstration states are performing successfully" (*Federal Register* 2006, p. 76560).

Ignored by this statement are two facts: 1) Jacobson et al. (2004) found that the provision of services by state merit–staffed Wagner-Peyser Act employees was more effective and efficient than provision of these services by the demonstration sites, and 2) the formal evaluation of the demonstrations relied on in the notice of proposed rulemaking had in fact been completed by Jacobson et al. and accepted by the department in early 2004—nearly three years before the notice of proposed rulemaking was published.

These proposed regulations could have forced affiliated One-Stop offices to close, leaving much of the country without any public employment services. Furthermore, under the proposed regulations, the Wagner-Peyser Act programs would only have existed as part of the remaining comprehensive One-Stop local offices. States would have been allowed to replace state merit employees with private employees funded under WIA, and the new staff would be indistinguishable from other local WIA employees. The goal of these regulations was to eliminate the Wagner-Peyser Act programs without legislative authority. The

Wagner-Peyser Act would have continued to exist as a matter of law but would have been stripped of its impact as a matter of fact.

Eliminating the Employment Service: Congress Responds

The Senate's Health, Education, Labor, and Pensions Committee was well aware of the regulatory maneuvers of the Bush administration. They saw the December 20, 2006, notice of proposed rulemaking as an attempt to circumvent their legislative failures. On January 17, 2007, Senators Edward M. Kennedy of Massachusetts and Patty Murray of Washington wrote to the leaders of the Senate Appropriations Committee requesting that they restrict the ability of the administration to carry out the proposed regulations.[11] Later that month, Congress acted on the request and used the budget appropriations process to prohibit the administration from implementing the proposed regulations during the remainder of fiscal year 2007 by barring the expenditure of funds to promulgate or implement the rule. The continuing resolution for the new appropriation stated in section 20601 that "none of the funds made available in this division or any other Act shall be available to finalize or implement any proposed regulation under the Workforce Investment Act of 1998, Wagner-Peyser Act of 1933, or the Trade Adjustment Assistance Reform Act of 2002 until such time as legislation reauthorizing the Workforce Investment Act of 1998 and the Trade Adjustment Assistance Reform Act of 2002 is enacted" (U.S. Congress 2007, pp. 21–22).

Thus, Congress prevented the department from making any major policy changes with respect to these three workforce statutes.

The prohibition on implementing regulations through the appropriations process, however, only lasts for one year. It would have to be renewed each year through the appropriations process. In December 2007, the Omnibus Budget Reconciliation Act, which funded the USDOL for the remainder of fiscal year 2008, contained virtually the same language and again prohibited the Bush administration from finalizing and implementing its proposed rule for another year.

In 2008, the Congress took no action to reauthorize the Workforce Investment Act. Decisions about the structure and content of the WIA programs and their relationship to the Employment Service awaited President Obama and the new Congress. It was not until August 2009 that the department withdrew the proposed rule, published in December 2006, stating that the withdrawal was based on a continuing congressional prohibition against publishing a rule until WIA was reauthorized.

Research and the Bush Policy Proposals

Eliminating and privatizing the Employment Service

The Bush administration's determination to get rid of traditional public employment services with their state merit–staffed employees was not based on any research findings that the traditional public employment services were not cost-effective. In fact, the department-funded evaluation of the public employment service showing they were cost-effective was ignored.

When the administration first proposed to eliminate the public employment service system in 2003, the Jacobson and Petta (2000) evaluation of the public labor exchange in Oregon and Washington states had already been completed and published by the department. While the study only examined two traditional state public labor exchange systems in the states of Washington and Oregon, it found that these public employment services yielded unusually high net benefits compared to most public expenditures. The benefit-cost ratios were greater than 1.0 for all users of the state public labor exchanges, but for UI claimants the ratios ranged between 1.2 and 4.5 (pp. 7–9). If this study had been consulted in developing policy, it would have encouraged the retention of traditional public employment services.

The key issue in making a policy decision should have been a determination of whether the nontraditional employment service offices available to all job seekers were more cost-effective than the traditional public employment service offices. The Clinton administration had set up a test in three states: Colorado, Massachusetts, and Michigan. In order to evaluate which approach worked better—the traditional model or the nontraditional model—the Jacobson et al. (2004) evaluation of the public labor exchange function in the United States evaluated six states separately and then compared the three demonstration states to the three traditional states. The results showed that the traditional approach worked better.

The administration's response to the Jacobson et al. (2004) evaluation was not to use it as a guide to policy development, but rather to suppress the research findings for four and a half years. The administration then undertook a policy that was directly contrary to the evaluation findings. During this period, several attempts to have the completed study released—from both inside and outside the department—were met with opposition from political leaders in the Employment and Training Administration. In March 2005, Congressman Ray LaHood (R-IL) requested a copy of the completed study. In May, DeRocco replied oddly that "the study was never completed," although the report had been completed and accepted by the department in February 2004 and the Westat research contract was closed out later that year.[12] Indeed, when the evaluation results were cited in the December 2006 *Federal Register* notice, they were misrepresented as having found that private employment services were as effective as public employment services.

Alan Krueger, former chief economist at the department, commented on the suppression of the research results. He wrote in the Economix blog of the *New York Times* that "the Bush administration . . . buried a careful study that found that outsourcing job placement services for the unemployed at the local level was less effective than traditional state public labor exchange services, and continued with its pursuit to contract-out and devolve a cost-effective program" (Krueger 2008).

He saw this effort as part of the larger privatization effort. "Just as it has tried to with other government functions such as Social Security, the Census, the Federal Emergency Management Agency and national defense, the Bush administration has been trying to outsource or eliminate services for the unemployed" (Krueger 2008).

Evaluating America's Job Bank

Until it was eliminated in June 2006, America's Job Bank appeared to compete successfully with private employment services. Woods and Frugoli (2004) conducted a national search of AJB and private job banks and found that AJB had more job openings listed than the private job banks for a number of occupations. They listed three occupations—computer programmers, secretaries, and welders—for which AJB had substantially more openings than two other all-purpose job search sites, Monster.com and CareerBuilder.com.

The department funded a study of the outcomes of America's Job Bank (TATC 2001). It showed that AJB had a substantial impact on helping workers find employment. Using a small sample of employer and job seeker participants, it made a number of findings. Employer postings on AJB attracted the submission of resumés; employers then interviewed 13 percent of the job seekers whose resumés were received, and 8 percent of the AJB job orders led to at least one hire (Woods and Frugoli 2004).

The America's Job Bank study examined data for the program year ending on June 30, 2001. For that year, it found the following:

New job orders posted:	6,962,692
New job openings posted:	11,228,690
New employers registered:	55,563
Total employers registered:	226,274
Resumé searches conducted:	8,234,049

TATC estimated that 79,000 total employers hired at least one person through AJB and that 345,000 workers were placed through AJB (Woods and Frugoli 2004). TATC concluded that AJB was an effective program.

Disseminating research

Little employment and training research was disseminated by the ETA after the first year of the Bush administration. A review process was established by which the deputy assistant secretary, Mason Bishop, received all completed research and evaluation reports for his personal review. The review process went very slowly, if it proceeded at all. In time, Bishop piled the reports high on the floor in a corner of his office. Inquiries about the status of the reports were met with replies that they were still under review. Eventually, the inquiries ceased.

The Jacobson et al. (2004) public labor exchange evaluation was completed in December 2003 and submitted to the department. As director of research, I submitted it to ETA program administrators and staff for their review in December. I was immediately informed by an e-mail from Bishop that "this report is NOT to go to anyone in ETA outside of the second floor"—the floor where the political leadership of the department was housed. Furthermore, I "should NOT be convening any meetings concerning this report."[13] The report did, however, go through a technical review by the ETA's research and evaluation staff, and comments were provided to the researchers at Westat. Those comments were incorporated into the final report, which was received by the department in February 2004. The final evaluation was accepted and determined to be adequate and completed, and the contract was closed out. That report was held by the assistant secretary's office and was not shared with anyone inside or outside of the Employment and Training Administration.

Shortly afterward, the book *Labor Exchange Policy in the United States* (Balducchi, Eberts, and O'Leary 2004) was completed in draft form and submitted to the department prior to its publication by the W.E. Upjohn Institute for Employment Research. This book and another, *Job Training Policy in the United States* (O'Leary, Straits, and Wandner 2004), were partially funded by the department under the Clinton administration, and departmental staff had been authorized by the USDOL to work on the book as authors and editors with other outside contributors. As is consistent with the rules of the federal Office of Government Ethics, they also were given permission to work on the publications during work time at the department, as long as this work did not interfere with completing their other work and they were not compensated for their work.

On February 6, 2004, I received an e-mail about the labor exchange book. The sender, the career deputy assistant secretary,[14] was "currently in discussion with the Solicitor's Office to obtain clarification on the appropriate role of Department staff in development" of the book, to determine the "appropriate review and clearance process of the draft within the Department," to "develop very clear guidance that would guide any ongoing and future efforts of Employment and Training Administration staff participating as authors or editors of outside publications . . . to clarify the authorization process to obtain approval to work on such activities in an official capacity." Meanwhile the career deputy asked me to "provide . . . [him] a copy of the grant agreement under which the publication was produced." I provided the grant agreement, but the guidance and clarification were never forthcoming.

The grant agreement revealed that the Upjohn Institute was legally bound to publish the two books upon completion at no cost to the department. All of the chapters of the books already had been reviewed by outside reviewers and by the editors of the volumes. Discussions continued for many months between the ETA and the Upjohn Institute, but, despite pressure placed on the Institute by the ETA political leadership not to publish the books, both books eventually were published. The ETA's leadership was able to delay publication, but they were not able to suppress the books.

In the years that followed, further dissemination of publications was severely limited. By 2006, the number of unpublished studies had grown considerably. The list included the following: a Westat five-year study, *Evaluation of Labor Exchange Services in a One-Stop Delivery System Environment* (Jacobson et al. 2004); a report to Congress on the H-1B job training programs that had been required by the American Competitiveness in the Twenty-First Century Act (P.L. 106-313); three five-year research plans for the periods 2002–2007, 2004–2009, and 2006–2011, all required to be submitted to Congress under Section 171 of the WIA; a study of the uses states had made of $8 billion in Reed Act unemployment insurance funds that had been distributed to them; at least eight miscellaneous studies, including evaluations of youth offender demonstration projects; two reports that were part of a large unemployment insurance research evaluation; and six studies that were part of the Administrative Data Research and Evaluation (ADARE) project. Many of these studies were initiated during the Clinton administration. The research findings frequently, but not always, were at odds with the Bush administration's initiatives. As the studies were completed, they were sent to Deputy Assistant Secretary Mason Bishop for his review. The studies sat in his office.

In November 2006, the Democrats won a majority in both houses of Congress. In January 2007, Senator Murray, the new chair of the Employment and Workplace Safety Subcommittee of the Senate Committee on Health, Education, Labor, and Pensions, which is responsible for workforce development issues, became aware that a number of departmental studies that might be of use to the subcommittee as it carried out its legislative work had not been distributed or published. She had acquired a list of most of the unpublished ETA studies. Senator Murray wrote to the department and requested the studies. After discussion with ETA political appointees, in February 2007 the administrator of ETA's Office of Policy Development, Evaluation, and Research sent the studies to Murray. Senator Murray shared them (for review purposes only) with a small number of researchers, but they were never publicly disseminated or used for public policy purposes.

At the OMB, a number of senior career staff and political appointees supported basing labor policy on rigorous research, but had not received research products on the major employment and training programs. At the same time, OMB staff became aware that research had been completed but not released. They read references to the unpublished research and spoke to some of the researchers who had conducted the research. In one case, they participated in a review of the research. Prior to becoming an OMB examiner, Joe Siedlecki had worked for Christopher King, director of the Ray Marshall Center for the Study of Human Resources at the University of Texas. Siedlecki was familiar with one of the unpublished studies—a quasiexperimental impact evaluation of WIA training programs authored by King and Kevin Hollenbeck of the Upjohn Institute. In 2006, Siedlecki, in his capacity as OMB examiner, requested but did not receive a copy of the King and Hollenbeck evaluation from the department.[15]

On April 8, 2007, OMB staff went to the Hart Senate Office Building and held discussions with Murray's staff. The OMB received the list of unpublished studies that had been completed and learned that the department had sent the studies to Senator Murray. OMB political and career staff were concerned both that the studies had not been publicly released and that the studies had been shared with Congress before the OMB had seen them. OMB staff wanted to reach their own conclusions about the appropriateness of new department policy initiatives, and they wanted to use the latest research in making those decisions. Later in April, OMB career and political staff met to decide what to do about the department's stonewalling on research and evaluation. The OMB adopted a four-part process: 1) an independent review of the quality of the suppressed studies, and the publication of the suppressed studies that were found to have merit by the independent reviewer; 2) the development and publication of an overdue five-year ETA research plan; 3) completion of three evaluation and demonstration projects; and 4) ETA collaboration with an independent organization to peer-review the design of all future evaluations.

On May 16, 2007, Mason Bishop was called to the New Executive Office Building to discuss the OMB's research and evaluation. Regarding the unpublished studies, Bishop tried to explain what had happened. He sought to justify his actions and those of Assistant Secretary DeRocco in suppressing the studies by criticizing the research as being of "poor quality" and, therefore, not appropriate for dissemination. OMB staff, however, directed that the studies be disseminated. After the meeting, the department sent the OMB the studies. Some of the studies were then provided to researchers for external review.

The OMB also raised a concern about the future use of research and evaluation funds. It proposed to take an active role in the ETA's research planning process to assure that funds were used for their intended purposes. OMB insisted that the department complete and publish a WIA five-year research plan in 2007—the department had ignored congressionally mandated deadlines to publish plans in 2002, 2004, and 2006.

Finally, OMB also took the unusual step of directly intervening in the current research and evaluation process. OMB staff informed Bishop that the ETA's research, demonstration, and evaluation allotment for the new program year beginning in July 2007 would be held up unless the department agreed to undertake three research efforts and revise its peer review process.

The proposed research projects consisted of 1) a long-term random assignment experimental evaluation of the Adult, Dislocated Worker, and Youth components of the Workforce Investment Act program that included a benefit-cost component; 2) a short-term, quasiexperimental evaluation of the WIA program (in addition to releasing the King-Hollenbeck quasiexperimental impact study); and 3) completion of the WIA Individual Training Account (ITA) Demonstration by conducting a second round of telephone interviews and a longer-term evaluation. The OMB was concerned that billions of federal dollars had been spent on the WIA program since its inception, and yet the program had never been rigorously evaluated. The OMB also thought that two quasi-experimental impact analyses could be used by the next administration to inform WIA reauthorization and that the random assignment evaluation, which would take at least five years to complete, could and should inform future policy decisions. The requirement that the ITA study be extended arose from staff concerns that the original follow-up survey to determine training outcomes had been conducted before some of the trainees had completed training, thereby limiting the usefulness of the research.[16]

To ensure that future evaluation efforts be of the highest quality, the OMB required the ETA to work with the Coalition for Evidence-Based Policy—an independent research organization that supports the development of rigorous evidence for program assessment. Thereafter, the department began to use the coalition to peer-review existing draft evaluations and participate in the review of designs of future evaluations, in particular those deemed by the ETA to have the potential for significant policy impact.

By 2005, Congress also had realized that something was wrong with the way the ETA was conducting research and evaluation. Congress had lost confidence in the department's management of two WIA budget accounts: 1) Pilots, Demonstrations, and Research, and 2) Evaluation. As a result, Congress directed the ETA to report to it on how these research funds were being used. The fiscal year 2006 appropriation conference report for the Omnibus Budget Reconciliation Act contained the following:

> The conferees direct that the Department submit a quarterly report beginning in January 2006 to the House and Senate appropriation committees on the status of awards made for pilot, demonstration, multi-service, research and multi-state projects under section 171 of the Workforce Investment Act. This quarterly report shall be submitted to the House and Senate committees on appropriations no later than 45 days after the end of each quarter and shall include the following information: a list of all awards made during the quarter, and for each award shall include the grantee or contractor, the amount of the award, the funding source of the award, whether the award was made competitively or by sole source and, if sole source, the justification, the purpose of the award, and expected outcomes. (U.S. House of Representatives 2005)

While Congress could not direct the department to carry out a specific research agenda, it did what it could to force the department to develop and implement a legitimate research plan.

In 2008, both Congress and the OMB put yet more pressure on the department to release the suppressed studies, but the department resisted. In July, the first study released was an analysis of the uses of the Reed Act distribution. A researcher at the Congressional Research Service had been asked by House Ways and Means staff to write the UI section of the "Green Book," which describes the programs under the jurisdiction of the committee. The researcher was aware of the Reed Act study and wanted to include an analysis of it in the Green Book. After the department declined a request for access to it, the researcher called congressional and OMB staff to ask for assistance. A PDF file of the study was posted on the ETA Web site on July 30, 2008.

The department, however, did not want to acknowledge that the Reed Act report had been withheld for four years. The Reed Act study therefore was hidden in plain sight. At the ETA's Web site, the study was not noted as a new release, did not appear in the chronological listing of research studies, and could not easily be found during a search of the site. There was no listing of the report and no link to the URL, so analysts could not search for the report using the USDOL search engine. The only way to find the paper was to know the URL and enter it on the Web. No one was informed about how to find the URL, so I received many questions about whether and where the studies had been posted and how to find them. A colleague had quietly sent me the URLs for all of the reports that were posted in August and September of 2008. Without that tip even I would not have been able to find the papers or inform others of how to find them. It was in this sense that this and the other reports were "hidden in plain sight."

Indeed, the Reed Act study had been given a number as an ETA occasional paper. Rather than giving it a 2008 release date, the ETA backdated it and gave it the number ETA Occasional Paper 2004-11, suggesting that it had been released in 2004.

Ryan Hess of the *Employment and Training Reporter* did not accept the 2004 release date. In an article titled "ETA Dusts Off Reed Act Paper," Hess (2008) reported that the study was actually released in 2008 and asked the department "why this was kept under wraps for so long." He reported the department's response as follows:

> "Over the years, there were a number of studies that ETA commissioned, and it received reports that were either of poor quality or not relevant to the Employment and Training Administration's direction," an agency spokesman told MII [Publications, which publishes E&TR]. "After recent discussions with [the Office of Management and Budget], ETA decided to issue a number of these reports by posting them online." (p. 14)

Thus, even after DeRocco and Bishop had left the department—in late 2007 and the beginning of 2008, respectively—the department still claimed that the unreleased research was of "poor quality," despite the fact that the studies in question were the product of third-party research that the department had sponsored, reviewed, and approved. The department correctly indicated that the USDOL's policy "direction" was contrary to the research. And the statement failed to mention that in the ETA's discussions with the OMB, it had been ordered to release all of the rest of the studies of which the OMB was aware.

Ironically, the method that the OMB used to require the release of the suppressed studies was the Bush White House management tool, the President's Management Agenda. The President's Management Agenda sets quarterly targets for the Department of Labor—and other executive branch agencies—to reach. OMB set September 30, 2008, as the deadline for publication of the rest of the suppressed studies. The cited studies were all released—though hidden in cyberspace—in August and September of 2008 (Table 6.5).

Dismantling the research process

As part of the effort to ensure that there would be no more unwanted research results, Assistant Secretary DeRocco removed most of the senior staff responsible for policy, research, and evaluation from the Office of Policy Development, Evaluation, and Research in the ETA. Gerri Fiala, administrator of the office, was "encouraged" to leave the department and did so after spending one year on an intergovernmental personnel assignment to a nonprofit agency. James Woods, director of evaluation, was reassigned to direct a strategic planning division in another office. I was removed from my position as director of research and demonstrations and transferred to another office. David Balducchi, the manager of demonstration projects, was similarly transferred and made the manager of an administrative unit. The director of policy, Terry Finegan, retired.

Much of the funding for research and evaluation was redirected to other areas that supported Bush administration initiatives. Funds for pilots, demonstrations, research, and evaluation were used less and less for research purposes and instead were diverted to nonresearch purposes or to projects of interest to the administration. Thus, the Bush administration's "war on science" scored a victory at the Employment and Training Administration (Mooney 2005).

Table 6.5 Selected Employment and Training Administration Research Studies Released in 2008

Research study	Release date	Completion date	ETA occasional paper number
Unemployment Insurance: Assessment of the Impact of the 2002 Reed Act Distribution	7/30/08	12/04	2004-11
Net Impact Estimates for Services Provided through the Workforce Investment Act	8/15/08	10/05	2005-06
Anatomy of a One-Stop: Baltimore City Eastside Career Center; Anatomy of Two One-Stops: Camdenton, Missouri, and Columbia, Missouri (2 papers)	8/29/08	No date (2006)[a]	2006-07, -08
Workforce Development in Rural Areas: Changes in Access, Service Delivery, and Partnerships	9/04/08	6/30/05	2005-07
Youth Offender Demonstration Project Process Evaluation. Final Report, Vol. 1.	9/04/08	6/06	2006-06
Youth Offender Demonstration Project Process Evaluation. Final Report, Round Two	9/08/08	6/04	2004-10
Evaluation of Labor Exchange Services in a One-Stop Delivery System Environment	9/11/08	2/04	2004-09
Unemployment Insurance and Reemployment among Older Workers	9/11/08	2/04	2006-09
Five Year Research Plan, 2002–2007 (3 papers)	9/14–15/08	No date (2002)[a]	2003-09 to -11
Five Year Research Plan, 2004–2009 (8 papers)	9/16/08	No date (2004)[a]	2005-08 to -15

[a] "No date" means there was no date printed on the documents when they were released; however, the author knew the year in which they were completed (in parentheses).

SOURCE: ETA research Web site at http://wdr.doleta.gov/research; undated and untitled table.

ABANDONING PROGRAM OVERSIGHT

By its actions, the administration showed that it was not interested in the stewardship of the statutorily established programs for which the ETA was responsible. Instead, the focus of the ETA was on the president's "demand-driven" system, which provided funds outside of the traditional public workforce system. During the 2004 presidential campaign, President Bush promoted the expansion of opportunities through the "ownership society," which called for the federal government to allow Americans to have the option of managing their economic and retirement security. Within the department, under the demand-driven banner, policy and discretionary funding efforts were launched to weaken workforce security protections that had been developed during the New Deal and Great Society eras. This new system was composed of three sets of discretionary grants that were more related to business development than employment development. They consisted of 1) Workforce Innovation and Regional Economic Development (WIRED) grants, 2) Community-Based Job Training Grants (CBJTG), and 3) High Growth Job Training Initiative (HGJTI) grants. "High growth" industries receiving funding included the retail industry, where funding went to a variety of mall developers such as Westfield, Glimcher, and Prime Properties. Community-based grants went to community colleges around the country that tended to be located in Republican-friendly areas, including Mesa Community College in Phoenix, Arizona.

The vast majority of all ETA discretionary funds were channeled into the demand-driven system. In January 2007, the Congressional Research Service (Lordeman and Levine 2007) found that between May 2002 and December 2006, nearly $732 million in discretionary ETA funding had been awarded through these grants. In essence, ETA—without congressional oversight—abandoned the federal-state workforce structure. The HGJTI ($287 million) and CBJTG ($250 million) grants were made in 14 sectors that ETA had identified as "high growth" sectors. The WIRED grants ($195 million) were made to 13 regions of the United States to "transform and rebuild their economies."

An audit by the department's Office of Inspector General (OIG), published in November of 2007, found that between July 1, 2001, and March 31, 2007, the ETA awarded 157 High Growth Job Training Initiative grants totaling $271 million. Only 23 grants were awarded competitively, while the rest were awarded noncompetitively. Examining a sample of the noncompetitively awarded grants, the audit found that "ETA could not demonstrate that it followed proper procurement procedures in 35 of 39 tested noncompetitive awards (90 percent)" (OIG 2007).

At the department, many ETA staff members were assigned to work almost full-time on the WIRED grants. They were not working on the ongoing workforce development programs that the department was congressionally mandated to operate, oversee, and manage. In mid-February 2007, at an ETA managers' retreat, Assistant Secretary DeRocco was asked by one staff member, "What should I do? I am spending so much time on my WIRED grant that I have no time for my regular work." DeRocco responded: "WIRED *is* your regular work!" Work priorities at ETA were clear.[17]

In effect, the demand-driven system became the real work of ETA staff, leaving little time for anything else. Travel to oversee state and local workforce development programs virtually stopped. Attendance at regional and national meetings was limited to trips to market the demand-driven system. The statutorily mandated programs of the department were largely abandoned for a new economic development initiative. The justification for this new initiative was a theory of trickle-down workforce development: if the department put money into regional economic development, new firms would become established, old firms would grow, and new jobs would flow from these firms.

One indicator of the administration's lack of interest in traditional workforce development programs was the reduction in the number of guidance letters sent out to regions and states concerning congressionally authorized programs (Table 6.6). Technical assistance and guidance sharply declined in all statutorily created programs. Between 2002 and 2007, the department issued few guidance letters relating either to the ES or to the reporting and analysis systems. Guidance regarding the UI system also declined. Only the development and issuance of Training and Employment Guidance Letters continued to function at a steady level, but the focus of the guidance switched to areas of interest to the Bush administration, including the acceleration of the foreign labor certification process.[18]

Table 6.6 Guidance Letters Provided by the ETA, 1999–2007

Year	Unemployment Insurance Program Letters	Training and Employment Guidance Letters	Employment Service Program Letters	Reports and Analysis Letters
1999	49	15	11	1
2000	33	22	2	0
2001	47	31	8	1
2002	30	27	0	0
2003	32	26	0	0
2004	31	36	0	0
2005	31	35	0	0
2006	30	30	0	0
2007	27	32	0	0

SOURCE: USDOL Web site http://wdr.doleta.gov/directives (accessed May 10, 2010); dissemination files from DOLETA's Office of Policy Development and Research.

THE STATES CONTINUE TO PROVIDE REEMPLOYMENT SERVICES

Despite the Bush administration's attempt to privatize public employment services during its eight years in office, Congress continued to appropriate Wagner-Peyser Act grants to the states each year, and, as a result, the programs survived at the state and local level. Even with federal neglect of state ES programs and state WPRS systems, the states continued to provide employment services. The level of services, however, declined with the drop in appropriated funds. The level of activity in the WPRS system is enumerated in Table 4.4. The ES's provision of reemployment services—ES reportable services and job search services—is described in Table 4.6.

The Bush administration had not succeeded in eliminating the Wagner-Peyser Act. In fact, no major federal workforce development legislation was enacted during the Bush years, and reauthorization of WIA and TAA remained for the Obama administration to tackle.[19]

State workforce agencies continued their work individually and cooperatively, especially through their coordinating agency, the National Association of State Workforce Agencies. Despite the lack of technical assistance that might have been provided by their federal partner, the states continued to operate their programs. Even America's Job Bank survived under a new nonprofit structure through the efforts of the individual states and NASWA.

LESSONS LEARNED

The lessons learned from the examination of reemployment services policy in this chapter are as follows:[20]

United States Employment Service. The USDOL should reestablish the United States Employment Service within its department and reestablish an active partnership with the states to oversee the operation of the public workforce system.

Privatization demonstration. The Jacobson et al. (2004) study found that 1) employment services provided by state workforce agency employees ("traditional employment services") are more cost-effective than employment services provided by private agencies and government agencies other than the state workforce agencies ("nontraditional" demonstration sites), and 2) traditional sites provide much greater access to reemployment services to a much wider population. Thus, demonstration authority granted in the mid-1990s to several states should be rescinded. Wagner-Peyser Act funds should be administered statewide under the control of the governors. All states should be required to administer their state employment services through their merit-staffed professional employees of state workforce agencies.

National electronic job bank. The department should actively support a national electronic job bank. It should either reestablish America's Job Bank as a departmental program or establish a partnership role with the National Association of State Workforce Agencies in operating the JobCentral National Labor Exchange.

Employment service funding. Funding of workforce development programs should reflect their relative cost-effectiveness. Funding for Wagner-Peyser Act programs should be substantially increased.

Reemployment Services Grants. Annual grants to support the WPRS system should be reestablished. Funding should be set at a higher level than the $35 million per year appropriated between 2001 and 2005. The full cost of providing comprehensive reemployment services to all workers currently being referred by the WPRS system is between $200 and $300 million per year.

Research and evaluation. The research and evaluation program should be revitalized and receive adequate staffing and funding. In a time of burgeoning deficits and fiscal austerity, the department should help people get back to work in the most cost-effective way possible. Because it has been a decade since the last evaluation of the employment services under the Wagner-Peyser Act, the department should undertake a new evaluation of the program.

Notes

This chapter was written with the assistance of David E. Balducchi, who made contributions throughout the chapter.

1. Initially, the federal UI program was the Bureau of Unemployment Compensation within the Social Security Board, while the United States Employment Service was part of the U.S. Department of Labor. The two organizations had to negotiate the colocation of the two programs at the local level as well as the services that ES would provide to UI claimants. They also agreed to act "as if they were a single agency." The federal UI and ES agencies were brought together by President Truman in a reorganization implemented under the Reorganization Act of 1949 (Altmeyer 1966, pp. 62–65, 175–178).

2. In a telegram to the governors on December 18, 1941, President Roosevelt requested the transfer of local ES offices from state employment services to the federal government under the direction of the U.S. Employment Service to assure "that we utilize to the fullest possible extent" workers "to increase our production of war materials . . . by centralizing work recruiting into one agency." The president was authorized to carry out this action through an appropriation measure that had been enacted earlier in 1941 (Altmeyer 1966, pp. 129–134).

3. Lawrence Katz, interviews with the author, August 21 and September 25, 2008.

4. Unemployment Insurance Policy Letter 35-95 stated, "The Department believes that SESAs [state employment security agencies] should move toward fully implementing telephone claims taking or other electronic methods of filing . . ."

5. Mary Ann Wyrsch, interview with the author, July 29, 2008.

6. The ES is permitted to operate affiliated One-Stop sites under the WIA. The WIA/Wagner-Peyser Act regulations state that "local Employment Service offices may operate as affiliated sites, or through electronically or technologically linked access points as part of the One-Stop delivery system (20 CFR 652.202, *Federal Register* 65, 156: 49462, August 11, 2000).

7. The Workforce Investment Act/Wagner-Peyser Act regulations state, "The Secretary has and has exercised the legal authority under section 3(a) of the Act to set additional staffing standards and requirements and to conduct demonstrations to ensure the effective delivery of service provided under the Act. No additional demonstrations will be authorized" (20 CFR 652.216, *Federal Register* 65, 156: 49464, August 11, 2000).

8. The caveat begins, "The evaluation is biased in favor of a conclusion that PLX [public labor exchange] services—particularly those offered in a traditional setting absent One-Stop Career Center integration—offer a more effective delivery mechanism than WIA service delivery provided in a One-Stop Career Center environment." The entire caveat can be found at http://wdr.doleta.gov/research/keyword.cfm?fuseaction=dsp_resultDetails&pub_id=2379&mp=y (accessed January 6, 2010).

9. See the section "Abandoning Program Oversight," on p. 232, which discusses these three programs.

10. Elaine Chao, statement at the release of the president's 2009 budget, February 5, 2008.

11. Edward M. Kennedy and Patty Murray, letter to Senators Tom Harkin and Arlen Specter, January 17, 2007.

12. Emily DeRocco, letter to Rep. LaHood, in response to his written request for a copy of the Jacobson et al. (2004) study, May 13, 2005.

13. Mason Bishop, e-mail to the author, December 22, 2003.

14. Different from Bishop, who was the political DAS, not the career DAS.

15. Joseph Siedlecki, interview with the author, December 29, 2008. Information in the next four paragraphs comes mainly from Siedlecki.

16. Ibid.

17. I attended this meeting.

18. Since Table 6.6 is a list of guidance letters posted on the ETA's Web site in October 2008, some guidance letters may have been issued and then removed from the Web site.

19. The department succeeded in gaining reauthorization of the Trade Adjustment Assistance in 2002, but not under the terms that were desired by the Bush administration. The TAA was not reauthorized after it expired in 2007. The American Recovery and Reinvestment Act of 2009 reauthorized TAA.

20. These recommendations were developed at the end of 2008. By the end of 2009, the Obama administration had addressed two of these recommendations with the February 2009 enactment of the American Recovery and Reinvestment Act. First, the act provided additional funding for the ES in the amount of $400 million. Second, from the new ES funds, $250 million was reserved for Reemployment Services Grants. These funds were made available through June 30, 2011.

7
Public Job Training
and Training Vouchers

As a result of post–World War II economic and trade policies, the U.S. Department of Labor has operated public job training programs for over five decades. The goal of national job training programs has been to improve the operation of labor markets by enhancing the skills of individuals facing barriers to employment. The programs have been unstable, with changing objectives, different target populations, varying program components, changing administration and operational methods, and fluctuating funding levels.

Early programs reflected concern about the loss of jobs resulting from automation. The Area Redevelopment Act of 1961 provided loans to businesses in depressed regions of the country as well as loans for job training. In 1962, the Manpower Development and Training Act program began and was administered as an intergovernmental partnership with the states. Initially funds were provided for dislocated workers, but after the enactment of the Economic Opportunity Act in 1964, the emphasis shifted to alleviating poverty by providing training to disadvantaged adults and youth. The Comprehensive Employment and Training Act (CETA) was enacted in 1973 under President Nixon. Under the new act the administration and operation of training programs devolved to the states and local entities, consistent with that administration's revenue sharing policy. CETA also provided work experience to unemployed workers in the form of public service employment. In 1982, the Reagan administration shifted course, supporting the enactment of the Job Training Partnership Act (JTPA). JTPA further decentralized training programs to the local level and eliminated public service employment. Program coordination between JTPA's locally administered Private Industry Councils and its partner workforce development agencies— the state-administered Employment Service (ES) and Unemployment Insurance (UI) programs—became even more difficult. Under JTPA, programs for disadvantaged adults and youth were retained, and a dislocated worker program was added, but funding levels for the programs were reduced (LaLonde 1995).

Since the mid-1990s, two major factors have altered the nature of training programs in the United States: 1) the introduction of One-Stop Career Centers, which further linked training programs with the ES and other partner agencies, and 2) the enactment of the Workforce Investment Act (WIA), with its introduction of training vouchers. These developments have taken place in the context of stagnant nominal funding throughout the 1990s and funding declines during the Bush II administration. (See Table 6.1.) These two developments were accompanied by further sharp declines in real funding levels. As a result, both the concept of universal access to workforce services (a concept central to the One-Stops) and the expectation of substantial availability of training services following core and intensive services have proven to be highly unrealistic.

This chapter examines both of these developments, concentrating on research and policy relating to the One-Stop centers and training vouchers. The chapter begins with a brief overview of selected research and evaluation findings regarding training programs, and then summarizes more recent research and evaluations. It then looks at recent training policy relating to the impact of One-Stops and training vouchers and assesses the extent to which policy has followed the lessons learned from research.

Much of this chapter analyzes training vouchers, including the Individual Training Accounts (ITAs) that were implemented under the WIA. Attention is also paid to new research findings from studies completed since WIA's implementation in 2000. Particular emphasis is placed on studies completed between 2001 and 2008 that were withheld by the U.S. Department of Labor and not published until the end of the Bush administration.

COST-EFFECTIVENESS OF U.S. TRAINING PROGRAMS: AN OVERVIEW OF EVALUATION RESULTS

Researchers have found a fundamental problem in the public provision of training by employment and training programs: the training that is provided is not extensive enough to have an economic impact equivalent to education and prolonged training. A comprehensive review of the evidence for government-sponsored training's effectiveness for low-income and dislocated workers in the United States and in other countries concludes that it is unlikely that short-term training programs could significantly increase the skills of the American labor force, even if they were significantly better funded. Government-sponsored training programs fail because they consist of short-term, low-cost training. The authors point out that a 10 percent rate of return on training would be very high. Thus, if training has an average cost of $3,000, the highest increase in annual earnings would be $300. Even such an optimistic outcome will not raise low-wage workers out of poverty or result in much of an improvement in the well-being of dislocated workers. Thus, vastly larger investments would be needed to significantly raise earnings and skills (Heckman, LaLonde, and Smith 1999; Heckman, Roselius, and Smith 1994).

As LaLonde (1995) explains, small public training programs have small effects on earnings: "We got what we paid for. Public sector investments in training are exceedingly small compared to the magnitude of the skill deficiencies that policy-makers are trying to address," he writes. "There also is evidence that existing services are ineffective for some groups. As a result, training dollars now going to those groups would be better spent by reallocating them toward other groups that benefit from these programs and also toward the development of new and probably more intensive high-cost services that can generate larger post-program earnings gains" (pp. 149–150).

LaLonde points out that the expenditure per participant declined under JTPA—and continued to decline under WIA. Similarly, he notes that while a year of education is associated with approximately an 8 percent increase in an average worker's earnings, the duration of job training is much shorter. As a result, lower effects on employment and earnings should be expected for short-term job training programs as compared to an additional year of schooling.

Surveying the evaluation literature for adults and youth, LaLonde finds that low-cost job search assistance (JSA) training—he considers JSA a form of training—for women can significantly raise their earnings. The result for skill and occupational training is more mixed, with women benefiting from on-the-job training and from classroom training that provides job-specific skills, rather than basic training. On the other hand, training for adult men and youth has far less positive results. For men, the effects on earnings are generally modest or nonexistent, while youth tend to experience no positive effects.

With respect to the services provided to dislocated workers, LaLonde reports three findings: 1) job search assistance is a cost-effective re-employment service, 2) workers who participate in short-run job training get no further benefit compared to JSA, and 3) female participants gain more from these programs than males. He cites his own work to indicate that longer-term rigorous, academic training for dislocated workers at community colleges appears to produce long-term benefits.

LaLonde concludes that, other than job search assistance, less intensive training, including training provided under USDOL programs, does not raise workers' earnings. He sees little reason to continue low-cost job training except for adult women, and recommends the development of new longer-term, more intensive training approaches, using demonstration projects to identify which approaches work. Short-term job training is not likely to have a significant impact on workers' earnings, even if the resources dedicated to training programs were to be significantly increased. Finally, he writes that current knowledge indicates that if training funds are scarce, those funds should be shifted to JSA, as JSA is more cost-effective than low-cost training (LaLonde 1995).

Summarizing what is known about the cost-effectiveness of training for dislocated workers, King (2004) finds that dislocated worker training has not been adequately evaluated. Only two experimental evaluations have been conducted—the Texas Worker Adjustment Demonstration and the New Jersey Experiment. He finds the Texas effects modest (Bloom 1990) and the New Jersey effects negligible. King reviews the Jacobson, LaLonde, and Sullivan (2002) study showing that community college training can have a substantial impact on earnings that can last for several years, but he is concerned by the methodology, which does not even use quasiexperimental methods. He regrets that the department did not complete the evaluation of dislocated worker training that it began toward the end of the JTPA program, and he would like to see a new comprehensive experimental evaluation of job training for dislocated workers.

Examining the industrialized nations, Martin and Grubb (2001) find that the experience of public training programs is mostly bleak:

Evaluations of public training programmes in OECD countries suggest a mixed track record. Some programmes in Canada, Ireland, Sweden and the United States have yielded low or even negative rates of return for participants when the estimated programme effects on earnings or employment are compared with the cost of achieving these effects . . . However, the picture is not entirely black: some public training programmes work . . . The most consistently positive results were recorded for adult women. The findings were less optimistic with regard to adult men . . . The most dismal picture emerged with respect to out-of-school youths: almost no training programme worked for them. (p. 25)

Thus, the weak training outcomes found in the U.S. evaluations are similar to the experience of other industrial nations.

NET IMPACT EVALUATIONS OF JTPA AND WIA PROGRAMS

The department has been operating training programs under JTPA and WIA for nearly 30 years. It has conducted evaluations and rigorous demonstration projects to look for training programs that work for disadvantaged adults, dislocated workers, and youth. In general, the results have not been positive.

The JTPA Program Evaluation (1996) and the Search for Effective Youth Employment Programs

The department funded an experimental evaluation of JTPA, covering the Adult and Youth programs (Bloom et al. 1997; Orr et al. 1996). The evaluation was based on a sample of 21,000 individuals drawn from participants in 16 JTPA service delivery areas.

The findings for the JTPA Adult Program participants were modest. Adult programs had a small but significantly positive effect on the earnings of men and women, but the effect on earnings as a percentage of prior earnings was twice as great for women as for men—about a 10 percent gain for women and a 5 percent gain for men. The effect of youth programs was insignificant for both males and females. The benefit-cost analysis yielded small positive benefits to society for adult men and women, but negative results for both female and male youth.

The JTPA Evaluation did not cover the JTPA Dislocated Worker Program. The department began work on a separate evaluation of the outcomes of dislocated workers, but these efforts were halted with the enactment of WIA.

Coinciding with the Republican takeover of Congress in 1995, the findings for JTPA youth participants had a devastating short-term impact on the program. The budgetary response to the youth findings of the JTPA Evaluation was immediate. Congress reduced the funding of JTPA Youth Program grants to states from $1.5 billion in FY 1994 to $0.3 billion in FY 1995. (See Table 6.1.) No department training programs had ever experienced such a precipitous decline. While funding of youth programs increased in succeeding years, approximating $1 billion in the late 1990s and the early 2000s, the program never reached the high funding levels of the early 1990s. Starting in the early 2000s, WIA Youth Program funding began to decline with the other components of the WIA program.

The dismal findings for JTPA-served youth resulted in a search for new youth options that might provide more cost-effective results. Two major demonstration projects were launched to test two program models based on local projects that appeared to be successful, in order to see if they could be replicated more widely and thus be models for new national programs. They were the Center for Employment and Training (CET) and Quantum Opportunity Project (QOP) models. Neither of these models, however, proved to be cost-effective.

The CET in San Jose, California, provides training in a worklike setting to out-of-school youth. An early evaluation of youth served by CET found the San Jose program to be highly successful with respect to employment, earnings, and other outcomes. The department attempted to replicate the model at 12 sites, conducting an experimental demonstration between 1995 and 1999, with 1,400 youth assigned to treatment and control groups. The final report followed up on the participants 54 months after random assignment. The evaluation found that replication was difficult and was only successfully completed in 4 of the 12 sites—the 4 sites operated by CET itself. While the structural model could be replicated, the staff could not. CET was found to be a unique organization with highly motivated leadership and staff. The 54-month results showed no earnings gains for the treatment group in the replication sites (Miller et al. 2006).

QOP was another departmental effort to serve disadvantaged youth, operating as a demonstration from 1995 to 2001. It was funded by the USDOL and the Ford Foundation. The demonstration provided after-school services to ninth grade students. Its primary goals were to increase high school graduation rates and enrollment in postsecondary education. Its secondary goals included improving high school course grades, improving achievement test scores, and decreasing risky behavior, including teenage pregnancy, crime, and substance abuse. An evaluation by Schirm, Stuart, and McKie (2006) found that the demonstration did not achieve any of its primary or secondary goals.

In contrast to the Youth Program, the JTPA Adult model survived, and the evaluation had little adverse impact on the funding of the Adult Program. Although the overall evaluation results for the Adult Program were not very positive, the positive impact on adult women helped to maintain support for the program. The JTPA Dislocated Worker Program, which had not been evaluated, was not affected by the release of the JTPA Evaluation. In fact, increasing concern about worker dislocation resulted in the JTPA Dislocated Worker Program being the only JTPA program to experience continued funding growth in the late 1990s.

The JTPA Evaluation caused much consternation among the supporters of youth employment programs. The loss of funding was devastating to youth employment programs at the state and local level in the mid-1990s. While problems were observed in the selection of the participating local sites, the evaluation appeared to be technically adequate and objective in its administration. Nonetheless, the JTPA Evaluation was blamed for the decline in the JTPA Youth Program.[1]

The JTPA Evaluation showed that politicians pay attention to research and evaluation results, especially if the message is strongly negative. The JTPA Evaluation experience made department administrators much more careful about evaluations conducted during the rest of the Clinton administration. Before an evaluation would be approved, questions were asked about what the potential impacts of the evaluations might be. Behind these questions lurked the implicit question of whether a new evaluation might have negative findings similar to those of the JTPA Evaluation.

WIA Evaluations

Evaluations of the WIA programs have followed an uneven, strange, and increasingly political path. While under the Clinton administration the initial evaluations followed a traditional path of making efforts to understand and improve the programs, during the Bush administration the conduct of the evaluations and the dissemination of their findings became increasing political.

With the enactment of WIA in 1998, the department quickly initiated a number of process evaluations to examine the program implementation. They were conducted by Social Policy Research Associates. The early implementation analyses studied how the programs were being adopted in the states and whether they were being implemented in accordance with the legislative intent. Individual studies were produced over several years, and the findings were summarized in a final evaluation report (SPRA 2004).

A number of additional evaluations were conducted for the department. A major eight-state field research evaluation was conducted by the Rockefeller Institute for Government. A net impact evaluation was conducted using administrative data as part of the Administrative Data Research and Evaluation (ADARE) project. Two states funded their own evaluations of federal and state training programs. In 2007, the Office of Management and Budget (OMB) mandated that the department conduct two evaluations of WIA programs: a quasiexperimental evaluation and a random assignment evaluation. Ironically, a Republican-controlled OMB belatedly compelled a resistant Republican-controlled Employment and Training Administration (ETA) to resume evaluation of the WIA program. Two antagonistic opponents on the role of evidence-based policy faced each other, and the OMB prevailed.

Rockefeller implementation study

The Rockefeller Institute for Government conducted an eight-state process evaluation of the WIA program for the department (Barnow and King 2005). Ten researchers conducted field studies in each of the eight states. Under the direction of Richard P. Nathan, all of the researchers used the same field research methodology.

The study was conducted in Florida, Indiana, Maryland, Michigan, Missouri, Oregon, Texas, and Utah. Findings of the report were organized into five major topics: 1) leadership, including the roles of employers and the private sector; 2) system administration and funding; 3) organization and operation of the One-Stop Career Centers; 4) service orientation and service mix; and 5) the use of the market mechanism, including the Eligible Training Provider list, Consumer Reports, performance standards, and training vouchers—i.e., Individual Training Accounts. The study was highly useful, even though the selection of participating states was not based on achieving a representative sample.

Seven-state net impact evaluation

The Hollenbeck et al. (2005) quasiexperimental evaluation examined the net impact of the WIA program in seven states: Florida, Georgia, Illinois, Maryland, Missouri, Texas, and Washington. The longitudinal administrative data for the evaluation came from the ADARE project, which makes available (through data-sharing agreements with state partners) data drawn from UI wage records, state workforce development programs, and other state and federal programs.

WIA participants who received WIA core, intensive, or training services were compared to a group who registered with the ES but did not receive WIA services. The treatment and comparison groups received employment services in either program year 2000 or 2001. Hollenbeck et al. (2005) conclude that "WIA services as currently provided in these states are effective and appear to be doing a good job of addressing WIA's state objectives" (p. v). The impact of receiving any WIA services, compared to the impact for those served by the ES, "increases employment rates by about 10 percentage points and average quarterly earnings by about $800." The impact of receiving WIA training services, compared to workers served by ES or WIA but not receiving training services, was "also positive, but generally smaller in magnitude than for the receipt of any WIA services."

Disaggregating the results, the impacts for WIA dislocated workers were consistently larger than for WIA adults. For both WIA adults and dislocated workers, impacts for women were greater than for men, "a finding largely consistent with the literature on training impacts."

Hollenbeck et al. (2005) completed their evaluation in October 2005, but it was embargoed by the ETA's political leadership, Emily DeRocco and Mason Bishop. Under pressure from the OMB, it was released three years later, in August 2008. Even though DeRocco and Bishop had by then left the USDOL, the Internet release of the evaluation on the department's Web site was accompanied by an unprecedented, disavowing preface called "Summary and Caveats," which sought to impugn the report and its conclusions by opining that the methodology of the researchers "may well have led to erroneous results."

State evaluations

Washingon State Community College study. Jacobson, LaLonde, and Sullivan (2002) studied the impact on dislocated workers of enrolling in community college courses. The study examined the universe of the 121,000 dislocated workers who filed valid claims for unemployment insurance in Washington State in the first half of the 1990s. A group of approximately 25,000 of those workers enrolled in at least one course provided at one of 25 community colleges.

The study identified "high return" classes—those that improved the annual earnings of participants. Participants experienced high economic returns from taking and completing courses that provided more technical academic and vocational skills—including courses in the health and engineering fields—and math and science classes.

The study findings suggest that substantial economic returns to training are concentrated in the high return classes. Thus, the department and state workforce agencies should encourage training program operators to provide job training in these areas, and to provide information to unemployed workers about the types of job training that can best increase their earning power.

State Workforce Investment Act evaluations. A number of states have been interested enough in the effectiveness of their training programs to fund program evaluations conducted by third parties. Two of these evaluations have been conducted by Kevin Hollenbeck. Washington had a third-party evaluation conducted for its employment and training programs; Hollenbeck and Huang (2006) conducted a net impact and benefit-cost evaluation of 11 state and federal workforce development programs operating in Washington State, including the WIA Adult and Dislocated Worker programs. The study used quasiexperimental methods, comparing the participant outcomes to those who registered with the ES but did not participate in the programs. Findings were generally positive, concluding that "the benefit-cost analyses show that virtually all of the programs have discounted future benefits that far exceed the costs for participants, and that society also receives a positive return on investment" (p. iii). Short-term net impact findings were positive for the WIA Adult and Dislocated Worker programs but not for the WIA Youth Program, while the long-term impacts were positive for all three programs. None of the three programs had a positive benefit-cost ratio from the perspective of the government sector, although the WIA Dislocated Worker and Youth programs had positive long-run ratios (pp. 7–9).

Hollenbeck and Huang (2008) also conducted a study of workforce program performance indicators for Virginia. Their performance indicators included gross and net impact indicators, and they recommended that Virginia use net impacts rather than gross impacts. Their net impact indicators flowed from a quasiexperimental evaluation for workers exiting programs between July 2004 and June 2005 using administrative data. For department-funded programs, the study covered the WIA Adult and Youth programs but not the WIA Dislocated Worker Program. The comparison group was workers who participated in the ES.

The net impact results—measured at two quarters after program exit—indicated the WIA Adult Program had a small positive impact of about 5 percent on earnings. These results were small compared to Vocational Rehabilitation programs, which resulted in nearly 20 percent earnings increases. The WIA Youth Program, however, had a small negative, significant impact on employment.

The longer-term net impact, measured at four quarters after program exit, indicated that the WIA Adult Program had a smaller, 3 percent positive impact on employment, while the WIA Youth program impact on employment was not significant.

The positive net impact of each of the WIA programs on quarterly earnings was between $400 and $500 two quarters after program exit. By four quarters after program exit, the positive effects on quarterly earnings had declined to less than $200 for WIA adults and to less than $100 for WIA youth.

How Much Job Training Do Employment and Training Programs Provide?

All department-funded employment and training programs provide more employment services than training services. Training services are limited for many reasons. One reason is the lack of demand from workers because most unemployed workers want to become employed immediately. Many workers do not want, and cannot afford, to wait to receive training before they go back to work. Second, the limited and declining budgets for programs with training components have meant that these programs only can afford to provide limited amounts of training. Training is considerably more expensive than other employment services. Accordingly, local agencies provide training services less frequently than they do employment services.

In addition, job training is frequently provided and funded by agencies other than the USDOL. Department programs fund only a small portion of the training that is provided by federal, state, and local agencies.

In 2003, Domestic Policy Council staff at the Bush White House asked Assistant Secretary DeRocco why ETA-funded training was so expensive. Naively, they were dividing the ETA's entire WIA appropriation by the number of workers receiving job training annually, and they were outraged that short-term training appeared to cost more than $20,000 per trainee. The erroneous assumption made by Domestic Policy Council (DPC) staff was that the ETA programs were solely training programs, and that they provided no other valuable employment and reemployment assistance services.

Since DeRocco could not explain the true cost per training participant, she asked Eric Johnson, the ETA's director of performance measurement, to prepare a response. Johnson knew that only a small percentage of ETA funds were being used to provide training and that WIA core and intensive services absorbed the majority of WIA funds. However, he was unable to respond to the DPC's concern directly, because the ETA cost accounting reports received from the states do not break down expenditures by the type of employment services provided. Johnson came and asked me, as ETA research director, to conduct a study to estimate training expenditures as a percentage of all ETA-funded programs.[2]

The resulting study (Mikelson and Nightingale 2006) estimated the amount and the portion of department employment and training program funds that are expended on job training. While it was widely known that U.S. "training programs" have always encompassed much more than training, the study estimated that in 2002, out of the $6.5 billion appropriated for employment and training programs, only between $1.1 and $1.7 billion (18 to 27 percent) actually was spent on training. Thus, approximately three-quarters (or more) of funding was spent on services other than training. The result is not surprising in a universal-access, One-Stop environment in which the great majority of workers only need core and intensive services. It also is not surprising given the finding that workers go through a complex triage process before they are referred to training. Counseling workers to determine whether core and intensive services will suffice or whether they should be referred to receive scarce training vouchers takes time—it requires several hours of counseling prior to referral to training (Table 7.1).

Not only are most ETA programs thought of as training programs, but among ETA programs the WIA programs are often thought of as "the" training programs of the department. In fact, other ETA-funded

Table 7.1 Estimated Expenditures on Job Training and Number of Trainees in U.S. Department of Labor Programs, 2002

Program/funding source	Low estimate ($000)	High estimate ($000)	Approximate no. of trainees
WIA—Dislocated Worker programs	280,215.0	467,025.0	93,400
WIA—Adult activities	303,237.0	505,395.0	101,000
WIA—Youth activities	47,801.4	159,338.0	63,700
Job Corps	207,100.0	207,100.0	52,800
Trade Adjustment Assistance	79,823.2	79,823.2	40,700
H-1B Technical Skills Grants	12,071.2	19,752.9	29,500
All other labor programs	217,141.7	308,823.9	113,900
Total estimate for labor programs	1,147,389.5	1,747,258.0	495,000

SOURCE: Mikelson and Nightingale (2006), p. 42.

programs (e.g., Trade Adjustment Assistance, or TAA) also provide a great deal of job training services. In 2002, the job training programs funded by the ETA provided training to a half-million workers. Since the WIA programs trained an estimated 258,100 individuals, WIA supplied only about half as much job training as was provided by ETA-funded programs.

While the Labor Department is a major provider of job training resources, other federal agencies provide a great deal of job training too. At the state level, referrals to job training are frequently provided by state agencies. Mikelson and Nightingale (2006) estimated that the USDOL accounts for approximately one-third of the federal expenditures on training made by all civilian federal agencies. The Department of Education provides considerably more job training than the Department of Labor, and a number of other domestic federal agencies also provide a significant amount of training (Table 7.2).

O'Shea and King (2001) examined the issue of who funds public job training services from the state perspective. They looked at the distribution of state expenditures in three states—Tennessee, Texas, and Washington—during the early implementation of the WIA program. They found that WIA core and intensive services frequently "absorb the available training dollars under WIA," so that states are left to fund much of the public job training using state training programs and advis-

Table 7.2 Federal Spending on Job Training, by Department, 2002 (excluding administrative cost; $ millions)

Department	Low estimate		High estimate	
	$	%	$	%
Labor	1,147.0	36.0	1,747.3	33.2
Education—Pell Grants	1,250.0	39.2	1,875.0	35.6
Education—all others	628.8	19.7	1,318.6	25.1
Health & Human Services	93.8	2.9	169.6	3.2
Veterans Affairs	40.4	1.3	121.1	2.3
Housing & Urban Development	26.9	0.1	26.9	0.1
Interior	3.1	< 0.1	5.1	< 0.1
Justice[a]	0.0	0.0	0.0	0.0
Total federal	3,190.0	99.3	5,263.6	99.6

NOTE: Percentages do not sum to 100 because of rounding.
[a] Justice's Serious and Violent Offender Program was not yet in operation.
SOURCE: Mikelson and Nightingale (2006), p. 40.

ing workers to apply for Pell Grants and direct loans, as well as other student loans.

The job training that private firms provide to their workers is subject to widely varying estimates. Mikelson and Nightingale (2006) examined four different surveys of firms and found that they spent about $50 billion per year on training. These expenditures included training costs and salary costs but not the cost of the administration of their training programs.

Estimates also vary about the number of employees who receive private sector–provided training each year. The answer depends on whom you ask. Surveys of firms suggest that approximately 70 percent of their workers receive training. However, surveys of workers yield much lower numbers. Workers employed by firms with more than 100 employees indicated that only 20 to 25 percent of workers received training. Training was also very unevenly distributed among workers; its provision varied principally by education. The study found that workers with more education were much more likely to receive training than workers who are less educated (Mickelson and Nightingale 2006).

Compared to all other sources of job training funding, department-funded job training programs are small. Indeed, other federal agencies provide more job training than the department does. Many of the job training referrals by the One-Stops are made to training funded by state programs and by other federal government agencies. The department also spends a small amount on training compared to the private sector; in fact, it spends 3 percent or less of the annual spending on private sector training. The number of workers receiving department-funded training amounts to considerably less than 5 percent of those who receive private sector training.

TRAINING VOUCHERS AND INDIVIDUAL TRAINING ACCOUNTS

Vouchers in the Provision of Public Services

A voucher is a "subsidy that grants limited purchasing power to an individual to choose among a restricted set of goods and services"

(Steuerle 2000, pp. 4–5). Vouchers are one of the many ways that the government can provide services. Vouchers must compete with other delivery mechanisms: direct government delivery, contracting out of government services, use of competitive public suppliers, or providing loans or cash payments. While vouchers have been widely used elsewhere in government, until the WIA was implemented in 2000 they were relatively untested in the workforce development system. Prior to WIA implementation, the workforce development system did not provide training services; it contracted out training services to both public and private providers. With the implementation of WIA, widespread use of training vouchers was introduced to customers, who can use them to purchase training services from either private or public training providers. The expected effect was not greater privatization of training services but an increase in consumer choice.

A number of characteristics are common to all voucher programs. The purpose of vouchers is to increase the supply of services from which consumers can choose. That is, vouchers are expected to create competition among service providers. Whether this happens or not depends on the initial and long-term number of suppliers or providers (which is heavily affected by population density), on entry conditions in the market, and on the degree of regulation in the market (e.g., in health care).

Vouchers also have an effect on the demand for the good or service in question. In exercising consumer choice, recipients are expected to have enough information to make an educated choice. In a "Free Choice" voucher model, customers choose job finding and training services on their own without the intervention of government officials.[3] But customers may not have the ability to make sound choices: they may lack either competence or resources. Problems might include lack of information as well as lack of interest or motivation. Information may be asymmetric in the sense that customers might have less information than do the service providers. In some cases, the complexity of decision-making may make training vouchers problematic, as when recipients must determine the quality and effectiveness of training providers as well as whether the training will match their own skills and abilities (Barnow 2000). Similarly, recipients might face a complex of choices that suggest the need for "Informed Choice," in which the recipient and the frontline government worker work together, with the government worker providing information to the recipient. Informed Choice has been identified as a concern in connection with the "bundling" of multiple services; it suggests that there might need to be an intermediate position between the freedom of providing cash without restraints and the restriction of providing in-kind services (Lerman and Steuerle 2000).

The above discussion also suggests that the sharing of information between government agencies and recipients might act as a substitute for making information available directly to the recipient. In this regard, frontline government workers can provide two things: 1) an assessment of an individual customer's abilities and skills regarding alternative occupations and 2) their personal knowledge about training providers in the local labor market. These mediated services may act, in part, as a substitute for the customer's direct, self-service use of the informational tools, such as labor market information, information on the track record of the training providers (i.e., WIA Consumer Reports), and the list of training providers who are permitted to receive the training vouchers (i.e., WIA Eligible Training Provider lists).

Vouchers may also increase prices if they increase the demand for a particular service. For example, there is evidence that the student loan program has had the effect of raising the price of higher education, and Section 8 housing vouchers have raised rents in areas of high usage. Furthermore, vouchers may raise prices if suppliers are allowed to discriminate between purchasers who use vouchers and those who do not (Steuerle 2000, pp. 18–19).

Models for Training Vouchers

Once WIA was enacted, the challenge for the workforce development system was to determine the effectiveness of training vouchers, something that has been largely untested in the workforce development context. A review of the use of vouchers for public training programs for disadvantaged and dislocated workers indicates that "there is little evidence that vouchers for these workers are effective and that they are a better alternative than other service delivery mechanisms" (Barnow 2000). Few precedents were found for the training voucher that became part of WIA. However, evaluations of two early voucher-like programs—the Seattle-Denver Income Maintenance Experiments for low-wage workers of the 1970s and the TAA program of the late 1980s—found that neither had positive impacts (Barnow 2000).

Not only was the use of public job training vouchers largely untested, but it was unclear what was meant by a training voucher. A number of different approaches to vouchers have been discussed and tried. Individuals receiving public training could be given more or less freedom to choose. Under past programs, frontline workers could provide more or less information and guidance about how to use these funds. As these precedents were analyzed along a continuum of the degree of freedom, information, and guidance they offered, three models emerged for providing public training vouchers. A number of studies have considered these models in reviews and evaluations of training programs and demonstrations (Table 7.3): early pre-WIA voucher programs; an early voucher demonstration under WIA; and the ITA Experiment, which tested alternative approaches to WIA training vouchers (Barnow and Trutko 1999; D'Amico et al. 2001; D'Amico et al. 2004; Public Policy Associates 1999).

An Informed Choice model represents the middle of the continuum. Although this model was not specified in the development of WIA, it became the operational model that was chosen by the great majority of service delivery areas and local boards both before and after the implementation of WIA. The Informed Choice model, when applied to individuals who, it is determined, are in need of training, has four main characteristics:

1) Assessment and counseling are provided to transmit labor market information, and to determine whether the proposed training is both appropriate for the customer and also in a demand occupation.

2) Training vendors are screened to determine the quality, outcomes, and cost of training.

3) Counselors and customers jointly make decisions, with frontline staff acting in the roles of guides, facilitators, and information brokers.

4) The voucher is limited both in time and dollar value.

In assisting customers, One-Stop centers provide information, assistance, and guidance with the goal of helping customers make the best choices on their own. One-Stop staff members provide labor market information, conduct assessments to assure that customers have a realistic view of their abilities, and provide information about the training programs and vendors. Frontline staff members play a guiding or facilitating role, but the final choice is the customer's.

In contrast, a Free Choice model gives the training participant maximum choice and may restrict the role of frontline staff. Individuals deemed in need of training are offered training vouchers. They can make use of them, if they wish, with no further guidance from workforce development counselors. They can make use of labor market information, vendor information, and assessment tools available at the One-Stop centers, but they can use the voucher for training in any occupation that is not restricted by law. They also can use the voucher to purchase training from any training provider on the state or local Eligible Training Provider list. This model is most like the policy concept that was considered in the early 1990s prior to enactment of WIA.

Finally, under a Directed Choice model, frontline workers provide labor market information, assessment, and training and vendor information as in the Informed Choice model, but they also play a stronger role. Rather than simply providing technical guidance from their own knowledge, frontline workers use their professional judgment about what program and which training provider to select for a customer. These staff members make use of their knowledge regarding training programs, demand for occupations and wages, customers' skills and abilities, customers' ability to successfully complete the training, and the best choices of training providers in the local labor market. Counselors can guide customers to more cost-effective training choices or restrict choices that are likely to be less cost-effective.

Development of Training Voucher Policy

The introduction of training vouchers—called Individual Training Accounts (ITAs)—under WIA was a sharp departure from past workforce development system approaches. Training vouchers also represented a move into untested waters. Under previous training programs—the Manpower Development and Training Act, Comprehensive Employment and Training Act, and Job Training Partnership Act programs—the USDOL, states, and localities contracted with private training providers to put workers in existing classes. Rejection of this

Table 7.3 Training Vouchers: Proposals, Demonstrations, and Programs

	Ross proposal	Pre-WIA vouchers (Barnow and Trutko 1999)	Career Management Account	ITA/ETP Demo	WIA (D'Amico et al. 2004)	ITA Experiment	PRAs (H.R. 444)	WRAs (H.R. 3976)
Dates	1993	Pre-1999	1995–97	2002	2003–04	2002–04	2003	2005
Type of choice	Free	8 Informed 1 free	Informed	Nearly all informed	Nearly all informed	Free/ informed/ directed	Free	Free
Voucher amt. ($)	1,200	2,000– 10,000	2,500– 8,500	1,700– 10,000	1,200– 10,000	3,000 & 8,000[a]	3,000 or less	3,000 or less
Avg. voucher amt. ($)								
modal	—	—	—	—	5,000	3,133	—	—
median	—	—	—	—	5,000	3,116	—	—
mean	—	—	3,292	—	—	4,764	—	—

NOTE: Blank = not applicable; — = not available.

[a] Maximum voucher amount during the demonstration. After the demonstration, the eight demonstration sites had caps ranging from $3,000 to $6,000; the modal value was $3,000, and the median value was either $4,000 or $4,500.

SOURCE: Barnow and Trutko (1999); D'Amico et al. (2004); D'Amico and Salzman (2005); Perez-Johnson et al. (2004); Public Policy Associates (1999); Ross (1993); H.R. 444 for Personal Reemployment Accounts; H.R. 3976 for Worker Recovery Accounts.

model for public training programs came as a result of a public policy movement to incorporate customer choice in the provision of government services. The customer choice approach was expected to make the delivery of government services more effective and efficient by making use of the market mechanism—i.e., to compete with or substitute for the usual way of providing government services. Policy gurus recommended vouchers for use at the local, state, and federal levels, citing successful implementation of voucher programs in a wide variety of contexts (Osborne and Gaebler 1992).

Prior to his election, Bill Clinton was associated with the centrist New Democrats, who adopted this customer choice approach in the early 1990s as a method of providing government goods and services. With respect to workforce development programs, the Progressive Policy Institute, also associated with the New Democrats, advocated a "market-based competitive system" under the emerging One-Stop center system, in which service providers would compete for customers who could make their own choices without being subject to the "control of the government bureaucracy" (Plastrik 1994).

Doug Ross, who became the first assistant secretary for employment and training in the Clinton administration, wrote a chapter in the Progressive Policy Institute's book *Mandate for Change* (Marshall and Schram 1993) that became a policy guidepost to the administration. He advocated a more competitive American workforce system, one that recognized that individual jobs could not be protected but would assure displaced workers a return to work through retraining.[4] Dislocated workers would receive education and retraining through Career Opportunity Cards—vouchers in the form of "smart cards." With the cards, workers could purchase job finding and training services that would "give Americans direct control of the education and career development resources that are the principal new source of economic security." Workers experiencing "a threat . . . to economic security" would be eligible for a smart card with a value of up to $1,200, "the approximate cost of one year of community college training," which could be used at any educational or training institution that provided performance information to state workforce agencies. These agencies would put this information into "*Consumer Reports*-type information regarding . . . completion rates, placement rates and starting wage rates" that would be available to individuals selecting training programs (Ross 1993, p. 67).

Thus, Ross embraced training vouchers as the preferred method of providing training and employment services, combining it with smart card technology. His concept of free choice allowed customers to assess the outcomes of service providers on their own. Ross would not have included a government role in the decision process; he did not propose assigning states and localities the task of assessing the quality of service providers and restricting training provider participation, as was done later through Eligible Training Provider lists under WIA. Ross supported giving workers free choice in selecting the kind of training they received and who provided it (Ross 1993, p. 68). Ross's voucher would have been funded at less than the current cost of most short-term training and did not provide for income support while workers attended a year of community college. Ross set the maximum value of his training vouchers low because the voucher would be made broadly available to all dislocated workers, not just to the small number of workers most in need of training services. Ross's free choice model did not prevail; in WIA, Congress adopted the informed choice model for its training vouchers.

The market model approach to training services was initiated by transforming the infrastructure for workforce development service delivery. Flowing from the Clinton administration's National Performance Review, a policy decision was made in 1993 to create a "system of competitive, One-Stop, career development centers open to all Americans" (Gore 1993, p. 49). This was followed by a One-Stop implementation grant initiative that preceded the enactment of WIA. One-Stop centers would provide universal access to what would become WIA core services. It was thought that training vouchers would eliminate the need to provide targeted training programs through three separate USDOL programs aimed at youth, disadvantaged adults, and dislocated workers. The Clinton administration hoped to create a more open process of funding eligibility and selection that would be facilitated by providing vouchers to all workers (Balducchi and Pasternak 2001).

The One-Stop centers were a budget initiative that began in the first year of the Clinton administration and ran from FY 1994 to FY 2000, during which time grants were awarded to develop One-Stop centers in all states. This initiative commenced under the JTPA, preceding WIA's enactment by five years. Curiously, the first, but unsuccessful, proposal to replace JTPA was the proposed Reemployment Act of 1994, which did not incorporate a provision permitting the use of vouchers (Balducchi, Johnson, and Gritz 1997; Balducchi and Pasternak 2001).

The use of training vouchers as a substitute for training assignment was first proposed by President Clinton as part of a policy proposal called the Middle Class Bill of Rights, after Congress failed to enact the 1994 Reemployment Act. Vouchers were seen as a way to bring the market to bear on job training programs. Rather than having job counselors in local workforce agencies choose who would receive what kind of training from which providers, customers would make their own choices. It was thought that vouchers would empower these customers to make their own decisions, resulting in improved training opportunities through the triumph of a newly created public training market (Balducchi and Pasternak 2001).

Early in the policy discussion, it was assumed that the market mechanism would result in customers making better choices than those made by training counselors. Consumers would demand the best possible training services for themselves. It was expected, however, that consumers would have good information both about which occupations to train for and which training providers to select. Customers would require information on which occupations were in demand and what wages they could expect when they completed training. It was also anticipated that they would glean information on which occupations offered the best long-term career paths and would use the information wisely. These assumptions about training vouchers are embodied in the free choice model. The assumptions, however, were faulty. States found it difficult and expensive to develop and maintain WIA's Consumer Reports and Eligible Training Provider lists, and the department lost interest in funding and supporting the labor market information programs that were the foundation of training vouchers. By the late 2000s, the information infrastructure essential to supporting training vouchers had collapsed.

Training Vouchers before the Workforce Investment Act

Implementation of training voucher programs began on a small scale even before the enactment of WIA. Some individual localities tried vouchers on their own. For example, the Atlanta Regional Commission first used vouchers under JTPA in 1991 to provide training to approximately 13,000 Eastern Airlines workers when the company went bankrupt. Given the size of the dislocation and the limited staff to serve Eastern's workers, the commission could not make use of the JTPA classroom training approach. The experience of the commission was that many of the dislocated workers served by the vouchers made poor training choices: they selected training for occupations that provided low wages or for which there was little likelihood of career development (e.g., cosmetology and bartending). In response to this experience, the commission began to build its own vendor list and monitor vendor performance (D'Amico et al. 2001, pp. II-2, II-3).

Shortly before WIA implementation, the department funded a study of the use of vouchers under JTPA. The researchers found that the voucher system using the informed choice model was in effect in eight of nine sites, while one site used the free choice model. They found that all agencies limited the time that vouchers could be used (generally to two years or less) and that most agencies also limited the dollar amount (to between $2,000 and $10,000) that could be paid for training. While agency payment was not always contingent upon placement of the training participant, it was usually contingent upon training completion. Agencies usually had a screening process to assess which training providers could be approved to provide training, based on training courses offered, costs, and outcomes. They also usually developed a list of approved providers based on past performance (Barnow and Trutko 1999).

As policy interest grew, the USDOL began to look further into vouchers in the mid-1990s. In anticipation of the possible enactment of individual training accounts (ITAs), the department conducted a Career Management Account (CMA) demonstration. This project was carried out from 1995 to 1997 at 13 sites (Public Policy Associates 1999). The demonstration was designed to provide models for a new workforce development program that would provide training using vouchers. The vouchers, however, were only used to provide training services to a sample of dislocated workers at each site. Sites continued to operate their nonvoucher programs while designing and operating a voucher program for between 200 and 1,208 participants per site, at an average of 335 participants per site. Voucher design varied widely between sites and included as recipients those determined to be most in need, unemployment insurance claimants most likely to exhaust their benefits, those nominated by One-Stop center staff, and some other interested dislocated workers. The maximum amount of the grant varied from \$2,500 to \$8,500. The average cost per participant was \$3,292. The CMA demonstration delivery system, however, largely failed to test the efficacy of nondirected customer choice. Sites continued to provide assessment, counseling, and labor market information. Participants were given the freedom to choose how to use their vouchers, but evaluation results indicated that a critical factor in customer satisfaction with the CMA demonstration was the strong role played by CMA case workers and the information provided to customers by frontline case workers to guide their training decisions.

The CMA demonstration sites used an informed choice model, but with widely varying designs and specifications. The process analysis conducted by Public Policy Associates provided a sense of some of the issues involved in implementing an informed choice model. However, the evaluation design did not permit the measurement of net impacts of the demonstration. Thus, the demonstration provides limited insight for making policy choices on the design and use of vouchers.

In response to the CMA demonstration, a number of demonstration sites continued to use the voucher approach after the 1995–1997 demonstration ended. Metro Portland, for example, initiated an Individual Learning Account approach under which customers made regular contributions to an account that could be used to pay for training or education, with contributions matched by employers and social service agencies. The Baltimore Office of Employment Development also continued the voucher approach after CMA ended, making case managers into coaches who helped customers make informed choices, and empowering those case managers to make decisions about customers with special needs (D'Amico et al. 2001, pp. II-2, II-3).

The Career Management Account demonstration provided limited information about how to make the transition from JTPA assignment to training slots. Upon enactment, WIA programs abruptly made the transition to training vouchers.

Vouchers under the Workforce Investment Act

In 1998, when the bill that became WIA emerged from negotiations between the Democratic administration and the Republican-controlled Congress, training vouchers were a key component of the new legislation. The question remained, however, as to whether the training vouchers would follow the free or informed choice model.

Section 134(d)(4)(F) of the WIA provides "consumer choice requirements" and states that "in general . . . training services . . . shall be provided in a manner that maximizes consumer choice in the selection of an eligible provider of such services." For eligible providers, such information must include "a description of the programs through which the providers may offer the training services" and "performance information and performance cost information."

Section 134(d)(4)(G) of the WIA states that "training services . . . shall be provided through the use of individual training accounts . . . and shall be provided to eligible individuals through the one-stop delivery system," with the following exceptions: on-the-job training, customized training, cases where there are insufficient numbers of eligible providers to allow for customer choice, and training services provided to special populations that face multiple barriers to employment.

Congress, however, made clear that it favored an informed choice approach. Both the House and the Senate indicated that although they supported Individual Training Accounts, their support was conditional. Senate Report 105-109 went beyond the language in WIA and said with respect to ITAs that "case management, such as general guidance or recommendations . . . will be provided to varying degrees, based on case-by-case judgment by the manager," while, after consulting an Eligible Training Provider list and Consumer Reports, "the ultimate decision about what field to pursue and which provider to select is the participant's." Similarly, House Report 105-093 observed "that the success of the use of skills grants is contingent upon several supporting elements" and went on to describe the reasons that Eligible Training Provider lists and Consumer Reports are needed.

The department, however, did not take a position on how the new Individual Training Accounts should be administered but delegated decision-making authority to the states and local boards. In the summary and explanations to the WIA regulations—20 CFR 660-671—published on August 11, 2000, in the *Federal Register*, the department stated that "Section 660.410 provides a definition for an ITA that seeks to provide maximum flexibility to State and local program operators in managing ITAs. These regulations do not establish procedures for making payments . . . rather they provide that authority to the State or Local Boards."

Thus, the federal government authorized states and localities to select the nature of Individual Training Accounts along a continuum from free to informed choice. By leaving the decision to the states and localities, the department effectively defaulted to the informed choice model, as that is what the pre-WIA experience suggested would be the states' and localities' choice.

The informed choice model received supportive assistance. Implementation was aided by various tools available to frontline workers and customers. Most important among them were labor market information tools developed in the 1990s that provided useful information, both for the selection of training that would result in good jobs and for the selection of training providers who could help workers get those jobs. The improved and more automated labor market information system— called America's Labor Market Information System (ALMIS)—was specifically developed to support a market-oriented training system under WIA. It was available to help ITA recipients make choices about which high-demand, high-wage occupations to train for in their local labor markets (Woods and Frugoli 2004).

Early Implementation Demonstration of WIA Training Vouchers

Because the training vouchers authorized by WIA had not received much testing prior to WIA enactment, the ETA's dislocated worker office was anxious to jump-start the process.[5] The result was a training voucher demonstration that provided funding for those state and local areas that were willing to be early implementers of training vouchers. These sites would be studied and the lessons learned would be shared with states and local areas that adopted training vouchers more slowly.

In March 2000, the USDOL selected 13 sites (six local workforce investment areas and seven states) to accelerate their participation in the ITA process through an Individual Training Account/Eligible Training Provider (ITA/ETP) Demonstration project. Twelve of these demonstration sites used the Informed Choice model. Only one site predominantly used the Free Choice model.

All sites had dollar caps on the Individual Training Account amounts, varying between $1,700 and $10,000. Given the way WIA performance was to be measured, sites had an interest in having their ITA recipients complete training and find subsequent employment. They maintained contact with ITA recipients during their training and tried to help solve any problems. Although the sites varied in how proactive they were, all sites contacted recipients at least once a month. Among training providers, proprietary schools were the most proactive in helping trainees get through training and in assisting trainees in finding jobs after completion. Community colleges were less proactive, although they too provided counseling and placement services.

The ITA/ETP Demonstration examined the implementation of ITAs in the demonstration sites through early 2002 (D'Amico and Salzman 2005). By that time, WIA programs had developed and matured. Local areas were more comfortable authorizing training, and the number of workers receiving training had increased above the depressed 2000 levels. Nearly all local areas were planning to primarily use ITAs rather than on-the-job, contract, or customized training. The ITA approach used by nearly all areas was the Informed Choice model, since local areas were concerned that individuals authorized to receive training should receive adequate information, guidance, and assistance from frontline staff. States increased the quantity of training they provided after the department informed the states that it was not advocating a work-first philosophy that deemphasized training. More training also could be provided as the costly WIA infrastructure for providing core, intensive, and training services was completed. Eligible Training Provider (ETP) lists were established and expanded. Many states found ways to make it easier for training providers to get on the list, including easing eligibility requirements and collecting most of the required data about training providers from unemployment insurance wage records. These ETP lists provided a substantial range of choices, although the range of choices increased in areas that were more urbanized. A system of WIA Consumer Reports was generally searchable on-line and provided information to support consumer choice, including basic information on training programs.

Implementation of Training Vouchers

A study of WIA implementation in eight states (Barnow and King 2005) found that overall training vouchers was a successful part of the

WIA system. They were popular both with participants and with the local workforce investment boards (WIBs). Participants appreciated the ability to make their own choices about training. Local WIBs found that vouchers worked well as long as they were able to guide participants' choices.

Using the Informed Choice approach, states and localities set maximum dollar amounts of the vouchers, the time within which they had to be used, and guided the participants' choices regarding training types and providers of training. Barnow and King noted that the USDOL also was conducting a training voucher experiment testing alternative types of vouchers. The study suggested that the evaluation of the department's experiment would provide evidence regarding how much guidance local workforce investment boards should provide to training participants.

Barnow and King went on to note that WIA permits exceptions under which training can be provided without using vouchers. They sought to examine how these exceptions were used but found too few cases to draw any conclusions about their efficacy and recommended a special study of these exceptions.[6]

Barnow and King also found a number of problems with the administration of vouchers. First, some states and localities had difficulty establishing the ETP lists reflecting training providers' success in placing training participants. Some state workforce agencies had technical difficulty developing the lists. Some training providers objected to providing the detailed information used to develop the lists. The study suggested that states could develop more efficient methods of developing the lists, and less intrusive methods for providing data from training programs that have few WIA enrollees.

Second, the maximum voucher amount was meant to be a ceiling, but some states found that training providers responded to the maximum by making it the floor for their training voucher charges. Third, the study also found that adults sometimes made inappropriate and overreaching choices in selecting training programs.

The U.S. Department of Labor funded another Workforce Investment Act implementation study, this one of 38 local workforce areas in 21 states between the fall of 1999 and January 2004 (D'Amico et al. 2004). The study found that 10 of the 14 sites visited used ITAs exclusively or nearly so, and that other types of training also were used.

Some rural areas used ITAs little or not at all. Local areas used customized training when they sought to align workforce development with economic development. And local areas used contract training to serve special groups such as the homeless and workers with disabilities.

D'Amico et al. (2004) also found that most local areas placed similar time limits on the use of vouchers—between one and two years. The maximum voucher amount, however, varied widely among 29 local areas—between $1,200 and $10,000. Among these areas both the median voucher and the mode were $5,000.

With respect to the degree of customer choice, the study found that the informed choice approach was used at virtually every site researchers visited. The researchers did find, however, that consumer choice was constrained when one of four conditions was present: 1) the number of training providers was limited, particularly in rural areas; 2) sites were in the process of making the transition to the more stringent standards of WIA subsequent eligibility; 3) dollar caps on training vouchers limited access to certain types of training; and 4) training providers encouraged potentially WIA-eligible workers to seek training at the One-Stops ("reverse referrals").

Exploring Voucher Options: The ITA Experiment

At the time the ITA/ETP Demonstration began, I encouraged the department to learn more about training vouchers and particularly about alternative designs for training vouchers. Since training vouchers were a given under WIA, the key policy question was which voucher design was most effective. The research unit chief, Jon Messenger, and I developed a design for an ITA experiment and presented it to the ETA's career deputy assistant secretary, Ray Uhalde. Before approving the proposal, Uhalde wanted to be sure that the three treatments were different enough that the experiment would likely yield significant results. Interestingly, he also raised the issue of whether the experiment might reflect adversely on the new WIA programs, as the Job Training Partnership Act Evaluation had on the JTPA program. The sensitivity to the program and budgetary impacts of the JTPA Evaluation was still raw four years after the evaluation was published.

The ITA Experiment reflected the WIA program requirement that before customers could be approved to receive WIA training funds they had to meet four qualifications: they must 1) be determined to be "in need of training," 2) have the skills and qualifications to complete the training, 3) have received at least one core and one intensive service, and 4) be unable to obtain funding assistance to pay for training from some other source. To meet each of these requirements, customers had to interact with WIA staff. For example, customers might have to do the following: demonstrate that they had unsuccessfully searched for work or had scored above a cutoff on an administered assessment form; take a basic skills test to determine their skills and qualifications; complete occupational counseling; and receive an intensive service such as a job search or career exploratory workshop, participate in a job club, or have their recent job searches reviewed (Perez-Johnson et al. 2004, pp. 32–35).

Mathematica Policy Research conducted the ITA Experiment for the department, testing three approaches to vouchers: the free choice, informed choice, and directed choice models (Table 7.4).[7] The goal of the experiment was to determine which model was most efficient by looking at participants' employment and earnings outcomes after they completed training and returned to work. The three approaches were tested in eight study sites in Arizona, Connecticut, Florida, Georgia, Illinois, and North Carolina. Approximately 8,000 WIA customers enrolled in the program between December 2001 and February 2004. Truncating the process, Deputy Assistant Secretary Mason Bishop

Table 7.4 The Three Approaches Tested for the Design of the ITA Experiment

	Approach 1, Directed Choice	Approach 2, Informed Choice	Approach 3, Free Choice
Award amount	Customized	Fixed	Fixed
Counseling	Mandatory, most intensive	Mandatory, moderately intensive	Voluntary
Could counselors reject customers' program choice?	Yes	No	No

NOTE: Under the ITA Experiment, directed choice = "structured customer choice"; informed choice = "guided customer choice"; and free choice = "maximum customer choice."
SOURCE: McConnell et al. (2006).

ordered Mathematica to produce an evaluation report before all the participants enrolled in the project had the opportunity to complete their training. As a result, Mathematica's initial "final evaluation report," completed in December 2006, produced no meaningful results. In the Spring of 2007, the Labor Branch of the Office of Management and Budget objected to the premature survey and ordered the department to contract for a second survey and a second final report. The contract was let, and the contractor proceeded with the second survey. A second final evaluation with longer survey follow-up was completed in 2009.[8]

The voucher design for the ITA Experiment was based on three key choices: 1) whether counseling is mandatory or not, 2) the size of the bonus, and 3) the ability of local staff to restrict customers' training choices. The informed choice model looks most like the approach participating sites had used before the experiment. Counseling was mandatory but, although the training provider had to be on the local or state Eligible Training Provider list, local staff did not ultimately restrict customer choice with respect to training type or provider. The maximum voucher amount was fixed for all customers, generally at a maximum of $3,000 at most sites. The free choice model differed from the informed choice model in that counseling—beyond what was provided under intensive services—was not mandatory. The directed choice model differed from the informed choice model in three respects: 1) local staff could restrict training by type and provider; 2) more intensive counseling was mandatory after assignment to WIA-funded training; and 3) the maximum voucher amount was customized for each customer, generally at a maximum of $8,000.

An interim report (Perez-Johnson et al. 2004) found that the free and informed choice approaches had been largely implemented as planned, but that the directed choice model had not. Local office staff found a number of reasons not to make counseling after training assignment mandatory, as was called for in the experimental design. Because they had followed an informed choice approach before the implementation of the experiment, counselors were more comfortable with that approach and believed it worked well. Counselors also were not comfortable with evaluating training appropriateness or cost-effectiveness. At the same time, they were reluctant to leave customers free to pursue training without any guidance, and in some cases did provide some unrequested counseling after assignment to training, but it was neither structured nor intensive.

The results of the study were most noteworthy with respect to the free choice model. Participants in the free choice model received far less counseling. Only 4 percent received counseling after training assignment, compared to 59 and 66 percent of the participants in the informed and directed choice groups, respectively. Free choice participants, however, were more likely to participate in training; 66 percent of them participated, compared to 58 and 59 percent of those in the informed and directed choice groups (Table 7.5). Despite not receiving counseling after assignment to training, free choice participants were no more likely to take training in low-wage jobs such as cosmetology and massage therapy than were participants in the other treatment groups.

ETA political and policy staff discussed the need for counseling as part of the operation of training vouchers during the life of the ITA Experiment. The Personal Reemployment Account (PRA) initiative included some of the features that superficially looked like the free choice model. After being briefed on the interim report of the ITA Experiment, ETA political officials seized upon the free choice model as the justification for the Bush administration's WIA reauthorization proposals of 2003 and 2005. In 2006, the free choice model was again used by the Bush administration—this time to justify the Career Advancement Accounts (CAAs) proposal.

The Bush administration's argument for the Personal Reemployment Accounts and Career Advancement Accounts ignored the fact that the ITA Experiment design provided counseling twice—once before and then once after the assignment to WIA-funded training. The policy justification for the PRAs and the CAAs concentrated on the impact of providing counseling *after* assignment to training, including the early indication that providing additional counseling after the training voucher offer did not increase training effectiveness. What the argument ignored was the fact that all participants who were assigned to training had already received a good deal of counseling—an average of five hours—*before* they were ever assigned to any of the three treatments. Counselors took time to determine who was in need of training and who was not. Since training is an expensive intervention and few training slots are available, counselors had to determine who would be most likely to benefit from training (McConnell et al. 2006, p. xxvi).

In the ITA Experiment, the free choice approach was shown to assure high rates of participation in training without fear that training would be

Table 7.5 Summary of Impacts of the ITA Experiment

	Means			Impacts	
	A1, Directed Choice	A2, Informed Choice	A3, Free Choice	Between A1 and A2	Between A3 and A2
Customers' experience obtaining an ITA					
Attended or was excused from an ITA orientation (%)	69	67	74	2	7***
Received counseling after an orientation (%)	66	59	4	7***	−55***
ITA take-up rate (%)	59	58	66	1	7***
Training outcomes					
In training any time during follow-up period (%)	64	64	66	1	3
In training at time of survey (%)	17	14	14	3**	1
Weeks in training	19	16	18	3***	2**
Employment outcomes					
Employed any time during follow-up period (%)	80	79	81	1	2
Total weeks worked during follow-up	30.8	29.9	29.6	0.9	−0.2
Total earnings in follow-up period ($)	17,032	16,464	15,724	568	−740
Receipt of UI and public assistance					
Received UI benefits (%)	66	66	67	1	2
Amount of UI benefits received ($)	3,412	3,266	3,483	146	217**
Received food stamp benefits (%)	20	19	20	1	1

NOTE: **statistically significant at the 95 percent confidence level for a two-tailed test; *** statistically significant at the 99 percent confidence level for a two-tailed test.

SOURCE: McConnell et al. (2006), p. xxii; 15-month follow-up survey and Study Tracking System, as of July 2004.

in low-demand, low-wage occupations. The 2006 report, however, does not reveal which of the three approaches is most effective, as measured by training completion, employment, earnings, and employment retention. The final report, with its net impact and cost-benefit analyses, was designed to provide useful information relevant to policymakers.

The 2006 ITA Experiment report (McConnell et al. 2006) contained an implementation analysis, a net impact analysis, and a benefit-cost analysis for the demonstration, which were based on outcomes 15 months after individuals were found to be eligible for WIA-funded training. The 2006 report had substantial shortcomings, however, because it cut off data collection too early. At the time of the follow-up interview that was used to assess outcomes, 17 percent of Treatment 1 participants were still in training, while 14 percent of Treatment 2 and 3 participants were still in training. Clearly the results, presented below, will change with a longer-term follow-up of treatment group members.

Furthermore, no control group could be constructed for this demonstration because the use of training vouchers was required for most WIA training participants. As a result, the ITA Experiment net impacts and benefit-cost analysis compared the treatment groups to one another. Because Treatment 2 (informed choice) had been the most used model before the demonstration, it was used as a baseline for comparison to Treatments 1 and 3.

Net impact analysis

Table 7.5 reveals significant differences in the way that customers experienced the receipt of Individual Training Accounts and in their training outcomes, but no significant differences in employment outcomes. Comparing the free choice option to the informed choice outcome, researchers found that customers in the free choice option were significantly more likely to be excused from orientation, significantly less likely to receive counseling after orientation, and significantly more likely to experience increased ITA take-up rates. There was no significant difference in the amount of training they received through the follow-up period or in whether or not they were in training at the end of the follow-up period. However, since substantial numbers of customers were still in training when the follow-up interview was conducted, only limited information was available on the impact of training after training completion. The lack of significant differences in employment outcomes remains true no matter which of the following three ways is used to measure the outcome of customers: 1) by their being employed at any time during the follow-up period, 2) by total weeks worked during the follow-up period, or 3) by total earnings during the follow-up period. Free choice participants received a larger amount of UI benefits, but there was no difference in the percentage of individuals receiving UI or food stamp benefits.

Benefit-cost analysis

The early benefit-cost analysis is not conclusive. The best comparator for the benefit-cost analysis is the benchmark estimates of net benefits. The results when comparing the informed choice (Approach 2) to the directed choice (Approach 1) option reveal that net benefits for society are not statistically different from zero. Net benefits for customers are not significant. The net benefits for the government sector (−$1,423) are negative and significant because the treatment is more costly (McConnell et al. 2006).

Comparing the informed choice (Approach 2) to the free choice (Approach 3) yields statistically insignificant results for society. The net benefits to customers are also insignificant. For the government sector, net benefits are negative and significant (−$816) because the government provides vouchers to a larger proportion of customers and pays out more in UI benefits and other transfer payments (Table 7.6).

With the information available at the time of the 2006 report, the researchers conclude that their "best estimates suggest that switching from Approach 2 to either Approach 1 or 3 would neither be beneficial nor costly to society as a whole." They also note that "Approach 1 costs the government about $1,400 more per customer eligible for training than Approach 2" and that "Approach 3 costs the government about $800 more per customer eligible for training than Approach 2" (McConnell et al. 2006, p. 107).

From a public policy perspective, a key issue for training vouchers is the comparative benefit-costs between informed choice (Approach 2) and free choice (Approach 3). The evaluators found that although the switch from informed choice to free choice resulted in a negative net benefit, the effect was insignificant using the 15-month follow-up survey data. On the other hand, the result was negative and significant

Table 7.6 Summary of ITA Experiment Benefits and Costs

	Approach 1 vs. Approach 2			Approach 3 vs. Approach 2		
	Customers	Government	Society	Customers	Government	Society
Total benefits ($)	920	−218	701	−387	−630**	−1,018
Total costs ($)	−97	1,205***	1,108***	−34	185*	151
Net benefits ($)	1,017	−1,423***	−407	−353	−816***a	−1,169

NOTE: * statistically significant at the 90 percent confidence level for a two-tailed test; ** statistically significant at the 95 percent confidence level for a two-tailed test; *** statistically significant at the 99 percent confidence level for a two-tailed test.
a Total does not sum correctly because of rounding.
SOURCE: McConnell et al. (2006), p.114.

using administrative data. The evaluation results could be substantially different, however, once the data from the second survey with its much longer follow-up period are incorporated into the study. The final report would be critical to understanding the outcomes of the ITA Experiment.

RESEARCH AND EVALUATION STUDIES INITIATED IN 2007

In June 2007, the OMB intervened in the ETA's research and evaluation effort—something it had never done before. The Republican political leadership of the OMB put pressure on the Republican political leadership of the ETA, insisting that the ETA conduct and release certain research. Indeed, the OMB withheld appropriated ETA research and evaluation funds from the department at the beginning of program year 2007, pending compliance.

The OMB withheld the funds because it wanted the ETA to conduct three employment and training studies. Two of them were evaluations of the WIA program—a long-term "gold standard" experimental evaluation and a short-term quasiexperimental evaluation. The third was the completion of the evaluation of the ITA Experiment after a second-round follow-up survey. With this longer follow-up, the evaluation could take into consideration longer-term outcomes following completion of job training and obtain more accurate net impact results. This would allow the ETA to better assess the relative strengths of the three training voucher models that were tested.

Even after the department agreed to conduct these three projects, the OMB continuously monitored the projects during the quarterly performance budgeting process. By means of this process, the OMB compelled the department to report on its efforts to complete and publish the WIA short-run evaluation and to contract for and begin design of the longer-term experimental WIA evaluation. In November 2007, the department complied with the OMB requirement and reported on its planned 2008 accomplishments in its *2007 Performance and Accountability Report* (USDOL 2007), in which it reported the following: "Rigorous Evaluation of Major Job Training Programs: DOL is contracting [for] an independent study of program effectiveness—using administrative data—to be completed by 2008. Also in 2008, a more rigorous, seven-year evaluation will begin to determine WIA services' impact on employment and earnings outcomes for participants."

The department dutifully initiated the quasiexperimental WIA evaluation in late 2007, which was conducted by IMPAQ International. To meet the OMB deadline, the contractor raced to complete and publish the evaluation by December 2008, attempting to get administrative data from 25 states but ultimately collecting data from only 17. The evaluation used two comparison groups: 1) UI claimants and 2) UI claimants who received services from the ES; the comparison groups were selected using propensity score matching. The state workforce agencies were informed about the evaluation through Training and Employment Notice 22-07, issued on December 21, 2007. The draft final evaluation was completed (but not published) by the end of December 2008, and it was submitted to the OMB before the end of the year, at which time the department stated its intent to complete its review of the evaluation and publish it.

From the OMB's perspective, the quasiexperimental WIA evaluation was a stopgap effort until the department could conduct a random assignment WIA evaluation. In early 2008, the department developed a statement of work for the experimental evaluation. Following a competitive procurement, the contract was awarded to Mathematica Policy Research in June 2008. Mathematica also developed an evaluation plan and design to conduct the project in 30 randomly selected localities around the United States.

The third OMB project was the completion of the Individual Training Account Experiment evaluation. The OMB learned that the follow-up survey for the ITA experimental demonstration project had been conducted too early, at Bishop's direction. The department thus was forced to conduct a second follow-up survey and prepare a final evaluation report by 2009.

TRAINING PROGRAMS AND TRAINING PUBLIC POLICY

JTPA operated from 1982 through June 2000. The Clinton administration tried to replace JTPA with the failed Reemployment Act of

1994 (H.R. 4040) and the later failed CAREERS Act of 1995–1996 (H.R. 1617). In 1998, the Clinton administration and the Republican-controlled Congress reached a compromise and enacted WIA. WIA operated under its authorizing legislation until September 2003, when the statute expired, and it thereafter was extended through temporary continuing appropriations. Attempts to replace WIA persisted throughout the Bush administration, as the administration proposed WIA reauthorization with each new Congress in 2003, 2005, and 2007. In each case, the separate WIA component programs were to be consolidated with the ES, but there were also significant differences among the bills, and these differences mostly reflected overall policy initiatives of the Bush administration. None of these efforts succeeded, and the task of replacing WIA awaited President Obama and the 111th Congress.

The 2003 Proposals

Workforce Investment Act reauthorization

House consolidation bill. The Bush administration unveiled its first WIA reauthorization proposal on March 6, 2003. The House bill, H.R. 1261, was introduced on March 13, 2003, and closely reflected the administration proposal. The bill, sponsored by Rep. Howard P. McKeon (R-CA), passed quickly in the House on May 8 as the Workforce Reinvestment and Adult Education Act of 2003, with voting along party lines—220 to 204.

The bill would have consolidated several formula-funded adult programs—the WIA Adult and Dislocated Worker programs, the Employment Service, and Reemployment Services Grants. These programs would have been combined into one formula program to create a revised Adult Program. Ten percent of the funds appropriated for the new Adult Program would have been reserved by the secretary of labor for dislocated worker grants (currently called National Emergency Grants), demonstration projects, and technical assistance. Youth programs would have remained a separate funding stream.

ITAs would have remained the primary method of providing training funds to individuals in the Adult Program. These funds could only be paid to Eligible Training Providers, as determined by the One-Stop operators. The sequencing of core, intensive and training services would have been eliminated in some cases. Up to 10 percent of adult funding could have been used for incumbent worker training (Lordeman 2003).

The WIA reauthorization bill included Personal Reemployment Accounts (PRAs) in section 113. PRAs were also proposed in the Back to Work Act (H.R. 444), which also failed to be enacted.

Senate bill. The Senate bill, S. 1627, was introduced by Senators Michael Enzi (R-WY), Edward Kennedy (D-MA), Judd Gregg (R-NH), and Patty Murray (D-WA) on September 17, 2003. The bill retained the current structure of WIA and Wagner-Peyser Act programs. It included no consolidation or block granting provisions. The Senate bill had bipartisan support and reflected widespread state support for the current system, including by the governors of both parties. It passed the Senate. With diametrically opposed bills, the House and Senate were not able to reconcile the bills, and they died. The department had supported the House bill, had opposed the Senate bill, and was unwilling to support a compromise between the two. The Senate was strongly opposed to the department's proposal, so WIA reauthorization went nowhere.

Personal Reemployment Accounts

H.R. 444, the Back to Work Act, was introduced by Jon C. Porter (R-NV) on January 29, 2003, as a separate bill from H.R. 1261, the WIA reauthorization bill. Porter introduced President Bush's proposal to provide PRAs—"Back to Work Accounts" —in the amount of $3,000 to UI beneficiaries who were found to be likely to exhaust their UI benefits using WPRS's profiling mechanism and who were eligible for at least 20 weeks of UI benefits. The accounts could be used for a broad number of purposes: job training, child care, transportation, relocation services, housing assistance, career counseling, and other expenses to help in finding a job. If the eligible workers found employment within 13 weeks of becoming unemployed, they could retain the unspent portion of the PRA as a reemployment bonus. (See Chapter 10 for further discussion of reemployment bonuses.) It was introduced as a small part of the president's larger economic stimulus package; H.R. 444 authorized $3.6 billion to establish PRAs, which would serve at least 1.2 million unemployed workers. Individuals could only be eligible to receive a PRA once, and they would have to work with One-Stop staff, who would inform them of the limitations on the use of the funds, work with them to develop a personal reemployment plan, and approve the drawing down of the PRA funds.

The PRAs would be available only to dislocated workers who were eligible for UI and were likely to exhaust their UI benefits. They would not be available to workers who had quit their previous jobs, who were new entrants or reentrants to the labor force, or who had lost their previous jobs but did not have a history of strong labor force attachment. They also would not be available to workers who qualified to receive UI benefits but who were not likely to exhaust their UI benefits as determined by the worker profiling mechanism. Thus, PRAs would not be available to many workers who would be eligible to participate in the WIA Adult or Youth programs.

The 2005 Proposals

In 2005, the Bush administration again supported WIA reauthorization, this time in the 109th Congress, based on a proposal to consolidate adult programs. The administration's bill was introduced in the House as H.R. 27 and was enacted on March 7. It was similar to H.R. 1261 from the previous Congress.

The House bill would have retained a separate WIA Youth Program but would have consolidated the WIA Adult and Dislocated Worker programs and the Employment Service, as well as Reemployment Services Grants. Ten percent of the funds for adult workers would have been retained by the secretary of labor for dislocated worker grants, demonstration projects, and technical assistance. National programs, such as the Job Corps and programs for migrant and seasonal farm workers, Native Americans, and veterans would have been retained. The bill would have modified the sequencing of core, intensive, and training services in some cases. It still would have provided training, primarily through ITAs.

Along with the consolidation of the adult programs, the other major controversy regarding the House bill was that it would have allowed religious organizations to operate job training programs and to take applicants' religious beliefs into consideration when hiring workers to provide these job training services.

The first Senate bill, S. 9, introduced by Senator Enzi, was nearly identical to the one passed in 2003, S. 1627. A new bill, S. 1021, was introduced by Senators Enzi and Kennedy on May 12, 2005. It was based on S. 9. The Senate incorporated S. 1021, as amended, into H.R. 27 and passed its version of H.R. 27 on June 29, 2006.

The Senate bill would not have consolidated the adult programs, continuing separate programs for WIA Adult and Dislocated Worker programs, the ES, and Reemployment Service Grants. Like the House bill, it would have modified the sequencing of services and retained ITAs, although it would have renamed them Career Scholarship Accounts. The Senate bill, however, did not contain the provision that would have allowed religious organizations to consider religion in hiring workers to provide job training services for department-funded programs.

The House and Senate took no further action after passing their separate versions of H.R. 27. Once again, they could not reconcile the differences between their bills, and the legislation died (Lordeman 2005; Naughton and Lordeman 2007). Once again, the department supported the House bill and was unwilling to compromise to come to agreement with the Senate.

The American Competitiveness Initiative and Career Advancement Accounts

Midway through the 109th Congress, the Bush administration changed course on workforce programs. In his 2006 State of the Union message, President Bush announced his American Competitiveness Initiative (ACI). Its purpose was to strengthen the U.S. economy in its ability to compete with other nations. It planned to commit $5.9 billion in FY 2007 and more than $136 billion over 10 years to invest in research and development, strengthen education and training, and encourage entrepreneurship and innovation. Training was one of six new initiatives. The workforce development system was expected to provide "job training that affords more workers and manufacturers the opportunity to improve their skills and better compete in the 21st century" (State of the Union Letter 2006). More specifically, Bush proposed in his initiative to "provide more flexible training to workers" by offering "training opportunities to some 800,000 workers annually, more than tripling the number trained under the current system" (State of the Union Press Release 2006).

Because it had no funding to back it up, the ACI served a political agenda. The workforce initiative was to be funded by taking existing WIA funds, leaving little to maintain the current system, and thus starving the existing public workforce development system. The training component of the American Competitiveness Initiative was called Career Advancement Accounts (CAAs). CAAs were a recycled form of training voucher that differed from past vouchers in that there would be no assessment or counseling whatsoever before awarding the vouchers. The CAA vouchers would consume 75 percent of the consolidated WIA-ES funds. Only an additional 3 percent of total funding would be available for administration. If ACI were enacted, state workforce agencies would be encouraged to take Internet applications, assess the applications without collecting further information, and then allocate funds and issue voucher awards. Thus, 78 percent of the current workforce development system funding would be taken for CAAs, and the state workforce development system would have to survive on the remaining 22 percent of its previous funding level, which would have proven catastrophic for the system. Fortunately for the workforce development system, ACI was not enacted.

December 20, 2006, Regulatory Initiative

On December 20, 2006, the department published a Notice of Proposed Rule Making in the *Federal Register*, which tried to alter WIA and Wagner-Peyser Act programs, but the department was prevented from doing so by the new Democratic-controlled Congress. The department initiated the rule-making after the Republican-controlled 109th Congress had failed to reauthorize the WIA and after the Republicans lost control of both houses of Congress in the November 2006 election. (See Chapter 6.) It was clear that the Bush administration had not been able to enact the type of WIA reauthorization bill it wanted in the 109th Congress.

The 110th Congress

If a Republican-controlled Congress had rejected the Bush administration's WIA reauthorization proposals in 2003 and 2005, a Democratic-controlled Congress certainly was not going to accept its 2007 proposal. In April 2007, Secretary Chao sent a department bill directly to Congress without White House review, once again recom-

mending consolidation of job training and employment service programs and making CAAs the heart of her proposal. The Chao proposal
went nowhere. No hearings were held on the proposal, either in the
House of Representatives or in the Senate.

After a considerable delay, on October 4, 2007, Rep. McKeon introduced H.R. 3747, the Workforce Investment Improvement Act of 2007.
It again proposed to consolidate WIA Adult and Dislocated Worker
programs with the ES and repeal the Wagner-Peyser Act. Controver-
sially, it would again allow religious organizations providing workforce
development services to hire workers exclusively from members of
their own religious faith. On October 23, the bill was referred to the
Subcommittee on Workforce Protections. No further action was taken
on the bill. Thus, over a six-year period, under both Republican and
Democratic Congresses, the Bush administration's approach to reauthorizing WIA had proven to be a political failure. Congress and stakeholders had rejected every attempt to consolidate, block-grant, or cash
out the public workforce system.

RELATIONSHIP OF WIA REAUTHORIZATION PROPOSALS TO RESEARCH FINDINGS

Bush administration training proposals were based on a misrepresentation of the research findings. The Bush administration sought to
justify CAAs based on the results of the ITA Experiment by misrepre-
senting its findings. Findings from the ITA Experiment were presented
to departmental career and political staff (Perez-Johnson et al. 2004;
McConnell et al. 2006). These results were used to justify the CAAs
because the free choice model had resulted in more training than the
other two models, and the report had not indicated that the benefit-cost
results were any worse. These findings were interpreted as justification
for not providing assessment and counseling before giving out training
vouchers.

But the interpretation of the free choice model findings was erroneous: the evaluation found that unemployed workers received a significant amount of counseling and assessment (an average of five hours)
before they were offered a training voucher. After they were offered

a voucher, they were more likely to start training, if they were not required to receive further counseling (McConnell et al. 2006, p. 26). Thus, the report revealed that workers may have made similar training choices after they received the training voucher, whether they received additional counseling or not.

The Bush administration made several claims in marketing its new proposals and in criticizing components of the existing public workforce system. However, the evidence did not support these seven claims:

Claim 1: Most of the cost of One-Stops is from wasteful and excess administrative overhead. The declining budget for running the One-Stops resulted in state and local workforce agencies doing the only thing they could do to deal with more customers while employing fewer staff: they substituted automated self-service for staff-assisted core and intensive services. The conversion of the public workforce system between the mid-1990s and the present to self-service tools does not represent excessive administrative overhead; it represents a substitution of capital for labor at a time of declining nominal resources and huge losses of frontline staff.

Claim 2: The Employment Service programs are duplicative of the Workforce Investment Act programs and should be eliminated. In fact, the ES and WIA programs are complementary. The ES provides WIA-type core and intensive services in most states and localities, while the WIA provides intensive and training services (Barnow and King 2005).

Claim 3: Only training is a worthwhile service. This claim ignores the extensive research literature on the effectiveness of the One-Stops and the ES in providing referrals to job openings, providing job search assistance, and administering the UI work test (O'Leary 2006).

Claim 4: A Free Choice training voucher model can be implemented without providing any counseling services. The Free Choice model contained in the Bush administration's CAA proposals was a misrepresentation of the Free Choice model tested in the ITA Experiment. In that experiment, individuals were not required to engage in additional counseling after they were offered a training voucher, but they received an average of five hours of counseling before they were offered a training voucher (McConnell et al. 2006, p. xxvi).

Claim 5: Short-term training is the answer. The WIA reauthorization proposals of the Bush administration would have provided vouchers that were likely to have been used largely for short-term training. Short-term training has been found to be less effective than long-term training or education (Heckman, LaLonde, and Smith 1999; LaLonde 1995).

Claim 6: Targeting is not necessary. The Bush administration's training proposal did not target based on need or likely success of training. Career Advancement Accounts, for example, would have been awarded based on limited information received from Internet applications. Demand for training funds would have greatly exceeded fund availability. Each year's funding would have soon been exhausted. Fund disbursement most likely would have been conducted on a first come, first served basis. CAAs would have ignored the fact that training as currently constituted is more cost-effective for some groups than for others (Barnow and King 2005; King 2004; LaLonde 1995).

Claim 7: The type of training provided does not matter. The Bush administration would not have provided any guidance about what kind of training to take. Training voucher recipients could have chosen high-return or low-return training programs. However, research shows that training targeted to fields such as math, science, and health services is most cost-effective. Such targeting is needed to have training succeed (Jacobson, LaLonde, and Sullivan 2002).

CONCLUSIONS

- Job search assistance appears to be more cost-effective than training, and, if WIA resources cannot be expanded significantly, existing resources should be transferred from training to job search assistance (LaLonde 1995).

- The conversion of local workforce offices to One-Stop Career Centers with universal access for all workers and the requirement and encouragement of having partners locate in these centers has put enormous demands and strains on these local offices. The One-Stop initiative was expected to have been accompanied by a substantial increase in the funding for employment and training programs. In the absence of funding increases, the state workforce agencies cut costs to serve the large flow of participants. The result has been heavy investment in automated resource rooms and the provision of self-service tools, while training is infrequently provided to participants and tends to be low-cost and of short duration.

- The Clinton administration briefly increased funding to accompany the One-Stop initiative and the proposed Reemployment Act of 1994. When the Democrats lost control of Congress in 1994, funding increases ended. Funding levels for WIA and ES programs were stable in nominal terms in the second half of the 1990s but then declined between 2001 and 2008.

- The decision to make job training vouchers a key component of the WIA training system was made based on little experience under the prior employment and training programs and without much evaluation (Barnow 2000). Training vouchers were implemented as part of the WIA program more because of ideology than evidence. It is not clear that training vouchers under WIA have been successful. On the other hand, ITAs using the Informed Choice model look very much like the training system that was used during the JTPA years, and thus ITAs do not represent a substantial change from the past.

- Effective job training should not be offered to workers without providing considerable staff-assisted employment services. Workers need guidance in whether to take training, what kind of training to take, and where to take the training. In the ITA Experiment, the procedures of the participating sites met this criterion. Counselors provided an average of five hours of counseling before training vouchers were offered to workers (McConnell et al. 2006).

- The Career Advancement Account proposal was fundamentally flawed. It would have offered training vouchers to workers over the Internet with no counseling. No research evidence exists that supports providing training vouchers without career counseling. The Bush administration would have used CAAs to slash the funding of One-Stop centers while creating an ineffective block grant program. As justification for the CAA initiative, advocates pointed to positive aspects of the Free Choice offer in the ITA Experiment that provided little or no counseling *after* the voucher was offered. The Bush administration's explanation of the Free Choice model, however, ignored the need for counseling *before* participants received the training voucher offer (McConnell et al. 2006).

- The department should pursue new program models for out-of-school youth and conduct a series of demonstration projects to test their effectiveness. Among the interventions that should be explored is a program of employment bonuses paid to out-of-school youth who remain employed for one year. Employment bonuses were successful when tested as part of the Youth Offender Grants in St. Paul, Minnesota, and West Palm Beach, Florida, but they were not tested rigorously using experimental methods (Jenks, MacGillivray, and Needels 2006).

- Policymakers should have more realistic expectations about the provision of training. Given the historic limitations on public funding for job training, it does not appear that both universal access to One-Stops and adequate funding for skill and occupational training can be achieved solely under WIA. Greater financial support is needed if long-term training is to be provided. Greater funding needs to be made available, either through a reauthorized WIA program or through another agency such as the Department of Education, with considerable training authority given to community colleges.

- Long-term training cannot be provided to experienced workers without also providing support services. The key to increased participation is income support throughout the period of participation in training. It may be valuable for policymakers to review the 10-year experience of MDTA, where 1.1 million disadvantaged and nondisadvantaged individuals completed training (Mangum 1973, p. 42), receiving a stipend in the form of UI-type weekly allowances.

Notes

1. I attended a small meeting of workforce researchers and practitioners at Johns Hopkins University several years after the publication of the JTPA Evaluation. During the meeting, an ardent supporter of youth programs accused Larry Orr, one of the principal authors of the evaluation, saying, "You killed the Youth Program!" Orr replied, "I prefer to think that I saved the Adult Program."
2. Eric Johnson, in a conversation with the author, 2003.
3. In this chapter the terms "free choice" and "informed choice" have been used in the discussion of vouchers in accordance with the workforce development literature. In the volume *Vouchers and the Provision of Public Services* (Steuerle et al. 2000), the terms "individual choice" and "structured choice" are used.
4. This approach sounds a lot like the concept of "Flexicurity," first advocated in Western Europe at about the same time. The difference is that when flexible labor market policy was implemented first in Denmark and later in other European countries, the policy was accompanied by much larger investments in employment and training programs—collectively called Active Labor Market Policy (ALMP)—than were provided in the United States.
5. Doug Holl of the WIA Dislocated Office wanted to conduct the ITA/ETA Demonstration, while I wanted to conduct the ITA Experiment. The result was an agreement on our parts to conduct both.
6. In program year 2003, the WIASRD report found that training without ITAs occurred in a substantial minority of cases. For the WIA Adult program, ITAs represent 55.0 percent of all training services, with Pell Grant recipients at 9.9 percent and non-ITA, non–Pell Grant recipients at 35.1 percent. For WIA dislocated workers, ITAs represented 65.9 percent; Pell Grants 4.8 percent; and non-ITA, non–Pell Grants 29.3 percent.
7. The names of the three options in the ITA Experiment are: 1) Maximum Customer Choice, 2) Guided Customer Choice, and 3) Structured Customer Choice, and they correspond to Free, Informed, and Directed Choice, respectively.
8. The results of this second evaluation are not yet known.

8
The Self-Employment Experiments and the Self-Employment Assistance Program

with Jon Messenger[1]

The U.S. Department of Labor sponsored two self-employment assistance (SEA) experiments in Massachusetts and Washington states during the late 1980s and early 1990s. This chapter examines these two experiments and the policy lessons learned from them. It discusses how the experiments led to the enactment of the federal SEA legislation. It also reviews the development and operations of the SEA programs that today operate in seven states.

Since the enactment of federal legislation in December 1993, states have been able to incorporate SEA programs into their unemployment insurance (UI) systems. SEA programs permit an exception to the UI work-search rule requiring UI claimants to search for a job in wage and salary employment each week, although other eligibility requirements for collecting regular UI benefits are maintained. Under the SEA program, unemployed workers who are eligible for UI can start their own businesses instead of searching for wage and salary employment. While they are starting their small businesses, they can collect SEA benefits in lieu of UI benefits in the same amount and for the same duration as their regular UI benefits. They receive entrepreneurial counseling and training to help them establish successful microenterprises.

The SEA experiments began in 1987, at a time when microenterprise and microlending were not well known or well regarded as employment and economic development strategies. It was only in the 1990s that microenterprise development became more popular, and it was not until 2006 that Muhammad Yunus was recognized by the Nobel Committee for his pioneering efforts in this area. Yunus and the Grameen

Bank, which he started in Bangladesh, shared the Nobel Peace Prize because the committee believed that lasting peace requires the reduction in poverty that can be facilitated through microcredit programs. In the United States, microenterprise is an alternative employment strategy available to American workers. In addition to the availability of the SEA program, microenterprise training is provided through state WIA programs.

Microenterprise Creation and Self-Employment Assistance

Most dislocated workers want to return to wage and salary employment. Self-employment, however, is a way to promote the reemployment of a small percentage of UI recipients. Establishment of individuals in self-employment is also an important subset of business start-ups. The growing recognition of both the contribution of microenterprises to the creation of employment opportunities and the relatively modest financial and managerial requirements of self-employment have generated interest in using self-employment as a tool for assisting unemployed workers to return to work. Unlike other services to assist the unemployed to obtain jobs, self-employment assistance is designed to promote direct job creation for unemployed workers—to empower the unemployed to create their own jobs by starting small business ventures. These microenterprises are typically sole proprietorships with one or at most a few employees, including the owner/operator.

While the primary goal of self-employment assistance is direct job creation for the unemployed worker, the microenterprises started by these individuals may also generate additional jobs that can be filled by other dislocated workers. Thus, a self-employment assistance program for dislocated workers provides an opportunity to integrate labor market policy and economic development policy in a synergistic relationship, helping dislocated workers to return to work while simultaneously providing a modest boost to economic growth and job creation in their communities.

In addition, an increasing number of dislocated workers are now coming from professional, technical, and managerial occupations—occupations that make them particularly well-suited for self-employment. In the Washington State demonstration, 37 percent of all participants came from professional, technical, and managerial occupations. In the Massachusetts demonstration, 45 percent of participants came from these occupations.

Encouraging self-employment is not a new workforce policy. It was a component of workforce development plans before SEA came on the scene. Indeed, self-employment programs were part of the Job Training Partnership Act (JTPA) programs. Entrepreneurial training was an authorized use of JTPA formula funds provided to the states for both disadvantaged and dislocated workers, and many states made use of that authority. Discretionary funding had also been provided for entrepreneurial training by the secretary of labor. For example, in 1986 8 of 90 dislocated worker projects funded from the JTPA Title III reserve account included an entrepreneurial training component (Wandner and Messenger 1992, p. 13). Similarly, today entrepreneurial training is one of nine types of training services that are allowable under section 134(d)(4)(D) of the Workforce Investment Act (WIA).

European SEA Programs

The impetus for the SEA program in the United States came from the development and adoption of self-employment programs for the unemployed in 17 other industrial nations. Self-employment programs began in 1979 in France, which adopted a lump-sum payment approach to provide capital to start a small business. In 1983, Great Britain started a program that provided periodic payments during the start-up period for workers starting their own businesses. Over the next decade, 15 other industrial countries adopted programs, following either the French or the British approach (Orr et al. 1994). These self-employment programs were designed to help unemployed workers "create their own jobs" by starting small businesses, usually microenterprises. Virtually all of the Western industrialized nations adopted self-employment assistance programs for the unemployed during the 1980s.

The Western European self-employment programs for unemployed workers provided the inspiration and key design components for the U.S. self-employment experiments. The two U.S. experiments followed the approaches of the French and British programs, which also were the models followed by other industrial nations. The French self-employment program provided eligible individuals with a single, lump-sum payment for business start-up capital; the five countries of Luxembourg, Norway, Portugal, Spain, and Sweden followed the French model. The British program provided eligible individuals with biweekly payments to supplement their earnings during the first year of business operations. Ten countries—Australia, Belgium, Canada, Denmark, Finland, Greece, Ireland, Italy, the Netherlands, and West Germany—followed the British model. Both of these programs also provided participants with business services, such as business training and counseling advice—although the availability of these services varied greatly by locality (Scott 1992, pp. 244–252).

U.S. policymakers gained an understanding of how these self-employment programs work in three ways. First, the German Marshall Fund encouraged American consideration of self-employment assistance programs by sponsoring three study tours for American visitors to observe microenterprises and microenterprise policy and programs in Western Europe. Second, the Organisation for Economic Co-operation and Development (OECD) studied microenterprise as an employment and economic development policy and disseminated its findings through its publications and through its sponsorship of meetings and briefings. Finally, the staff of the Corporation for Enterprise Development studied the European programs and promoted the adoption of self-employment programs in the United States (Orr et al. 1994).

While designing the U.S. self-employment experiments in 1988, staff from the USDOL, state workforce agencies, and a research contractor participated in the third German Marshall Fund–supported study tour and visited France, Great Britain, and Sweden to observe firsthand the self-employment programs in those countries.[2] The French and British programs were examined as models of how unemployed workers could become self-employed business owners. The Swedish program was examined because of its efficient and effective administration. The designers of the demonstration projects drew on the experience of these countries in adapting the self-employment concept to the U.S. environment. Both the French and British models were tested in the United States. Administrative procedures used in the experiments made use of lessons learned in Britain and Sweden.

Today SEA programs—called start-up incentives in Europe—are more prevalent and tend to be larger in the European Union than in the United States. Start-up incentives provide funds to individuals in the form of lump-sum grants, periodic payments, or loans, and may include entrepreneurial counseling and training. For 2004, start-up programs were reported to exist in 20 of the 25 European Union member countries (European Commission 2006). Start-up programs remain particularly popular among the early European Union members of Western Europe. Fourteen of these countries report having such programs—Austria, Belgium, Finland, France, Germany, Greece, Ireland, Italy, Luxembourg, Norway, Portugal, Spain, Sweden, and the United Kingdom. The program has also been adopted by six of the new European Union member countries in Eastern Europe—Bulgaria, the Czech Republic, Estonia, Hungary, Lithuania, and Slovakia. Among the new members, these programs have been initiated, in part, as a policy to encourage the transition to a market economy. The great majority of the countries that participate in these programs have more participants than the United States. In 2003, the largest users in terms of numbers of participants were Germany (237,253), Spain (93,033), and France (51,146). Of the countries reporting program activity, participants in these programs range from 0.1 to 12.9 percent of the participants in their UI programs. Compared to the United States, European participants are a much larger proportion of UI participants in every country with a program, reaching 12.9 percent in Germany, 9.5 percent in Ireland, and 4.9 percent in Italy. Nevertheless, most programs amounted to less than 2 percent of UI expenditures (Table 8.1). By contrast, there were only 1,342 individuals entering the U.S. Self-Employment Assistance program in 2003, representing a tiny fraction of 1 percent of all UI claimants.

Germany has a strong commitment to promoting self-employment by unemployed workers. Programs associated with the German unemployment compensation program have more participants than any other European country. One program—the "transition benefit" ("Überbrückungsgeld")—was introduced in 1986 to promote the transition from unemployment to self-employment. The program looked more like the U.S. Self-Employment Assistance program in that it made payments for six months in the amount of the monthly UI benefit amount, but it added to that amount a lump-sum social insurance contribution for new firms.

The second program—the "business foundation grant" ("Existenzgrundungszuschuss")—was added in 2003. It was more needs-based and provided benefits for up to three years, but only to workers whose annual wage income was less than 25,000 euros. Benefits were a fixed amount for all beneficiaries, and they declined over time, from EUR

Table 8.1 Number of Participants in Unemployment Insurance and in Start-Up Incentives in European Union Countries, 2004

Country	UI participants	Start-up participants	Start-up/UI (%)
Austria	591,498	3,952	0.67
Belgium	575,093	517	0.09
Bulgaria	—	—	—
Czech Republic	169,109	6,002	3.55
Estonia	51,052	287	0.56
Finland	126,098	2,643	2.10
France	2,261,436	51,146	2.26
Germany	1,842,405	237,253	12.88
Greece	—	—	—
Hungary	109,654	5,203	4.74
Ireland	71,884	6,855	9.54
Italy	277,319	13,584	4.90
Lithuania	—	—	—
Luxembourg	7,744	15	0.19
Norway	112,918	262	0.23
Portugal	184,859	1,686	0.91
Slovakia	74,750	2,958	3.96
Sweden	206,116	5,601	2.72
Spain	2,358,392	93,033	3.94
United Kingdom	2,458,030	3,492	0.14

NOTE: — = not available.

Participants. The measure of participants used above is dependent on the availability of data. The "stock" (S) was generally used since it is more frequently available; it is a measure of participants as an annual average stock. In some cases, the stock measure was not available (or unreasonably small), so the number of "entrants" (E) was used; "entrants are participants joining the measure during the year (inflow)." See below for usage by country.

Unemployment insurance. This consists of "full unemployment benefits" (line 8.1 of the publication) that are considered to be unemployment insurance rather than unemployment assistance programs (or other means-tested programs).

Short-time compensation (STC). Called short-time work or partial unemployment benefits (line 8.2). Line 8.2 includes compensation for formal short-time working arrangements and/or intermittent work schedules, irrespective of their cause, and where the employer/employee relationship continues.

Start-up incentives. Include loans or grants to individuals (line 7). Include only transfers to individuals, not to employers.

SOURCE: European Commission (2006).

600 per month the first year, to EUR 360 per month the second year, and finally to EUR 240 per month the last year. Together Germany spent EUR 2.7 billion on the two programs in 2004 (Table 8.2), $3.3 billion at the exchange rate in effect in the middle of that year (*European Employment Observatory Review* 2005).[3] This compares to only $5.1 billion spent in the United States on the WIA and Job Corps programs in FY 2004.[4]

The primary goal of Germany's two self-employment programs was employment rather than economic development. The programs sought to create jobs for the entrepreneurs, with some additional jobs created by the entrepreneurs' new businesses. This new employment could either be higher income jobs or "marginal jobs with low-volume (low-income) self-employment . . . in the form of 'mini-jobs'" (*European Employment Observatory Review* 2005). The German government's emphasis, thus, was on reducing high levels of unemployment, whether it be with jobs that fully employed workers or jobs that kept them underemployed.

In July 2006, the two self-employment programs were combined into a start-up grant ("Grundungszuschuss") to cover living expenses and social insurance contributions for the first few months of self-employment. The start-up grant is available to unemployed workers who still have entitlement to at least 90 days of unemployment benefits. To qualify for the grant, applicants must show that they have the skills to carry out the businesses they plan to start. They also have to produce a letter to the employment agency from a knowledgeable body—such as a chamber of commerce, guild, industry association, or bank—that the proposed new business is potentially sustainable.[5]

The start-up grant is paid in two phases. For the first nine months, UI claimants receive grants equal to their unemployment benefit levels (60 percent of claimants' last net income for single claimants and 67 percent for workers with families) to cover living expenses plus EUR 300 a month for social insurance payments. The monthly EUR 300 for social insurance payments can be paid for an additional six months if the claimants can show that they are operating their businesses full time. Self-employment programs grew steadily from 2000 to 2004: the number of individuals receiving funding rose from 92,953 to 351,673. From 2005 through 2007 the programs declined because of stricter requirements to qualify and because of lower unemployment rates.[6]

Table 8.2 Entrants, Participants, and Expenditures for German Self-Employment Programs, 2000–2007

	Entrants				Expenditures	
Year	Transition benefits	Business foundation grant	Start-up grant	Total entrants	Expenditures (millions of euros)	Expenditures per participant (euros)
2000	92,953			92,953	750.4	8,100
2001	96,385			96,385	804.6	8,300
2002	125,096			125,096	1,005.9	8,000
2003	158,820	95,198		254,018	1,681.3	6,700
2004	183,497	168,176		351,673	2,726.8	7,800
2005	156,888	91,020		247,908	3,200.3	12,900
2006	108,398	42,813	33,569	184,780	—	—
2007	176		125,919	126,095	—	—

NOTE: Data fields are blank for the years before programs began or after ending, indicating "not applicable." — = not available. Transition benefits were also known as the bridging allowance. The business foundation grant was also known as the start-up subsidy or "Me Inc."
SOURCE: Wiessner (2008).

In Germany, a total of 850,000 individuals became self-employed in 2007. Close to 20 percent of them moved from unemployment to self-employment. Thus, the start-up grant plays a significant role in increasing business start-ups. An evaluation of the German self-employment programs showed high rates of business survival. After two years, 70 to 80 percent of the businesses were still active, while only 7 to 13 percent of participants were unemployed.[7]

THE SELF-EMPLOYMENT ASSISTANCE EXPERIMENTS

The Self-Employment Assistance Experiments Begin

In 1987, Congress appropriated an additional $5 million to the Employment and Training Administration's (ETA) research budget to conduct a series of experiments to help reemploy dislocated workers. In January 1987 three ETA staff members met to discuss how best to allocate these research funds. They were Ray Uhalde, the ETA's policy and research deputy director; Carolyn Golding, director of the Unemployment Insurance Service; and I, who was then director of UI research. We discussed whether to proceed with a self-employment demonstration project. Given the lack of precedent for such a program in the United States, Uhalde and Golding doubted that SEA could work. Expecting a low take-up rate by UI claimants and noting the high failure rate of small businesses, Uhalde believed that prospects for success of a self-employment experiment were low.[8] I also was uncertain about the efficacy of SEA in the United States, but argued for testing the approach.

Despite the ETA's reservations, in February 1987 I received approval to test the effectiveness of self-employment programs for unemployed workers. From nearly a dozen states that responded to an August 1987 solicitation to test the French lump-sum-payment SEA model, Washington State was selected as the site in which to conduct the experiment. A grant agreement between Washington and the USDOL was signed in September 1987.[9] Designed to test the cost-effectiveness of the self-employment option for unemployed workers who were eligible to collect UI, the Washington project offered one-time lump-sum payments for initial start-up and capitalization of new business ventures.

Before the Washington self-employment experiment began, however, Congress directed the USDOL to conduct a second SEA demonstration. Then-congressman Ron Wyden (D-OR) proposed that the department conduct an experiment to test the feasibility of providing self-employment assistance in the form of periodic payments to unemployed workers in three states. The UI program would be authorized to pay this periodic self-employment allowance in lieu of regular weekly or biweekly UI payments (Orr et al. 1994).

In December 1987, Congress enacted Section 9152 of the Omnibus Budget Reconciliation Act of 1987 ("Demonstration Program to Provide Self-Employment Allowances to Eligible Individuals"), which authorized the Department of Labor to proceed with self-employment demonstration projects in three additional states. There were several notable aspects of this legislation. First, Congress mandated that the demonstration be conducted as a classical experiment in which workers were randomly assigned to treatment and control groups. Second, Congress specified that the demonstration use the British approach of providing periodic payments to UI claimants starting up small businesses. Third, Congress required that the self-employment allowances paid to treatment group members be funded from the state accounts in the federal Unemployment Trust Fund. Thus, the demonstration would be funded out of existing trust funds, rather than through new appropriations. Finally, the demonstrations had to have a neutral effect on the federal budget. If the operation of the demonstration project resulted in "excess cost" above the amount the state would have paid out in regular UI benefits, the state would have to pay that amount into its own account in the Unemployment Trust Fund (Orr et al. 1994; Wandner and Messenger 1992).

Some members of Congress were skeptical about a self-employment demonstration and did not want to dedicate any new funding to the project. Enactment of the demonstration project was conditioned on the "excess cost" provision. The provision was imposed on the Wyden amendment because, in its absence, the amendment would have imposed new federal budgetary costs, which would have had to be offset with equal cost reductions under existing federal budget rules. However, this provision had serious consequences for the self-employment demonstration design. It also had an adverse effect on state participation because of the risk of repayment costs. On the other hand, it made it more likely that permanent SEA legislation would be enacted if it could be shown that an SEA program would either be cost-neutral or have a positive impact on the federal budget (Orr et al. 1994).

Although Congress did not appropriate funds to carry out the design, administration, and evaluation of the Wyden demonstration, the department—with some reluctance—proceeded with this second self-employment demonstration project. The department competitively selected three states (Massachusetts, Minnesota, and Oregon)[10] to participate in this project as well as a research contractor (Abt Associates, with Battelle Institute as a subcontractor) to design, monitor, and evaluate the projects in these three states and in Washington State. The projects were designed through the cooperative efforts of the participating states, the ETA, and the research contractors. The project designs and the operational procedures were informed by the study tour of self-employment assistance programs in Great Britain, France, and Sweden.[11] When it was time to implement the project, however, Minnesota and Oregon dropped out after reviewing the project design and facing the possibility of having to pay excess costs from their own state funds.

Design of the U.S. Self-Employment Assistance Experiments

Ultimately the department sponsored experimental demonstration projects in Washington and Massachusetts. These projects, called the Unemployment Insurance (UI) Self-Employment Demonstration Projects, were designed to assist UI recipients interested in self-employment in creating their own jobs by starting a business venture. In both Washington and Massachusetts, the projects were jointly operated by the state employment security and economic development agencies.

The self-employment experiments tested packages of self-employment assistance for UI recipients on permanent layoff; these packages comprised a combination of "self-employment allowances" and business development services consisting of business training, counseling, technical assistance, and peer support. The Massachusetts experiment also added an additional targeting process designed to identify those UI recipients considered likely to exhaust their UI benefits. The employment security agencies offered and paid the self-employment allowances, while the economic development agencies and local service providers delivered the business development services. The Washington demonstration tested financial assistance in the form of lump-sum payments, while the Massachusetts demonstration tested biweekly payments equal to an individual's regular UI benefits.

All costs of the Washington demonstration project were funded by department research resources. The Massachusetts demonstration project allowance payments, however, were funded from the Massachusetts state account in the federal Unemployment Trust Fund, while state funds were used to provide business development services for project participants. Project operations in Washington State took place between 1989 and 1991. Operations in the Massachusetts demonstration took place during three distinct enrollment periods, the first of which began in 1990; the third and final enrollment period was completed in early 1993.

Both of the self-employment experiments included a sequence of intake activities that served to screen out those UI recipients with insufficient interest in or motivation for self-employment. For example, UI claimants interested in self-employment were required to attend an initial orientation session, which provided them with information about the demonstration and a reality check about the pros and cons of self-employment. Individuals who attended this session then had to submit a timely, complete, and acceptable application to be eligible for selection into the projects. Thus, out of a large number of UI beneficiaries eligible to participate in the self-employment demonstrations, only a small percentage—3.5 percent in Washington State and 1.9 percent in Massachusetts—actually completed the intake activities and qualified for selection into the projects (Benus et al. 1995).

Implementation Process Results of the SEA Experiments

Table 8.3 shows basic implementation process results of the Massachusetts and Washington Self-Employment Demonstration Projects. The top line of the table indicates the total number of UI claimants who were identified as being in the target population in the Washington and Massachusetts demonstrations. All of these individuals received an invitation to attend an orientation session about the project in their respective state. As the table indicates, there was a precipitous

Table 8.3 Participation in UI Self-Employment Demonstration Activities

	Massachusetts	Washington
Invited to orientation (target population)	63,921	42,350
Attended orientation	2,658	3,167
% of invitees	4.2	7.5
Submitted application	1,515	1,932
% of attendees	57	61
% of invitees	2.4	4.5
Randomly assigned	1,222	1,507
% of applicants	80	78
% of invitees	1.9	3.5
Treatment group	614	755
Control group	608	752
Attended initial training session	573	640
% of treatment group	93	85
Attended all training modules (WA) or all biweekly training workshops (MA)	305	630
% of treatment group	50	83
Attended one or more business counseling sessions	569	529
% of treatment group	93	70
Mean hours of business counseling received, per person	7.5	1.5
Received lump sum payment		451
% of treatment group		60

NOTE: Blank = not applicable.
SOURCE: Benus et al. (1995).

decline at the very first step in the process of self-screening based on individuals' interest in and motivation for self-employment. Of those individuals invited to attend a project orientation, only 4.2 percent in Massachusetts, and 7.5 percent in Washington, actually attended an orientation session to learn about the demonstration. This suggests that self-employment only appeals to a relatively small percentage of the unemployed.

The orientation session and application process provided another significant screen for winnowing the target population. Of those individuals who attended an orientation session, only 57 percent in Massachusetts, and 61 percent in Washington, actually submitted an application to participate in the demonstration. It is reasonable to attribute this result to the design of these two self-screening steps. The orientation session included a strong reality check for interested individuals by emphasizing the very real risks—as well as the potential rewards—associated with self-employment. The application was, in essence, a self-assessment tool designed to force individuals to think through some of the difficult issues involved in starting a business (e.g., who the likely customers would be for the business) and thus make them think hard about whether self-employment was a realistic option for them.

As a result of this self-screening process, the vast majority of claimants who submitted an application were accepted for random assignment into the demonstration or a control group—80 percent in Massachusetts and 78 percent in Washington. The remainder of applicants were screened out of the demonstration because they submitted unacceptable applications. The reasons for rejection of applications included submitting late or incomplete applications, and business ideas that were either too vague or of a prohibited type (e.g., pyramid schemes, political organizations). However, applications were not evaluated based on the likelihood of success of the business. This was considered to be the individual's responsibility. In total, 614 individuals in Massachusetts and 755 individuals in Washington were randomly selected into the treatment group for their respective demonstrations, and an equivalent number were assigned to control groups.

Both the Massachusetts and Washington self-employment experiments provided selected individuals with a series of business training seminars, as well as unlimited individual business counseling and technical assistance for the duration of their participation in the demonstration. Both projects also offered participants some form of peer support, through regular Entrepreneur Club meetings in Washington and less formal networking opportunities in Massachusetts. Attendance at all the business training seminars plus at least one counseling session was mandatory (unless specifically waived by the business counselor because of one's previous experience). Development of a business plan was also mandatory, although this process was more formalized in Washington than in Massachusetts because a formal business plan was a requirement for receipt of a lump-sum payment. The peer support activities were entirely voluntary in both projects.

The Washington demonstration provided UI recipients selected for the treatment group with lump-sum self-employment allowances to serve as business start-up capital. These payments were equal to the remainder of their entitlement for UI benefits. To obtain the payment, Washington participants were required to complete a series of five milestones: 1) complete four business training modules, 2) develop an acceptable business plan, 3) open a business bank account, 4) satisfy all licensing requirements applicable to the business, and 5) obtain adequate financing (the amount of start-up funding identified as necessary in the business plan, taking into account funds available from the lump-sum payment).

The Massachusetts demonstration provided treatment group members with biweekly payments, termed self-employment allowance payments, equal to their regular UI benefits, to supplement their earnings while they were planning and establishing their new businesses. To continue receiving these biweekly payments, Massachusetts participants had to participate in a total of seven required training seminars—an initial one-day training session on starting a business (the "Enterprise Seminar") and a series of six half-day workshops on specific business-related topics (e.g., marketing)—plus at least one business counseling session. Massachusetts participants also were required to work full-time on activities related to starting their businesses and to submit a written self-certification to that effect.

As Table 8.3 indicates, the majority of treatment group members attended the required business training sessions. Eighty-five percent of project participants in Washington completed the first training module, and 93 percent of Massachusetts participants completed an initial training session (the Enterprise Seminar). A much higher percentage of individuals attended all training sessions in Washington (83 percent) than in Massachusetts (50 percent). Higher attendance likely was due to the fact that training was front-loaded in Washington, with all four modules provided over a one-week time period, while in Massachusetts the remaining six biweekly training workshops were provided over a 12-week period, over which time many participants opted to drop out of the demonstration and returned to searching for wage and salary jobs. Thus, the self-screening process continued throughout the period of participation in project activities, particularly in the Massachusetts demonstration.

There also was a substantial difference in the business counseling and technical assistance services received by project participants in Massachusetts and Washington. While most participants in both projects received at least one counseling session (93 percent in Massachusetts and 70 percent in Washington), the mean number of hours of business counseling received in Massachusetts was five times greater than in Washington—7.5 hours per treatment-group member versus only 1.5 hours. There are two explanations for this large difference. The strongest explanation is that the strong monetary incentive of obtaining the lump-sum payment—which is equal to the individuals' remaining UI benefit entitlement—caused individuals to move as quickly as possible through the business planning process so as to obtain the maximum payment amount. In addition, front-loading the business training services in Washington might have resulted in less opportunity for interaction between project participants and counselors than the more extended period of training workshops provided in Massachusetts.

Of those 755 individuals selected for the Washington project, 451 completed the five milestones required to qualify for the lump-sum payment. These individuals received payments averaging $4,225 each to start their own microenterprises. Project participants in Massachusetts received average biweekly self-employment allowance payments of $530 to $540 per person while they were working full-time on planning and operating their businesses. In addition, Massachusetts also offered project participants needing substantial start-up capital special assistance in obtaining bank loans from private institutions, although in practice this help was rarely needed (because of the relatively low start-up costs of the home-based service businesses that dominated business start-up by Massachusetts participants) and even more rarely used.

Net Impacts of the U.S. Self-Employment Assistance Experiments

Evaluation results from the self-employment experiments clearly indicate that self-employment is a viable reemployment option for some unemployed workers. As indicated above, the potential target population for a self-employment assistance program for unemployed workers is relatively small: only 2 to 4 percent of UI recipients are interested in pursuing self-employment. However, of those individuals who are interested in becoming self-employed, a large proportion—

about half—actually do start a business. These results are consistent with the experiences of self-employment programs for the unemployed in other industrialized nations. For example, participation rates in the national self-employment programs for the unemployed in France and Great Britain have averaged approximately 2 percent a year, and programs in Germany and Australia have averaged 1 percent participation or less (OECD 1995, p. 9).

A final report on the SEA Experiments in Massachusetts and Washington was completed and published by the department (Benus et al. 1995). The findings in the report were based on telephone follow-up surveys with the treatment and control groups, which were conducted an average of 31 months after random assignment in Massachusetts and an average of 33 months after random assignment in Washington.[12] Survey data was supplemented by data from state UI wage records, from an automated management information system for each project, and from on-site observations. The report also included a benefit-cost analysis from three different perspectives: project participants, the government, and society as a whole. A summary of the net impacts of the Massachusetts and Washington demonstrations is presented in Table 8.4.

Self-employment assistance significantly increased the number of business starts by treatment group members compared to the control group. In Washington, 63 percent of participants entered self-employment at some point following their enrollment in the demonstration, versus 41 percent of control group members. In Massachusetts, 58 percent of project participants entered self-employment, compared to 47 percent of controls. Business starts in Washington were primarily in the services and in retail trade, although they included some small-scale manufacturing businesses. In Massachusetts, the great majority of business starts were in the services industry, but there were some in wholesale and retail trade.

Contrary to the widely held belief that most new businesses fail within three years of start-up, most of the new microenterprises started by demonstration participants survived: 61 percent of Washington participants and 74 percent of Massachusetts participants who were self-employed at some point since random assignment were operating their businesses at the time of the follow-up survey nearly three years later. However, based on the survey data, business survival rates for the control group were very similar to the survival rates for treatment group

Table 8.4 Summary of UI Self-Employment Demonstration Net Impacts

	Massachusetts			Washington		
	Treatments	Controls	Impact	Treatments	Controls	Impact
% self-employed since random assignment	58	47	12**	66	44	22***
Length of first UI spell (weeks)	26.5	24.5	−1.8***	19.3	11.6	−7.6***
Total benefit payments in dollars since random assignment (UI + lump sum payments in Washington)	7,400	6,567	−876***	6,750	5,442	−1,300***
Annual time in self-employment (months)	2.6	1.7	0.8*	3.4	1.1	2.3***
Annual self-employment earnings ($)	2,627	1,439	1,219	3,029	703	2,157**
Annual time in wage and salary employment (months)	4.4	4.1	0.6	5.2	4.5	−0.7**
Annual wage and salary earnings ($)	10,119	7,797	3,053**	9,920	8,414	−1,744**
Total time in employment since random assignment (months per year)	7.4	5.8	1.9***	7.8	6.7	1.1***
Total annual earnings since random assignment ($)	14,664	10,056	5,940***	14,259	13,173	205

NOTE: All impact estimates presented in this table are regression-adjusted impacts derived using ordinary least squares (OLS). * coefficient significantly different from zero at the 0.10 level (two-tailed test); ** coefficient significantly different from zero at the 0.05 level (two-tailed test); *** coefficient significantly different from zero at the 0.01 level (two-tailed test).
SOURCE: Benus et al. (1995).

members noted above.[13] Thus, while the self-employment assistance provided by the demonstration increased the total number of businesses, the demonstration did not improve the chances of survival of those businesses that were started by treatment group members vis-à-vis businesses started by control group members.

Both the Washington and Massachusetts demonstrations promoted rapid reemployment—and reduced the duration of unemployment and the receipt of UI benefits—among project participants. The Washington demonstration reduced participants' duration of unemployment by an enormous 7.6 weeks. Clearly, this result was driven by the strong monetary incentive of the lump-sum payment, which declined rapidly over time (since the payment was essentially a "cash out" of the individual's remaining UI benefit entitlement). While weekly UI benefit payments were thus reduced, this reduction was more than offset by the substantial cost of the lump-sum payments to Washington participants who started a business. When lump-sum payments are factored into the equation, total benefit payments to participants were significantly higher ($1,300) than UI benefits paid to the control group. In contrast, the Massachusetts demonstration—which provided participants with biweekly SEA payments but no lump-sum payments—reduced participants' unemployment by 1.8 weeks compared with the control group, resulting in a net savings in combined UI and SEA payments of $876 per participant.

In terms of employment and earnings, self-employment assistance, as expected, increased participants' annual time in self-employment and annual earnings from self-employment compared with the control group (although the earnings increase was not statistically significant in Massachusetts, possibly because of the relatively small size of the sample). In Washington, the demonstration also reduced total time in wage and salary employment. This was also an expected outcome, since the demonstration was promoting self-employment and it is reasonable to expect that at least some of the participants would have obtained wage and salary jobs in the absence of the demonstration.

An unexpected finding, however, was that the Massachusetts demonstration also increased wage and salary employment among project participants. Although apparently counterintuitive, this finding seems more reasonable when one considers the differences in the program models tested in Massachusetts and Washington. As noted earlier, the sequence of self-employment assistance services in Massachusetts was more spread out compared to the front-loaded sequence of services in Washington (designed to allow participants to expedite receipt of the lump-sum payment). This difference resulted in a much longer period of interaction between participants and their business counselors in Massachusetts than in Washington, and five times greater use of business counseling services in Massachusetts, as noted earlier. With this additional one-on-one assistance plus more time to carefully work through their options, Massachusetts participants may have been better equipped to target a niche for themselves in an existing firm than participants in the Washington demonstration.

Overall, then, the self-employment assistance provided in the demonstration significantly increased participants' total time in employment (i.e., the combination of self-employment and wage and salary employment) after they were randomly assigned to the project. On an annual basis, demonstration participants were employed 1.1 months longer than the control group in Washington and 1.9 months longer than the control group in Massachusetts. This result is due to the fact that positive self-employment and negative wage and salary employment impacts somewhat offset each other in Washington, while both of these effects are positive and additive in Massachusetts. This phenomenon is even more pronounced in terms of total earnings. In Washington, demonstration participants' total annual earnings after random assignment were only $205 higher than the controls' earnings—not a statistically significant increase. In contrast, the additive effect in Massachusetts resulted in a dramatic increase in the total annual earnings of project participants, compared to the control group—a net annual earnings increase of $5,940 per treatment group member over the three-year follow-up period.

In summary, then, the results of the UI Self-Employment Demonstration in Massachusetts and Washington indicate the following:

- The self-employment assistance programs provided in the demonstrations increased business starts among project participants, reduced the length of their unemployment, and increased their total time in employment—which includes self-employment plus wage and salary jobs. In addition, the Massachusetts demonstration also had a substantial positive impact on participants' earnings.

•   When placed into a benefit-cost framework, both self-employment assistance program models proved to be cost-effective for project participants and society as a whole.[14] The program model tested in Massachusetts proved cost-effective to the government sector as well, while the Washington program model produced substantial net costs to the government.

The final report finds that SEA for the Massachusetts model is a viable reemployment option for unemployed workers and that the benefits of such a program exceed its costs. The report concludes, "These results indicate that SEA is a cost-effective approach to promote the rapid reemployment of unemployed workers and should be permanently incorporated into the U.S. employment security and economic development system" (Benus et al. 1995, pp. x–xi).

SELF-EMPLOYMENT ASSISTANCE LEGISLATION

Policy and Research Environment

Interest in self-employment increased over the life of the SEA experiments. This interest, both inside and outside of government, made for a much more favorable public policy environment for implementing an American SEA program, especially after rigorously evaluated demonstrations showed that they could be cost-effective in the United States.

Private foundations, including the Charles Stewart Mott and Ford foundations, encouraged microenterprise programs, especially for disadvantaged workers and for women. Foundation support funded a demonstration attempting to help welfare recipients start their own small businesses. Although the SEA experiments did not serve a disadvantaged population, the foundations became more interested in self-employment assistance as evaluation results became available.

The Corporation for Enterprise Development is a nonprofit organization that promotes microenterprise. It had been a key player in organizing the first two German Marshall Fund trips to look at European microenterprises and government-sponsored microenterprise programs. Its president, Robert Friedman, was central to this effort and continued to push for expanded emphasis on microenterprise policy in the United States.

Interest in microenterprise programs was also increasing within the federal government. A number of federal agencies began implementing small microenterprise programs and projects, but these efforts were small and uncoordinated. Constance R. Dunham, a staff economist at the Council of Economic Advisers, had a strong interest in microenterprise policy. From her position in the Executive Office of the President, she called monthly meetings of executive-branch cabinet agencies that dealt with microenterprise to inform and coordinate microenterprise policy across the federal government. As an economist, she was particularly interested in the SEA experiments, since their use of experimental methods would yield results that would show decisively whether self-employment programs worked for a UI population.

In the early 1990s, worldwide interest in self-employment as an employment option became apparent. Evidence from developing countries about the importance of microenterprise—such as the widespread availability of microloans from the Grameen Bank in Bangladesh—was broadly recognized. In 1990, at its seventy-seventh annual meeting, the International Labour Organization recognized and discussed microenterprise as an employment strategy. International Labour Organization staff prepared a monograph on this issue (ILO 1990). Carolyn Golding, who by that time had become deputy assistant secretary for employment and training, attended the meeting as a U.S. representative and spoke about the SEA experiments. The experiments had seemed marginal when they began, but a few years later they became part of the broader policy debate.

The early 1990s were a time of change for self-employment in the United States and around the world. During the 1990–1991 recession in the United States, establishing a microenterprise became a legitimate alternative to seeking wage and salary employment. Progressive firms like General Electric were paying for transition services that included helping laid-off workers set up their own businesses. Following the breakup of the Soviet Union, the department, working with the World Bank, had a hand in helping Eastern European nations make the transition to market economies. Golding played an important role in setting up comprehensive programs, first in Poland and Hungary (where the programs included SEA programs), then in Russia and Albania.[15]

By 1991, the interim reports for the Massachusetts and Washington self-employment experiments were completed, and they were published the next year (Benus et al. 1992; Johnson and Leonard 1992). The interim reports consisted of analysis of the implementation of the projects, but they did not include net impact and cost-benefit analyses. The reports showed that the Massachusetts model held promise as a cost-effective employment creation approach.

When Larry Katz reviewed the Massachusetts interim report he found it to be encouraging and believed that self-employment assistance might be a sound new policy initiative if it was narrowly targeted using the worker profiling mechanism. Robert Reich was the main proponent of SEA. He liked the idea, and he found the research to be supportive. When SEA was enacted in 1993, it was based on a combination of research and intuition.[16]

When Alan Krueger came to the department as the new chief economist, he thought that SEA had been oversold. He correctly thought it would be small—attracting no more than 2 percent of the UI claimants who received a participation offer—and he was afraid that most participants would fail in their attempts to set up a microenterprise.[17] It was not until the final report was released in 1995 that the SEA's cost-effectiveness was demonstrated; thus the final report was not available when the temporary program was enacted (Benus et al. 1995). When SEA was made permanent in 1998, however, the legislation had a solid research base.

Enacting Federal Legislation Authorizing the SEA Program

By 1991, the department had completed the operational phase of the two congressionally authorized SEA experiments and the interim evaluations. The Massachusetts study was sent as an interim report to Congress. In April 1992, Sen. Harris Wofford (D-PA) introduced amendments to reform the federal-state UI program (S. 2614). These amendments were principally drafted by David Balducchi, a USDOL employee then working for Wofford as a Congressional Fellow. The amendments included a provision to allow all states to participate in SEA programs. In June 1992, Rep. Wyden introduced a single-purpose SEA House bill (H.R. 5306). The SEA provision was incorporated into a large tax bill (H.R. 11) that was passed by the House and the Senate, but President George H.W. Bush ultimately vetoed it.[18]

Soon after the beginning of the 103rd Congress on February 4, 1993, Senator Wofford introduced a new bill (S. 320) that contained several features of the previous bill, including Self-Employment Assistance. Then, on March 27, Wofford and four cosponsors (Senators Bill Bradley [D-NJ], John Kerry [D-MA], Ted Kennedy [D-MA], and George Mitchell [D-ME]) introduced a single-purpose bill (S. 1045) to make SEA available in all states. According to Wofford, the bill "would make self-employment a reemployment option under our unemployment compensation system." A companion House bill (H.R. 1154) was introduced by Rep. Wyden and five cosponsors (Representatives Rob Andrews [D-NJ], Ralph Hall [R-TX], Tom Ridge [R-PA], Olympia Snowe [R-ME], and Jolene Unsoeld [D-WA]). Later, Senate and House sponsors received support from the Clinton administration, and the SEA provision was incorporated as an amendment to the North American Free Trade Agreement (NAFTA),[19] signed into law by President Clinton on December 8, 1993, with a five-year sunset clause.[20]

Secretary Reich was supportive of, but not active in, the SEA legislative effort. He had been introduced to the program during roundtable discussions in his office with Larry Katz, Darla Letourneau, me, and others. He was actively interested in the evidence behind the proposal and whether an SEA program would work. The research evidence convinced him, and he became an advocate for the program.[21]

The SEA initiative had broad support in the department. Carolyn Golding had raised SEA during a policy meeting with Reich. She was surprised when Kitty Higgins responded, "What about the Massachusetts experiment?" Golding realized then that Higgins would be a key player in getting SEA enacted, and she was. Higgins was active throughout 1993 in moving many policy initiatives forward, including SEA.[22]

The department had initially included the SEA program option as part of the administration's proposal in September 1993 to provide a final extension of the Emergency Unemployment Compensation (EUC) program for long-term unemployed workers. However, this provision was not included in the bill reported out of the House Ways and Means Committee for the EUC extension legislation: SEA was too controversial to add to an extension of UI benefits. In a single-purpose bill, it stuck out and could not gain support.[23]

Reich was actively involved in the legislative effort to enact NAFTA. He unsuccessfully tried to win support from Democrats for

NAFTA by promising that the administration would push for passage of the legislation that provided additional funding for employment and training programs. However, most Democrats were unwilling to support NAFTA, and they would not trade their support for more employment and training funds.[24]

The environment for enactment of SEA quickly changed. The NAFTA treaty was signed by President George H.W. Bush in December 1992 before he left office. President Clinton adopted and championed the agreement and urged Congress to ratify it. NAFTA was supported by most Republicans but opposed by most Democrats. The Clinton White House needed Democratic votes, and several Democrats came to the White House to get something for their vote for NAFTA. Rep. Wyden was one of them. He had first proposed the SEA experiments in 1987. In 1993, he came to the staff of the "NAFTA war room" in the White House and asked for support for SEA legislation. The White House was supportive and referred Wyden to the Department of Labor. Since the department had already (unsuccessfully) proposed SEA provisions, it readily added its support to the Wyden proposal. The NAFTA bill containing the SEA provision received sufficient numbers of Democratic votes in the House and Senate and was enacted into law. The SEA provision was able to prevail because the NAFTA bill was laden with many extra provisions and did not face strong opposition, although some members of Congress questioned whether SEA should be a part of the UI program. Wyden and the USDOL proposed the SEA as a permanent provision, but it was enacted as a temporary bill, sunsetting in five years.[25]

Reich was pleased to gain Wyden's support for NAFTA, and he was pleased to get SEA enacted. He wanted to make SEA permanent, but because of budgetary constraints, all the administration could get was a five-year program.[26] Congress mandated that the department conduct an evaluation of the SEA program. Making SEA permanent would be considered after the evaluation was completed.

Federal Self-Employment Assistance Legislation

With enactment in 1993, Self-Employment Assistance became part of federal UI law. The federal SEA legislation amends the Federal Unemployment Tax Act at section 3306(t). The provision also makes

SEA a permitted use for incurring expenditures from the Unemployment Trust Fund under section 303(a)(5) of the Social Security Act. The statute authorizes but does not require states to offer self-employment assistance as an additional tool to help speed the transition of dislocated workers into new employment. To establish SEA programs, states must enact legislation that conforms to the federal legislation.

Under the act, states that operate SEA programs select those UI beneficiaries who are eligible for the program by identifying those claimants who are most likely to exhaust their entitlement to UI benefits, using the worker profiling mechanism to identify unemployed workers likely to become long-term unemployed. Self-employment program participants are required to work full-time on starting a business. They are also required to participate in self-employment activities (such as entrepreneurial training, business counseling, and other activities) to ensure that they have the skills necessary to successfully operate a business.

In February 1994, the department issued federal guidelines regarding temporary self-employment programs that would expire in five years.[27] States had the flexibility to establish their own programs within those guidelines. To do so, each state first had to do three things: 1) enact conforming state legislation to establish its self-employment program; 2) develop a plan describing how the SEA program in that state would operate, including assurances that entrepreneurial training would not be paid for out of the Unemployment Trust Fund; and 3) then submit the state plan to the department for review and approval (Wandner 1994a).

The SEA-authorizing legislation called for the department to conduct an evaluation of SEA and submit the results to Congress. The evaluation was completed in December 1997 and transmitted to Congress (Vroman 1997).

On October 28, 1998, section 3 of the Noncitizen Benefit Clarification and Other Technical Amendments Act of 1998 repealed the Self-Employment Assistance termination date, thus making permanent the authorization of the SEA program. States with SEA programs, and particularly the new SEA state of Pennsylvania, had been pressing Congress to make the program permanent.

In December 1998, the department issued revised guidelines to reflect that the Self-Employment Assistance program had recently become permanent. While the other provisions of the 1994 state guidance remained in force, the new guidance eliminated the requirement that states submit plans and get approval for their SEA programs prior to implementing them. States would still have to submit their proposed SEA legislation to the department for review to assure that it was in conformity with federal legislation. The guidance stated that after five years of SEA state experience, states could best learn how to implement programs from other states (USDOL 1998).

IMPLEMENTATION AND OPERATION OF THE SELF-EMPLOYMENT ASSISTANCE PROGRAM

State Implementation of Self-Employment Assistance Programs: Early Results and Evaluation

Among the department subagencies, implementing Self-Employment Assistance was primarily the responsibility of the Unemployment Insurance Service. From a federal perspective the SEA provisions amended the federal unemployment insurance law to allow UI payments to individuals who were not actively seeking wage and salary employment, but the other major employment and training programs were not greatly involved. The JTPA program provided entrepreneurial training, but such training was very limited and picked up little of the SEA training costs. At the state level, participation in SEA was optional. States had to amend their state UI laws to permit UI claimants to participate in the program. The state UI staff would also have to find funding for entrepreneurial training, although the training funds could come from the JTPA/WIA program.

After enactment of Self-Employment Assistance, the department had to develop guidance for the states. Mary Ann Wyrsch, the UI Service's administrator, delegated implementation to the UI Experiments group and the UI legislative division. Since SEA was a voluntary state program, she did not get involved either in the legislation or its implementation. Her concern was that as a nontraditional use of UI tax dollars, the program should be crafted to avoid moral hazard and that it be implemented carefully.[28] During 1994, when most of the implementation effort was ongoing, the national UI staff was busy on other issues.

Unemployment remained high, and the Emergency Unemployment Compensation (EUC) program continued to operate. Many new policy initiatives were being launched, including the UI flexibility provisions of the Reemployment Act of 1994.

Much of the knowledge about the SEA program resided with Jon Messenger, the project manager for the SEA experiments. As a result, he and I worked on the design of the new SEA program. Messenger was the main author of the SEA procedures and guidance to the states, assisted by other members of the Unemployment Insurance Service.

The department moved quickly in the two months after the SEA legislation was enacted. It issued program guidance to the states about how to implement SEA programs on February 16, 1994, as Unemployment Insurance Program Letter No. 14-94 (Wandner 1994b, pp. 72–94). The guidance advised the states about the enactment of the SEA provision. It described the Massachusetts SEA experiment and the availability of the interim report on its demonstration project. It described the new federal legislation in detail, interpreted it, and explained how states could voluntarily adopt the SEA program as part of their state UI programs. Furthermore, it described the plans that states would have to submit to the department after enacting state legislation and before implementing their SEA programs. Finally, it included appendices that provided three additional things: 1) the language from section 504 of the NAFTA law dealing with SEA, 2) draft language for states to include in their state UI laws to implement SEA programs, and 3) a commentary on the draft language to explain the department's interpretation of the proposed state legislative provisions as well as how states might implement SEA.

Two key issues in the SEA guidance to the states for implementing the state SEA legislation were 1) assuring that there were no "excess costs" and 2) funding business development services—including entrepreneurial training, counseling, and technical assistance—that needed to be provided to SEA participants. The lesser of the issues was excess cost. It was nearly impossible to estimate excess costs in an ongoing SEA program without a control or comparison group, so the issue gradually disappeared for operating state SEA programs. More troubling was the provision of business development services, which required new funding, something that was not easy to find.[29] To the extent that the state UI programs are the main stewards of the SEA program, UI programs have to identify the funding source for these services, as the

Unemployment Trust Fund is prohibited from providing training funds. The UI program has to partner either with the WIA programs or with the Small Business Administration, neither of which has proven easy to partner with.

After the issuance of the 1994 guidance, states began enacting SEA legislation and sending implementation plans to the department. The department set up a small group within the UI Service to consider implementation issues. Each state SEA plan was reviewed to ensure that it met the federal requirements, including actuarial and technical design standards, such as maintaining cost neutrality and targeting the program using worker profiling methods.

After the SEA program was made permanent in 1998, SEA began settling down into one more component of the UI program. In 1999, the department issued new guidance that relaxed the requirements for state implementation of SEA programs (Messenger, Peterson-Vaccaro, and Vroman 2002, pp. 149–150; USDOL 1998). The USDOL's oversight of the establishment of SEA programs was lessened. States were no longer required to submit SEA implementation plans and have them approved before they could initiate new state SEA programs.

States began to establish SEA programs in 1995 and 1996. In April 1995, New York was the first state in the nation to implement an SEA program under the NAFTA-authorizing legislation. Three other states implemented SEA programs by the end of 1996: Maine, Oregon, and Delaware (in order of implementation). These four states each submitted an SEA annual report on program activities and outcomes for the year ending June 1996. Although the data in these reports were preliminary, describing the very beginning of four state SEA programs, they provided a glimpse of the early use of self-employment assistance as a reemployment tool for the unemployed.

Between July 1995 and June 1996, nearly 2,000 individuals participated in the Self-Employment Assistance program in the above four states. Most participants, about 1,800, were in the New York SEA program. The other SEA states served substantially smaller populations than New York, and the New York program operated more than a year longer than those of other SEA states.

The results in New York are particularly interesting. New York had the only Self-Employment Assistance program in 1995 that was operational long enough to obtain early data on SEA program outcomes. New

York conducted a survey of SEA participants in early 1996 based on a survey developed by the department for the SEA annual report.[30] The survey results indicated that 84 percent of all New York SEA participants were reemployed at the time—either in self-employment (58 percent), wage and salary jobs (14 percent), or both (12 percent).

Since the Self-Employment Assistance program was enacted as a temporary five-year program, the 1993 legislation required that the department conduct an early evaluation of the SEA program (Vroman 1997) to determine whether to make the program permanent before it expired in December 1998. The study concluded that the SEA program would likely remain a small program, with a take-up rate of perhaps 1 to 2 percent of UI claimants. Nevertheless, it also concluded that SEA was a useful tool for workforce development policy, and that public policy would do well to have a wide array of tools to deal with worker dislocation issues. Because of the limited scale of the program as well as data and funding constraints, the study did not conduct a benefit cost analysis but found that SEA was too small a program to pose a threat to the UI trust fund.

Vroman described the political, administrative, and technical barriers that states would face in enacting and implementing Self-Employment Assistance (Vroman 1997). He found that, as of 1996, only 7 of the 10 states that enacted legislation had completed the complex process of implementing the program. At that time, SEA was an innovation that was largely confined to the coastal states; among states with programs, only Minnesota was in the interior. Of the coastal states, the programs in New York, New Jersey, Oregon, Maine, and Delaware operated statewide; in California the program was only implemented in six local areas. As required by law, states used their worker profiling mechanisms to select potential participants. States, however, set their profiling thresholds to make access to their SEA program either expansive or restrictive. Thus, the profiling threshold varied from a more accessible 0.40 probability of exhausting UI to a more restrictive 0.70 probability. All the states provided counseling, technical assistance, and entrepreneurial training. These services were mostly funded by the JTPA's Dislocated Worker program and the Small Business Development Centers (SBDCs), but some funding also came from the governors' JTPA discretionary funds, in-kind services, UI penalty and interest funds, and state-financed training funds. The key finding, however, was how small the SEA program was and how small it continues to be. The results can be seen in Table 8.5. Payments to SEA enrollees were less than 1 percent of UI regular-program first payments in all states except Maine, where they approximated 4 percent.

Implementation from 1995 to the Present

By 2008, 12 states had enacted SEA programs: California, Connecticut, Delaware, Louisiana, Maine, Maryland, Minnesota, New Jersey, New York, Oregon, Pennsylvania, and Rhode Island. However, since 1995, SEA has been largely an East Coast phenomenon; of the 12 states that have adopted SEA, only 4—Louisiana, Minnesota, California, and Oregon—lie beyond the eastern seaboard (Table 8.6).

In 2008, seven states had active state SEA programs: Delaware, Maine, Maryland, New Jersey, New York, Oregon, and Pennsylvania. These states report data on the SEA programs to the department. The Louisiana program became operational in January 2005, but the program received no applications and did not become effective.[31] Washington State has a program called "Self-Employment Assistance," but it is a form of commissioner-approved training, and it was not enacted under the federal SEA provisions.[32]

Since 1995, SEA program data have been reported by participating states along with other data about benefit receipt and payment for the regular UI program. Table 8.7 presents the reported data on the num-

Table 8.5 Flow of Participants into the Self-Employment Assistance Program in Five States, 1996

	New York	New Jersey	Oregon	Maine	Delaware
Regular UI program first payments	541,784	312,370	145,835	47,439	26,755
No. attending SEA orientation	3,902	513	141	240	—
No. SEA applications	2,241	252	—	177	—
No. enrolled in SEA	2,195	156	111	134	17
No. completing SEA	1,751	—	76	—	14

NOTE: — = data not available.
SOURCE: Vroman (1997).

Table 8.6 Self-Employment Assistance: Legislation and Program Implementation, 1995–2008

State	Effective dates of legislation	Implementation
California[a]		Not implemented
Connecticut[b]	(See below)	(See below)
Delaware	1996	1996–present
Louisiana[c]	1/1/2005	2005–present
Maine	1995	1995–present
Maryland	2000	2000–present
Minnesota[d]	4/19/1995–1/1/1999	Not implemented
	2003–2008 (for Project GATE)	2003–2004
New Jersey	1998	1998–present
New York	1995	1995–present
Oregon	1996	1996–present
Pennsylvania	1997	1997–present
Rhode Island[e]	(See below)	(See below)

NOTE: blank = not applicable.

[a] California developed an SEA plan that was approved by the department, but it never implemented a statewide program; California has legal authority for a program, but it is not operational (USDOL 2008b).

[b] Connecticut no longer has an SEA provision in its state UI law (USDOL 2008b).

[c] Louisiana has SEA legislation but has never implemented it, according to David Fitzgerald.

[d] Minnesota also never implemented its SEA legislation, according to Charles Hartfiel.

[e] Rhode Island never implemented its SEA program, but it does operate a state self-employment program that is separate from its UI program, according to Ray Fillipone.

Washington State enacted SEA in 2006, but the program is a form of commissioner-approved training and is not an SEA program under federal law; it is set to expire on July 1, 2012 (USDOL 2008b). Washington has never submitted reports to the department on its program.

SOURCE: Legislative dates from state legislation and interviews with state and federal staff. Implementation dates from data reported by states to USDOL in federally required report, the ETA 5159 report.

ber of individuals entering SEA. The program is very small; it only reached 3,170 participants in 2002 and has declined sharply since then. Even among SEA states, the program is highly concentrated: only seven states have active programs. Four state programs serve more than 100 participants a year, but none of the programs serve as many as 1,000 participants. The data reveal that the program is used most in a few states: New Jersey, New York, and Oregon. New Jersey entrants have remained fairly level over time, while reported participants have declined in New York and temporarily ended in Pennsylvania.[33] Maine has also contributed to the flow. Delaware and Maryland have had few entrants.

For individual states with SEA programs, new participants represent less than 1 percent of UI first payments in all cases except Maine in 2004 and 2005. Maine's SEA participants reached a high of 1.5 percent of regular UI first payments in 2004. In other states, the maximum has been below 1 percent—0.3 percent in Maryland, 0.3 percent in New Jersey, 0.6 percent in New York, 0.2 percent in Oregon, and 0.1 percent in Pennsylvania. For the United States as a whole, SEA has only reached 0.0007—or less than one-tenth of one percent—of regular UI first payments.

The small size of the Self-Employment Assistance program can be measured in a number of ways. The number of workers entering SEA has only reached as high as 3,200 per year, and annual payments have amounted to less than 70,000 weeks compensated and $17 million in benefits paid (Table 8.8). These are very small numbers compared the regular UI program, which paid $43.1 billion to 10.1 million beneficiaries in 2008.

A number of states, however, have active microenterprise programs that are not tied to the UI program. States sometimes find that their own state programs are more flexible and easier to implement. States have a particularly difficult time finding funding for microenterprise counseling and training, which states must fund themselves. Since the Unemployment Trust Fund cannot be used to fund training, neither UI nor ES administrative funds can be used to provide SEA training. Thus, since funding of entrepreneurial training through the WIA programs has been minimal, it sometimes has proven easier to conduct microenterprise programs outside the umbrella of USDOL-funded programs.

While the WPRS program provides reemployment services to dislocated UI beneficiaries, in states without SEA programs workers only receive assistance to return to wage and salary employment. If these reemployment services are not effective, workers may be referred to training. In states with SEA programs, the WPRS system offers two options: 1) provision of reemployment services to aid the return to wage and salary employment, and 2) referral to the SEA program so

Table 8.7 Self-Employment Assistance: Number of Individuals Entering Program by State, 1995–2008

					States				
Year	DE	MD	ME	MN	NJ	NY	OR	PA	Total
1995			44	—		608			652
1996	17		127	—	2,041	32			2,217
1997	5		120	—		2,839	49	786	3,799
1998	—		90	—	321	1,270	66	541	2,288
1999	—		59		569	1,837	18	416	2,899
2000	1	26	98		491	1,654	18	229	2,517
2001	—	125	109		834	1,480	278	301	3,127
2002	17	22	118		524	1,634	305	550	3,170
2003	43	11	202	45	486	70	338	147	1,342
2004	56	10	481	235	557	475	166	9	1,989
2005	31	21	351	102	626	309	204	0	1,644
2006	21	21	252		632	177	226	0	1,329
2007	22	21	201		496	369	295	152	1,556
2008	35	15	130		477	219	507	86	1,469

NOTE: Blank = not applicable, as the program was not in operation in that year in that state. — = not available, meaning either there were zero referrals or data were not reported. Data are for the eight states that have enacted SEA legislation and implemented state programs. California enacted an SEA program but never implemented it. Minnesota did not implement its original SEA program; it became effective on April 19, 1995, and was repealed effective January 1, 1999. Minnesota then implemented a temporary SEA law allowing the state to participate in the federal self-employment demonstration project, Project GATE, which operated between 2003 and 2005, according to Charles Hartfiel. A Louisiana SEA law became effective on January 1, 2005, but the state has not reported on its inactive program, according to David Fitzgerald. Maryland SEA data is in error; according to Susan Bass, Maryland's SEA director at the time, the Maryland SEA program served 571 participants during the period 2003–2007, but the reported data shows fewer than 100 total participants. Bass also indicates that the Maryland program has always served between 100 and 200 participants. As a result, I have replaced the number of reported 2001 Maryland participants—4,227—with an estimate of 125 for that year. SEA data for Puerto Rico for 2001 appeared in the ETA 5159 report; it has been removed since Puerto Rico has not enacted an SEA program.

SOURCE: Unemployment Insurance Data Base; ETA 5159 report.

claimants can begin setting up their own small businesses (Messenger, Peterson-Vaccaro, and Vroman 2002, pp. 142–143).

Under federal law, both WPRS and SEA use the worker profiling mechanism to identify UI claimants who are likely to exhaust their entitlement to UI benefits. When profiled UI claimants report to One-Stop Career Centers, a small proportion of them are interested in setting up their own small businesses. These claimants can choose to be referred to the SEA program. Although it is mandated that referrals to SEA be made through the WPRS system, few SEA states report that they make these referrals, and those that do appear to refer very few workers. The number of reported referrals has not been more than a few thousand. A substantial amount of nonreporting and underreporting has occurred.

Table 8.8 Self-Employment Assistance Program Data, 1995–2008

Year	SEA referrals from WPRS	Number of individuals entering SEA	SEA weeks compensated	SEA benefits paid ($)
1995	660	652	5,591	1,364,676
1996	2,649	2,217	26,603	6,507,709
1997	2,356	3,799	42,111	10,968,804
1998	831	2,288	37,740	9,587,764
1999	1,434	2,910	32,726	9,718,240
2000	2,735	2,517	38,913	13,209,451
2001	2,552	3,127	37,787	12,501,211
2002	4,950	3,170	50,057	17,159,098
2003	874	1,342	25,228	8,966,567
2004	1,293	1,989	41,978	14,603,948
2005	1,468	1,623	38,983	13,928,325
2006	1,292	1,329	32,370	14,599,974
2007	1,522	1,556	35,139	13,645,131
2008	1,489	1,469	67,360	10,307,763

NOTE: Data has been adjusted to remove reported data for three states that submitted SEA report data without having SEA programs: Puerto Rico, reporting the number entering SEA for 2001; Oklahoma, reporting SEA weeks compensated for 2005; and Kentucky, reporting SEA benefits paid for 2003.

SOURCE: Unemployment Insurance Data Base (UIDB). For "Number of individuals entering SEA," "SEA weeks compensated," and "SEA benefits paid," data are from ETA 5159 report. "SEA referrals from WPRS" data are from ETA 9-048 report.

All states with SEA programs are expected to make use of the WPRS program to refer workers to the SEA program, since both programs must consider the likelihood of exhausting UI benefits as a condition of participation. Of the seven states with SEA programs, however, only four—Maine, New Jersey, New York, and Oregon—report that they use the WPRS system to identify individuals to refer to the SEA programs (Table 8.9). In those states, referrals reached nearly 5,000 in 2002 but have remained at fewer than 1,500 since then. Only New Jersey has reported that referrals to SEA regularly occur before workers are enrolled in the SEA program. Maine, New York, and Oregon report using the referral mechanism to some extent, while Delaware, Louisiana, Maryland, Minnesota, and Pennsylvania do not report using worker profiling referrals.

All or most workers entering the SEA program should be referred by the WPRS system, since SEA participants are required to be profiled. Comparing the data in Tables 8.6 and 8.8 suggests that is not the case. New Jersey reports that all individuals entering the SEA program have been referred. New York and Oregon have been reporting that a substantial portion of SEA entrants are referred from WPRS, but the percentage has been declining sharply in New York. Maine reports a small number of referrals, while the other states report no referrals. Low referral rates appear to reflect a lack of reporting or an underreporting rather than a lack of use of worker profiling as the referral mechanism to the SEA program.

States found the process of implementing the SEA program burdensome. They were not accustomed to setting up a plan for a new program, as was required under SEA. Until 1999, they were required to establish such a plan and submit it to the department. After the enactment of a permanent SEA program in late 1998, however, the USDOL removed this requirement.

Self-Employment Assistance programs appear to be effective at starting businesses with reasonably high survival rates. The Washington State experiment fostered businesses that experienced a 63 percent survival rate after 15 months, while the Massachusetts experiment had a 77 percent survival rate after 13 months. By comparison, the survival rates of firms participating in European self-employment programs were not as high (OECD 1995). All SEA programs in Europe and the United States, however, had survival rates that were at least 40 percent

Table 8.9 Number of Individuals Referred to SEA from WPRS by State, 1995–2008

					State					
Year	DE	LA	MD	ME	MN	NJ	NY	OR	PA	Total
1995				29	—		583	48		660
1996	17			38	—	308	2,102	184		2,649
1997	6			11	—	677	1,512	50	—	2,256
1998	—			9	—	313	494	15	—	831
1999	2			6		545	859	24	—	1,436
2000	—		—	11		492	2,203	29	—	2,735
2001	—		—	5		834	1,552	161	—	2,552
2002	—		—	10		2,990	1,677	273	—	4,950
2003	—		—	42	—	486	73	273	—	874
2004	—		—	64	—	557	552	120	—	1,293
2005	—	—	—	87	—	626	446	307	—	1,466
2006	—	—	—	54		632	206	401	—	1,293
2007	—	—	—	136		496	412	478	—	1,522
2008	—	—	—	24		477	275	713	—	1,489

NOTE: Blank = not applicable, as the program was not in operation in that year in that state. — = not available, meaning either there were zero referrals or data were not reported. Data are for the nine states that have enacted SEA legislation and implemented state programs. Erroneously reported data have been removed for states that have not enacted SEA programs: Connecticut for 1999–2003, Georgia for 1997, Iowa for 1995, Nebraska for 1996 and 1998–2004, New Hampshire for 1996, and Washington for 2002.
SOURCE: Unemployment Insurance Data Base; ETA 9048 report.

12 months or more after businesses left the program (Table 8.10). In comparison, for all new firms that opened a single establishment in the United States in 1998, 66 percent were still in existence two years after their birth and 44 percent were still in existence four years after (Knaup 2005). Self-employment programs for the unemployed appear to do quite well compared to all new establishments in the United States and compared to similar programs in Europe.

While the SEA program is very small today, it could have a much larger effect on the U.S. economy if the program were implemented nationwide. If participation in a national SEA program reached 1 or 2 percent of regular UI beneficiaries and if the participants had 50 percent business start rates, the SEA program could yield 50,000 to 100,000

Table 8.10 Survival Rates of Businesses for Participants in Self-Employment Programs

	Intake year	Months since leaving program	Survival rate (%)
Australia	1990	12	54
Denmark	1989	12	40
France	1986	54	51
Netherlands	1985	36	52
United Kingdom	1991	7	71
United States			
Washington	1990	15	63
Massachusetts	1990–92	13	77

SOURCE: OECD (1995); Benus et al. (1995).

business starts. At that level, SEA would contribute an additional 8 to 16 percent to the estimated 637,100 U.S. business starts in 2006 (SBA 2008)—a significant increase.

Selected State Case Studies

Of the 13 states with SEA legislation, six do not have active programs. California has legal authority for a program, but it is not operational. Connecticut no longer has an SEA provision in its state UI law (USDOL 2008b). Louisiana has SEA legislation but has never implemented it. Minnesota also never implemented its SEA legislation. Rhode Island never implemented its SEA program, but it does operate a state self-employment program that is separate from its UI program.[34] In 2006 Washington State enacted a program called Self-Employment Assistance, but it is a form of commissioner-approved training and is not subject to the USDOL's reporting rules for SEA. The Washington State SEA provisions expire on July 1, 2012.[35]

Louisiana

Louisiana enacted SEA legislation in 2004, and its program became operational on January 1, 2005, yet Louisiana has not reported any SEA activity. Workers were not interested in the program, and the state received no applications. The lack of interest resulted from the requirement that participating UI claimants needed to take part in entrepreneurial training. Interest was lacking despite the fact that free training was available through Louisiana's technical schools. After Hurricane Katrina struck Louisiana, the program became inactive. As of 2008, no state staff members were dedicated to the program, and it was not being promoted by the state workforce agency.[36]

Maryland

Maryland enacted its SEA program and implemented it in 2000. The Maryland UI program searches for UI beneficiaries to participate as part of the WPRS profiling process. Each Sunday night, WPRS participation notices are sent out to new UI claimants. Claimants with worker profiling exhaustion probabilities of 0.4 or greater are sent a WPRS notice that also includes an invitation to compete for a spot participating in SEA. SEA applications are received from approximately 2 percent of those who are invited to compete. Participants must be ready to start their own business after receiving training, provided by the organization Women Entrepreneurs of Baltimore. The rigorous entrepreneurial training course lasts eight weeks. Training fund limitations restrict the number of training courses to only four each year; about 30 students are in each class, and about 115 have participated each year in recent years. Recently, annual training costs have been approximately $300,000, or $2,600 per trainee. In the past five years, 571 workers have participated in the program. Since the Maryland SEA program began in 2000, staff members estimate that participants have numbered between 100 and 200 each year.[37]

The SEA program is considered to be very successful by Maryland, but the program is constrained by limited and unstable training fund availability. Local Workforce Investment Boards have been unwilling to provide entrepreneurial training because of the adverse effect on WIA performance outcomes. Since participant income following training is generally not in wages and salaries, WIA program operators get no credit when the standard outcome measures of entered employment, earnings, or retention are used. As a result, training funds generally come from the governor's WIA reserve funds and occasionally from the state's UI penalty and interest account.

The Maryland agency collects only limited SEA data. A work-search exemption for SEA participants is the only item in Maryland's automated UI reporting system—the rest of the SEA system is run off the mainframe, and the SEA program does not transmit the SEA data to the reporting staff in the labor market information unit. As a result, the SEA data reported to the department does not reflect the true size of the Maryland SEA program. Rather than the actual figure of 571 participants over the past five years, a federal report (Table 8.6) counts fewer than 100 participants. Table 8.8 does not capture the fact that between 50,000 and 75,000 UI claimants are invited to apply for SEA each year through the worker profiling process.[38]

Minnesota

Minnesota enacted a program, effective on April 19, 1995; however, the Minnesota program was not implemented. The state workforce agency prepared to implement the program, but then staff members looked at the complexity of program operation (e.g., the data collection and analysis required by the department to determine the cost-effectiveness of the program) and the expectation of limited net return to Minnesota (i.e., the small number of jobs created relative to the effort to set up the program). As a result, the state agency decided not to implement the program and asked the state legislature to repeal the authorizing legislation. In 1998 the SEA statute was repealed, effective January 1, 1999.[39]

In 2002, Minnesota applied to participate in Project GATE, a department-funded microenterprise demonstration project. Since the presence of an SEA program was a condition of participation, Minnesota enacted a temporary SEA program for the duration of the project, from 2003 to 2005. The Minnesota SEA program ended with the completion of the Project GATE demonstration project.[40]

New York

New York was the first state to enact SEA legislation, in mid-1994. Implementation of the SEA provisions began in January 1995. The program had bipartisan support: it was enacted in the final year of Governor Mario Cuomo's Democratic administration and implemented at the beginning of Governor George Pataki's Republican administration. John E. Sweeney, commissioner of the New York State Department of Labor when the program was implemented, saw the SEA program as an opportunity for his agency to change its policy response to unemployment and encourage "an active approach to job creation which relies on the abilities of people to create their own businesses." The SEA program also fit with the "overall economic development strategy for the state of New York," which was centered on the "growth of small and medium sized enterprises." As a result, the SEA program became an integral part of that process (OECD 1995; Sweeney 1995).

As the program commenced, Carolyn Peterson-Vaccaro, the first director of the New York SEA program, emphasized that the key to its success was to have the USDOL and the state labor departments educate and train state and local staff about the SEA program and include as many staff members as possible in the process. She also emphasized the need to establish good working relationships with the private sector. She believed that the success of the New York program was dependent on existing businesses that volunteered to assist the program and on the Small Business Development Centers, which provided counseling and training to SEA participants in New York (OECD 1995).

The early political support was crucial, but equally important was the program's careful design and planning. Shortly after enactment of SEA, a New York project team of field and central office staff began meeting in September 1994 to plan program implementation. The team studied the evaluation results of the Massachusetts and Washington experiments, took what could be applied to New York, and adapted other aspects of the program to New York's needs. A crucial aspect of the New York law and its implementation was that, while the New York Department of Labor would run and manage the program, two other agencies—the State University of New York's SBDCs and the New York State Department of Economic Development—were given the critical role of providing entrepreneurial training. The problem other state SEA programs encountered—lack of resources for SEA training— was avoided in New York by giving this responsibility to the agencies that specialized in providing entrepreneurial training. Strong political support for the SEA program ensured that the other state agencies would provide funding for SEA training (Sweeney 1995).

The resources per participant needed for the training component of the early New York SEA program were modest in comparison to the eight-week training course provided by the Maryland SEA program: New York SEA participants were only required to take 20 hours of training that included topics such as starting a business, developing a business plan, marketing strategies, financing, and dealing with taxes and regulations. The program was initially designed to serve up to 1,000 entrepreneurs at a time and to serve up to 2,500 entrepreneurs per year (Sweeney 1995).

Table 8.7 shows that the New York program provided self-employment assistance to more than 2,000 UI claimants a year in 1996 and 1997. It continued to serve more than 1,000 claimants a year between 1998 and 2003. Beginning in 2004, however, the annual number of participants dropped sharply and has not reached 500 participants per year since then.

Self-Employment Assistance programs are small programs. They depend a great deal on who runs the program. Carolyn Peterson-Vaccaro ran the New York SEA program from 1995 until the end of 1998. During her tenure, enrollment surged. She actively promoted the program among UI and ES staff. Because of the lack of training funds, Peterson-Vacarro and her deputy director aggressively looked for entrepreneurial training funds, and the largest sources of entrepreneurial training funds were two organizations funded in part by the Small Business Administration (SBA)—the SBDCs and the Service Corps of Retired Executives. She worked with the regional SBA director, who was willing to support SEA with significant amounts of training resources at no cost to the SEA program.[41]

After Peterson-Vaccaro left for another job in the New York Labor Department in 1998, support for SEA ebbed. Peterson-Vaccaro continued to encourage the program until the spring of 1999, when she transferred to the New York governor's office. Once she left the New York Department of Labor she had little to do with the SEA program.[42]

Since 2002, New York has experienced a decline in applications and approvals for the SEA program. In 2002, 1,670 applications were received, and 1,625 were approved. In 2008, between January and September, 164 of 326 applications were approved.[43] The decline in SEA participation can be attributed to a number of factors.

First, New York no longer has an SEA director who coordinates the efforts of the UI program and the One-Stops. The New York UI program has the lead role in operating the SEA program: it pays the SEA allowance, but it does not provide any services. As in almost all states, UI no longer has an active presence in the One-Stops. It pays all UI benefits from two telephone call centers. Job Service staff members administer the SEA program in the New York local offices, but it is not a priority for them. No one brings these two organizations together and ensures that they are working cooperatively on the SEA program.

Second, while 20 hours of entrepreneurial training continues to be required, the New York Department of Labor does not pay for the training and no longer has an outside source of funding. In general, SEA participants pay for their own training. The One-Stop staff guides participants to privately provided entrepreneurial training courses and training providers. The SEA program ended its statewide relationship with the SBDCs and with the Service Corps of Retired Executives, which had provided counseling and training. UI claimants interested in SEA get limited support.

Third, while all UI claimants with a profiling score of 0.7 or greater are invited to apply, SEA applications are down greatly. Marketing of and support for the SEA program by the One-Stop staffs is minimal, and the UI staff members have a limited working relationship with One-Stop staff members, who operate the program in the One-Stop local offices. Many UI staff members are ambivalent about the program. From a UI benefit payment perspective, they see an inequity between the SEA participants who can work full time on setting up their own businesses and draw SEA allowances, and other claimants who cannot receive UI benefits if they work at all in wage and salary employment or in self-employment.[44]

Pennsylvania

The Pennsylvania SEA program began in 1997. It continues to operate, and the program impacts are being monitored by the Pennsylvania UI staff with follow-up surveys. For the period January through September 2006, the SEA program had 201 participants, who started 113 new businesses. Those businesses reported income totaling $228,239 and employed 19 workers earning $260,373 in wages during this period.[45] While Pennsylvania failed to report any participation in the SEA program to the USDOL for 2006, it would appear that the Pennsylvania program has operated continuously since 1997, but that the reporting for the program has been uneven.

PROJECT GATE EXPERIMENT

When the World Trade Center buildings fell on September 11, 2001, Lower Manhattan below Houston Street was temporarily closed, and most business in the area came to a halt, including those in Chinatown. In an effort to help Chinatown recover, Secretary of Labor Elaine Chao asked the Employment and Training Administration to develop a one-time effort to help rejuvenate the area. Initially, ETA research staff proposed conducting a microenterprise development demonstration, which Secretary Chao strongly supported. Consultation by ETA staff with the SBA, however, revealed that the SBA had already initiated a demonstration program in Chinatown in conjunction with Pace University. With that information, ETA research staff recommended a multistate micro-enterprise demonstration outside of New York City using experimental methods. Secretary Chao approved both the project and its funding, and personally awarded grants to the participating states and requested project briefings. "Project GATE" had begun.

Project GATE (Growing America Through Entrepreneurship) was funded in 2002 and began operation in late 2003; operations ended in 2005. Its goal was to assist people to create or expand their own small businesses in three states—Maine, Minnesota, and Pennsylvania. These states were chosen in part because they were all believed to have SEA legislation and SEA programs that were in operation.[46] The local sites in which the project operated were: Philadelphia and Pittsburgh, Pennsylvania; Minneapolis/St. Paul and northeast Minnesota; and Portland, Lewiston, and Bangor, Maine.

A large-scale outreach was conducted in each site to make people aware of the program. The outreach was conducted by five means: 1) providing information in the One-Stop Career Centers, 2) inserting fliers in envelopes with UI benefit checks, 3) creating a GATE Web site, 4) conducting a grassroots campaign, and 5) marketing through mass media. Individuals were not randomly assigned into treatment and control groups until they had expressed a strong interest in participating, as indicated by registering with the program, attending an orientation, and completing a project application. Altogether, 4,201 interested individuals were assigned to either a treatment group or a control group; the two groups contained equal numbers. Members of the treatment group were offered an assessment, classroom training in entrepreneurial skills, and individual and ongoing technical assistance (Benus et al. 2008a).

Almost every local-area resident in the project sites was eligible to participate in Project GATE. Individuals were required to be 18 years of age or older, and they had to be a state resident who could lawfully work in the state. They had to want to start or improve a small business. Unlike participants in the SEA demonstrations, participating individuals could be employed, unemployed, or out of the labor force, and they did not have to be collecting UI. Project GATE was designed, however, to be part of the workforce development system and its institutions. The gateway to entering the demonstration was the One-Stop Career Centers. The One-Stops conducted the outreach for the project, and they provided the orientation session that potential members of the treatment and control groups attended. During its operation, Project GATE was an additional employment service that the One-Stops could offer to those who were interested in starting or expanding a small business.

Although Project GATE was funded by the department, it was a partnership with the Small Business Administration. The SBA assisted in linking participants to business loans. Its SBDCs played an important role at the local level, providing assessments, training, and technical assistance at all sites except Philadelphia. These services also were provided by community-based organizations and universities in some sites.

The demographics of the 4,201 applicants for Project GATE were diverse and differed widely by site. Across all sites, applicants were, on average, 54 percent male, 42 years of age, 54 percent white and not Hispanic/Latino, and had 14 years of education. Ninety percent were born in the United States, 96 percent were U.S. citizens, 35 percent had household incomes of less than $25,000, and 68 percent had household incomes of less than $50,000 (Benus et al. 2008a, p. 53).

Individuals who attended the assessment received an estimated 15 hours of services, consisting of 1 hour in assessment, 12 hours in training, and 1 to 2 hours in technical assistance. However, a significant percentage of participants dropped out of the program after the assessment, with one-quarter of participants receiving no training or technical assistance. Forty-two percent of participants received both training and technical assistance. Participants spent approximately 16 weeks in the program.

Although it served a much wider population, Project GATE was designed by making use of lessons learned from the earlier UI self-employment assistance experiments, including these design and implementation procedures. The close relationship between these experiments was facilitated by the fact that the principal investigator for Project GATE, Jacob Benus, was also the principal investigator for the SEA experiments.

The interim report concluded that Project GATE was largely implemented as planned and that it could be replicated successfully on a wider scale. The final evaluation would include a net impact analysis and a benefit-cost analysis (Benus et al. 2008a).

The implementation of Project GATE has had a confounding effect on the SEA entrant data for the three participating states: Maine, Minnesota, and Pennsylvania. For the period in which the project ran, from 2003 to 2005, Maine and Minnesota reported Project GATE participants as SEA entrants, while Pennsylvania did not. The inclusion of Project GATE participants increased Maine's count of entrants in SEA in all three years. Minnesota reported its SEA program activity only during those years, since the state does not operate an ongoing SEA program.

CONCLUSIONS AND LESSONS LEARNED

Cost-effective. Results from the UI Self-Employment Demonstration project in Massachusetts showed that self-employment assistance is a cost-effective strategy for helping some unemployed workers to become reemployed. SEA gets those workers back to work faster by helping them to create their own jobs. A small number of states developed, implemented, and are operating SEA programs to assist unemployed workers to move from unemployment into self-employment.

Small program size. Few states have adopted the program: only seven states have active programs. Few individuals use Self-Employment Assistance programs in the states that have programs. Self-employment assistance is likely to be appropriate only for a small number of workers in the United States—up to 2 percent of the unemployed—based on experience to date.

Foreign experience. Twenty European Union countries have start-up programs. Participation in some of these programs has been larger than in the United States. In three EU countries, Germany, Ireland, and Italy, self-employment programs are a great deal larger than in the United States, and these programs are part of a broad policy to expand employment and encourage entrepreneurship.

Lack of entrepreneurial training. A key reason for the small size of the SEA program is the lack of permanent, reliable sources of entrepreneurial training. In Program Year 2005, only 359 WIA Adult and Dislocated Worker program exiters in the entire nation received entrepreneurial training—approximately seven entrepreneurial trainees per state. Similarly, in CY 2005, only 1,623 individuals participated in the SEA program, mostly because of the lack of entrepreneurial training resources. The incentives to providing this training clearly need to change.

Federal indifference. The USDOL has not promoted the SEA program in recent years. Without encouragement or technical assistance and guidance, the program lost its policy momentum. The few states that have implemented this program either have seen participation declines or steady participation at very low levels.

Sustainability. Small employment and training programs like SEA are difficult to implement and sustain. Few staff in the local offices know about them or have the ability to help them flourish. There is little coordination between the UI program, which pays for self-employment allowances, and the One-Stops, which both administer the program and either provide participants with entrepreneurial training and other re-employment services or refer them to such training and services.

Reporting problems. Reporting for the program is frequently inaccurate. Because the program is a stepchild within the UI program, the SEA program frequently has weak links to the rest of UI, including to the state workforce agency reporting unit.

Potential impact on new business formation. Although the Self-Employment Assistance program is small in the states in which it exists, it could have a modest but significant impact on the U.S. economy if the program were implemented nationwide and encouraged by the USDOL and the state agencies. If participation in the national SEA program reached 1 or 2 percent of regular UI beneficiaries and if the participants had 50 percent business start-up rates, the SEA program could yield 50,000 to 100,000 business start-ups per year. At that level, SEA would have contributed an additional 8 to 16 percent to the 637,100 U.S. business start-ups in 2007 (SBA 2008).

Recommendations

The federal government could do a great deal more to encourage states to adopt and use the Self-Employment Assistance program. The Department of Labor should do three things:

1) Provide states with information, guidance, and technical assistance;

2) Encourage states to enact SEA programs;

3) Encourage states to provide entrepreneurial counseling and training through their Workforce Investment Act programs. Disincentives to providing entrepreneurial training that stem from the WIA performance measures should be removed by developing new performance measures for the outcomes of the SEA program.

The department should work with the Small Business Administration and encourage it to provide entrepreneurial training and counseling services to SEA and WIA participants. The SBA should be encouraged to become a partner in the SEA program and in the provision of entrepreneurial services to the WIA Adult and Dislocated Worker programs.

Funding of entrepreneurial training is a key problem that must be addressed if the SEA program is going to work well and expand in the future. In most states with SEA programs, the program is considered to be a UI program, and thus support from other agencies is weak. SEA allowances can be funded from the Unemployment Trust Fund, but entrepreneurial training and other business development services cannot. Other funding sources such as the governor's WIA discretionary funds or the UI penalty and interest fund are currently being used in some states, but they are too small and vary too much over time to be reasonable ongoing sources of funding. State and local WIA entities cannot be expected to provide WIA funds for entrepreneurial training when self-employment income is not reflected in the WIA common performance measures, which use UI wage records to determine whether workers entered wage and salary employment. Participation in the WIA entrepreneurial training program is punished by the WIA performance measurement system, which is based on UI wage records. Funding of entrepreneurial training could be encouraged in three ways:

1) A separate entrepreneurial training account could be created within the WIA Dislocated Worker Program to encourage the provision of entrepreneurial training services. The account would be available to all states with SEA programs. This new account would encourage states with existing SEA programs to expand them, and other states to enact these programs. The initial funding level would not have to be large—$10 million would allow training for more than 3,000 workers—a sharp increase from the less than 2,000 UI beneficiaries participating in SEA in 2007. As SEA participation increases over time, the account funding level also should increase.

2) States should be encouraged to have their SBDCs, Service Corps of Retired Executives, and state departments of commerce participate in the SEA program and provide counseling and training.

3) The Department should work with the Small Business Administration to have the SBA encourage state SBDCs and the Service Corps of Retired Executives to provide counseling and training to both SEA and WIA participants.

Congress should encourage state use of the SEA program. One incentive would be to have SEA benefits paid out of the Federal Unemployment Tax Act (FUTA) account in the Unemployment Trust Fund rather than from the state accounts, as is currently the case.

Notes

1. Jon Messenger wrote much of the section of this chapter titled "The Self-Employment Assistance Experiments" (p. 297).
2. I led a group of 14 individuals who were expected to participate in the self-employment demonstration projects on this study tour, which was funded by the German Marshall Fund. The German Marshall Fund also funded two earlier study tours of senior officials to examine policy aspects of the European programs.
3. The mean midyear value of the euro was 1.22 to the dollar in 2004.
4. $5.1 billion was the entire Training and Employment Services account for FY 2004.
5. Markus Franz, e-mail message to the author, November 19, 2008. Franz at the time was the counselor for labor and social affairs at the German Embassy in Washington.
6. Ibid.
7. Ibid.
8. Ray Uhalde, in an interview with the author, August 12, 2008.
9. The ETA's Field Memorandum 81-87, dated August 11, 1987, requested USDOL regional office staff to recommend states to participate in a Self-Employment Demonstration Project.
10. The department decided to proceed with a demonstration in three states. In response to a call for state applicants in a *Federal Register* notice dated March 1, 1988, five states applied to participate in the Three State Demonstration: Alaska, Iowa, Massachusetts, Minnesota, and Oregon. After extensive negotiations, Massachusetts, Minnesota, and Oregon were selected to participate.
11. The project officer at the German Marshall Fund, Ann Heald, recommended that the study tour visit Sweden because of Sweden's efficient management of its self-employment program. Tour participants studied the Swedish operational methods as well as its program design. They also brought back the British self-employment program forms as an aid to designing project forms and determining what project data elements to collect. I was the director of the study tour.
12. The net impact estimates for the Massachusetts demonstration presented in this section are based on the results of the first and second cohorts out of the three cohorts of project enrollments. Since the third cohort of participants did not complete participation in demonstration activities until 1993, only one round of follow-up surveys was completed with these individuals, and the follow-up period was substantially shorter than for the first and second cohorts (19 months versus 31 months). In addition, changes in state UI policy arising from enactment of the Emergency Unemployment Compensation (EUC) Act of 1991 substantially altered the implementation of the demonstration for Cohort 3. Benus et al. (1995) presents a full discussion of these changes.
13. The term "survival rates" indicates the number of project participants or control-group members who were self-employed at the time of the follow-up survey, divided by the total number of participants who entered self-employment at some point during the three-year follow-up period.

14. The measurable benefits to society from the demonstration accrue because of earnings and asset gains among project participants. It is assumed that society derives value from additional market output that is equal to the value of this additional compensation. These measurable benefits are then compared to the costs of self-employment demonstration administration and service costs. There are other potential benefits of self-employment, such as community economic development and psychological well-being, that cannot be readily quantified. The methodology that was used for calculating demonstration benefits and costs is described in the final report.

15. Carolyn Golding, interview with the author, December 5, 2008.

16. Lawrence Katz, telephone interview with the author, August 21, 2008.

17. Alan Krueger, telephone interview with the author, October 13, 2008.

18. David Balducchi, note to the author, July 18, 2005.

19. Self-Employment Assistance was enacted as part of Title V (Transitional Adjustment Assistance) of the North American Free Trade Agreement (NAFTA) Implementation Act (P.L. 103-182).

20. Section 3 of the Noncitizen Benefit Clarification and Other Technical Amendments Act of 1998 amended NAFTA to repeal the SEA termination date, making the SEA program permanent.

21. Robert Reich, interview with the author, November 21, 2008.

22. Golding, interview.

23. Katz, phone interview.

24. Reich, interview.

25. Katz, phone interview.

26. Reich, interview.

27. See Unemployment Insurance Program Letter 14-94, "Provisions Relating to Self-Employment Assistance," in Wandner (1994a), chap. 3.

28. Mary Ann Wyrsch, interview with the author, July 29, 2008.

29. Jon C. Messenger, comments on draft of this chapter, October 23, 2008.

30. According to the SEA annual report for 1996, prepared by the New York State Department of Labor and titled *Taking Care of Business: The Self-Employment Program, Annual Report*, 392 out of the 675 program participants surveyed responded to the survey, for an overall response rate of 58 percent.

31. David Fitzgerald, interview with the author, October 23, 2008. Fitzgerald was at that time chief of benefits for the UI program.

32. The Washington State SEA program does not conform to the federal SEA program. Under the Washington provisions, the state continues to pay regular UI benefits, rather than self-employment allowances in lieu of regular UI benefits. The Washington State law requires participants to be in full-time entrepreneurial training, while federal SEA law requires participants to be working full time to set up a business. This information was supplied by Jamie Bachinski in an e-mail message to the author, December 31, 2008.

33. See discussion below about the continuing operation of SEA in Pennsylvania.

34. Ray Fillipone, interview with the author, October 3, 2008.

35. The Washington State program, however, is listed as a federally conforming SEA

program in the Comparison of State Unemployment Insurance Laws (USDOL 2008b).

36. Fitzgerald, interview.

37. Susan Bass, interviews with the author, April 23 and June 9, 2008. Bass was then the director of the Maryland Self-Employment Assistance Program.

38. Ibid.

39. Charles Hartfiel, in an interview with the author, June 6, 2006. Hartfiel was at that time the Unemployment Insurance administrator for Minnesota.

40. Ibid.

41. Carolyn Peterson-Vaccaro, interview with the author. Peterson-Vaccaro was the first director of the New York Self-Employment Assistance Program.

42. Ibid.

43. Mark Rickert, interview with the author, October 1, 2008. Rickert was the assistant director of the Unemployment Insurance Program for New York State.

44. Ibid.

45. Peter Cope, e-mail message to the author, January 25, 2007. Cope was then the director of the Pennsylvania Bureau of Unemployment Compensation Benefits and Allowances.

46. When Secretary Chao went to Minnesota and announced that the state was being given a grant to participate in the program, the state workforce agency realized that the USDOL was not aware that the state program had terminated. The state legislature quickly introduced a temporary bill to allow Minnesota to waive the work-search requirement for participants in Project GATE who were UI beneficiaries. It was enacted during a 2002 special session of the state legislature and became effective in 2003. As a result, workers enrolled in Project GATE in 2003–2005 are reflected in the Minnesota reports submitted to the U.S. Department of Labor for the SEA program.

9
Work Sharing

with David E. Balducchi

INTRODUCTION

Work sharing—also called short-time compensation (STC)—was the experiment that did not happen.[1] As work sharing emerged as a U.S. public policy issue in the 1970s, the Carter administration announced a 1977 plan to have the federal government take a leadership role by launching a rigorous demonstration project using experimental methods. Soon after it was launched the plan fizzled. The demonstration was canceled, and it was left to the states to pursue and lead this program. Since then, both the states and the federal government have wielded leadership at different times in work sharing policy, and while the USDOL conducted two program evaluations, it has not pursued a rigorously evaluated demonstration.

Work sharing attempts to reduce layoffs by compensating a larger number of workers with partial unemployment insurance (UI) benefits in place of a total layoff for a smaller number of workers. For example, an employer can place 50 workers on a 20 percent hours reduction—to a four-day week—instead of achieving the same hourly reduction by temporarily laying off 10 workers. In 17 states, individual firms, with the support of their employees, can file work sharing plans with a state UI agency. If the state agency approves the plan, work sharing can be used for a period of time, generally up to one year. During that time, workers can receive work sharing benefits for weekly work reductions of 10 percent or more, usually a one-day reduction. Work sharing benefits are calculated as a prorated share of a worker's weekly UI benefit amount. Work sharing benefits are deducted from the total normal entitlement workers have for UI benefits, and work sharing plus UI benefits cannot exceed that entitlement during a one-year period. The benefits paid are charged to the employer in accordance with normal state UI experience-rating provisions.

Work sharing has been advocated by some policy analysts as a program that could improve the behavioral impact on workers in relation to the UI program. The American UI program has been found by some analysts to have a pro-layoff bias. Factors mentioned as contributing to this bias include incomplete UI experience rating, which encourages additional layoffs once firms reach maximum tax levels, and a UI partial benefit formula that permits only very limited hours of work per week. The effect of these disincentives sits heavily with the UI program, so it is not surprising that reforming the UI program has been seen as part of the solution. One proposal has been for greater adoption and utilization of work sharing (Abraham and Houseman 1993, pp. 132–147).

For a state to adopt a work sharing program, the state legislature must enact work sharing provisions as part of the state UI statute. In the absence of special legislation, workers who experience a modest reduction in their weekly hours of work would not receive UI benefits under regular state UI partial benefit formulas. These normal partial benefit formulas are designed to pay benefits to workers whose hours are so sharply reduced that they are in need of income support, so they are usually only available to workers who work no more than one or two days a week. Work sharing has the effect of suspending and superseding these normal UI partial-benefit payment provisions.

Work sharing is available in a number of European countries and in Canada. It was first implemented in the United States in 1978 in California. Today, it is an optional UI program that states can adopt as part of their UI system. The program was authorized by Congress through legislation enacted in 1982 and again in 1992. Nationally the program is small and infrequently used, but it is more important in a small number of states, and it represents an additional, targeted program used by employers to ease the problems associated with unemployment.

WORK SHARING IN OTHER COUNTRIES

Work sharing was first developed in Germany in 1927, and it operated briefly under the Weimar Republic. After World War II, Germany reestablished work sharing, and work sharing spread throughout Western Europe and to Canada. It was a popular program in Europe for several decades, but prior to the Great Recession of 2007–2009 it had declined in usage as Europe became more concerned with labor market flexibility and less concerned with job security. Given work sharing's long history in Europe, European work sharing programs can shed light on work sharing policy options for the United States.

Work Sharing in Germany since World War II

Work sharing in Germany has been modified and adapted in the post–World War II period. Its procedures were adopted as part of the Employment Promotion Act of 1969. It has been supported by the tripartite employment policy participants: government, labor, and management, working as partners. Work sharing attempted to support the stabilization of employment, labor-management relations, and society in general (Jensen 1995, pp. 7–10)

Work sharing ("short-term working allowance") is popular in Germany, particularly in times of economic downturn. When the economy weakens and employers have reduced orders, as a first step employers generally lay off temporary or contract workers. If that reduction is not sufficient, employers' second step frequently is to apply to participate in work sharing with the Federal Employment Agency. As part of the request, a firm must demonstrate that it faces a cyclical problem and that the prospects for recovery are good. If the request is approved, working hours may be reduced substantially, even by up to 100 percent.[2]

The German work sharing program is generous and highly flexible. For employees, work sharing replaces a larger share of lost income—60 percent for single workers and 67 percent for workers with families—than in the United States. At the same time, work sharing benefits do not reduce workers' entitlement to regular UI benefits. Workers who face a subsequent layoff can receive full entitlement to their UI benefits. Work sharing is attractive to employers because it reduces the cost of wages in a time of crisis. Work sharing benefits are not an additional cost to the employer: UI taxes are funded by a flat payroll tax on employers and employees, and the benefits are not experience-rated, as they are in the United States. Thus, use of work sharing by employers reduces wage and salary costs but imposes no additional UI contribution. On the other hand, employers must maintain their contributions to pension and national health insurance funds at the same rate as if the workers were working full time.[3]

As laws restricting worker dismissals tightened over time in Germany, the rules for work sharing were loosened. Work sharing plans were limited to six months before 1969. Since then, the normal six-month plan has been subject to extension, first to 12 and later to 24 months. Today, work sharing can be drawn for six months, but can be extended for up to 24. Work sharing program oversight attempts to assure that layoffs would have occurred if an employer's work sharing plans had not gone into effect (MaCoy and Morand 1984, pp. 53–58; Vroman 1992).[4]

Use of the German program has been highly cyclical. Use has been greatest early in a recession and then has declined as the recession advances. During past major recessionary years, work sharing recipients have numbered half or more of the workers receiving UI benefits. Although there was a downtrend in the utilization rate through the 1980s, the percentage reduction in the work week for participating workers increased (Vroman 1992, pp. 22–27).

Work sharing use increased to more than 200,000 participants in 2002, in response to the 2001 recession, but declined sharply thereafter. The cost of the program reached almost 700 million euros. The average cost per participant has been 3,000 to 4,000 euros. In late 2008, the financial and economic crisis in Germany led to a sharp increase in the number of applications to the Federal Employment Agency, particularly in the auto industry. The number of applications for work sharing is viewed by Germans as one indicator of the economic situation in the country, and the 2008 economic downturn was reflected in the increased use of the work sharing program (Table 9.1).[5]

Several critical differences exist between the German and U.S. work sharing programs. U.S. employees are less inclined to use a program that provides less wage replacement and reduces future eligibility for regular UI benefits. U.S. employers are less likely to use a program that is experience-rated and results in increased direct cost to themselves. By contrast, work sharing is particularly attractive to German employers facing stringently enforced advance notice provisions, because it provides greater short-run flexibility and wage bill reductions. The U.S. work-sharing program suffers lower participation from being more closely tied to this country's UI program, which has less generous UI benefit payment levels and a financing system that assigns employers direct responsibility for the benefit costs of their former employees.

Table 9.1 Expenditures for Participating Workers and Employers in Short-Time Work in Germany, 2000–2007

Year	2000	2001	2002	2003	2004	2005	2006	2007
Participants	86,052	122,942	206,767	195,371	150,593	114,607	66,482	68,317
Employers	—	—	—	—	—	10,718	6,561	8,333
Expenditures (euros, in millions)	—	—	607	687	637	416	150	—
Expenditures per participant (euros)	—	—	2,900	3,500	4,200	3,600	2,300	—

NOTE: — = not available.
SOURCE: Eichhorst and Zimmermann (2007) for expenditures and for participants 2000–2004; e-mail message from Markus Franz on November 22, 2008, for participants and employers 2005–2007.

The U.S. institutional structure encourages adjustments of employment, while the German system encourages adjustment of hours. According to Abraham and Houseman (1994a, p. 32), the difference in "labor adjustment lies not in the adjustment of total labor input, but rather in its division between adjustments to the number of workers employed and adjustment to hours per worker. German companies rely much more on adjustment of average hours, including the use of short-time work, to reduce labor input during downturns; American companies make greater use of employment adjustment, and by implication layoffs."

Much of this difference in employment adjustment is in timing. In a recession, U.S. employment adjusts downward very quickly, while in Germany adjustment takes place with a lag. In Germany, work sharing tends to be used during the first year of a cyclical downturn, as employers substitute a decline in hours for a decline in employment. German employment declines tend to take place after this delay of about one year. Thus, work sharing acts to stabilize employment in the short run, although it does not prevent long-term downward adjustments (Abraham and Houseman 1994b, pp. 86–94; Vroman 1992, pp. 27–30).

Work Sharing in Europe

By the mid-1990s, work sharing programs had been adopted by a dozen nations: Austria, Belgium, Denmark, France, Germany, Great Britain, Italy, Luxembourg, the Netherlands, Norway, Sweden, and Canada (Cook, Brinsko, and Tan 1995). All had the same goal: that of retaining jobs during a cyclical downturn by substituting hours reductions for reductions in employment. But the programs varied among themselves as well as differing in some critical ways from the U.S. program.

A comparison of programs in Belgium, Canada, France, and Germany as they existed in the mid-1990s shows a variety of program designs. For most programs, the government required both employer and worker approval of submitted work-sharing plans. Plans could stay in effect for widely varying periods, with the maximum program length ranging from 6 to 24 months. Canada had minimum and maximum weekly reductions in hours, but Belgium and Germany had no such limits: the reductions could run from 0 to 100 percent. Replacement rates generally varied between 50 and 60 percent in Belgium, Canada, and France, but could be as much as 68 percent in Germany. Work sharing benefits were generally paid at the same level as regular UI benefits. Employers needed to retain full fringe benefits. Benefits did not count against UI eligibility. Funding was either from a nonexperience-rated, flat payroll tax or from general revenue (Cook, Brinsko, and Tan 1995).

The European Union (EU) collects data on work sharing programs through its statistical agency, Eurostat. Its 2004 data (European Commission 2006) shows short-time working allowances and partial unemployment benefits programs operating in six countries: Austria, Belgium, Finland, Germany, Luxembourg, and Spain (Table 9.2). The programs in Austria, Germany, Portugal, and Spain were listed as short-time working allowances. Work sharing participants varied from being less than 1 percent of the country's basic UI program participants up to nearly 15 percent. The programs in Finland and Germany were bigger than those in participating U.S. states, but the programs in Austria, Belgium, Finland, Luxembourg, and Spain were roughly similar in size. In the six countries that have short-time work or partial unemployment benefit programs, half have short-time work programs that are smaller than business start-up incentive (self-employment assistance) programs.

The pre–Great Recession decline in European use of work sharing was related to a shift in the overall labor market policy toward "flexicurity." Beginning in the mid-1990s, Denmark became one of the innovators of the flexicurity movement. Flexicurity tries to balance flexibility in the labor market with high levels of workforce security. Employers are more free to lay off workers. Employees are not guaranteed job security in their current jobs (labor contracts become flexible), but a combination of active labor market policies, lifelong learning strategies, and "modern social security systems" (including broad coverage of UI, pensions, and health care) is designed to create greater workforce security as workers move between jobs. Adoption of flexicurity spread throughout Europe, and by 2005 the European Union had adopted flexicurity as a central principle of its European Employment Strategy (European Commission 2005, 2007).

The movement toward flexicurity has had a negative impact on work sharing in Europe. Flexicurity is the antithesis of contractual labor arrangements, "which discourage or delay transfers" (European Commission 2007). Work sharing in Europe came to be seen as a tool that delays necessary adjustment, especially in cases such as Germany,

Table 9.2 Participants in UI, Short-Time Compensation (work sharing), and Start-Up Incentives in European Countries, 2004

Country	Unemployment Insurance	STC	STC/UI %	Start-up	Start-up/ UI %
Austria	591,498	480	0.08	3,952	0.67
Belgium	575,093	34,158	5.94	517	0.09
Bulgaria	—			—	—
Czech Rep.	169,109			6,002	3.55
Estonia	51,052			287	0.56
Finland	126,098	18,837	14.94	2,643	2.10
France	2,261,436			51,146	2.26
Germany	1,842,405	150,593	8.17	237,253	12.88
Greece	—			—	—
Hungary	109,654			5,203	4.74
Ireland	71,884			6,855	9.54
Italy	277,319			13,584	4.90
Lithuania	—			—	—
Luxembourg	7,744	484	6.25	15	0.19
Norway	112,918			262	0.23
Portugal	184,859			1,686	0.91
Romania	—			—	
Slovakia	74,750			2,958	3.96
Sweden	206,116			5,601	2.72
Spain	2,358,392	48,385	2.05	93,033	3.94
United Kingdom	2,458,030			3,492	0.14

NOTE: blank = data not applicable; — = data not available.

Participants. The measure of participants' use above is dependent on the availability of data. The "stock" (S) was generally used since it is more frequently available; it is a measure of participants as an annual average stock. In some cases, the stock measure was not available (or unreasonably small) so the number of "entrants" (E) was used; "entrants are participants joining the measure during the year (inflow)."

Unemployment insurance. This consists of "Full unemployment benefits" that are considered to be unemployment insurance rather than unemployment assistance programs or other means-tested programs.

Short-time compensation (STC). Called short-time work or partial unemployment benefits. Includes compensation for formal short-time working arrangements and/or intermittent work schedules, irrespective of their cause, where the employer/employee relationship continues.

Start-up incentives. Include loans or grants to individuals.

Work sharing and start-up incentives. Include only transfers to individuals, not to employers.

SOURCE: European Commission (2006).

where it was used on a large scale to address the problem of structural unemployment in East Germany after reunification. Flexicurity encouraged greater use of active labor market policies (ALMPs) and less use of UI-related programs such as work sharing.

By contrast, the self-employment assistance (SEA) programs are seen as a key component of European active labor market policies. Eighteen EU countries have "start-up incentive" programs, far more than the number that have work sharing programs. None of the newer members of the EU have a work sharing program, whereas five of the new countries (Bulgaria, the Czech Republic, Lithuania, Romania, and Slovakia) have start-up incentive programs. Thus, work sharing is a program for a small number of Western European countries with higher per capita incomes.

Despite the retreat from work sharing during much of the 2000s in Europe, work sharing returned as a preferred public policy during the Great Recession in many European Union countries. Germany was the greatest user of work sharing. Assessing the European response to the Great Recession, the European Commission considered work sharing to be one of the key public policy responses to weakening demand for labor (European Commission 2009).

DEVELOPMENT OF SHORT-TIME COMPENSATION PROGRAMS IN THE UNITED STATES

Origins of Work Sharing in the United States

Work sharing is not new to the United States. It was used somewhat as a voluntary, private, uncompensated program during both the Hoover and Roosevelt administrations without government involvement.[6] However, it declined and largely disappeared when three things happened: 1) economic conditions worsened as the Depression dragged on, 2) a federal-state UI program was enacted that compensated total layoffs but did not compensate work sharing arrangements, and 3) large-scale reemployment occurred at the end of the 1930s as production increased for national defense. During the 1950s and 1960s, the availability of UI benefits made layoffs more acceptable to employers (Abraham and

Houseman 1993, p. 134; MaCoy and Morand 1984, pp. 158–164; Platt 1956).

As restructuring of the U.S. economy began in the 1970s, the concept of government-based work sharing was first introduced in New York in response to employment problems and civil rights concerns. It was considered by the New York state legislature in 1975 but not enacted. In 1978, California was the first state to enact a work sharing program. Enactment was prompted by concerns about potential state government layoffs that might result from adoption of Proposition 13, a tax-cutting referendum that imposed state spending limits. Without work sharing, state budget cuts were expected to result in permanent layoffs of state employees. The work sharing program was enacted but never used for this purpose. Instead it was used by the private sector and became a small but popular program. The California state government strongly supported and promoted the program in its first few years of operation. In May 1981, California sponsored a national work sharing conference in San Francisco to promote the adoption and use of work sharing (Best 1981, pp. 87–89). Fourteen other states followed California's lead between 1982 and 1988, but the pace of expansion since then has slowed: only four states have adopted work sharing since 1988 (Table 9.3).

Six Phases of Work Sharing Policy

In the United States, work sharing policy has gone through six distinct phases. In the first phase, states developed work sharing policy with little federal policy or involvement. This phase lasted until 1982. The second phase overlapped with the first phase and began in 1980 when Congress seized upon the state policy innovations, resulting in the enactment of a temporary federal work sharing law in 1982. The third phase—the single period of active federal stewardship—lasted from 1982 until expiration of the temporary federal law in 1985, during which time eight states enacted work sharing laws. The fourth phase was a seven-year period of federal laissez-faire. State work sharing programs continued to operate, and the prior period of federal activism helped encourage seven additional states to enact work sharing laws. In the fifth phase, the recession of 1990–1991 prompted renewed congressional attention, resulting in enactment in 1992 of the permanent federal work sharing law. In the sixth phase, from 1992 through the present, the

Table 9.3 Summary of State Work Sharing/Short-Time Compensation Laws, 2008

State	Initial year of program	Limit on number of weeks	Reduction in hours worked (%)	Require full or health fringe benefits	Special STC tax, maximum rate (%)
Arizona	1982	26	10 to 40	Optional	Yes[a]
Arkansas	1985	26	10 to 40	Full	No
California	1978	[b]	10 or more	Optional	No
Connecticut	1992	26	20 to 40	Full	No
Florida	1984	26	10 to 40	Optional	Yes, 1.0
Iowa	1991	26	20 to 50	Optional	No
Kansas	1988	26	20 to 40	Optional	[c]
Louisiana	1986	26	20 to 40	Full	No
Maryland	1984	26	10 to 50	Optional	No
Massachusetts	1986	26	10 to 60	Health	[d]
Minnesota	1994	52	20 to 40	Full	No
Missouri	1987	26	20 to 40	Optional	No
New York	1986	20	20 to 60	Full	No
Oregon	1982	26	20 to 40	Optional	[e]
Rhode Island	1991	26	10 to 50	Optional	[f]
Texas	1986	52	10 to 40	Optional	No
Vermont	1986	26	20 to 50	Optional	No
Washington	1983	26	10 to 50	Health	No

NOTE: Illinois enacted work sharing in 1983, but the law expired in 1988. Louisiana enacted work sharing in 1986 but no longer operates the program.

[a] 1.0% if negative reserve ratio is less than 15%; 2% if 15% or more.

[b] California: no limit, but total paid cannot exceed 26 times the weekly benefit amount (WBA).

[c] Excludes negative-balance employers.

[d] Negative-balance employers are treated as reimbursers.

[e] If benefit ratio is greater than tax rate, reimburse excess at end of quarter.

[f] All short-time compensation (STC) benefits are charged to STC employer regardless of base-period charging rule.

SOURCE: USDOL (2008b).

U.S. Department of Labor has failed to implement most aspects of the federal work sharing law and policy, while 17 states continue to operate existing work sharing programs, and one additional state enacted a work sharing law.

Phase I—State initiation of work sharing (1975–1982)

Prior to 1982, states were on their own in developing compensated work sharing policies. Early in this period, coalitions of labor and business began promoting work sharing schemes as an outgrowth of the severe recession of 1974–1975. Until the "Great Recession," the 1974–1975 recession caused the greatest job loss since the Great Depression. The federal government enacted, and states implemented, a string of UI benefit extensions that allowed claimants to draw up to 65 weeks of benefits. Twenty-four states had to borrow from the federal UI trust fund to be able to afford to pay UI benefits and then qualified for generous repayment schedules. These activities made state government officials and business and labor organizations familiar with the UI programs and may have made states more amenable to trying modifications to their state UI programs—one such approach being work sharing.

New York State was the first to consider enacting state work sharing legislation. Initially the program was thought of as a social program to protect employment gains of minorities and women. Support for work sharing initially arose from the New York City Commission on Human Rights. Subsequently, Lillian Poses, a member of the Governor's Task Force on Unemployment for the state of New York, became the chief sponsor of a work sharing proposal that bore her name. The Poses Plan became part of a broader bill designed to improve the employment situation in general and the labor market position of women and minorities in particular. The legislation was introduced in the New York State Assembly in June 1975 but died in committee (Ittner 1984, pp. 121–122).

In 1978, when California became the first state to enact a work sharing program, State Senator Bill Greene of East Los Angeles, chair of the senate labor committee, championed the program and secured its passage. Business and organized labor were initially skeptical of the program but soon came to support and promote it (Lammers and Lockwood 1984, p. 62). While anticipated state employee layoffs never occurred, California's work sharing program was instead used by the private sector, and it soon became a small but popular program, supported by Governor Jerry Brown and the state's Employment Development Department (EDD). The program grew rapidly, as yearly enrollment of employers increased from 474 in 1979—the first full year of program operation—to 2,567 in 1982.[7] In May 1981, the EDD hosted a national work sharing conference in San Francisco. Business and labor groups, as well as the Council of State Governments, the National Governors Association, and state officials from New York and Pennsylvania, cosponsored the conference.[8] Featuring Congressman Pete Stark (D-CA), who supported federal work sharing, the conference provided national exposure for California's policy, and it stimulated other states to adopt programs (Best 1981, pp. 87–89; Ittner 1984, p. 128).

California's implementation was followed by legislation in Arizona in 1981 and Oregon in 1982. Importantly, the champion of the Arizona program was the Motorola Corporation. In the 1970s, Motorola was trying to implement a no-layoff policy for its employees, and at the time believed that the best way to achieve this goal was to utilize a UI-based work sharing program.[9] Motorola, whose largest production facility was in Phoenix, first approached the Arizona Department of Employment Security in 1977, asking for that department's support for an Arizona work sharing program. The Arizona workforce agency was initially skeptical, but it was won over to the program (St. Louis 1984). Motorola continued to support work sharing for a number of years and was instrumental in gaining enactment of work sharing programs in other states where it had operations—Florida, Illinois, and Texas. Motorola also encouraged work sharing by supporting a detailed case study of the implementation of the Arizona program (Morand 1990, pp. 314–315).

Interest in work sharing by the federal government stirred in 1977. The impetus for action came from civil rights concerns and studies of the work sharing program experience in Europe. Policy analysts were considering the possibility of adapting the program to the U.S. environment (Henle 1976; Levitan and Belous 1977). One of those analysts, Peter Henle, became the assistant secretary for policy, evaluation, and research at the department in 1977. Under his leadership, the USDOL conducted research and analysis, followed the progress of the California program, and decided to conduct an experiment that would test the efficacy of work sharing in major metropolitan labor markets. The department made the decision to conduct the project, selected a research contractor, and began the design for the demonstration and its evaluation.[10] Sites were considered and visited, and preparations for the experiment began. The AFL-CIO, however, expressed strong disapproval of work sharing and of the experiment, and the business community did not support the program. The Carter administration canceled plans for the experiment (MaCoy and Morand 1984, pp. 120–134).

The period 1975–1982 was one of work sharing innovation in New York, California, Arizona, and Oregon. Those states developed policy and programs without the guidance of the federal government. The USDOL became interested in the program, but ultimately it did little during this period. The department was more noteworthy for what it failed to do: it did not challenge state work sharing programs as contrary to federal UI law, although federal law provided no explicit authority to implement work sharing programs.

Phase II—Enacting temporary federal legislation (1980–1982)

That states led the way in initially implementing work sharing is not surprising, considering the history of social legislation in the United States. As compared to other industrial nations, the United States came late to the social-insurance policy table. For example, the United States enacted public old age pensions and UI as part of the Social Security Act of 1935. Germany had led the way with a national old age pension in 1889, and it was followed by 28 other, mostly industrial, nations through 1929. The United States only enacted social insurance programs after the concepts and operational details of such programs had been worked out by other nations, and after the economic collapse of the Great Depression had revealed the exposure of its workers to unemployment and poverty (Sass and Munnell 2006). In a similar manner, the United States ignored the development of work sharing among industrial nations until the 1970s.

In 1982, the federal government enacted a temporary work sharing law, following the lead of California, Arizona, and Oregon. The AFL-CIO had opposed work sharing for many years, but it reversed its policy in August 1981, when its executive council issued a resolution supporting compensated work sharing, provided that employee safeguards were incorporated into any legislation. Work sharing had strong support from the Committee on Economic Development and Motorola's Washington, D.C., lobbyists. The combination of state, business, and labor backing ultimately was sufficient to gain political support to enact a federal work sharing law (Ittner 1984, p. 128).

Rep. Patricia Schroeder (D-CO) introduced work sharing legislation in June 1980, a recession year. Her purpose was to ease recessionary job losses (Schroeder 1984, pp. ix–xi). The Reagan administration initially opposed federal work sharing, asserting that a federal law was not needed, since three states had already implemented work sharing provisions without federal work sharing authority. Two years later, when the United States faced another recession, federal work sharing legislation was enacted as part of the Tax Equity and Fiscal Responsibility Act (TEFRA) of 1982 (P.L. 97–248). The law passed with support from business, organized labor, and state employment security agencies.[11] Before enactment, the legislation was amended to address concerns held by employers and organized labor regarding potential abuses of the program. The concerns included three points of worry: 1) initiation of work sharing without the permission of the other party; 2) employers conducting layoffs first and then instituting work sharing later, instead of using work sharing as a substitute for layoffs; and 3) excessive use or duration of work sharing programs (Ittner 1984, pp. 129–134). TEFRA provided for a three-year experimental work sharing program and required the department to develop a model for state work sharing legislation, establish deadlines, and conduct research.

The federal law was complex; it consisted of three components with a total of 11 different elements. The three components were 1) a statutory definition of work sharing, 2) provisions for employer work sharing plans that would be developed prior to program implementation, and 3) the method of taxation to pay for work sharing benefits. Four elements defined what an authorized work sharing program would be and how it could operate as part of the regular UI program. The definition described the nature of a work sharing program. Six other elements enumerated the requirements of a qualified employer plan. These elements mostly reflected the concerns of business and organized labor about potential program misuse. One final element specified that the tax provisions for work sharing had to be charged to employers in a manner similar to the way they are charged under state UI laws—as a safeguard to ensure that the cost of work sharing would be borne by the participating employer and not passed on to other employers. Thus, the final bill fulfilled Schroeder's basic interest in offering a simple, voluntary approach to work sharing, while allaying the fears of business and organized labor about what might go wrong in a largely untested program (Ittner 1984, pp. 126–132).

During this second phase, state work sharing policy and programs got the attention of Congress. Congress considered temporary work sharing legislation and, with the impetus of a recession, enacted it.

Phase III—Policy under the temporary federal legislation (1982–1985)

While the temporary law was in effect, the department developed model state legislative language and administrative guidelines. The language was published and distributed to the states in July 1983. The department's model legislation authorized states to enact companion laws, as long as they addressed the three components of the federal law. Thus, the model state laws contained 1) definitional elements, 2) qualified employer plan requirements (i.e., administrative components and eligibility provisions, including maintenance of health and retirement benefits), and 3) UI tax-charging provisions for employers participating in work sharing. In addition, the model legislation contained administrative provisions relating to the scope and identification of affected employer units and participants, as well as a requirement that participating employers report their work sharing activities to the state workforce agencies (USDOL 1983, pp. 5–21).

With enactment of a temporary work sharing law and the distribution of federal guidance, states began to consider whether to adopt work sharing as part of their employment policy strategy. The authority for states to operate work sharing programs under federal law commenced on September 4, 1982, and lasted until September 3, 1985, although states would continue to operate their work sharing programs without express legislative authority until that authority resumed with new federal work sharing legislation, enacted in 1992. During this phase, the states of Arkansas, Florida, Illinois, Maryland, New York, Texas, Vermont, and Washington enacted work sharing laws.[12]

The majority of state work sharing programs were implemented during the 1980s. The states that initiated programs back then envisioned work sharing as a component of their active labor market policy. Efforts to enact work sharing legislation generally began with discussions between progressive lawmakers, employers, governors, and the state employment security agency administrators. The USDOL provided technical assistance to the states. For example, in 1984, then–Arkansas governor Bill Clinton developed an economic initiative in response to continuing high levels of unemployment. Clinton's goal was "to accelerate job and income growth," and work sharing was conceived as a small human-capital component of a broader initiative.[13] Clinton's staff contacted the USDOL, requesting information about work sharing, which staff members then used to develop the work sharing portion of the state legislative package.[14] Clinton's economic package was presented to the state legislature in 1985 and enacted the same year (Clinton 2004, pp. 317–318).

Congress, however, wanted further information about the effects of work sharing before making the program permanent. Section 194 of TEFRA therefore required the department to report to Congress on state work sharing programs. Between 1982 and 1983, Mathematica Policy Research, under a contract with the USDOL, evaluated the work sharing experience of California, Arizona, and Oregon (Kerachsky et al. 1986). The evaluation found the following:

- Work sharing participation reduced the number of layoff events;
- Although total hours of regular UI collection were lower for employers participating in work sharing, the average total compensated unemployment (including both regular UI and work sharing benefits) was more expensive for those firms;
- Work sharing participation helped firms save on the hiring and training costs that would have been associated with layoffs; and
- The administration of work sharing benefit payment activities on a per-layoff equivalent basis was more expensive to the state than the administration of regular UI.

The evaluation failed to find the administrative and behavioral problems feared by interest groups. For example, organized labor had been concerned that work sharing would negatively impact the receipt of fringe benefits, particularly private and public pensions and health insurance, as well as provoke other potential employer program misuse. Also, the Labor Department and business were concerned that administrative costs might be excessive and might shift the tax burden to nonparticipating employers. The evaluation report minimized concerns about these potential adverse impacts.[15] At the same time, the study did not find that work sharing provided net benefits to the government because of the associated higher total costs to the Unemployment Trust Fund.

The 1982 legislation called for the appointment of an advisory committee composed of business, labor, and public members to oversee the work sharing evaluation. The department selected the members of this committee from groups and individuals who were interested in and supportive of the program.[16] The advisory group reviewed the plan for the evaluation and supported the comparison group methodology for the study. When the final evaluation was completed, however, the group objected to the results, which they believed inaccurately portrayed the work sharing programs. They requested an outside review of the evaluation by a Congressional Research Service economist, who challenged the selection method of the comparison group.[17] The Mathematica evaluation was completed and submitted to the department in late 1985 and published in 1986. The report was submitted to Congress along with comments from the advisory committee. In its comments, the committee was highly supportive of work sharing, criticized the Mathematica evaluation, expressed its conviction that there were no barriers to making work sharing permanent, and endorsed making the program permanent (Morand 1990, pp. 317–320).

Phase IV—Federal laissez-faire (1985–1992)

From September 1985 to July 1992, federal work sharing legislative authority lapsed. Yet state work sharing programs continued, and seven new states—Connecticut, Iowa, Louisiana, Missouri, Kansas, Massachusetts, and Rhode Island—enacted and implemented programs. As in Phase I, during Phase IV states enacted and operated work sharing programs without express federal authority.

The policy distinction between Phases I and IV is that, while in both phases states were left to themselves, in Phase IV state actions were informed by expired 1983 guidance to develop state legislation. At the same time, the department continued to collect and publish legislative and reporting data on state work sharing programs, and it conspicuously raised no issues of conformity with federal UI law, which no longer included a federal work sharing provision.

With the end of the temporary federal law, the department did not actively pursue work sharing policy or promote and support work sharing programs. The states with existing programs continued to operate them as if the federal law were still in place, and new states adopted work sharing using the expired guidelines. Stakeholder groups closely followed state work sharing programs, and the work sharing evaluation required under the temporary federal law produced mixed results. Congress, however, neither reacted to these findings nor reconsidered work sharing policy until unemployment rose substantially in the final two years of this phase.

Phase V—Enacting permanent federal legislation (1990–1992)

The 1990–1991 recession provoked further legislative efforts to help the long-term unemployed. In the fall of 1991, Rep. Stark, an early supporter of work sharing, developed a bill to revive a federal work sharing law. In November 1991, President George H.W. Bush signed the Emergency Unemployment Compensation Act (P.L. 102–164) to provide emergency unemployment benefits to long-term unemployed workers who ran out of regular unemployment benefits.

In January 1992, Stark introduced H.R. 4115 to make work sharing a permanent part of the UI program. During this period, Senator Harris Wofford (D-PA) developed a similar bill for Senate consideration. Wofford introduced S. 2614 in April 1992.[18] That bill sought to make work sharing permanent and provide for other UI reforms. Both bills included the detailed work sharing elements contained in the temporary work sharing law. In addition, Wofford's bill added a new provision to allow workers to receive employer-sponsored training to enhance job skills on their nonwork days while receiving work sharing benefits.

The Emergency Unemployment Benefits program was to expire in June 1992. Unemployed workers and interest groups seeking to continue the program deluged Congress with phone calls and letters. On June 9 the House passed H.R. 5260 to extend the emergency benefits program. A section of H.R. 5260 contained a limited version of the Stark bill, which allowed states to pay work sharing benefits. On June 19 the Senate passed its version of H.R. 5260, which contained similar work sharing language. Wofford urged the House and Senate conference committee to expand the work sharing program elements to include the maintenance of health and pension benefits and employer-sponsored training. On July 2, the conference committee adopted the stripped-down House bill, adding the Wofford provision to permit employees to participate in employer-sponsored training programs.

Congress enacted this bill. There is no legislative history as to why the House and Senate conference committee did not incorporate the more detailed work sharing elements contained in the 1982 temporary federal law (U.S. Congress 1992). One possible explanation is that, after a decade of work-sharing experience in the United States, any impetus for added benefit, tax, and administrative requirements had dissipated, especially as work sharing evaluation results had not borne out the initial fears of either employers or organized labor. Another is that Congress did not think the more detailed protections were necessary, as the secretary of labor retained general authority to promulgate regulations necessary to carry out the purposes of the act. In any case, Congress was anxious to complete action on an extension of unemployment benefits before departing for the July 4 recess.

On July 3, 1992, the first President Bush signed H.R. 5260 as the Unemployment Compensation Amendments (P.L. 102–318), which extended the benefits program and made work sharing a permanent part of the federal UI program. Similar to the temporary law, the Unemployment Compensation Amendments of 1992 required the department to develop model state work-sharing legislative language, establish guidelines and provide technical assistance to states, and conduct research. Dissimilar, however, was the elimination of the safeguards and restrictions on states, employers, workers, and unions. Section 401(d) of the act simply authorizes the use of the UI trust fund to pay work sharing benefits and provides a definition of work sharing that contains five elements:

1) Individuals whose work weeks are reduced by at least 10 percent are eligible for work sharing unemployment compensation;

2) The amount of unemployment compensation payable to any individual is calculated as a pro rata portion of the unemployment compensation that is payable to the individual if the individual is totally unemployed;

3) Eligible employees are not required to meet the availability for work or work search requirements while collecting work sharing benefits, but are required to be available for their normal work week;

4) Eligible employees may participate in an employer-sponsored training program to enhance job skills if such program is approved by the state workforce agency; and

5) The employer reduces the number of hours worked by employees in lieu of imposing temporary layoffs.

The elements are straightforward and are essentially definitional. The first three items repeat the definitional elements contained in the 1982 legislation. Item Five—requiring that work sharing be used when reducing the number of hours in lieu of layoffs—became part of the definition, whereas in the temporary legislation it was a requirement of a temporary employer plan. The fourth item was new and is not definitional; it embodies the Wofford provision to permit but not require employees to receive employer-sponsored training while engaging in work sharing. All earlier safeguards for business and organized labor that had been added to the temporary law were eliminated, reflecting the lack of political pressure to retain them. With the substance of the qualified employer plan removed, all references to such a plan—and to the requirement that work sharing benefits be taxed to employers like other UI benefits—were eliminated.

The effect of the federal work sharing legislation was to authorize the payment of work sharing benefits from the Unemployment Trust Fund under section 303(a)(5) of the Social Security Act and section 3304(4)(E) of the Federal Unemployment Tax Act (FUTA). Each state has an account within the Unemployment Trust Fund from which it pays UI benefits, and over the history of the UI program the fund has been carefully protected by federal policymakers to prevent its use for any purpose other than the payment of UI benefits. Under the permanent legislation, work sharing was defined as a UI program, and states were authorized to use funds in their Unemployment Trust Fund accounts to pay for work sharing benefits.

Phase VI—Work sharing policy under permanent legislation (1992–present)

Since the enactment of the permanent work sharing law, the department has neither distributed model state language nor provided guidance to states for implementing and operating work sharing programs. This inactivity reflects a controversy within the department about whether the new federal law was potentially defective. The crux of the dispute was whether the narrow provisions of the permanent law preclude the secretary from interpreting the law and exercising his or her discretion in administering it. While officials at the department were sorting through their policy options, the 1992 presidential election ceded the issue to the new Clinton administration.

Clinton political officials determined that the 1992 legislation required corrective action. They concluded that it limited the enforceable work sharing provisions to the five that were contained in section 401(d) of P.L. 02–318. Because the section did not include expansive language, such as that "the program meets such other requirements as the Secretary of Labor determines are appropriate," they opined that the secretary was constrained by the provisions as enumerated. If true, the secretary could not, for example, permit a state provision relating to maintenance of health and retirement benefits. Departmental officials also questioned whether states that had work sharing laws with greater protections than the federal permanent law (e.g., a requirement that labor agree to a work sharing plan) would be out of conformity with federal law. The department proposed corrective language in the House (H.R. 4040) and Senate (S. 1964) versions of the new administration's omnibus bill to update and restructure the nation's workforce development system—the Reemployment Act (REA) of 1994.

Section 251 of the proposed Reemployment Act of 1994 included language to correct the apparent technical deficiencies in the federal work sharing law by "clarify(ing) certain provisions of current law" and by adding several additional elements (USDOL 1994a).[19] The work sharing definition included in the REA bill contained nine elements, retaining the five elements of the 1992 Act and adding four additional elements. Two elements were adopted from the 1982 temporary law requiring the employer to produce a plan and permitting the maintenance of health and pension benefits. The state could require such a plan or the retention of such benefits, but only if it expressly chose to do so. The eighth element made employer participation voluntary—as it was under the 1982 act for organized labor and state workforce agencies. Finally, the ninth element gave the secretary discretion to impose "such other requirements as the Secretary of Labor determines are appropriate." It was this last provision that was considered key to allowing the secretary to provide guidelines and flexibility to the state work sharing programs.

The proposed Reemployment Act did not pass in 1994, and it was not reintroduced in 1995, when the Republicans had gained control of both houses of Congress. With the bill's demise, hope of resolving the work sharing policy dispute also faded. Further efforts at workforce development reform during the rest of the Clinton administration did not include revisions to federal work sharing policy.

In 1995, Representatives Ron Wyden (D-OR) and Amo Houghton Jr. (R-NY) introduced H.R. 1789 to make permanent the SEA programs and make technical changes to federal work sharing law. Subsequently, Rep. Sander Levin (D-MI) introduced technical amendments to work sharing in the 105th Congress (H.R. 3597) and in the 106th Congress (H.R. 1830). Representative Jim McClery (R-LA) introduced similar legislation in both sessions of the 107th Congress. Again, the work sharing provisions were not enacted. During this period, Congress did enact other workforce development bills, including the Workforce Investment Act (WIA) of 1998 and the Temporary Extended Unemployment Compensation Act of 2002, without fixing the work sharing program. In the absence of congressional action, the department has remained silent about whether the state work sharing laws are consistent with federal UI law. The department has not issued work sharing guidance, encouraged state participation in the program, or provided any technical assistance. Nevertheless, states have continued to use the program, and the department recognizes work sharing as an integral part of some state UI programs. Indeed, the department collects and publishes statistics on state work sharing programs and summarizes work sharing legislative provisions in its annual report comparing state UI laws.

Between 1985 and 2007, the number of beneficiaries under the program grew by more than a factor of 10, from 4,387 to 48,924. Similarly, work sharing beneficiaries as a percentage of regular UI program beneficiaries also grew by more than a factor of 10, from an insignificant 0.05 percent to 0.64 percent (Table 9.4).

In 2008, with unemployment increasing, interest in work sharing increased as well. Participation increased sharply in 2008 and exploded in 2009. Articles began appearing in newspapers about the increasing use of work sharing in some work sharing states, and policy interest increased.[20] On August 28, 2008, Barack Obama spoke approvingly of

Table 9.4 Work Sharing/Short-Time Compensation (STC) and Regular UI First Payments, 1982–2009

Date	STC first payments	Regular UI first payments	STC/regular UI first payments (%)
1982	2,649	11,648,448	0.02
1983	1,593	8,907,190	0.02
1984	3,189	7,742,547	0.04
1985	4,387	8,363,411	0.05
1986	12,956	8,360,752	0.15
1987	23,019	7,203,357	0.32
1988	25,588	6,860,662	0.37
1989	32,474	7,368,766	0.44
1990	44,922	8,628,557	0.52
1991	94,813	10,074,550	0.94
1992	97,619	9,243,338	1.06
1993	65,557	7,884,326	0.83
1994	53,410	7,959,281	0.67
1995	45,942	8,035,229	0.57
1996	41,567	7,995,135	0.52
1997	32,498	7,325,093	0.44
1998	47,728	7,341,903	0.65
1999	36,666	6,967,840	0.53
2000	32,916	7,035,783	0.47
2001	111,202	9,868,193	1.13
2002	93,797	10,092,569	0.93
2003	83,783	9,935,108	0.84
2004	42,209	8,368,623	0.50
2005	40,238	7,917,294	0.51
2006	39,854	7,350,734	0.54
2007	48,924	7,652,634	0.64
2008	96,388	10,052,694	0.96
2009	288,618	13,986,381	2.06

NOTE: The data for work sharing is incomplete: Connecticut and Maryland report other work sharing activity, but they generally do not report first payments; Arkansas has a work sharing program but has stopped reporting on it.

SOURCE: USDOL, Office of Workforce Security, required reports relating to the Unemployment Insurance Program, ETA 5159 reports for the regular UI program and for work sharing.

work sharing in his acceptance speech at the Democratic convention in Denver. Talking about what he believed are positive changes in behavior by Americans, the soon-to-be-elected president said, "I've seen it in the workers who would rather cut their hours back a day than see their friends lose their jobs." On a national stage, the Democratic candidate for president appeared to support work sharing in its most common form—a 20 percent reduction in the work week.

OPERATION OF U.S. WORK SHARING PROGRAMS

Program Provisions of the States

As experience has revealed few employer or labor abuses of the programs, states adopting work sharing have frequently, like California, relaxed their statutory provisions. California, for example, has an open-ended limit on the duration of work sharing plans and on the range of hours reduction, no requirement for maintenance of fringe benefits, and no special tax over and above its normal UI tax schedule (Table 9.2). Other states limit the duration of work sharing plans; all but two have durations of 26 weeks. All states allow a reduction of hours of between 20 and 40 percent during use of work sharing, but some states reduce the minimum percentage of hours to 10 percent. One state (Massachusetts) allows a maximum hours reduction of up to 50 percent. The hours reduction limits are prompted out of a concern that reductions should be modest and appropriate to the goals of work sharing. Thus, it has become accepted that reductions should be at least one-half day per week (10 percent), but generally should not be the majority of the week. Operationally, however, there has been no need for this concern. Work sharing has effectively become a program that reduces the work week from five days to four days—a 20 percent reduction.[21]

Even though employers tended to maintain fringe benefits during the use of work sharing, unions remained concerned about the potential reduction that could be imposed by employers. As a result, seven states have mandated that employers continue to provide either full fringe benefits or at least health insurance benefits. In most states, work sharing benefits, like other UI benefits, are charged to the employers. The first states that enacted work sharing programs—California, Arizona, and Oregon —were concerned about large-scale misuse of the program, particularly by firms that experienced great layoff activity, e.g., firms with negative balances in reserve ratio states. Over time this concern has diminished, and protective provisions are used less. Today seven states—including Arizona and Oregon, but no longer California—impose supplemental taxes or reimbursable provisions on some employers using work sharing. Without these additional tax charges, some employers could make use of work sharing at no additional cost if they already paid the maximum state UI tax rate. Some employer interest groups, thus, have been concerned that their members would end up picking up the tab for the negative-balance firms using work sharing. Nonetheless, 12 of the work sharing states have no special tax provisions.

Other work sharing provisions are not controversial. Work sharing benefits are calculated in several different ways, but all approaches tend to pay a percentage share of the weekly UI benefit amount, relating to the percentage reduction in the work week. State laws determine how many weeks of work sharing can be collected and what the total payment amount can be for individual participants. Each employer plan must be submitted to the state workforce agency for approval.

Many states with work sharing programs have been satisfied with them. In fact, in many cases state workforce agency officials have been the programs' champions. For example, the Kansas work sharing program received enthusiastic support from the Kansas officials, one of whom perceived it as an employer service, stating, "Now I've got something to offer employers rather than talking to them only about their taxes."[22] Other state administrators have been less enthusiastic. Some see work sharing as diluting the insurance features of the UI program, often increasing UI employer taxes and sometimes merely delaying instead of averting layoffs (Walsh et al. 1997).

One indication of satisfaction with existing work sharing programs is that the work sharing provisions, other than those dealing with taxes, have remained unchanged for over a decade. Since 1996, only three changes to work sharing laws have been made. Two states, Kansas and Rhode Island, have added a special tax provision, while Missouri removed its special tax.

States without Work Sharing Programs

Of the 53 state UI programs in the United States—the District of Columbia, Puerto Rico, and the Virgin Islands are "states" under federal UI law—only 18 have work-sharing laws. Louisiana adopted work sharing in 1986 but does not operate the program. The other 35 have not enacted such programs. A 1997 survey of all states (Walsh et al. 1997) revealed that the three main reasons for not adopting work sharing have been 1) lack of understanding about the program, 2) lack of support by key stakeholders, and 3) perceived disadvantages of the program. Lack of understanding included simple lack of information, but it also included a lack of understanding of the difference between work sharing and the basic UI partial benefit formula. Not only UI claimants but also some UI directors and state agency administrators lack this information. The current work sharing program has not been publicized by the department since the early 1980s, and there have been no recent private or public policy efforts to provide information or encourage its adoption.

The lack of support by stakeholders reflects a wide variety of groups who either have not provided active support or who have actively opposed the work sharing program. These groups might include the state workforce agency or its advisory council, state legislators, business, and labor. From the analysis of the reasons for the adoption of work sharing by 18 states (Walsh et al. 1997), it is clear that adoption requires strong support and initiative from one or more key stakeholders, with other stakeholders acquiescing. Work sharing is not a program that supporters can push through over active resistance.

According to the survey results, nonparticipating states perceived the disadvantages of work sharing to include an additional burden on the Unemployment Trust Fund (eight states) and additional administrative burdens and costs (six states). Some of these states also thought that the program was inappropriate because of the state's industrial composition—i.e., not enough manufacturing firms, not enough large firms, or too many agricultural and seasonal firms. Behind this perception seemed to be the belief that work sharing is best suited to large manufacturing firms. Thirteen states also believed that their existing UI programs were sufficient without work sharing, but some of the respondents erroneously thought that work sharing was similar to partial UI benefits.

In 2006, North Dakota enacted a one-year work sharing demonstration project but did not implement it. Thus, there has been no expansion of the work sharing program since Minnesota enacted the program in 1994.[23] The Walsh et al. (1997) survey found that 27 of the 34 non-work-sharing states either definitely or probably would not adopt work sharing. Only five states said they would consider adoption.

Scope and Operation of the U.S. Program

Work sharing programs are small, but states and employers have experienced wide variations in their use of the program. State goals for their work sharing have also varied, but it has worked best when the programs have been used to bridge temporary declines in the demand for the services of workers.

Size of the program

There is a separate work sharing report (the ETA 5159 work sharing report) that participating states submit to the department. These reports show that work sharing is a small program (Table 9.4). Between 1990 and 2008, work sharing benefits have been paid annually to between 32,000 and 111,000 U.S. workers who are covered by the UI system. These beneficiaries are a very small percentage of the 8–10 million workers who have been beneficiaries of the regular UI program in recent years. In fact, these beneficiaries have represented between 0.4 and 1.1 percent of regular UI beneficiaries through 2008.

While the work sharing program is very small nationally, it is highly countercyclical. In recessions, overall work sharing first payments have risen sharply as a percentage of regular UI first payments. From a norm of between 0.4 and 0.7 percent in the late 1980s, the percentage rose to 0.9 percent in 1991 and 1.1 percent in 1992. It returned to the norm, but again rose to 1.1 percent in 2001, declining to 0.9 percent in 2002 and 0.8 percent in 2003. Nationally, these figures are small compared to those of some European nations with work sharing programs.[24]

Work sharing, however, has been a much more important component of the UI program in the few states that keep the program fully operational. Table 9.5 shows that while work sharing claims were 1.1 percent of all beneficiaries in the United States in the recessionary year 2001, most states did not have work sharing programs. For the seven states that made greatest use of the program in that year, work sharing was much more important, amounting to over 3.0 percent of all beneficiaries. These states and their percentages are Rhode Island (6.2), Kansas (6.0), Missouri (6.0), Vermont (5.0), Arizona (4.9), New York (3.6), and California (3.2).

Coming out of the 2001 recession, six of the above seven states (Arizona being the exception) continued to have work sharing first payments at better than 1.5 percent of regular UI first payments. Thus, work sharing is popular among employers and employees alike in a small number of states. Today there is more persistent use of work sharing by employers in periods of both low and high unemployment in a half-dozen states with work sharing programs. The other work sharing states make only limited use of the program.

The first two work sharing states, California and Arizona, reached their highest levels of participation during the 1990–1991 recession. It should be noted, however, that Arizona's participation was heavily influenced in the 1980s and 1990s by the large-scale participation of one establishment, the Phoenix plant of Motorola (Kerachsky et al. 1986; Vroman 1992). Motorola was instrumental in getting work sharing enacted in Arizona, then made great use of the program for a number of years, but subsequently abandoned the program.[25]

Other states still have work sharing programs on their books, but they are either not supported or they are inactive. Louisiana's program is inactive. The Louisiana agency was initially interested in the program but then found that program administration was labor intensive for state government and for workers. The Louisiana program required that information be provided on a weekly basis about hours worked and whether workers were on vacation or not. The result was limited use, after initial interest. Louisiana firms now use temporary layoffs or a "skip week" option, whereby workers work for a week or two and then are laid off for a week or two, so that they collect full UI benefits on an intermittent basis. Louisiana no longer dedicates any staff to the work sharing program and does not encourage participation.[26]

The work sharing program in the United States has significant barriers to participation in states with work sharing programs. As the state survey indicates, the most immediate barrier is a lack of information. State UI central offices administer the program, but few of them provide much information or outreach. Local UI call centers and One-Stop

Table 9.5 Work Sharing First Payments as a Percentage of Regular First Payments, 1982–2008

State	1982	1983	1984	1985	1986	1987	1988	1989	1990	1991	1992	1993	1994	1995
AR[a]					—	0.3	0.2	0.4	1.5	0.6	8.2	0.1	—	—
AZ	2.5	0.3	0.6	—	6.7	2.4	2.7	0.7	2.4	2.4	4.1	2.6	1.6	1.7
CA	—	0.1	0.3	0.4	0.7	1.4	1.9	0.3	2.2	3.5	3.3	3.4	2.5	1.9
CT[b]											0.1	0.6	—	—
FL			—	—		0.5	0.8	0.5	0.5	1.6	1.3	0.6	0.7	0.6
IA										0.8	—	0.1	—	0.1
KS								0.8	1.4	5.0	3.9	2.5	1.8	3.9
LA[c]					0.0	0.1								
MA								—	—	—	0.3	0.3	0.1	0.1
MD[b]				—	—	0.3	0.3	0.1	—	—	0.5	—	—	—
MN													0.1	0.5
MO						0.1	0.2	0.4	1.2	2.6	2.1	1.7	3.0	2.1
NY						0.1	0.3	0.2	1.0	2.1	2.4	1.2	1.0	1.1
OR			—	—	—	0.1	0.1	0.3	0.2	0.6	0.7	0.4	1.7	0.5
RI										0.0	2.9	1.4	1.9	1.4
TX					—	0.7	0.3	0.2	0.6	1.0	0.6	0.5	0.4	0.4
VT					—	0.0	—	—	—	—	0.6	1.1	0.7	1.3
WA			0.0	0.0	—	0.1	0.7	0.8	0.9	1.8	2.0	1.6	1.5	1.6
US	0.0	0.0	0.0	0.0	0.2	0.2	0.4	0.4	0.5	0.9	1.1	0.8	0.7	0.6

State	1996	1997	1998	1999	2000	2001	2002	2003	2004	2005	2006	2007	2008
AR[a]	—	—	—	—	—	—	—	—	—	—	—	0.2	1.3
AZ	2.9	1.7	3.1	2.2	1.1	4.9	2.4	1.5	0.7	0.4	0.0	1.9	1.7
CA	1.8	1.6	2.6	1.7	1.2	3.2	2.6	2.3	1.4	1.5	1.3	1.8	2.2
CT[b]	—	0.0	—	—	—	—	—	—	—	—	—	—	—
FL	0.5	0.5	0.2	0.5	0.3	1.0	0.6	0.4	0.1	0.1	0.1	0.1	0.3
IA	0.0	0.0	0.1	0.5	0.0	0.0	0.1	0.4	0.0	0.0	0.0	—	—
KS	3.7	3.8	2.9	3.7	3.0	6.0	4.0	3.2	1.8	2.1	2.4	3.2	—
LA[c]													
MA	0.1	0.2	0.2	0.1	0.0	1.1	2.8	2.3	0.6	0.4	1.0	0.9	1.1
MD[b]	—	—	0.1	—	—	—	—	—	—	—	—	—	—
MN	0.2	0.1	0.2	0.3	3.0	2.1	2.3	2.1	0.7	0.8	1.0	1.5	2.2
MO	1.4	2.5	3.9	2.2	3.5	6.0	4.1	4.3	3.5	3.8	5.3	4.9	6.2
NY	1.2	0.8	1.0	1.1	1.2	3.6	2.5	2.2	1.2	1.5	1.2	1.3	1.3
OR	0.4	0.1	0.3	0.4	0.2	1.5	1.3	1.5	0.6	1.3	2.0	0.9	1.6
RI	1.6	1.0	2.3	2.7	1.3	6.2	3.7	5.6	3.6	3.9	4.4	4.5	8.1
TX	0.2	0.2	0.3	0.3	0.6	1.1	0.7	0.7	1.3	1.1	1.1	1.7	2.2
VT	1.9	0.9	2.3	4.9	1.6	5.5	5.5	4.0	3.5	5.0	2.0	2.9	5.0
WA	1.4	1.0	0.8	0.9	1.2	2.0	1.7	1.5	0.8	0.5	0.6	1.0	2.8
US	0.5	0.4	0.7	0.5	0.5	1.1	0.9	0.8	0.5	0.5	0.5	0.6	1.0

NOTE: Required reports submitted to USDOL as the ETA 5159 (work share) report, for the years 1982 through 2005. Data erroneously submitted by Puerto Rico and the Virgin Islands have been removed; they have never enacted work sharing programs. — = no data is available for years after state work sharing legislation was enacted. Blank = not applicable.

[a]Arkansas has a work sharing program but stopped reporting on it.

[b]Connecticut and Maryland report other work sharing activity but generally not first payments.

[c]Louisiana's program expired in 1986. Illinois enacted a program in 1983 but allowed it to expire in 1988; no benefits were ever paid under the program.

SOURCE: USDOL, ETA 5159 reports.

centers have little information about the program because they do not have an operational role to play. As a result, most employers indicate that they learn about the program by word of mouth. In the states where work sharing usage is highest, publicity appears to be the most important reason for its high usage. In the last U.S. evaluation, the five states with the greatest work sharing participation rates were found to have used publicity and outreach campaigns, and some of them also had involved local offices to provide information about the program (Best 1988, p. 62, cited in Jensen 1995, p. 27; Walsh et al. 1997, Chap. 4, pp. 1–45). Such publicity, however, could only be expected to raise state participation modestly.

Countercyclical versus structural unemployment

Work sharing is a highly countercyclical program. Since it is primarily designed to deal with temporary downturns in the demand for labor, it is expected to be little used during periods of economic expansion, when employers' demand for labor is increasing. Employer interest and use in it is generated by the onset of recessions. As a result, the work sharing program can be thought of as a work stabilization program used by employers during recessions when they expect to have only temporary declines in their need for labor.

Work sharing also has been used to address structural unemployment. Such use was much greater in Germany than in the United States. Germany has used work sharing extensively for structural adjustment; this occurred first in the coal and steel industries, allowing more time for adjustments to be made by natural turnover and retirements. Later it was used to assist in the absorption of East German workers in the 1990s.

In the United States, work sharing has only been considered as a method to ease structural adjustments for particular firms or industries. In the late 1980s and early 1990s, for example, the USDOL's Bureau of Labor-Management Relations and Cooperative Programs advocated work sharing as a tool to be used by labor management committees in individual firms to deal with impending structural unemployment.[27] Work sharing was one of a number of tools that the department recommended to employers and employees dealing with structural unemployment problems through labor-management committees. For example, in the early 1980s, the department recommended the use of work sharing to deal with structural problems in the steel industry (USDOL 1985).

The increasing importance of structural unemployment in the United States, however, has also reduced interest in work sharing. Firms are frequently more desirous of downsizing than they are concerned about retaining their current workforce. The early champion of work sharing, Motorola, abandoned that concept as it began its own structural adjustments. Its competitor, Hewlett-Packard, began using temporary workers, not work sharing, to address variations in the demand for labor, and Motorola determined that if it wanted to remain competitive in its industry, it could no longer engage in work sharing. Unions still support work sharing, but they also have responded to employers' changing employment policies. John Zalusky of the AFL-CIO said, "Since it is not very high on employers' agenda, it isn't very high on ours either" (Jensen 1995, p. 6).[28]

Employer and worker use of work sharing in the United States

Work sharing was expected to be used by a wide variety of firms, varying by industry, size, and financial status. However, in practice, program use in the United States has been limited. To the extent that firms use work sharing, those firms have been concentrated among large firms in the durable manufacturing industry. These firms tend to experience high levels of unemployment. Rather than simply substituting work sharing for layoffs, they have tended to continue to use layoffs as their primary means of reducing their labor force, while using work sharing as an additional reduction tool (Walsh et al. 1997). Work sharing primarily has been used by firms to retain their most highly skilled workers. Thus, rather than being a general-purpose, countercyclical work sharing program, the U.S. program seems to be a narrow-niche program.

Although interest in work sharing declined during the late 1990s, it increased again with the recession of 2001. As unemployment rose, some economists became concerned about the shortcomings of America's UI system, in which large numbers of workers were ineligible for or had exhausted unemployment benefits. The National Employment Law Project, the Economic Policy Institute, and the Center on Budget and Policy Priorities issued a report, *Failing the Unemployed* (Emsellem et al. 2002), that characterized state UI systems as beset with inequities and strict requirements, which shut too many workers out of benefits. The report urged state lawmakers to enact UI reforms, including work sharing in states where the programs were not up and running (Cadrain 2002).

An analysis of the program as it existed in California in 2002 (MaCurdy, Pearce, and Kihlthau 2004) is quite revealing. It shows that work sharing was used by a small number of employers (0.9 percent of firms that paid UI benefits), and that their use was limited; e.g., work sharing weeks compensated generally have been less than 1.5 percent of UI weeks compensated except in periods of recession. Employers who used work sharing in California in 2002 were usually larger, higher-wage, more likely unionized, and more likely to be in the manufacturing sector than non–work sharing, UI-paying firms. Work sharing firms had an average employment of 239 workers, compared to 40 workers for non–work sharing firms. They paid average wages of $39,200 per year, compared to $34,400 for non–work sharing firms. Seventy-three percent of work sharing firms had been paying UI taxes for 11 years or more, compared to 48 percent for non–work sharing firms. Nineteen percent of the work sharing firms were unionized, compared to 9 percent of the non–work sharing firms. Whereas manufacturing accounted for 11 percent of the firms paying UI benefits, such firms constituted 62 percent of firms that used work sharing. While only 0.9 percent of UI-paying firms used work sharing, for manufacturing firms the figure rose to 5.5 percent. Among manufacturing firms, work sharing was concentrated in firms in two-digit Standard Industrial Classification codes; in these categories, the firms wanted to retain high-skilled workers who tended to be trained on the job: electronics producers, industrial machinery producers, fabricated metal producers, instrument manufacturers, and furniture manufacturers (MaCurdy, Pearce, and Kihlthau 2004).

Employees using work sharing in California in 2002 tended to be older and better paid than workers collecting regular UI, indicating that they were more skilled than other workers. Seventy-one percent of work sharing participants were 35 years of age or older, compared to 63 percent for non–work sharing claimants, and their 2002 earnings were 40 percent higher than those of non–work sharing claimants. They were mostly in the manufacturing sector. They also collected fewer weeks of benefits (MaCurdy, Pearce, and Kihlthau 2004).

Rhode Island is one of the largest users of work sharing. The state workforce agency believes strongly in the program as a method of reducing unemployment. Agency staff members believe that the program benefits greatly from extensive agency marketing of the program to employer and worker organizations, resulting in statewide support for the program. The state promotes work sharing in many ways: directly contacting employers after layoffs, placing stories in newspapers, prominently offering work sharing as part of the Rhode Island employer services package, describing it in the monthly bulletin sent to employers, making presentations to employer groups and labor unions, and marketing it on the agency Web site. The result of all of these efforts is strong support from the governor and labor unions, and awareness of the program by the state chamber of commerce. Support from employers has spread by communication among employers. Employers learn about the program from employers who have used the program. Employers and workers have responded strongly, with a very high rate of use since 2001 (Table 9.5) and a doubling of use in the two years ending in October 2008.[29]

Rhode Island's administrative costs for work sharing are greater than those for regular UI and greater than the UI administrators would like. Rhode Island would like to emulate its neighbor Massachusetts, which has completely automated the work sharing payment process, including employers' weekly reporting of claims through the Internet. By contrast, while Rhode Island has automated the application process for employers, work sharing payments are still made manually. If the Rhode Island agency had the funding it would fully automate the work sharing payment process, using the Massachusetts approach. Nonetheless, the agency is strongly in favor of work sharing, and it believes that it is good for the Rhode Island economy as well as for employers and workers.[30]

In 2001 and 2002, Massachusetts automated its work sharing program during the surge in work sharing activity in response to the 2001 recession. Massachusetts had to administer between 200 and 300 employer plans during 2003. It went from a fully manual to a fully automated system. Deloitte and Touche built the Massachusetts system, using USDOL administrative funds. Internet-based, the three-step system allows employers to 1) apply to participate, 2) submit their work sharing plans and have them approved, and 3) submit their weekly work sharing payment transactions. As a result, the process is fully automated for the state workforce agency, employers, and participating workers.

Massachusetts is happy with the software, which it has made available to other states such as Vermont, since it is in the public domain. The Massachusetts UI director has also sent the program and its documentation to the USDOL and to the National Association of State Workforce Agencies for use by all state workforce agencies.[31]

The level of work sharing participation is lower in Massachusetts than in Rhode Island. This is due in part to Massachusetts's lower unemployment rate, but it is also because Massachusetts has done considerably less outreach than Rhode Island. Information about work sharing is available on the agency Web site and was promoted in a 2008 mailing to employers, but agency staff have not met with employer and labor groups to promote the program. With sharply increasing unemployment in 2008, the news media became more interested in work sharing, and the Massachusetts program received increased media coverage. However, only 88 employers were participating in the program in October 2008.[32] In January 2009, as the recession worsened, Massachusetts had 92 businesses enrolled in the program, with 1,300 workers receiving work sharing benefits. By that time applications had surged, with another 100 firms and another 1,700 workers waiting to participate (Crimaldi 2009).

During the Great Recession of 2008–2009, state work sharing programs experienced the highest usage by employers in the history of the federal-state UI system. In January 2008, as the recession began, a study on the stalemate in federal work sharing policy was published in *Publius* (Balducchi and Wandner 2008). As stakeholders, policymakers, and the press looked for public policy options to counter the recession, the article was widely read.

During 2009, a number of organizations began to advocate legislative action and increased use of work sharing during the recession. Neil Ridley (2009) of the Center for Law and Social Policy and Jon Messenger (2009) of the International Labour Organization provoked additional stakeholder interest in separate policy briefs describing the attributes of work sharing as an alternative to layoffs. In October, the National Association of State Workforce Agencies approved a new policy urging Congress and the U.S. Department of Labor to support enactment of work sharing in all states. In December, Sara Rix of the AARP hosted a national forum on work sharing policy to educate members and stakeholders in how to create successful work sharing initiatives

(AARP 2009). During the same period, work sharing received praise from economists such as Katharine Abraham, Susan Houseman, Mark Zandi, and Dean Baker.

The Congressional Research Service issued a report on work sharing to Congress by Alison Shelton (2009), and several bills were introduced in the House and Senate to correct the deficiency in the federal work sharing law and expand state participation through incentive grants. Given the unprecedented usage of work sharing during the Great Recession in the 17 states that operate programs, favorable testimonials from employers and workers contained in news stories from Steven Greenhouse (2009) of the *New York Times* and others, and endorsements from opinion makers and interest groups, it appeared possible that national work sharing policy might be revisited.

WORK SHARING IMPACTS AND COST-EFFECTIVENESS

Evaluations of work sharing programs in the United States and abroad have revealed mixed results. California conducted an early evaluation to determine whether to make permanent its initial, temporary program (Best 1988). The U.S. government conducted two evaluations, both mandated by the 1982 and 1992 federal work sharing legislation (Kerachsky et al. 1986; Walsh et al. 1997). The 1986 study was conducted in three states: Arizona, California, and Oregon. The 1997 study was conducted in five states: California, Florida, Kansas, New York, and Washington. There have been two large-scale evaluations of the Canadian program (Employment and Immigration Canada 1984; Ekos Research Associates 1993) and many smaller analyses of the program.

Because of the small size of the work sharing program and the high cost of running random assignment experiments, U.S. work sharing evaluations made use of comparison group methodologies. While analysis of the program evaluations that used random assignment experiments and comparison group methodology indicates that comparison groups cannot replicate experimental results (LaLonde 1986), comparison group studies are the best available guide to how work sharing programs work.[33] Nonetheless, the U.S. evaluations (Kerachsky et al. 1986; Walsh et al. 1997) have been limited in scope—in part because of a lack of data and limited funding for the evaluations. There were no benefit-cost analyses in the two national evaluations.

The Canadian evaluations, conducted in 1984, 1993, and 2005, are more comprehensive. They estimate program costs and benefits to society, even though sometimes the sources of data have been indirect. The Ekos 1993 study determined that work sharing is highly cost-effective, estimating the benefit-cost ratio of work sharing to be 2.6 to 1. The estimated cost of the program was incurred by the government in the form of increased total (UI plus work sharing) benefit costs of $52 million. This sum was composed of the costs of deferral of the UI waiting period, of filing for work sharing by those who would not file for regular UI benefits, and of paying UI benefits for post–work sharing layoffs. The estimated benefits ($137 million), however, were far less rigorously calculated. The benefits included $92 million in reduced stress from layoff avoidance (i.e., improved health and reduction in the use of social work and counseling services, police, and courts), $27 million in improved attitudes toward work (i.e., reduced future unemployment and UI costs), and $18 million in reduced hiring and training costs. The first two benefits were deemed to accrue to society, while the third accrued to employers. The study notes, but does not estimate, the cost of delayed adjustment to structural economic change in the form of labor hoarding.

The Canadian evaluations may provide some guidance about provision of training to workers while they are collecting work sharing. U.S. federal work sharing legislation permits states to allow workers to engage in training during the hours they are receiving work sharing so that they can increase their work skills. The three Canadian evaluations found that the offer of training resulted in low levels of take-up. In fact, in the evaluation of "Work Sharing while Learning," a program that was part of a larger initiative to support workers and communities in regions of high unemployment and operated between 2002 and 2004, Canadian researchers found no take-up of the program—no one participated. Firms did not participate in WSWL because of three factors: 1) the high cost of formal training, 2) heavy reliance on cheaper on-the-job training, and 3) difficulty in scheduling formal training on specific days of the week, since firms needed flexibility in production. The study also found that employees, particularly senior employees, were willing to participate in work sharing only if they could engage in leisure activities during their days off (HRSDC 2005).

Impacts on Employees

When surveyed, employees taking part in work sharing believe they are better off, and they support its use. Work sharing helps workers retain more of their prior earnings than layoffs do. There are also a number of nonpecuniary gains that worker surveys have consistently identified. Finally, the main distributional effect of work sharing appears to be a sharing of wage loss between more and less senior workers, so that less senior workers are better off with work sharing.

The California and Canadian studies found that between their earnings and their work sharing payments, participating workers maintained between 81 and 94 percent of their prior compensation. The studies found that workers on layoff received between 45 and 60 percent of their previous compensation.[34] These wide differences in income retention are reflected in workers' financial satisfaction during their work sharing and layoff experience. In the 1993 Canadian study, 15 percent of workers on work sharing were dissatisfied with their financial situation, while 41 percent of California workers on layoff were dissatisfied (EDD 1982; Ekos Research Associates 1993). Fringe benefits appeared to be nearly universally retained by workers during periods of reduced hours, whether states had rules requiring retention or not. In the U.S. evaluation, over 90 percent of employers in each state maintained full benefits, including the two states that did not have a fringe benefit retention provision in their work sharing law (Walsh et al. 1997, Chap. 5, p. 6).

The California and Canadian studies attempted to estimate some nonpecuniary effects of work sharing as well. Workplace improvements that were cited included skill maintenance, labor-management relations, and worker morale. Other personal factors included increased leisure, psychological and physical well-being, and quality of life (EDD 1982; Ekos Research Associates 1993).

The main distributional effects of work sharing relate to workers by level of seniority and demographics. Less senior workers were found to experience financial gains from the program since they avoided experiencing layoffs. The avoidance of layoffs and the improved financial position of these workers are paid for by the more senior workers who, in the absence of work sharing, would have experienced no wage loss. Thus, all of the U.S. and Canadian evaluations have found that there is a transfer of earnings from more senior to less senior workers.

Since the participants in work sharing consist largely of more senior employees who would have experienced no reduction in hours in the absence of work sharing, some resistance to work sharing might be expected from them. However, it appears that there was a good deal of solidarity among workers. In the California evaluation, only 6 percent of workers opposed the initial decision to use work sharing (Best 1988).

When work sharing was considered for adoption in the United States in the 1970s, it was expected that it would have a significant effect on helping women and minorities retain their jobs. Women and minorities were expected to be overrepresented among program participants. The California and first Canadian evaluations, however, did not find benefits to women and minorities, but they did find benefits to younger adults. The first U.S. study found that the demographic characteristics of workers on layoff were similar for the work sharing group and the comparison group.

The latest U.S. work sharing study (Walsh et al. 1997, Chap. 6, pp. 16–21) compares new work sharing claimants with new UI claimants and finds no statistically significant results. It does not show that women, youth, or minorities gain significantly from retaining their jobs because of work sharing. According to Walsh et al., women and youth made somewhat larger usage of work sharing, but these results were not significant. Older workers tended to use work sharing less than other age groups. This underrepresentation could be because of either firm-level decisions or worker preferences. No statistical difference was found among race and ethnic groups.

Impacts on Employers

Reducing layoffs

The 1997 U.S. study tried to estimate the number of layoffs work sharing firms would have had in the absence of work sharing, using a comparison group. The researchers found that they could not answer this question because the comparison group was not comparable. Work sharing–user firms were dissimilar to nonusers in a number of dimensions. Work sharing firms' total charges (UI plus work sharing) were much larger than those of the comparison group, and these results were significant for all states. Compared to non–work sharing users, work sharing–user firms' charges for the regular UI program were significantly greater in two states (Florida and Kansas) and approximately the same in two more states (New York and Washington). The Florida and Kansas charges were so much larger that they could not be reasonably attributed to the use of work sharing. The study also examined the states' mass layoff use. It found that a higher percentage of work sharing users also experience mass layoffs than in the comparison group.

Using work sharing instead of layoffs

The 1986 U.S. work sharing evaluation found that on average work sharing–user firms were approximately eight times as likely to use layoffs as work sharing, in terms of the hours their employees spent on work sharing and UI (Kerachsky et al. 1986, pp. 186–190). This high use of layoff utilization calls into question work sharing's role as an employment stabilization tool (Cook, Brinsko, and Tan 1995; Vroman 1992). The 1986 findings also call into question the comparability of the treatment and comparison groups.

The findings from the 1997 evaluation (Walsh et al. 1997, Chap. 6, pp. 4–5) are similar, although more modest. Expenditures on UI for layoffs varied between 1.6 and 3.6 times as much as expenditures on work sharing among the five states studied. The evaluation confirms the finding of the 1986 U.S. study that work sharing–user firms had high levels of UI charges, both in general and compared to work sharing charges. For the study year 1992, the average percentage of total charges to UI (UI plus work sharing) varied from 62 percent in Florida to 78 percent in Washington. At the same time firms were using work sharing, they also were making heavy use of the UI program. This suggests that work sharing was not so much a layoff reduction program for these firms as a part of their overall labor force reduction strategy.

Repeat use of work sharing

Some firms use work sharing repeatedly. The 1997 U.S. study found that some work sharing firms made use of work sharing in more than one year. For the five states that the study examined in 1991–1993, work sharing–user firms' use of the program was split into use in 1–4 quarters, 5–8 quarters, or 9–12 quarters. The range of use was from New York, where nearly half (45 percent) of firms used the program in 9–12 quarters, to Florida, where only 5 percent of firms did. The other states varied between 12 and 16 percent. High rates of repeaters resulted in enactment of a limitation on work sharing use in Washington State, where firms are required to be off work sharing for 12 months following three years of usage before they can renew a work sharing plan. California considered enacting such legislation in 1995 but took no action (Walsh et al. 1997, Chap. 6, pp. 1–34).

Repeat user firms were examined to see if they had also experienced high UI costs, since firms at the maximum UI tax rate had an incentive to use work sharing at no additional cost. High UI-cost firms were strongly represented in New York and Kansas, but not in California, Washington, or Florida (Walsh et al. 1997, Chap. 6). As noted above, Kansas was one of two states that later added special tax provisions to its work sharing law.

A key issue is whether usage of work sharing has an impact on firm productivity. To date, the U.S. studies have not made estimates of the effects on productivity for firms using work sharing. Analysis of the early effects of the Canadian program found no measurable effects (MaCoy and Morand 1984, p. 111). The later Ekos Research Associates (1993) study also did not find any increase in productivity for Canadian work sharing firms, but it found a tendency for work sharing firms to retain employees even in the face of structural problems. Such a delay of an adjustment by layoff is likely to decrease productivity. Work sharing firms were found to be more profitable in the short run, but with no long-term improvement in profitability.

Impacts on the Government

Effect on the UI trust fund

Analysis of the cost of work sharing to the UI trust fund is an issue that is unique to the United States, because work sharing in this country is funded by the UI program and both work sharing and UI costs are experience-rated. The work sharing evaluations that have considered the cost to the UI trust fund are the California evaluation (EDD 1982) and the two national evaluations. All three studies have found that the total cost to the UI trust fund of work sharing and UI costs is greater for work sharing–user firms than for a comparison group of firms. The California study found that total cost for work sharing–user firms was about 16 percent greater.

The 1986 national study found that employer participation in work sharing increased the total benefit charges paid to the firms' employees as well as the firms' UI payroll taxes. The net effect on the UI trust fund was less clear. The study made qualitative estimates showing that there would be significant negative impacts on the trust fund in the short run, as work sharing charges increase rapidly with the onset of a recession but the response by UI tax rates is much slower. In the long run, however, the study concluded that work sharing should not affect the UI trust fund adversely, because work sharing benefits are subject to both stronger experience rating and reduced noncharging (Kerachsky et al. 1986, pp. 169–184).

To determine the effect of work sharing on the Unemployment Trust Fund, the 1997 work sharing evaluation analyzed the UI tax charges of work sharing–user firms that had 9–12 quarters of use in a three-year period. In 1992, California and Washington high-use firms did not have higher levels of charges than low-use firms. However, in New York and Kansas UI charges for high users were more than double those of low users, indicating an adverse impact on the Unemployment Trust Fund in these states (Walsh et al. 1997, Chap. 6, pp. 11–13).

Administrative costs

Automation has a big impact on work sharing administrative costs. The California and 1986 national evaluations examined administrative costs to the UI program before the increased automation of UI benefit payments in the 1990s. Kerachsky et al. (1986, pp. 217–220) found that work sharing costs were much greater for regular benefits—more than twice as great—because of the expectation that there would be approximately five times as many claimants receiving benefits compared to the regular program, assuming a 20 percent work-week reduction. These costs do not include the costs associated with approving the plan and responding to inquiries about the program.

After a decade of increased UI automation in the 1990s, Walsh et al. (1997, Chap. 4, pp. 17–19) found that costs continued to be high for states that did not automate the work sharing component of their UI programs. States reduced their administrative costs by reducing the layers of approval for work sharing plan submissions. Texas automated its plan approval process and accelerated approval of work sharing plans. For the claims-taking process, similar streamlining took place, as over half of the states switched to employer-filed claims, and five of these states allowed employers to submit ongoing claims forms without claimant signatures. Of the other states, four states automated the claims-taking process and three states were building work sharing into their voice response systems for UI claims taking. As a result, all work sharing states reduced the administrative burden through employer filing and automated claimant filing. Even though the automation of work sharing claims was nearing completion by 1997, a state survey found that concern about administrative cost was nevertheless a reason that six states gave for not adopting work sharing (Walsh et al. 1997, Chap. 4, p. 8).

The cost of work sharing administration was a study in contrasts. The three work sharing states that were fully automated responded that their costs of administration were actually less per claim than the cost of regular UI, because work sharing claimants do not come into the local offices and are not subject to work search requirements. The other states found the program more expensive because its administration is labor intensive. The lesson to be learned was to automate the work sharing program, and states responded. In 1997, only three states were fully automated, one was partially automated, and four more were building work sharing into their new, automated telephone claims-taking processes (Walsh et al. 1997, Chap. 6, Table 4.9). Today, the UI program is highly automated, using telephone and Internet claims-taking. There is no reason to expect that administrative cost would be a barrier to work sharing adoption, especially if states adopt the most automated work sharing software available, as in Massachusetts.

LESSONS LEARNED

Small size and employer usage. Work sharing in the United States is a small program and is likely to remain small, but it could be a great deal larger than it is today. Only a third of the states have work sharing programs, and state participation could be increased. Moreover, within the work sharing states, most employers and workers make little use of the program. That could increase if state agencies provided more information about the program, and if business and labor supported the programs the way Rhode Island does.

Unemployment reduction. Work sharing reduces unemployment in cases where layoffs are temporary. Workers share the reduction in hours and are cushioned in their earnings loss by the receipt of work sharing benefits. However, work sharing does not necessarily eliminate unemployment in work sharing firms. When employers use the work sharing program, it frequently supplements rather than substitutes for layoffs. Over time, these firms use both employment reductions and hours reductions to achieve the labor force reductions they seek to achieve.

Skilled worker retention. Employers who use work sharing tend to be large employers, concentrated in durable manufacturing, with persistent unemployment problems. They tend to engage in large and persistent layoffs, making heavy use of the UI program. Similarly, workers who use the work sharing program tend to be skilled, experienced, high-wage manufacturing workers. Employers put these workers on work sharing so they have the opportunity to call them back to full-time work and reduce their risk of losing key workers (MaCurdy, Pearce, and Kihlthau 2004). Used in this manner, work sharing is a tool to retain skilled workers who are needed to maintain a productive U.S. manufacturing sector.

Federal policy. The USDOL has not actively supported the work sharing program. A more active public policy would require either a broader interpretation of the 1992 permanent work sharing federal law or enactment of a technical amendment to the law.

- Interpretation. The department could interpret the 1992 work sharing amendments to the Social Security Act and FUTA as permitting the provisions of the 1982 work sharing amendments and any other requirements that the department deems appropriate. This interpretation would be issued under the existing authority of the secretary of labor to interpret the UI provisions of the Social Security Act and FUTA – of which work sharing is one. Initially, an ETA policy letter could be issued expressing this interpretation. A subsequent regulation could codify this interpretation, if needed.

- Legislation. Following a legislative route, a work sharing amendment could adopt the language proposed in Section 251 of the proposed Reemployment Act of 1994. The key item in that language gives the department explicit authority to guide and interpret the program so that the "program meets such other requirements as the Secretary of Labor determines are appropriate."

Increasing state adoption and usage. Work sharing will not achieve its potential as a workforce development tool unless more states adopt work sharing. States that have adopted it would have to use it more extensively.

- The department should adopt a positive policy toward work sharing. It then needs to provide guidance and technical assistance regarding state enactment of work sharing legislation. The department also should promote the use of the program and provide forums for state-to-state exchange of information. States such as Rhode Island would be eager to provide support to other states.[35] In addition, the department should provide financial support for states that wish to fully automate their work sharing administration, reducing the cost of program administration.[36]
- For states, the barriers to participation are lack of knowledge, lack of interest, and political opposition. Furthermore, some states are concerned about the fact that introducing a work sharing program is likely to lead to a small increase in expenditures from their state UI trust fund accounts. Promotion of the program by the department and the work sharing states is likely to encourage adoption, especially in times of high unemployment.

Increasing employer and worker usage. Analysts have recognized a variety of barriers and disincentives to expansion of work sharing that affect employers and employees.

- For employers, barriers include lack of information, experience rating of work sharing charges, administrative complexity—at least for smaller firms—and a preference for reducing employment rather than hours.

- For employees, the main barriers are charging work sharing benefits against UI benefit entitlement and the low work sharing rate of replacement of lost wages compared to other countries.

It appears that the state workforce agencies could overcome the concerns of employers and workers and increase participation if they actively supported and marketed the work sharing program in a manner similar to Rhode Island's approach.

Work sharing and labor market flexibility. Work sharing should not interfere with labor market flexibility. Use should be encouraged to retain jobs during temporary layoffs, especially during cyclical economic downturns. It should not be encouraged for use to stop or slow structural adjustments.

Training and work sharing. Training during receipt of work sharing is not likely to have widespread use in the United States: the Canadian inability to encourage training use is apt to be repeated here. The inflexibility of production and workforce scheduling and the preference for on-the-job training is likely to have a negative effect on use of formal training during work sharing usage. The next work sharing evaluation in the United States should examine the use of training during work sharing periods.

Work sharing evaluations. The United States should conduct another national work sharing evaluation that includes a benefit-cost analysis. The evaluation would likely be a quasiexperimental impact analysis, despite problems of setting up valid comparison groups. While it would be preferable to conduct a rigorous work sharing evaluation using an experimental design, the small size of the program and the high cost of an experimental evaluation might argue against conducting such an evaluation.

Notes

1. This chapter uses the terms work sharing or short-time compensation (STC) for this program. Work sharing is a generic name and should more properly be called compensated work sharing, because of a history of uncompensated work sharing that was incorporated into some labor-management agreements. Some states (e.g., New York) have used the term "shared work" to describe the program. In Europe the program is most frequently called short-time work, and payments are called short-time working allowances.
2. Markus Franz, e-mail message to the author, November 22, 2008. Franz at the time was counselor for labor and social affairs at the German Embassy in Washington, D.C.
3. Ibid.
4. Ibid.
5. Ibid.
6. This section draws and expands upon Balducchi and Wandner (2008).
7. Similarly, the number of employees enrolled in the program also grew rapidly, from 8,245 in 1979 to 99,332 in 1982.
8. While the USDOL did not sponsor this event, I attended on behalf of the department and made a presentation at the conference.
9. Robert Galvin, CEO and chairman of Motorola, took a personal interest in work sharing and encouraged its adoption in all states in which Motorola had production facilities. He wanted the USDOL to take an active role in promoting work sharing, as he made very clear in a meeting with me and another department staff member, Robert Crosslin, at Motorola's headquarters in Schaumberg, Illinois.
10. I worked with the office of the assistant secretary for policy, evaluation, and research to design the experimental evaluation and visited states that were potential sites for study.
11. Business support was led by the Motorola Corporation and the Committee for Economic Development. At the national level, the AFL-CIO executive council supported work sharing, while California unions provided state support among organized labor. For the state workforce agencies, Therman Kaldahl, president-elect of the Interstate Conference of Employment Security Agencies (now called the National Association of State Workforce Agencies), testified in favor of work sharing legislation in 1980 (Ittner 1984).
12. Illinois enacted temporary work sharing legislation in 1983, and the state legislature allowed the program to expire in 1988.
13. Work sharing does not create human capital, but it may retard the depreciation of human capital for workers. It also may ensure access to human capital by employers when they decide to expand production.
14. I was one of the department staff providing technical assistance to Arkansas, New York, and other states.
15. Massachusetts eliminated the issue of higher administrative cost by completely automating the work sharing administrative process. Massachusetts is making its automated system available to other state workforce agencies at no cost.

16. The advisory committee included Frank W. Schiff, vice president and chief economist of the Committee for Economic Development; Casey F. Koziol, vice president and director of personnel administration for Motorola; and John Zalusky, an economist with the AFL-CIO. They were all strong advocates of the work sharing program.

17. As the organizer of the advisory group and project officer for the evaluation, I found the experience to be a difficult one. Trying to set up an objective and rigorous evaluation with a highly respected evaluator, Mathematica Policy Research, resulted in a quasiexperimental evaluation design that was challenged and was difficult to defend. An unrelated problem resulted from the insistence of one of the participating states, California, that it be allowed to draw samples of participants itself, assembling the evaluation database and then removing the personal identifiers. The result was a data set that appeared to be highly flawed. The final product yielded ambiguous results and sparked contention about how to assess the evaluation. The difficulty of coming to agreement about the design and results of a quasiexperimental evaluation won me over to the use of experimental methodology. The year after the completion of the work sharing evaluation, I proposed the initiation of the UI Experiments.

18. David Balducchi worked on Senator Wofford's staff and assisted in the drafting of S. 2614.

19. In developing specifications for the REA legislation, the department issued a series of consultation papers (see USDOL 1994a), each of which endorsed work sharing and proposed revisions to its definition through a technical amendment.

20. See Smith (2008); Nickisch (2008). Nancy Dunphy, deputy commissioner of the New York State Department of Labor, told a Washington, D.C., audience in November 2008 that New York was again experiencing an increase in work sharing and that, while only 18 states have this job-saving provision in their UI laws, other states should consider adopting it.

21. As the recession worsened in late 2008 and early 2009, greater work reductions occurred, with 40 percent reductions—to a three-day work week—becoming more prevalent.

22. William Clawson, UI chief, Kansas Department of Human Resources, interviewed by David E. Balducchi, March 22, 1993.

23. In early 2010, seven states introduced work sharing bills in their state legislatures, reflecting concern about high unemployment during the Great Recession.

24. The Advisory Council on Unemployment Compensation (1995, pp. 189–190) and Cook, Brinsko, and Tan (1995) reviewed the work sharing program and its evaluations. They are supportive of the work sharing program but express concern about its "minimal utilization," especially compared to the high German usage rates. They express the hope that some of the impediments to greater utilization can be overcome.

25. The representative of Motorola who promoted federal and state work sharing legislation, Casey Koziol, explained that Motorola sought to implement a no-layoff policy in the early 1980s. Work sharing was a tool for Motorola to use to reduce labor costs during periods of low labor demand. Motorola was forced to abandon

this no-layoff policy—and its use of work sharing—when its competitors adopted a policy of hiring contract employees and laying them off during periods of slack demand.

26. David Fitzgerald, chief of benefits, Louisiana UI Program, in an interview with the author, October 23, 2008.
27. William L. Batt Jr. was the bureau's advocate for work sharing. He later supported the program's adoption and use in Connecticut.
28. Casey Koziol, vice president and director of personnel administration for Motorola, in a telephone conversation with the author, 1995.
29. Ray Fillipone, assistant director of income support for the Rhode Island Department of Labor and Training, and Kathy Catanzaro, WorkShare program manager, interview with the author, October 3, 2008.
30. Ibid.
31. Edward Malmborg, Massachusetts UI director, interview with the author, October 28, 2008.
32. Ibid.
33. The first U.S. evaluation was criticized by both the labor and business members of an advisory committee that was legislatively established to review the evaluation (Morand 1990, pp. 317–334). The heart of their criticism was that the comparison group of firms was not selected correctly. The members could not, however, recommend criteria for comparison group selection that would answer their concerns. (The subsequent evaluations in the United States and Canada raise the issue of whether there are any criteria for drawing a valid comparison group.) Many of the advisory committee's other criticisms were based on case studies and the committee's hopes for the program. Unfortunately, one area where the committee members were clearly wrong was in their hopes that work sharing would emerge as a larger, more substantial program (Morand 1990, p. 334).
34. In the 1993 Canadian study, this measure of replacement during layoff is of wages rather than of compensation.
35. Fillipone and Catanzaro, interview.
36. Vroman (1992) and Cook, Brinsko, and Tan (1995) suggest that employers should administer work sharing as is done in Germany, but automation of work sharing administration in the United States obviates the need for this approach.

10
Reemployment Bonus
Experiments and Public Policy

INTRODUCTION

The idea of reemployment bonuses originated in 1974 in Japan, where unemployed workers can receive a cash bonus for accepting a new job, but they cannot receive reemployment bonuses more frequently than once every three years. Reemployment bonuses also have been used in South Korea since 1995 (Martin and Grubb 2001; Wandner 2002).

Between 1984 and 1989, four reemployment bonus experiments were conducted in the United States. They provided varying levels of lump sum payments to permanently separated workers who took new, full-time jobs within six to 12 weeks after becoming unemployed and held those jobs for at least three to four months. These experiments were conducted to learn about the behavioral response of unemployment insurance (UI) recipients to the availability of UI benefits. Researchers designed a reemployment bonus system intended to speed the return to work of dislocated workers in a manner that would benefit employees and might be cost-effective. The concept behind these experiments was that UI claimants would be better off if they went back to work sooner and took similar jobs that paid similar wages to the jobs they would have taken in the absence of their bonus offers. Bonus offers were tested to see if the government sector could be better off financially, which would be true if the cost of offering bonuses was offset by a decrease in UI payments to unemployed workers and an increase in tax receipts during their longer periods of employment.

The reemployment bonus experiments were completed in the early 1990s, but as of today reemployment bonuses have not been implemented as part of U.S. labor market policy. The Clinton administration proposed federal reemployment bonuses in 1994, but the legislation was not enacted. In 2003, the Bush administration proposed Personal

Reemployment Accounts (PRAs), which included a reemployment bonus component targeted to dislocated workers. While that legislation was not enacted, PRA demonstration projects began in 2005. The Bush administration proposed PRAs as part of the Workforce Investment Act (WIA) reauthorization later that year. Because of a new administration initiative, the PRA initiative was abandoned in 2006 and was replaced with a proposal for training vouchers—Career Advancement Accounts—which became a component of President Bush's new emphasis on an "ownership society."

Reemployment Experiments

Some job-ready dislocated workers might delay searching for or taking a new job. The reemployment bonuses tested in the experiments provided an incentive to speed the return to work. The treatments consisted of the bonus offer by itself or the bonus in conjunction with the provision of job search assistance (JSA). Reemployment bonuses provide incentives to motivate workers to return to work and to encourage adjustments to structural economic change. These demonstrations encouraged dislocated workers to recognize and act upon the likely reality that their old jobs were gone forever and that there were steps that they could take to prepare for new employment. The bonuses provide incentive payments to individuals for successful early reemployment in suitable jobs. The purpose of these payments is to encourage dislocated workers to intensify their job search efforts and accept suitable new employment within a specified time period.

The intent in providing bonuses is not to encourage workers to take short-term jobs or jobs below their earnings potential. Rather, reemployment bonuses are offered as lump-sum payments, with the amount of the payment equal to some portion of the individual's entitlement to UI benefits. Tying the reemployment bonus to UI benefits can equalize the bonus incentive across claimants, since each person's bonus would be the same proportion of their UI benefit entitlement and would also be related to their usual wage level. To encourage participants to consider a longer time horizon and accept only suitable jobs, those individuals who qualify for reemployment bonuses can only receive a bonus payment after they maintain employment for some minimum specified period of time.

While the reemployment bonus experiments attempted to encourage permanently separated workers to find new jobs quickly, the bonuses might have had an adverse effect on employers, if workers subject to recall had responded to the bonus offers. More specifically, the reemployment bonus experiments answered two questions related to this concern: 1) What effect does a reemployment bonus have on workers subject to recall? 2) Can the effect be large enough that it would induce some workers to seek new employment? The answer is that no such impact was found (O'Leary, Spiegelman, and Kline 1995, pp. 267–268).

HISTORY OF EXPERIMENTS

The Illinois Reemployment Bonus Experiment was conducted in 1984–1985, sponsored by the Illinois Department of Employment Security and funded by state reserves for the Employment Service (ES) program. These reserves are monies held centrally by each state to supplement funding allocated to operate local ES offices (Woodbury and Spiegelman 1987). The experiment was designed, overseen, and evaluated by staff of the W. E. Upjohn Institute for Employment Research. The Upjohn team was interested both in the theoretical and empirical economic implications of a bonus and in the potential for developing a cost-effective program. The state of Illinois was hoping to identify and implement a cost-effective program that would increase incentives to return to work.

The apparent success of the Illinois Experiment encouraged further experimentation. The experiment reduced UI durations by just over one week without any reduction in postunemployment wages for the treatment group. It was also cost-effective for the UI trust fund: for each dollar spent on the reemployment bonus payment, UI regular benefits were reduced by more than two dollars. Reemployment bonuses looked like an ideal program to implement. But before reemployment bonuses could be considered for policy purposes, the research and policy community had some remaining questions. Could the results of the experiment be replicated? If replication was successful, what would be the best bonus offer level and time limit (qualification period) for designing the most cost-effective program?

Independent of the Illinois Experiment, the USDOL sponsored the New Jersey Experiment, which included a reemployment bonus treatment group (Corson et al. 1989). This project was designed and became operational in 1985 and 1986, before the results of the Illinois Experiment became available. The New Jersey Experiment was not designed to replicate or validate the Illinois Experiment.

In 1987, with the evaluation of the Illinois Experiment completed and the New Jersey Experiment operations over, the department sponsored two additional reemployment bonus experiments. These experiments used the Illinois model rather than the New Jersey model as their starting point for design and replication. The projects were funded using a portion of the $5 million that had been specifically added to the department's fiscal year 1987 budget to fund additional UI Experiments.

Two reemployment bonus demonstrations were conducted in 1988 and 1989—one in Pennsylvania and one in Washington State (Corson et al. 1991; Spiegelman, O'Leary, and Kline 1992). In contrast to the Illinois demonstration, these experiments had much more modest results. While half of the 10 treatments tested by the two experiments provided net benefits to claimants, society, and the government sector as a whole, only two of the treatments provided net benefits to one particular component of the government sector—the UI trust fund.

To better understand the results of the reemployment bonus experiments, a pooled analysis was conducted of the Pennsylvania and Washington State data (Decker and O'Leary 1992, 1995). The analysis controlled for differences between the two experiments and resulted in added precision to the estimate of impacts. The increased precision, however, did not improve the outcomes; reemployment bonuses were found to be cost-effective only to claimants.

In most cases, research and policy reviews of reemployment bonuses have been with regard to a broad, untargeted program, rather than more narrowly targeted programs like Worker Profiling and Reemployment Services (WPRS) and Self-Employment Assistance (SEA) that make use of a worker profiling mechanism. These reviews created modest expectations for reemployment bonus programs. These expectations have been further dampened by external validity concerns about an ongoing program. More recently, however, O'Leary, Decker, and Wandner (2005) found reemployment bonuses to be more promising if they are more narrowly targeted to UI claimants using the WPRS targeting process.

DESIGN OF THE REEMPLOYMENT BONUS EXPERIMENTS

Overview

All of the reemployment bonus experiments had eligibility requirements that had to be met before unemployed workers could participate in the projects as members of the treatment or control groups. The requirements were selected to do three things: 1) assure that workers filed for or drew UI benefits, 2) deal with UI administrative concerns, and 3) select workers who had experienced some degree of work displacement. Treatment design dealt mostly with the determination of the potential bonus amount, the period of time during which workers could qualify for the bonus, and the conditions under which they could receive the bonus.

All four experiments took place in single states. Selection of participating local offices was conducted with varying concern about how representative the participating local offices were of the state as a whole. Sampling of claimants within each local office was conducted using random assignment methods. The sample size was selected considering the need for precision for individual treatments and any subgroups that would be analyzed.

Eligibility Requirements

Eligibility requirements varied greatly

All the reemployment bonus experiments had requirements relating to the filing and eligibility for UI benefits. For the New Jersey Experiment a project participant had to be a recipient (monetarily and non-monetarily eligible); for the other experiments the participants had to be monetarily eligible at the time of the offer (Table 10.1). It was desirable to make the offer early, and in some cases prior to the receipt of a UI first payment, to speed the early intervention nature of the reemployment incentive. Nonetheless, in all of the experiments, bonuses could only be received by a participant who had become a UI recipient. The purpose of making an offer before a final determination of UI eligibility was to speed the intervention and to seek a cost-effective outcome.

Table 10.1 Eligibility Requirements for the Reemployment Bonus Experiments

	Illinois	New Jersey	Pennsylvania	Washington
Unemployment Insurance eligibility criteria	Initial claims only.	First payments only.	Initial claims only. Regular UI claims. Initially satisfy monetary eligibility conditions. Not separated from job due to a labor dispute. Sign for a waiting week or first payment within six weeks of benefit application date.	Initial claims only. Eligible to receive benefits from the state UI trust fund. Monetarily valid claims at the time of filing.
Dislocated worker criteria	Eligible for full 26 weeks of potential duration. Register with Job Service. (Excludes workers on temporary layoff and in union hiring hall.) Age at least 20 and not older than 54.	Age 25 or greater. Three years' tenure on prior job. Exclude temporary layoffs: expect recall on a specific recall date. Union hiring hall exclusion.	Union hiring hall exclusion. Exclude employer attached: must not have a specific recall date within 60 days after benefit application.	

The extent of dislocated worker screening criteria varied greatly. Screening was extensive in New Jersey, while it was nonexistent in Washington. The Illinois and Pennsylvania experiments fell in between. Although the experiments were focused on permanently separated employees, the degree of screening varied, largely because of analytical differences in the evaluations of the experiments. Evaluation analysis of subgroups was expected to make the experiments more comparable and to focus on subgroups in need of services, including groups having greater difficulty returning to work.

Serving dislocated workers

The policy goal of the experiments was to serve permanently separated unemployed workers, who might also share other characteristics of dislocated workers. The dislocated worker screens used in the experiments were not necessarily the same as those that would be used in an operational program. At the time of initiation of the experiment, no consensus had emerged about what those screens might be, and, as long as sample sizes were large enough, the screens could be simulated by imposing more restrictive screens on the experimental participants after the fact.

The experiments also represented different philosophies. The New Jersey and Illinois experiments were conducted earlier and imposed screens restricting the age and tenure of participants. By the time the Pennsylvania and Washington experiments were conducted, there was greater understanding that screening on the basis of age might not be permissible in an ongoing, federally sponsored program and that a strong tenure screen might need to be relaxed in an operational system. In addition, the Washington design was explicitly based on the expectation that any more restrictive screens would be imposed analytically on the experimental data after the fact.

Developed in 1993, profiling was required for use with reemployment bonuses in the "UI flexibility" provisions of the proposed Reemployment Act of 1994 and again as part of Personal Reemployment Accounts (PRAs) in 2003. As a result, any future reemployment bonus program proposal likely will use the same worker profiling targeting process. Thus, designs of the reemployment bonus operating systems should incorporate a worker profiling mechanism, and the profiling mechanism should be used to adjust the estimated impacts when applied to the reemployment bonus experimental data.

Design of the Experiments

The goal of the early experiments was to have a significant impact on worker behavior. The level of the bonus amount had to be sufficient to motivate unemployed workers to seek the bonus. The duration of the bonus offer had to be long enough to allow for success in seeking new employment. In Illinois, policymakers wanted the bonus design to be cost-effective to the government sector as well as to the UI trust fund. By contrast, in New Jersey the bonus amount was intentionally set high to assure that there would be a large response to the offer. In this sense, the New Jersey Experiment was a "first pass" at a reemployment bonus, with the expectation that fine tuning would have to be done in the future if the experiment had its expected impact.

The Illinois design provided a fixed $500 bonus amount, about four times the UI weekly benefit amount (WBA) at the time. Treatment group members had to become reemployed within 11 weeks of initially filing their UI claims. Since the bonuses were offered soon after filing for UI benefits—when claimants registered with the local Employment Service—and the claimants were eligible for up to 26 weeks of UI benefits (not including extended benefits), researchers believed the experiment could yield cost-effective results.

In New Jersey, the bonus offer was one-half of the remaining UI benefit entitlement at the time a new job was taken. It was designed as a UI benefit cash-out program, so that claimants could receive a portion of their remaining UI entitlement as a reward for not exhausting their entitlement. The offer generally was made in the eighth week of UI benefit receipt, when claimants would have about 18 weeks of potential duration remaining, if they qualified for the maximum duration of benefits. As a result, the initial offer averaged $1,644—about nine times the UI weekly benefit amount. By its value declining over time, the New Jersey offer was designed to encourage rapid search for and taking of a job. The declining offer also tended to encourage a cost-effective outcome, since it encouraged reemployment at the beginning of the qualification period. This offer could result in large declines in unemployment durations. In New Jersey, unlike Illinois, however, there was no assurance that the treatment group members would be eligible for a full 26 weeks of benefits.

The Pennsylvania and Washington design reflected what had been learned in Illinois, and reflected that experiment's promise of apparent success. (The New Jersey design was set aside.) The bonus offers were multiples of the worker's weekly benefit level. This approach was appropriate given the finding that claimants in the Washington Experiment who received less than the UI maximum weekly benefit responded more strongly to bonus offers than those constrained by the UI maximum benefit amount (O'Leary, Spiegelman, and Kline 1995, p. 267). From the Illinois experience, a bonus equivalent to approximately four weeks of UI benefits offered each week for approximately 11 weeks seemed adequate. (The offer of half of the remaining entitlement used in the New Jersey Experiment was clearly too much.) The new experiments tested benefit levels that bracketed the Illinois bonus amount (four times the WBA) and tested some qualifications that were similar to the earlier offers as well as others that were about half as much.

The resulting design provided for four treatment groups in Pennsylvania and six in Washington (Table 10.2). The dimensions of each design were the level of the bonus (high and low in Pennsylvania; high, medium, and low in Washington) and the qualification period or duration of the bonus offer (short and long).

The Pennsylvania and Washington experimental designs were developed at the same time and were coordinated. The Washington Experiment had an offer of four times the weekly benefit amount and a qualification period that tended to be about 10 ½ weeks. The Pennsylvania long-qualification-period (12-week) treatments paid either three or six times the UI weekly benefit amount, thus bracketing Illinois's offer of four times the weekly benefit amount. Some of the bonus offers were similar. The short qualification/high bonus offer and long qualification/high bonus offer treatments were nearly identical between the two experiments (Decker and O'Leary 1995, p. 536). As a result, it was hoped that the evaluation findings of the two experiments would be complementary and reinforcing.

In all of the experiments, participants had to work a minimum period of time, the "reemployment period," before they were eligible for a reemployment bonus. In Illinois, Pennsylvania, and Washington, the reemployment period was four months—defined as 16 weeks in Pennsylvania. This parameter was not considered to be sensitive to variation, so there was no experimental variation within any of the experiments

Table 10.2 Treatment Design for the Reemployment Bonus Demonstrations

Illinois

Bonus offer	Qualification period	Bonus payment	Reemployment period
$500	11 weeks	1	4 months

New Jersey

Bonus offer	Qualification period	Bonus payments	Reemployment period
Half of remaining UI entitlement; initial offer good for two weeks, then declines by 10% per week in each successive week.	12 weeks	2 (60% after 4-wk. reempl. period; 40% after 12-wk. reempl. period.)	4 weeks; 12 weeks

Pennsylvania

Bonus offer	Qualification period 6 weeks	12 weeks	Bonus payment	Reemployment period
3 × WBA	Low bonus, short qualification period	Low bonus, long qualification period	1	16 weeks
6 × WBA	High bonus, short qualification period	High bonus, long qualification period		

Washington

Bonus offer	Qualification period (0.2 × potential UI duration) + 1 week	(0.4 × potential UI duration) + 1 week	Bonus payment	Reemployment period
2 × WBA	Low bonus, short qualification period	Low bonus, long qualification period	1	4 months
4 × WBA	Medium bonus, short qualification period	Medium bonus, long qualification period		
6 × WBA	High bonus, short qualification period	High bonus, long qualification period		

NOTE: WBA = weekly benefit amount.

(Robins and Spiegelman 2001). New Jersey was an outlier, with a four-week reemployment period to receive the first reemployment bonus payment and 12 weeks to receive the second payment.

Qualifying for Bonus

To be eligible to receive a reemployment bonus, treatment group members in Illinois had to take new jobs, earning at least $30 per week, and hold them for four months. The New Jersey Experiment required workers to take a new job, which could not be temporary, seasonal, part-time (under 32 hours per week), and could not be provided by a relative or by the immediately preceding employer. As a tenure requirement, the worker had to hold that job for four weeks to get 60 percent of the bonus and for 12 weeks to get the remaining 40 percent (Corson et al. 1989, pp. 121–123). In Pennsylvania, workers had to start working in a new job, which could not be part-time (under 32 hours per week). Workers had to continuously hold the new job for 16 weeks. In Washington, workers had to take a new job, which could not be part-time (under 34 hours per week). The tenure requirement was continuous employment for a period of four months.

Thus, the common qualification requirement was to start a full-time job—defined three different ways—with a new employer and hold it for a three- to four-month period.

Site Selection

In all cases except in Illinois, the site selection process attempted to make the sites reasonably representative of the state as a whole. In Illinois, however, 22 local ES offices were selected, but they were all located in northern and central Illinois. Site selection ensured that a variety of rural and urban sites would be represented, but the selection process was largely for administrative convenience.

In New Jersey and Pennsylvania, site selection was based on survey sampling methodology. In New Jersey, 10 sites were chosen from a total of 38 local UI offices. Fourteen local offices were excluded as being too small to support the experiment. Local offices were then stratified geographically to assure that they were representative of the state in terms of mix of industries, local office setting, and other characteristics. Finally, 10 local offices were randomly selected, with the probability of selection based on local office size, as measured by their claimant population.

In Pennsylvania, 12 local UI-ES offices were randomly selected from 12 clusters selected based on UI–Job Service geographic regions within the state and the average duration of UI receipt. In Washington, 21 of 31 ES offices were selected. Of the 10 offices excluded, seven were the smallest offices in the state and were found not to be able to support the experiment, two were participating in another experiment, and one was excluded because of its integration with the Portland, Oregon, metropolitan area.

DEMONSTRATION FINDINGS AND ANALYSIS

Demonstration Findings

The demonstration findings derive from two outcome measures— the impacts on 1) UI receipt and 2) postunemployment earnings—and the benefit-cost analysis.

Impact on receipt of UI

The UI receipt impacts of the experiments are summarized in Table 10.3. The Pennsylvania and Washington data are regression-adjusted estimates from a pooled sample (Decker and O'Leary 1995). The results of the reemployment bonus experiments generally show a significant decline in benefits received in the benefit year. The results are largest in the Illinois Experiment, with a reduction in benefits of over one week.

The results for Pennsylvania and Washington are uneven and much smaller. The most generous bonuses—high bonus/long eligibility— had the greatest impact, but the results are not consistent for the other treatments. These results are disappointing in that they do not show a graduated impact, increasing from low bonus to high, and the size of the impacts is smaller than for the Illinois Experiment. The pooled data analysis for the Pennsylvania and Washington experiments confirm the smaller UI impacts of the two new experiments, yielding an estimate of half a week, which is less than half the result in Illinois.

**Table 10.3 Estimated Impacts of the Reemployment Bonus Treatments on
UI Outcomes and Earnings**

Treatment	Weeks of benefits in benefit year	Earnings ($ per claimant)
Illinois	−1.15***	8 (Qtr. 1)
New Jersey	−0.97***	176** (Qtr. 1)
	(benefit year)	
	−0.44**	79 (Qtr. 2)
	(2nd year)	
	−1.72***	46 (Qtr. 3)
	(over 6 years)	
		79 (Qtr. 4)
Pennsylvania		
PT 1 low-short	−0.63*	19 (Qtr. 1)
PT 2 low-long	−0.39	87 (Qtr. 1)
PT 3 high-short	−0.46	116 (Qtr. 1)
PT 4 high-long	−0.84***	70 (Qtr. 1)
Washington		
WT 1 low-short	−0.04	−178** (Qtr. 1)
WT 2 med.-short	−0.25	−54 (Qtr. 1)
WT 3 high-short	−0.71**	63 (Qtr. 1)
WT 4 low-long	−0.59**	36 (Qtr. 1)
WT 5 med.-long	−0.31	−42 (Qtr. 1)
WT 6 high-long	−0.80**	102 (Qtr. 1)
Combined		
PA-WA treatments	−0.51***	26 (Qtr. 1)

NOTE: New Jersey earnings are based on interview data. * significantly different from zero at the 90 percent confidence level (two-tailed test); ** significantly different from zero at the 95 percent confidence level (two-tailed test); *** significantly different from zero at the 99 percent confidence level (two-tailed test).

SOURCE: Illinois: Woodbury and Spiegelman (1987); New Jersey: Corson and Haimson (1996), pp. 27, 36; Pennsylvania, Washington, and combined: Decker and O'Leary (1995).

The New Jersey data are not comparable because that treatment included mandatory participation in job search assistance. Nonetheless, the combined impact of the offer of both JSA and the reemployment bonus is less than that for the reemployment bonus alone in Illinois during the first benefit year (Corson et al. 1989). The New Jersey Experiment, however, included a six-year follow-up study, and the total six-year result yielded an effect nearly double the first-year effect. It also exceeded the Illinois one-year impact. In the New Jersey Experiment, both the JSA-only and the JSA-plus-reemployment-bonus treatments had long-term effects on UI receipt, indicating that these two treatments led to jobs that were more stable, and the reemployment bonus contributed to this stabilization (Corson and Haimson 1996).[1]

Impact on postunemployment earnings

The postunemployment earnings of participants in the reemployment bonus experiments answered the question, "Did the experiments produce a less favorable job match, resulting in lower earnings in the new jobs?" The reemployment bonus offer might have induced unemployed workers to take a less suitable job at a lower wage, in order to take advantage of the bonus offer. The results from all four experiments, however, show that this did not happen.

Table 10.3 presents the earnings impacts for the experiments. There is no significant change in earnings for the Illinois, Pennsylvania, and Washington participants in the first quarter of employment following UI claims status, with one exception—that of a negative and significant impact for one Washington treatment. These findings are confirmed by the pooled data analysis for the Pennsylvania and Washington experiments, which also find no significant impact. The New Jersey Experiment shows positive results for the first quarter after the UI claim, but these results reflect, in part, the presence of the offer of job search assistance.[2] The conclusion is that reemployment bonuses result in more rapid reemployment because of more intense job search, and not from a willingness to take less favorable jobs or jobs with lower earnings.

Benefit-cost analysis

From the benefit-cost analysis of the Illinois Experiment, the net benefits from the perspective of the UI trust fund were both dramatic and promising when the analysis was published as the lead article in the September 1987 issue of the *American Economic Review*. The evaluation estimated that the net benefits per claimant were $90. The bonus offer was found to have reduced benefit payments by $2.32 for each $1.00 in reemployment bonuses paid, for a benefit-cost ratio of 2.32.

These strong positive results spurred the replication and extension of the experiment in Pennsylvania and Washington. The Illinois results, however, were not confirmed. Only 2 of the 10 treatments in these two states produced net benefits to the Unemployment Trust Fund. The results for the pooled sample were negative for the government sector and for society but positive for claimants.

The first goal of the Pennsylvania and Washington experiments was to replicate the Illinois Experiment. In Washington, the medium/long treatment (WT5) duplicated Illinois. No treatment in Pennsylvania duplicated the Illinois design, but the low/long (PT2) and high/long (PT4) treatments effectively bracketed the Illinois design. None of these three treatments produced net benefits for the UI trust fund. Three Pennsylvania treatments provided net benefits to the government sector as a whole.

The second goal of the new experiments was to fine-tune the design of the Illinois Experiment to find the most cost-effective combination of bonus amount and qualification period. Since there was no graduated and increasing impact on UI receipt as the bonus amount increased and the qualification period lengthened, this goal was not achieved either.

The conclusions from these new studies were that 1) the basic findings of Illinois could not be duplicated, and 2) no reemployment bonus design would pay for itself. The new experiments were not cost-effective to the UI trust fund. They also did not appear to result in net benefits for the government sector. Meanwhile, the New Jersey results were positive to all sectors, but these results were not comparable to the other studies (Table 10.4).

Explaining the Results

Failure to confirm the results of the Illinois Experiment led researchers to search for the reasons for the observed results. One response was the pooled data analysis for Pennsylvania and Washington, noted above. It was hoped that pooling data would provide more insight into the effects of the new experiments by improving the precision of the individual state estimates. The results of this analysis, however, only confirmed the results of the two separate evaluations (Decker and O'Leary 1995).

Further analysis of the Illinois results was conducted, looking for explanations for its stronger findings compared to the other three experiments. Davidson and Woodbury (1991) found that the favorable results of the Illinois Experiment may have been due to the availability of temporary emergency-extended UI benefits, known as Federal Supplemen-

Table 10.4 Estimated Net Benefits of the Reemployment Bonus Experiments ($ per claimant)

| Treatment | Claimant | Government | | Society |
		UI trust fund	Gov't total	
Illinois	—	90	—	—
New Jersey	400	45	165	565
Pennsylvania				
PT1 low-short	−312	41	−53	−365
PT2 low-long	142	−1	42	184
PT3 high-short	127	−10	28	155
PT4 high-long	171	−31	20	191
Washington				
WT1 low-short	−168	−71	−122	−289
WT2 med.-short	−87	−65	−91	−178
WT3 high-short	198	−37	23	222
WT4 low-long	−224	51	−16	−241
WT5 med.-long	−124	−79	−117	−241
WT6 high-long	328	−80	19	347
Pennsylvania and Washington combined	14	−25	−21	−7

NOTE: For New Jersey, results estimates were broader than the UI Trust Fund and include the entire U.S. Department of Labor. — = not available.
SOURCE: Illinois: Woodbury and Spiegelman (1987); New Jersey: Corson and Haimson (1996), p. 93; Pennsylvania, Washington, and PA-WA combined: Decker and O'Leary (1995).

tal Compensation (FSC), during the first half of the period of operation of the project. These benefits continued to be available after initially being enacted to ease the impact of the 1980–1982 recession. Thus, they provided up to 26 additional weeks of extended benefits to UI recipients who had exhausted their entitlement to regular UI benefits. The potential savings to the UI trust fund for FSC-eligible UI claimants was much greater because of their much greater total UI entitlement, i.e., up to 52 weeks. Workers eligible for FSC were found to be much more responsive to the reemployment bonus than those not FSC-eligible. While the benefit-cost ratio for all claimants was found to be 2.32, the ratio for those not eligible for FSC was about 1.4, which is closer to that for the average for Pennsylvania (Davidson and Woodbury 1991; O'Leary, Spiegelman, and Kline 1995, p. 267). The much more favorable impact of the reemployment bonus offer for FSC-eligible claimants provides a partial explanation for the much greater cost-effectiveness of the Illinois Experiment.

Comparisons have also been made between the individual experimental results. The stronger results of the Pennsylvania Experiment relative to Washington have been examined. One conclusion was that the tighter labor market in Pennsylvania during the 1988–1989 experimental period may have made it easier to find a job (O'Leary, Spiegelman, and Kline 1995, p. 267).

For individual experiments, subgroup analysis has been conducted. One subgroup that has been analyzed is dislocated workers. This target group was reflected to some extent in the selection of the eligible population to varying degrees in Pennsylvania, New Jersey, and Illinois, but not in Washington. In the Washington evaluation (Spiegelman and Woodbury 1987, pp. 116–120, 193, 202–203), the impacts and cost-effectiveness of the experiment for dislocated workers are analyzed, but this analysis is restricted to a subgroup of participants having only one dislocated worker characteristic (long tenure). A benefit-cost analysis for such long-tenure workers results in a conclusion that from "the perspective of the UI system, or the government as a whole, none of the alternative bonus offer programs look particularly attractive as a dislocated worker program" (Spiegelman, O'Leary, and Kline 1992, p. 202). A more recent analysis of worker dislocation described below, however, examined a much wider range of factors that are associated with worker dislocation.

Another explanation for the larger impact on UI receipt of the Illinois Experiment compared to that of New Jersey was in the design of the bonus offer—a constant $500 reemployment bonus in Illinois, which might have had a different effect on UI spells of unemployment than the New Jersey declining bonus (Decker 1994). Despite differences in the size and structure of the two bonuses, their offer had a similar impact on exit rates from UI receipt during the bonus qualification period. It was only after the end of the bonus qualification period that UI exit rates began to differ. For the Illinois Experiment, there was no impact on exit rates after the qualification period, while in the New Jersey Experiment there was a significant decline in exit rates. Thus, the New Jersey Experiment reduced UI receipt more among short-duration claimants than among long-duration claimants, who are more likely to exhaust their benefits. By contrast, the Illinois model had a substantial impact on long-duration claimants, reducing UI exhaustions. This finding provides part of the answer to why the Illinois model had a greater impact on UI receipt than the New Jersey Experiment. It does not, however, explain why Illinois' constant bonus had a greater impact than the Pennsylvania and Washington bonuses.

Reemployment Bonuses with Worker Profiling

Generally, the evaluation of the four reemployment bonus experiments was conducted and reviewed with the assumption that a permanent program would have the same eligibility conditions as the individual experiments. As we have seen, however, the experiments had greatly different eligibility criteria, from simple UI eligibility criteria in Washington State to the addition of more rigorous screening for characteristics associated with permanent worker dislocation in the other three experiments. New Jersey had the most rigorous worker dislocation screening.

In the Washington State experiment it was recognized that an operational program would likely need more rigorous screening to better target dislocated workers. As was seen above, the evaluation considered the impact of restricting eligibility to dislocated workers, but its analysis only dealt with one factor associated with dislocation, i.e., job tenure.

While the Washington Experiment did little targeting analysis, other analysis has shown that selection of dislocated workers to participate in reemployment bonuses and other reemployment services could be more effective and efficient. The six-year follow-up study of the New Jersey Experiment (Corson and Haimson 1996) revealed the impact that profiling could have on the net impact results of the UI Experiments. The study conducted a simulation of what would have been the impact on the original New Jersey evaluation findings if the operational profiling mechanism adopted for use in New Jersey starting in 1994 for the WPRS program had been in use during the experimental period in 1986–1987. It found that "using a profiling model to target reemployment services on workers with high probabilities of UI benefit exhaustion directs reemployment services to a group of workers who are likely to benefit from the services. These estimates also imply this approach to targeting is a relatively efficient way to provide services. Services are directed to a specific group of displaced workers who can benefit more from the services than a broader group of displaced workers, thereby generating relatively large savings in UI receipt for the given level of expenditures on services" (Corson and Haimson 1996, p. 75).

The original Pennsylvania reemployment bonus evaluation (Corson et al. 1991) included no analysis of targeting bonuses to dislocated workers. Corson and Decker (1996), however, found that the effectiveness of the reemployment bonuses offered in Pennsylvania would have increased if profiling had been used to select participants rather than using the broad screens that were used in the experiment. Setting the minimum probability of exhaustion at 0.7 for eligibility for a bonus, profiled workers were found to experience a longer duration of unemployment than unprofiled workers. The unemployment duration results were statistically significant.

This analysis suggests that the impacts and cost-effectiveness of a reemployment bonus could be increased by focusing on using worker profiling. It also suggests that some of the concerns about the external validity of these experiments could be reduced by targeting a permanent program with worker profiling. External validity concerns could be allayed in a number of ways, including these three: worker profiling would 1) target a small group of workers; 2) target only permanently separated, laid-off workers having characteristics of dislocated workers; and 3) create uncertainty about who would be selected.

Without profiling, potentially all UI beneficiaries could be eligible for an offer of a reemployment bonus, much as was the case in the Washington Experiment. Potentially about eight million U.S. beneficiaries could have been offered a bonus in 2007. With a bonus receipt rate of, say, 25 percent, approximately 2 million (8 million beneficiaries × 0.25) UI beneficiaries a year might receive a bonus. By contrast, while virtually all new UI claimants are profiled, only about 10 percent of them are referred to reemployment services. These workers are referred to a variety of reemployment services, and those that are not job-ready are referred to education and training services. Only a portion of these profiled UI claimants would be likely to be offered a reemployment bonus. However, assuming that all referred workers were offered reemployment bonuses, and again assuming a 25 percent receipt rate, approximately 200,000 (8 million × 0.1 × 0.25) reemployment bonuses would be paid each year, to less than 3 percent of UI beneficiaries. In general, for any group of laid-off workers applying for UI benefits, only a small portion would be offered a bonus. Such a small program would result in unemployed workers' having less knowledge about the program and a likely small behavioral response.

Targeting permanently separated, laid-off workers would be done in the first part of the worker profiling process. Workers would then be selected using a statistical model with input of personal and labor market characteristics. The result is that workers who would be offered a reemployment bonus would not be on temporary layoff and would be less likely to be among the short-term unemployed.

Employees and employers would not be certain whether individual unemployed workers would be referred to reemployment services or not. Furthermore, they would not be sure which of these referred workers would be offered a reemployment bonus. For permanently separated workers, referral to reemployment services would depend on the personal and labor market characteristics that go into the worker profiling model. Referral would further depend on the budget constraint of the state workforce agency, which can refer varying numbers of workers, either to reemployment services or to reemployment bonus offers. With worker profiling, labor representatives, employers, or fellow workers would not be likely to advise workers to collect a reemployment bonus, since such a small percentage of these workers would actually receive the offer.

An analysis simulating profiling of reemployment bonuses was conducted with data for the Pennsylvania and Washington experiments, the two experiments that seemed to have the greatest policy relevance (O'Leary, Decker, and Wandner 1998, 2005). The analysis made use of profiling of reemployment bonuses for two reasons: First, reemployment bonuses seemed to be policy-appropriate only for permanently separated dislocated workers. This conclusion had already been confirmed by the adoption of worker profiling as a component of the Clinton administration's 1994 targeted reemployment bonus proposal. Second, the Pennsylvania and Washington state results were modest, with half of the treatments in those two states found to be cost-effective to society and to the government sector, but only two treatments found to be cost-effective for the UI system. As a result, no optimum reemployment bonus design had been found.

Worker profiling was conducted using the model proposed by the USDOL (1994b), estimated separately for Pennsylvania and Washington based on data from the experiments from 1988 to 1989. Profiling was applied to individuals in both the treatment and control groups in each state. Two thresholds for profiling were applied, setting the likelihood of exhausting entitlement to UI at 50 and 75 percent. Starting with the full sample of participants in the two experiments, profiling reduces the samples to those who meet the profiling probability levels. The results presented in Table 10.5 reflect the model for the experiment period, with a likelihood of exhaustion set at 50 percent.

The net benefit results of the analysis of the profiled reemployment bonus data showed that profiling improved the results from the perspective of the UI program. When using mean values across all treatments in each state, results with profiling generally were stronger than results without. Setting the profiling threshold at 50 percent was more cost-effective than at 75 percent. The result of comparing bonus amounts (high and low in Pennsylvania and high, medium, and low in Washington) and eligibility period (short and long in both states) showed that the combination of low bonus amount and long eligibility period was the most cost-effective. These estimates "suggest that such a targeted bonus offer would yield appreciable net benefits to the UI trust fund if implemented as a permanent national program" (O'Leary, Decker, and Wandner 1998). The policy recommendation was for adoption of a low bonus amount of about three times the weekly benefit amount and

Table 10.5 Pennsylvania and Washington Reemployment Demonstrations, Summary of Net Benefits from the Perspective of UI System ($)

Demonstration and treatment	Based on full sample (no profiling)	Based on claimants above 50th percentile using profiling model
Pennsylvania bonus offers		
Low bonus/short qualification	40	−119
Low bonus/long qualification	24	108
High bonus/short qualification	−56	−138
High bonus/long qualification	−28	68
Washington bonus offers		
Low bonus/short qualification	−62	−2
Low bonus/long qualification	9	110
Medium bonus/short qualification	−88	6
Medium bonus/long qualification	−129	−141
High bonus/short qualification	−76	−97
High bonus/long qualification	−132	−94

SOURCE: O'Leary, Decker, and Wandner (1998).

a long qualification period of about 12 weeks. Using the 2008 national average weekly benefit amount, the bonus amount would average $900.

External Validity Concerns: Response to the Demonstration Findings

Overview

In evaluating and reviewing the reemployment bonus experiments, researchers have pointed to four types of external validity concerns: 1) low take-up rates for qualified treatment group members, 2) potential for induced insured unemployment, 3) subsidizing short-term layoffs, and 4) potential and unknowable displacement effects.

In the evaluation of the Illinois Experiment, the possible impacts of external validity issues were discussed, including take-up rates and displacement, but only the take-up issue was analyzed (Woodbury and Spiegelman 1987, pp. 526–528). Later studies have looked at all of these issues. Different researchers have placed emphasis on different external validity concerns.

Increased bonus take-up rates

The reemployment bonus experiments leave unresolved the question of what the actual rate of receipt of a reemployment bonus would be in an ongoing program. While that question cannot be answered, an upper limit can be estimated by determining what the increase in receipt would be if the take-up rate were 100 percent. This approach takes into consideration the fact that in an ongoing program, UI claimants eligible for a reemployment bonus would be far more likely to be aware of the bonus offer, and that they would be more likely to apply for and receive the bonus. Such an estimate is clearly an upper bound estimate because some eligible workers did not apply for reasons other than lack of information, and ongoing programs never experience 100 percent participation rates.

For the Illinois Experiment, Woodbury and Spiegelman examine the issue of take-up rates. Of the 4,186 treatment group members, 25 percent qualified for the bonus but only 13.6 percent received the bonus. Thus, since only 54 percent of the treatment group members who qualified for the bonus collected it, Woodbury and Spiegelman (1987, pp. 527–528) estimate what would have happened if take-up rates had risen to 100 percent with no accompanying decline in UI benefit receipt or unemployment. They calculate that the result would be a decline in the benefit-cost ratio from 2.32 to 1.26.

Among the four reemployment bonus experiments, the range of take-up rates varied from 53 to 80 percent. This implies that if all eligible claimants collected the reemployment bonus, the cost of the program would increase by as little as one-fifth and by as much as one-half.

Induced insured unemployment: delayed switchers

While it is possible that reemployment bonuses could induce the incidence of a spell of unemployment ("induced incidence") that would not occur in the absence of the bonus, this issue has not been raised or analyzed. Rather, the chief concern of policymakers has been the potential for a delay in switching from an old job to a new job ("delayed switching"), which would create a brief period of unemployment during which a bonus could be collected.

Delayed switching of jobs might result in the offer of a reemployment bonus only under limited conditions. Under current UI law, a bonus offer could be made only to workers who suffer a layoff. They cannot voluntarily quit and qualify to receive UI. Workers also cannot have sought and secured a job prior to the date of the layoff. In the absence of the reemployment bonus, these workers would have taken new jobs without an intervening period of unemployment. To take advantage of the potential reemployment bonus offer, these workers would then have to delay the start date of the job or reject the job offer.

Meyer (1996, p. 48) addresses the issue of delayed switching because he finds that the fraction of layoffs that do not result in unemployment range from 18 to over 30 percent.[3] Delayed switching would be of particular concern if laid-off workers could search for new work prior to their layoff date, accept a job offer only after a period of intervening unemployment, and collect a reemployment bonus for taking the new job. Delayed switching could be discouraged, however, if one reemployment bonus administrative step were expanded. Namely, prior to the payment of a bonus, the UI agency would have to determine from the new employer whether the employee had experienced continuous employment for three or four months. At the same time, the date of the employer's job offer could be collected, with a bonus eligibility requirement that the job offer date could be no earlier than the date of the reemployment bonus offer.

The concern about induced unemployment is related to the concern that employed workers could self-select into the program once it became operational. This occurrence would be of particular concern if a reemployment bonus program was untargeted and open to all UI recipients. Workers might know with certainty that if they met the program criteria they would qualify for and receive the bonus. With use of worker profiling for targeting, however, a small portion of permanently laid-off workers would be offered a reemployment bonus, and this concern should be greatly reduced.

Induced filing: nonfilers for UI benefits

A large portion of potentially UI-eligible unemployed workers never file for benefits—especially those unemployed workers who experience short spells of unemployment. Introduction of a reemployment bonus would raise the value of UI receipt and likely induce some UI nonfilers to file for benefits. Meyer (1996, pp. 43–44) discusses this issue, and he suggests that it would have a potentially large effect, citing an estimated "fraction of eligibles receiving UI ranging from 0.55 to 0.83."[4] Meyer goes on to estimate that the increase in the percentage of unemployed workers filing for benefits would be between 7 percent and 12 percent, while the actual percentage could be higher because of the likely disproportionately heavy participation rate by short-duration unemployed workers, who previously would not have found applying worthwhile.

The goal of a reemployment bonus program, however, is to shorten the duration of long-term unemployed workers. Using worker profiling to make reemployment bonus offers, nonfilers might be encouraged to apply for UI benefits in the hope of being offered a reemployment bonus. However, to the extent that induced filers represent short-term unemployed workers, the worker profiling process is likely to assign them a low probability of exhausting their UI benefit entitlement, and they would not receive a reemployment bonus offer. Given a low bonus offer (e.g., three or four times the UI weekly benefit amount) and a low probability of being offered the reemployment bonus, short-duration unemployed workers may continue to find little incentive to file for UI benefits.

Subsidizing short-term layoffs

Unemployment insurance is an important supplement to wages in layoffs. It can affect the behavior of employers and employees. For example, employers and employees formerly counted on workers receiving UI benefits each July in the automobile industry because of model changeovers. Meyer (1996, p. 45) suggests that reemployment bonuses could become an incentive to lay workers off. He notes that under the eligibility criteria of the experiments, reemployment bonuses cannot be provided to workers who return to their previous employer. He notes, however, that some workers on layoff are not subject to recall, and they might receive a bonus. It is doubtful that this incentive would come into play for at least three reasons under any likely potential federal legislation. First, under the eligibility conditions, workers on temporary layoff would not be on permanent layoff, would not pass the profiling screening, and therefore would not be offered a bonus. Second, if workers on temporary layoff eventually were informed that they were not subject to recall, a bonus would not be offered to them because they would no longer be newly unemployed. Third, the worker profiling mechanism is likely to exclude them from eligibility whether they are subject to recall or not, since they are not likely to have the characteristics of the long-term unemployed.

Displacement effect

A reemployment bonus could result in displacement if workers responding to the bonus offer sought and took jobs that would have otherwise gone to other unemployed workers. In an ongoing program, this adverse effect could affect those unemployed workers who were offered a bonus but did not find a job or those who were never offered a bonus. The displacement effect could be small if bonus recipients found jobs with little or no impact on other unemployed workers. Alternatively, the effect could be so great that there would be little or no increase in total employment; there would be a redistribution of jobs from other workers to reemployment bonus recipients.

The displacement effect was seriously examined in connection with the Pennsylvania and Washington experiments. In the Pennsylvania Experiment (Corson et al. 1991, pp. 205–216), the evaluation explicitly attempted to estimate displacement effects. Analysis of these estimates, however, found that their statistical power for detecting a significant displacement effect was extremely limited. The results were not statistically significant.

Davidson and Woodbury (1993) estimated the displacement effect of the reemployment bonus experiments using a partial equilibrium matching model of the labor market. They found that there would be little displacement of UI-eligible workers who were not offered a bonus. They found larger impacts for UI-ineligible workers who were never offered the bonus. Overall, they found that 30–60 percent of the gross employment effect of a reemployment bonus program would be offset by displacement of the UI-ineligible workers. Even though the gains to UI-eligible workers would be greater than the losses to the UI-ineligible workers, there would be no way of offsetting the losses in a reemployment bonus program.

In an earlier study, Davidson and Woodbury (1990) concluded that "reductions in covered (program participant) unemployment do not come at the expense of increased uncovered (nonparticipant) unemployment, and in this sense the bonus program entails no displacement effect."

The Advisory Council on Unemployment Compensation (1995) reviewed the results of the reemployment bonus experiments. It expressed concern about the potential displacement effect of reemployment bonuses, especially in a world of involuntary unemployment in which job openings are sufficient for only a small number of job seekers. They dismissed the effects of reemployment bonus incentives as "marginal at best."

It seems difficult to believe that there would be a substantial displacement effect for a reemployment bonus, particularly during nonrecessionary times when the U.S. labor market is characterized by reasonably strong employment growth. In addition, the potential size and impacts of a narrowly targeted reemployment bonus program appear to be too small to have an appreciable displacement effect. In an economy where annual new hires averaged over 50 million between 2001 and 2007 (BLS 2008), it would not be likely that offers of reemployment bonuses in an ongoing program would be as high as 500,000, and bonus receipt would be far lower. Generally, the displacement effect of an ongoing reemployment bonus program seems likely to be very small.

The effect of targeting reemployment bonuses

Offering a large, untargeted reemployment bonus as a permanent part of the UI program could certainly encourage entry into the UI program. Workers would know that they are eligible for a bonus, and filing for UI benefits could increase as a result. However, the application of worker profiling to reemployment bonuses decreases the number of individuals who are potentially eligible for reemployment bonus offers and increases the uncertainty that the offer will be made. A program with targeting that uses worker profiling thus is likely to "temper any potential entry effect" (O'Leary, Decker, and Wandner 1998, 2005).

Summary

External validity issues regarding reemployment bonuses were raised as part of the evaluation of the Illinois Experiment, but with considerable confidence of a positive net outcome because of the large positive impact of the experiment in general. With the weak Pennsylvania and Washington results that followed, the tide turned. The Illinois results were called into question, and the new, modest results were not clearly cost-effective. Analysis of external validity turned opinion against the reemployment bonuses.

While these concerns about external validity appear to be exaggerated, they are real. In particular, take-up rates in an ongoing program would clearly increase and would result in small increases in filing for UI benefits. The other effects appear likely to be small.

Given some external validity concerns, the cost-effectiveness of the largely untargeted reemployment bonuses would have to be raised appreciably before they could be recommended for public policy use. Worker profiling is a targeting device that would substantially increase this cost-effectiveness.

POLICY IMPLICATIONS OF REEMPLOYMENT BONUSES

While reemployment bonuses have not been implemented as a part of the UI program, bipartisan policy interest in establishing them as a federal initiative has emerged since the early 1990s. Two legislative proposals were developed by the executive branch and introduced by members of Congress. The Clinton administration proposed the Reemployment Act of 1994, and the Bush administration proposed Personal Reemployment Accounts in 2003.

Reemployment Act of 1994: A Failed Legislative Proposal

The next year the department proposed to implement reemployment bonuses as part of the proposed Reemployment Act of 1994 (USDOL 1994a); the bill was introduced but never enacted because the Democrats lost their majority in Congress later that year. Part E of the legislative proposal contained UI flexibility provisions that would have amended the Federal Unemployment Tax Act. The amendment would have permitted states to change their state UI laws to allow the payment of reemployment bonuses to certain workers and short-time compensation to workers who are working reduced hours for an employer. It also would have made the self-employment assistance program permanent, which was later accomplished.

The UI flexibility provisions arose from late-night brainstorming sessions held by Secretary Reich at the department. The sessions developed solutions to alleviate a jobless recovery from the 1990–1991 recession. The UI flexibility provisions offered a way to help the unemployed and, at the same time, work around funding problems that were hindering the providing of reemployment services. They presented an initial opportunity to use UI funds—"a big pile of money," as Reich characterized the funds—in an environment in which funding was scarce. Reich hoped to use more UI funds in the future to fund the retraining for dislocated workers, but the opportunity never presented itself.[5]

Reich reviewed the evidence supporting the reemployment bonuses and was convinced that they would be effective, if there was careful targeting using the worker profiling mechanism. He was also involved in discussions about the potential moral hazard problem that would exist if an operating reemployment bonus program encouraged entry into the UI program by workers who were seeking only to obtain the bonuses.[6]

Section 252 of the proposed Reemployment Act contained a reemployment bonus provision that would have allowed states to enact reemployment bonus provisions in such a way that the bonuses could have been as large as four times the weekly benefit amount. (The U.S. average weekly benefit in 2008 was approximately $300, so the average maximum bonus offer under that bill would have been approximately $1,200.) Eligibility for the program was restricted to individuals who met four conditions: 1) they were unemployed, eligible for UI, and determined as likely to exhaust their entitlement to UI; 2) they found full-time employment in no more than 12 weeks; 3) they found employment with a new employer; and 4) they retained full-time employment for not less than four months.

Thus, the reemployment bonus provisions of the proposed Reemployment Act were modeled after the design of the Pennsylvania and Washington reemployment bonus experiments in all of their key components (Table 10.6). The program would have had four characteristics: 1) it was targeted to UI beneficiaries who were likely to exhaust their UI benefits as determined by the worker profiling mechanism; 2) the benefit level for the bonus was set at the most cost-effective level; 3) the bonus calculation was a multiple of the UI weekly benefit amount to encourage wide participation; and 4) a single delayed payment was made to try to assure that good, long-term job matches were made.

The reemployment bonus provisions of the Reemployment Act did not look like the provisions of the Pennsylvania and Washington Reemployment Bonus Experiments by accident. Policymakers at the department were intent on learning from the experiments and designing actual programs that were likely to be cost-effective when applied in the field. The evaluators of the reemployment bonus experiments were asked to share the policy implications that came from their evaluations. The researchers and policy analysts in the department worked closely with the departmental policymakers to develop the final proposals.

Department staff had read Bruce Meyer's analysis of the reemployment bonuses and had tried to deal with his questions about UI program entry effects in an ongoing program. In the department's 1994 reemployment bonus proposal, staff members added worker profiling to the proposal to attempt to prevent entry problems. Department staff believed that applying the worker profiling mechanism to reemployment services would result in a more targeted, more cost-effective program that would limit or eliminate entry effects. However, their beliefs were not supported by analysis until 1998, when O'Leary, Decker, and Wandner (1998) "profiled the bonus." The authors had conducted this study because they wanted to simulate profiling the bonus to estimate whether a more targeted reemployment bonus program would be more cost-effective and less subject to moral hazard problems.

Nonetheless, in 1994 the department took a leap of faith when it endorsed the reemployment bonus policy. The results from the research showed that UI recipients responded to the offer of reemployment bonuses and went back to work sooner and did not take lower-wage jobs. However, the bonus offers without the targeting of worker profiling were not cost-effective for the Unemployment Trust Fund. Meyer argued that reemployment bonuses without targeting would perform worse in an ongoing program than in the experiments. Larry Katz believed that reemployment bonuses were a good idea and that they would be more cost-effective when the offer of the bonuses was contingent upon participants' being profiled. He was wary, however, of reemployment bonuses because of Meyer's concerns.[7] When Alan

Table 10.6 Reemployment Bonuses: Demonstrations and Legislative Proposals

	Pennsylvania demonstration	Washington demonstration[a]	Proposed Reemployment Act of 1994	PRAs (HR 444)
Eligibility				
UI eligibility	Yes	Yes	Yes	Yes
Dislocated worker selection criteria	Screens	Screens	Profiling	Profiling
Design options				
Bonus amount[b] ($)	900	600	1,200	3,000
	1,800	1,200		
		1,800		
Bonus calculation	WBA multiple	WBA multiple	WBA multiple	Flat amount
Qualification period	6 wks.	6 wks.	12 wks.	13 wks.
	12 wks.	11 wks.		
Reemployment period	16 wks.	4 mos.	4 mos.	0 wks./ 6 mos.
Number of payments	1	1	1	2
Most cost-effective profiled design				
Bonus amount ($)	900	900		
Qualification period	12 wks.	11 wks.		

[a] For the Washington demonstration, the qualification period was based on UI potential duration. Qualification period here is based on assumption that individuals qualified for full 30 weeks.

[b] Pennsylvania and Washington demonstration bonus amounts were determined as multiples of the UI weekly benefit amount. Here, bonus amounts are calculated as multiples of the early 2008 national average weekly benefit amount of about $300.

SOURCE: Corson et al. (1991); O'Leary, Decker, and Wandner (2005); Spiegelman, O'Leary, and Kline (1992); USDOL (1994b); HR 444.

Krueger became chief economist in August 1994, the decision to proceed with reemployment bonuses had already been made; otherwise he would have advised against it. He too was convinced by Meyer's arguments.[8] Both Katz and Krueger believed that the research results for reemployment bonuses were weaker than those for comprehensive job search assistance and self-employment assistance. It was not until four years after the Reemployment Act was proposed that O'Leary, Decker, and Wandner (1998) demonstrated that profiling the bonus could raise reemployment bonuses' cost-effectiveness and narrow their targeting in a manner that could reduce concerns about UI program entry effects. By proposing the Reemployment Act of 1994, policymakers anticipated the research.

The academic community had been on a roller coaster regarding reemployment bonuses. The high point was in 1987, when the *American Economic Review* featured the Spiegelman and Woodbury (1987) article on the Illinois reemployment bonus experiment. In the next few years, however, further analysis clouded the optimism. Economists developed great doubts about the Illinois—and later the Pennsylvania and Washington—results. By 1994 the doubters predominated.[9] The analysis of O'Leary, Decker, and Wandner (1998, 2005) did not show up as a working paper until 1998 and did not appear in an economic journal until 2005. By that time, most economists had lost interest in reemployment bonuses.

The reemployment bonus provisions of the proposed Reemployment Act show that public policy can study a set of carefully designed demonstration projects and develop policy in a manner that combines a close look at the research results with—as happened in 1994—a leap of faith.

Personal Reemployment Accounts: Another Failed Legislative Proposal

President Bush announced Personal Reemployment Accounts (PRAs) as part of an economic stimulus package on January 7, 2003. On January 29, 2003, legislation to create PRAs was introduced in the House of Representatives as H.R. 444, the Back to Work Incentive Act of 2003.[10] Under H.R. 444, UI claimants deemed likely to exhaust their entitlement to benefits would be offered a $3,000 PRA that could be used to purchase reemployment services, including training, or could be used as a reemployment bonus. Reemployment services could be bought from public or private providers. Each reemployment service purchased would be drawn down against the $3,000 PRA. Workers would be eligible for a reemployment bonus if they became employed within 13 weeks of becoming unemployed, but they could continue to collect UI benefits until they became reemployed. The amount available to pay the bonus would be $3,000 or the PRA balance, if reemployment services were purchased. A reemployed worker would be immediately eligible for 60 percent of the bonus upon becoming reemployed. The remaining 40 percent would be payable if the worker retained the job for six months (Levine and Lordeman 2005).

Conceptually, PRAs have two components. One is a human capital account to help workers improve their human capital while they search for work, providing them with their choice of training and intensive services, as well as support services, including transportation and child care services. The other component is an incentive to search for work in the form of a reemployment bonus. Together, the PRAs "offer a new, innovative approach designed to provide unemployed Americans additional flexibility, greater choice, and more control over their employment search, as well as a reemployment bonus for those who find a job quickly" (House Education and Workforce Committee 2005).

Personal Reemployment Accounts: Policy Development

The Council of Economic Advisers (CEA), under the leadership of its chair, R. Glenn Hubbard, developed the concept and design of PRAs in late 2002.[11] The intent of Hubbard's proposal was to make employment and training programs more market-oriented. A proposal that linked a training and reemployment service voucher offer and a cash bonus offer as an incentive to speed the return to work was an attractive market-oriented package. But a reemployment service voucher and a reemployment bonus are conceptually very different. The key to making the PRAs work would be how they were meshed together.

PRA also served another function. Because the United States was coming out of a recession, PRAs were part of a larger proposal to distribute approximately $10 billion to the states as an economic stimulus package. The design of the PRAs would reflect concern about rapid stimulus, even though most of the stimulus package disappeared as the economy improved. Nonetheless, the $3.2 billion for PRAs survived. The market orientation of PRAs continued to make them an attractive proposal.

In the rush to give President Bush a new economic proposal by the beginning of 2003, the CEA had very little time to conduct the staff work necessary to develop the PRA proposal. Tom DeLeire was the staff labor economist at the CEA that year, on leave from Michigan State University. Under time constraints, DeLeire reviewed the literature on the reemployment bonus experiments. He consulted with Meyer, who had written a journal article on the UI Experiments—including the reemployment bonus experiments—that was widely read (Meyer 1995). Meyer provided broad policy advice about reemployment bonus legislation. He did not recommend an optimal reemployment bonus design for incorporation into the PRAs.[12] The Mathematica and Upjohn Institute researchers who conducted and evaluated the reemployment bonus experiments were not consulted—even though they could have provided practical advice on program design—nor were departmental staff who had worked on the reemployment bonus experiments.

The CEA had done enough analysis to get the basic design of the PRA reemployment bonus component right. The CEA justified PRAs based on the four reemployment bonus experiments that had been conducted as random assignment experiments. The evaluations of the experiments "showed that a bonus of $300–$1,000 motivated the recipients to become reemployed, reduced the duration of UI by almost a week, and resulted in new jobs that were comparable in earnings to those obtained by workers who were not eligible for the bonus and remained unemployed longer" (Council of Economic Advisers 2003).

The targeting of the PRA program design was taken from the reemployment bonus experiments: PRA offers were to be made to UI claimants who were likely to exhaust their benefits, using the same worker profiling methodology being used by the WPRS and SEA programs.

In its annual report, the CEA described PRAs as "not intended as a replacement for UI but rather . . . as a new component of the UI system. They would be offered as an additional option to those UI recipients who, under current UI rules, are referred to reemployment services" (Council of Economic Advisers 2003, pp. 123–126). Thus, PRAs would be a supplement to the UI program, and they would be targeted to workers using existing methods for referring UI claimants to reemployment services.

Most of the design decisions about the PRAs were driven by budgetary concerns and by the primacy of the voucher portion of the PRAs. There would be no entitlement to PRAs. They would only be offered up to the exhaustion of a total appropriation of $3.6 billion. This appropriation was estimated to be sufficient to serve 1.2 million beneficiaries (in Program Year 2003) who were "very likely" to exhaust their entitlement to UI benefits. Qualifying unemployed workers would be given an account valued at $3,000 that could be used to purchase reemployment services, training, and supportive services, although core reemployment services would continue to be provided free of charge. Workers who found a job within 13 weeks of receiving their first UI payment would be able to retain the balance of the account as a reemployment bonus.

In the 2003 *Economic Report of the President*, the council left open the timing and number of payments under the PRAs: "States would have the option of providing the cash balance as a single lump sum or in two installments of 60 percent and 40 percent, the latter after the recipient had been on the new job for six months" (Council of Economic Advisers 2003). Thus, the CEA would have permitted a single delayed lump sum payment as in the experiments, but in the interest of rapid infusion of funds into a weak U.S. economy, supporters of H.R. 444 opted for the second approach.

It is not possible to reconcile the CEA's reading of the reemployment bonus experiment literature with the Bush legislative proposal. CEA staff believed that the bonus amount was too large and that it was being paid too soon. As the proposal moved from an early public policy initiative to a legislative proposal, a series of changes were made that had more to do with ideology than rigorous public policy analysis. These decisions certainly did not reflect the findings of the research.

Once the CEA had completed its analytical work, most of the development of PRA legislation was turned over to the Domestic Policy Council. The Domestic Policy Council worked with the ETA's political staff to complete the development of the legislative proposal. USDOL research and policy staff who had worked on the experiments and on the development of the reemployment bonus proposal in the UI flexibility component of the proposed Reemployment Act of 1994 were aware of the development of the PRA proposal. They were requested to supply some background materials, but they were not included in discussions about the PRA program design.

In the fall of 2002, I initiated a meeting with the ETA's deputy assistant secretary, Mason Bishop, to provide him with information he could use in developing an effective and practical PRA design. The meeting did not go well. The presentation was met with disinterest, and he asked no questions about the information presented. No further meetings occurred. The negotiations between the Domestic Policy Council and the department thus were not informed by the research findings. At one point in these discussions, DeLeire asked to speak to me. Assistant Secretary Emily DeRocco said no.[13]

The lack of careful policy development meant that the PRAs had a number of design flaws. The most important was that the reemployment bonus offer was too large. The bonus was that large because the bonus offer was driven by the voucher offer amount, and no consideration was given to decoupling the bonus offer from the voucher amount. A reasonable training voucher amount would have been much larger than the reemployment bonus offer. The bonus offer should have been in the range that the reemployment bonus experiments found to be most cost-effective. (The national UI average weekly benefit amount in 2003 was $254, so the reemployment bonus offer should have been no more than three or four times that amount, or no more than $1,000. Thus, the PRA bonus offer was at least three times as great as it should have been.)

In 2003, it appeared that the PRA proposal might be enacted. Departmental research staff suggested that further analysis be conducted to support the PRA initiative: analyses based on prior experiments could help anticipate what would happen if PRAs were implemented, could allow the department to give guidance about how states could design and implement the bonus component of the PRAs, and could provide detailed administrative procedures for offering and paying the bonuses. Of particular concern was the fact that the department was proceeding with PRA demonstrations without prudent planning: the demonstrations were announced without careful consideration of how they should be designed and implemented.

Analysis of Personal Reemployment Accounts

Thus, to prepare for the implementation of PRAs, either as demonstration projects or as a national program, the department commissioned two studies to assess the likely impacts of the program and methods by which the program could be implemented. The studies built upon existing data sets and evidence about the two components of the PRAs: the reemployment bonuses and the training vouchers.[14]

Decker and Perez-Johnson (2004) of Mathematica based their analysis on the ongoing ITA training voucher experiment as well as the Pennsylvania reemployment bonus experiment that Mathematica had conducted. The training voucher experiment tested a pure voucher option that looked much like the human capital account voucher portion of the proposed PRA program. Individuals could use the pure vouchers in the manner they thought best to purchase training. Counselors in the One-Stop Career Centers would meet with pure voucher recipients, but the recipients were free to make training decisions on their own about what kind of training to buy and whom to buy it from. The preliminary findings from the interim evaluation were that unemployed workers who were offered a pure voucher were more likely to receive training than individuals who received more counseling and direction, but they took training in similar areas to individuals offered the other voucher designs.

Decker and Perez-Johnson divided their study into three parts. The first part dealt with predicted impacts of the PRA reemployment bonus offers with respect to bonus receipt rates, impacts on UI receipt, and entry effects into the UI program. These were compared to the results under the reemployment bonus experiments. Decker and Perez-Johnson estimated that a $3,000 bonus offer would substantially increase the rate of receipt of the bonus, from as little as 11–22 percent up to about 30 percent. The increase in participation was expected both because of the higher bonus offer amount and because the first installment of the bonus would be payable immediately rather than after four months on the new job. They also predicted that reductions in UI receipt would be greater because the bonus offer would be larger and because it would target a population that was likely to have longer UI durations in the absence of a bonus offer.

The second part of the study dealt with PRA design, trying to help states decide how large to make the PRA offer, whether it should be $3,000 or set at a lower amount. Decker and Perez-Johnson pointed out trade-offs in setting the PRA level: a level of $3,000 was approximately twice as great as the largest reemployment bonus level set under the experiments, but it would still be less than most local Individual Training Account offers under WIA. Lowering the overall offer below $3,000 would bring the reemployment bonus offer closer to tested levels, but it would exacerbate the inadequacy of a training voucher. However, lowering the offer would also allow PRAs to serve more UI recipients.

The third part of the study developed recommended procedures for states to follow in developing and implementing their PRA programs. Decker and Perez-Johnson developed procedures that could make it easier for states to implement PRAs. They opted for simplicity to allow quick implementation and to accommodate a temporary three-year program that would be established under H.R. 444. They adapted procedures from the Pennsylvania Reemployment Bonus Experiment, thus providing procedures for offering bonuses, verifying employment, and making payments; the procedures were similar to those that would have to be developed under PRAs.

In another Personal Reemployment Account study, O'Leary and Eberts (2004) simulated the effects of PRAs using detailed transaction-level administrative data from the state of Georgia. They first estimated the costs for intensive, training, and supportive services based on state expenditure levels, relative utilization of each service, and relative valuations for the services. The simulations estimated the average cost per offer of a $3,000 PRA to help states estimate how many offers to make during an enrollment cycle. The simulations also determined the likely pattern of use of the reemployment bonus, reemployment services, and income maintenance payments. Estimates were made under a baseline that assumed no behavioral response to the bonus offer, as well as estimates assuming a one- or two-week reduction in UI receipt.

Under the baseline estimate, O'Leary and Eberts (2004) determined that 40 percent of workers would receive a first payment under the reemployment bonus, while only 27 percent would remain employed and receive the second payment. They estimated the costs associated with the PRA offers for the bonus, purchase of services, and UI exhaustee payments at approximately $2,500, with small increases as the behavioral impact increased because of higher bonus recipiency. They concluded that a $3,000 bonus offer would not be cost-effective, while a smaller targeted bonus could be.

O'Leary and Eberts estimated the number of PRAs that could be offered, assuming 100 percent take-up of the PRA offers. They also estimated a likely take-up rate of approximately 80 percent, based on

the reemployment bonus experiments and the resulting increased number of PRAs that could be offered. They estimated the sensitivity of
their estimates of the number of PRAs that could be offered to changes
in the assumed prices for services and found that the results were quite
stable. They found that reducing prices of services by half would result
in the ability to increase the number of offers by roughly 20 percent.
Because of lack of data, they could not determine, however, how the
imposition of prices for services that were previously offered free of
charge would change the demand for services by workers who would
be offered the PRAs.

O'Leary and Eberts estimated the likelihood that workers would go
to either extreme: either only purchase services and not pursue a bonus,
or pursue the bonus and not purchase any services. They found that an
individual who purchased services and did not pursue the bonus would
have to either experience an increase in earnings of 14 percent or, failing that, return to work six weeks sooner, to compensate for not receiving the full bonus offer. They determined that past research evidence
made either of these results unlikely. Thus, as was to be expected with
an overly generous bonus offer, the PRA design strongly encouraged
pursuing the bonus.

For individuals who did not receive bonuses, O'Leary and Eberts
considered whether $3,000 would be sufficient to purchase a bundle
of services. They found that there likely would be a shortfall of funds.
They also estimated the increase in the number of PRAs that could be
offered as the statewide maximum PRA offer was lowered.

In the Washington and Pennsylvania experiments, recipients of
bonuses did not experience lower wages than the control group. While
O'Leary and Eberts posited that paying workers the first bonus payment
immediately upon their becoming unemployed might result in lower
wages, they did not have data from which to estimate whether or how
much wages might decline.

Thus, these two analyses predicted a number of adverse outcomes if
PRAs were to be implemented. The PRA bonus offer was too large, so
the reemployment bonus outcome would be cost-ineffective. Moreover,
the overly large bonus would result in higher participation and receipt
than a lower and more reasonable bonus offer. The training offer would
be lower than the cap for training offers under WIA programs in most
states, and thus use of the PRA to fund training would be limited, and
training participation rates would be low.

Personal Reemployment Account Demonstrations

H.R. 444 was not enacted in 2003, but the Bush administration was still eager to try out PRAs. In August 2004, the USDOL announced plans to implement a PRA demonstration project. States were asked to apply. On October 29, 2004, Secretary Elaine Chao announced that seven states—Florida, Idaho, Minnesota, Mississippi, Montana, Texas, and West Virginia—had been awarded a total of nearly $7.9 million to participate in a demonstration project that would allow unemployed workers to use personal reemployment accounts to find new jobs. The demonstration project was designed to test the effectiveness of PRAs (USDOL 2004).

To fund the demonstration, each state had to agree to obligate its entire fiscal year 2005 Wagner-Peyser Reemployment Services Grant (RSG) allocation to the project. Nationally, the Reemployment Services Grants totaled $34 million in FY 2005. The PRA grant funds for these seven states otherwise would have been used to provide reemployment services to unemployed workers found to be likely to exhaust all of their entitlement to UI benefits under the WPRS system. The Bush administration had decided to terminate the Reemployment Services Grants after fiscal year 2005 funding, which for some ETA programs only became available for program year 2005. Thus the RSG funds were exhausted in June 2006. Because the administration had eliminated the grants from the president's budget request, department policymakers were glad to have the demonstration states terminate their funding of these WPRS reemployment services a year early. The department supplemented these Reemployment Services Grant funds by providing each state with an additional $750,000 in federal discretionary funds from the ETA's budget to support the demonstration.

Preparation for proposed PRA legislation and the PRA demonstration project was conducted by department staff and by research contractors, who tried to make the best of a botched PRA design by using research findings to make the design and implementation of the demonstration projects work as well as possible. They used data and analysis from the reemployment bonus and training vouchers experiments, and they conducted simulations using state administrative data. Technical assistance and an evaluation were conducted by a contractor, Mathematica Policy Research.

The department developed the basic demonstration design, which closely followed the legislative design embodied in H.R. 444. The states would offer PRAs of $3,000, with funding available to make a total of 2,000 offers for the seven participating states. States would charge participating workers for services other than WIA core services. They also had to develop their own cost list for all reemployment services. Reemployment bonuses would be paid to workers who received PRA offers and found full-time jobs by their thirteenth week of UI receipt. The bonus consisted of two payments, one paid upon employment and consisting of 60 percent of the account balance, the other payable after six months on the job and making up the remaining 40 percent.

The department gave the states options with respect to the design. They could choose the reemployment bonus amount to be the balance of the $3,000 PRA offered, or some lesser amount. Four states—Florida, Minnesota, Mississippi, and Montana—chose to offer individuals the remaining balance in their account, as in the legislation. Texas, Idaho, and Minnesota, however, developed methods to reduce the bonus offers below $3,000. States also determined the cost of services. Six of the states developed cost lists, while Idaho chose to offer all of its services through community colleges which already had developed price structures. States could offer the PRAs statewide or in selected local workforce areas. West Virginia was the only state that offered PRAs statewide (Hess 2004, 2005).

The PRA demonstration project began in 2004 in the seven selected states. In 2006, the department awarded a second round of funding to three of the original states—Idaho, Minnesota, and Mississippi—and provided new funding for Hawaii. The eight states received a combined total of $12.5 million from the department to establish PRAs for a minimum of 3,543 workers. In fact, since not all workers used up all of the funds in their individual accounts, a greater number of workers were allowed to enter the project—4,038 in the original seven states.[15]

Claimants' participation in the demonstration projects was voluntary. The average acceptance rate was 64 percent, varying from a low of 46 percent in Minnesota to a high of 88 percent in Mississippi.

The evaluation of the PRA demonstration found that, as expected from the prior analyses, individuals who were offered PRAs were not interested in receiving training and did not expend much of their vouchers on training. Less than one-tenth of disbursements were used to pro-

vide funds for participants enrolled in training, and virtually no participants purchased intensive services (Table 10.7).

Because of the overly generous reemployment bonus, participation
in the bonus increased greatly beyond the level found in the reemployment bonus experiments, with 45 percent of disbursements going to
the payment of reemployment bonuses. While a rigorous net impact
and cost-benefit analysis was not conducted because of project design
weaknesses and lack of data, the bonus offer was so large that the reemployment bonus component of PRA could not have been cost-effective.

The most flexible form of funding was "supportive services." This
use of funds functioned, in effect, as a piggy bank that workers could
break open any time they wanted. Forty-six percent of disbursements
were used to fund supportive services. Allowable supportive services
fell into three categories: 1) assistance with respect to a specific job
offer; 2) intensive services, training, or logistical support for job search
(e.g., child care and transportation); and 3) general expenses relating to
job search activities. In the states without restrictive policies regarding
the purchase of supportive services, the great majority of disbursements
fell into this category. The largest purchases for supportive services were
for the following: vehicles, including mileage; utilities, rent, and mort-
gage payments; clothing, uniforms, and supplies; and health screening
and other medical expenses. Child care was a smaller purchase amount
(Kirby et al. 2008, p. 56). Given the chasm between the intended and
actual uses of the PRAs, the demonstrations were a disaster.

Personal Reemployment Accounts and Public Policy Issues

As the above discussion demonstrates, the Bush administration's
reemployment bonus portion of the PRAs differed in two major ways
from the reemployment bonuses tested in the four earlier experiments:
1) the timing and 2) the size of the reemployment bonus payment.

First, as tested in the experiments and as proposed in the Reemployment Act of 1994, only a single bonus payment would be made, and it
would only be made to individuals who find a job and retain it for at
least four months. The timing of the payment was based on what was
learned from the three reemployment bonus experiments. The minimum reemployment period before individuals would receive a single
reemployment bonus payment was four months in Illinois, 16 weeks in

Table 10.7 PRA Demonstration Project, Average Disbursement per User as a Percentage of Total Expenditures

	States with restricted supportive purchases			States with broad allowable supportive service purchases				All states
	MS	WV	FL	ID	MN	MT	TX	
Type of disbursement								
Total bonuses	94	83	59	37	33	13	29	45
Intensive	0	1	1	0	1	0	0	1
Training	2	13	2	20	7	17	14	9
Supportive	4	17	41	63	67	87	71	55
Total services	6	17	41	63	67	87	71	55
Total expenditures	100	100	100	100	100	100	100	100

SOURCE: Kirby et al. (2008), p. 56.

Pennsylvania, and four months in Washington. The purpose of the delay was to be certain that an individual obtained and retained a new job. For Illinois, Pennsylvania, and Washington, "the four-month interval was believed to be sufficiently long to avoid encouraging claimants to accept short-term employment simply to qualify for a bonus" (Robins and Spiegelman 2001, p. 39). The test of finding a job comparable to that which would have been found in the absence of the bonus offer was that 1) the reemployment bonus induced taking jobs that paid the same wage and 2) the new job was held for a reasonable period of time.

Second, the bonus amounts tested in the Pennsylvania and Washington reemployment bonus experiments were two, three, four, and six times the UI weekly benefit amount. Given an average weekly benefit amount of approximately $250 in the United States in 2005, these reemployment bonus amounts translated into $500, $750, $1,000, and $1,500. Analysis of the cost-effectiveness of the Pennsylvania and Washington reemployment bonuses after applying worker profiling to the original data yielded a determination that the low bonus offer was the most cost-effective. Thus, a reasonable maximum bonus offer based on the findings of these two experiments would have been no more than four times the weekly benefit amount—that is, $1,000 or less.

As proposed, however, a PRA bonus could be as large as $3,000, which was considerably outside the range of reemployment bonus offers experimentally tested. The offer amounts for the Pennsylvania and Washington state experiments were carefully selected to test the full range of possible cost-effective options. Thus, there was no justification for such a large reemployment bonus offer when smaller bonus offers had produced a significant impact on speeding claimants' return to work and smaller bonus offers were more cost-effective.

CONCLUSIONS

Reemployment Bonus Effectiveness

A number of lessons were learned from the bonus experiments:

- As predicted by job search theory, cash bonuses have a significant impact on job search behavior and lead to a reduction in the average duration of unemployment, resulting in a desirable speeding of reemployment. Larger bonuses also had the largest impacts on reducing unemployment durations.

- As expected from the empirical literature on UI work disincentives, the bonuses had no effect on wages, indicating no decline in the quality of jobs taken in response to the offer of reemployment bonuses. There also was no evidence that the bonuses had any effect on worker attachment to their previous employers, as they had no effect on worker recall to their prior jobs.

- On the other hand, because unemployment durations were not directly related to the dollar level of the bonus offer, there was not the continuously increasing effect that might have been expected. The large effect of intermediate-level bonuses makes findings less certain about what would be an optimum bonus.

- Reemployment bonuses are not cost-effective if they are not targeted to populations that have some or all of the characteristics of dislocated workers.

- A more targeted program using profiling promises to be cost-effective and to minimize external validity problems related to implementation of an ongoing program.

- The reemployment bonus experiments made sense from a public policy perspective. They gave legitimacy to reemployment bonuses, a concept that was initially met with considerable skepticism. The lessons learned from the experiments were applied in developing the legislative specifications for the proposed Reemployment Act of 1994.

- The design of the PRAs did not make sense. The reemployment bonus offer should have been much smaller than the PRA amount—no more than three or four times the average weekly benefit amount. The reemployment bonus offer should have been decoupled from any training voucher and should have been offered in a much smaller dollar amount than the training voucher component.

Research Implications for a Reemployment Bonus Design and Operation

Worker profiling. Use of worker profiling with a statistical model would target the appropriate population—dislocated workers who are likely to be unemployed for a long time. An offer of a reemployment bonus to workers who are likely to remain unemployed for a long time should result in larger reductions in compensated durations of unemployment.

Worker profiling also would reduce any concern about induced unemployment. The program would be narrowly targeted and offered to a small portion of UI claimants. This targeted group would have certain characteristics—e.g., long tenure, likely long unemployment durations—that would make claimants less likely to incur a spell of unemployment simply to receive the bonus. Use of a statistical model would also create uncertainty about eligibility even among those workers who might be eligible, reducing policy concern about entry into the UI programs to receive a reemployment bonus.

Ascertaining the job offer date. Before paying a reemployment bonus, the UI agency should check with the new employer to determine whether the employee satisfies the continuous, full-time employment requirement for the specified period of time. At the same time, consideration should be given to determining when the job offer was made, and specifically whether it was made prior to the beginning of the spell of unemployment. This approach would reduce the risk that a worker would delay acceptance of a new job to incur a period of intervening unemployment in order to receive a bonus.

Bonus design. A reemployment bonus should be constructed to be a multiple of the weekly benefit amount. It should not be in the form of a fixed dollar amount, in order to avoid higher usage by low-wage employees than by higher-wage employees. This design would be in accord with job search theory and labor supply models that predict that low-wage workers would make greater use of a fixed dollar amount bonus offer. Based on the Illinois data, however, there is only weak confirmation of this hypothesis (Meyer 1996, p. 270).

Bonus size. The bonus size should be moderate, in order to provide a sufficient incentive to get unemployed workers to respond and speed their early return to work, but not so large as to greatly change their labor market behavior, e.g., prompting them to move from employment to unemployment. A bonus of between three and four times the weekly benefit amount would be reasonable. In 2008, the average bonus offer would have been approximately $900 if the bonus had been set at three times the weekly benefit amount (and approximately $1,200 if set at four times the weekly benefit amount).

Bonus offer timing. The bonus should be offered as early as possible during spells of unemployment. It should be offered as soon as individuals are determined to be eligible to receive UI. Alternatively, the bonus could be conditionally offered at the time of filing a UI initial claim. It could be offered to claimants who are determined to be monetarily eligible and who are profiled as dislocated workers. This approach assumes that states can make monetary determinations and conduct profiling on a real-time basis. The offer, however, would be conditional on claimants meeting nonmonetary eligibility stipulations, such as being involuntarily separated from a previous job.

The resulting program would be an effective instrument to encourage job-ready, dislocated workers to accelerate their return to employment. It would be a small program, with only a modest impact on local labor markets. It would not be a solution to unemployment by itself but one of many tools to encourage and enable unemployed workers to return to work.

Reemployment Bonus Policy

The research lessons learned about reemployment bonuses were used by the USDOL to develop the reemployment bonus provisions proposed in the Reemployment Act of 1994. The reemployment bonus design came directly from the conclusions drawn from the evaluations of the Pennsylvania and Washington state experiments.

In contrast, the reemployment bonus provisions in the Personal Reemployment Accounts legislative proposal and in the PRA demonstration project made no sense. The bonus offer was too large: the offer level was twice as large as the largest bonus tested by any of the experiments. As a result, the PRA reemployment bonus could not be cost-effective.

Reemployment bonuses still make good public policy sense. With refinements, reemployment bonus provisions that mirror those contained in the bill that would have become the Reemployment Act of 1994 should be adopted as a five-year sunsetting program that would be evaluated before being made permanent.

Notes

1. The New Jersey results reveal that the reemployment bonus had a significant effect on the long-term stabilization of employment. Both the JSA-only treatment and the JSA-plus-reemployment-bonus (RB) treatment had long-term impacts on UI weeks paid, although the impact of JSA-plus-RB was greater. For JSA-only, there were significant impacts in the first and second year, but not for the entire six-year period. For the JSA-plus-RB treatment, there was a significant effect for the entire period, as well as for each of the first two years.

2. In the New Jersey Experiment, however, the JSA-only treatment had no significant first-quarter effect on earnings. We must conclude that the reemployment bonus offer—in combination with the JSA offer—had a positive effect on earnings in the first quarter. There was, however, no significant effect for the JSA-plus-RB treatment for any of the six years of follow-up, or for the six years as a whole.

3. Bruce D. Meyer, in an interview with the author, August 25, 2008.

4. Vroman (1991) finds that over half of the individuals identified as nonfilers thought they were not eligible. While this response was the nonfilers' perception rather than their factual knowledge of the situation, many of these respondents were probably correct. The USDOL attempted to independently confirm this response with a study based on a follow-up 1993 CPS supplement (BLS 1997). The study was intended to match respondents' survey responses with their quarterly wage data to determine whether they were monetarily eligible. Because of a small non-filer sample, the Census Bureau did not conduct the match.

5. Robert B. Reich, in an interview with the author, November 21, 2008.

6. Ibid.

7. Larry Katz, in an interview with the author, September 25, 2008.

8. Alan Krueger, in an interview with the author, October 13, 2008.

9. Ibid.

10. On January 4, 2005, two bills were introduced in the 109th Congress that would have authorized PRAs as part of the WIA: H.R. 26, a stand-alone bill, and H.R. 27, a bill to reauthorize the WIA. The provisions of both bills were identical, and they, in turn, were identical to those of H.R. 444, which had been passed by the House of Representatives in the 108th Congress.

11. Much of the discussion in this section is based on an interview by the author with Tom DeLeire on July 19, 2005.

12. Meyer, interview.

13. Tom DeLeire, interview with the author, July 19, 2005.

14. I proposed these two projects to assist in the implementation of the PRA demonstration projects, not just to ensure that program managers and public policy officials would have a more realistic expectation about the likely outcomes of implementation of the PRAs.

15. Data and analysis for the PRA demonstration projects in Kirby et al. (2008) are restricted to the seven original states because Hawaii entered the project late.

11
Summary and Conclusions

This book has examined the impact that research has had on U.S. employment and training policy and programs over the past 25 years. It has identified employment programs that work and employment programs that do not work. Some programs that work have been pursued, but so have programs that have had little objective analysis. Sometimes policymakers wait for the results of research before acting, but often they make decisions without or despite research findings. At other times policymakers are totally uninterested in the research findings or, for political reasons, want to subvert and suppress them.

Over the past 25 years, there were two periods when interest in research was greatest at the Department of Labor (USDOL). In 1985–1987, Secretary of Labor Bill Brock sought ways to make American workers more competitive in the world economy and was willing to invest in research to find optimal approaches. Later, from 1993 to 1997, when Robert Reich was Secretary of Labor, the department took a particular interest in examining research findings and applying them to formulate public policy. By contrast, during the George W. Bush administration, when Elaine Chao was secretary of labor and Emily DeRocco was assistant secretary for employment and training, many research findings were ignored, misrepresented, and suppressed.

The intellectual framework for this book has been best stated by Bill Brock. (See Chapter 2.) Since the 1980s, Brock has believed that for U.S. workers to succeed in a global economy the government must invest in human development. Human development requires investments in training and education, as well as in what Brock calls "job transition assistance." This book has looked both at job transition assistance and job training. Job transition assistance includes public labor exchange services, comprehensive job search assistance, unemployment insurance eligibility reviews, reemployment bonuses, self-employment assistance, and work sharing. All of these job transition interventions seek to help workers shift from unemployment to new jobs smoothly, quickly, and efficiently. Job training includes skill and occupational training provided in the classroom and on the job.

439

RESEARCH USED OR MISUSED

For most of the past decade, employment research has been neglected. The USDOL's program of applied employment research withered, and existing research findings were not used to support public policy. Looking to the future, employment policy can and should be guided by research findings. While many knowledge gaps remain, much is known about what works and what does not work.

PROGRAMS THAT WORK

Much of the analysis in this book has concentrated on program interventions for dislocated workers that were tested by the experiments and by policy-oriented research. Together, the research has revealed a number of programs and approaches that work.

Comprehensive Job Search Assistance

The Worker Profiling and Reemployment Services (WPRS) system was based on the New Jersey Experiment and a number of other rigorous tests of the effectiveness of comprehensive job search assistance. The body of completed research reviewed in the USDOL (1995b) publication *What's Working (and what's not)* convinced researchers and policymakers that WPRS made sense and would be a cost-effective intervention.

An important component of WPRS was its early intervention approach. Unemployed workers would receive comprehensive job search assistance in the first few weeks of their job loss. Since the targeted workers were found to be likely to exhaust their entitlement to UI benefits, providing job search assistance services early offered the prospect of reducing the compensated unemployment of these workers so that WPRS would provide net benefits to the government sector.

Another key component of the WPRS system was its narrow targeting to a specific group of dislocated workers—those likely to exhaust their unemployment insurance (UI) benefits. Worker profiling became an allocation and targeting device to get reemployment services to the unemployed workers who could make more effective and efficient use of the limited funding that was available.

Meyer (1995) recommended providing comprehensive job search assistance to a broader group of workers, rather than targeting the smaller group most likely to exhaust their UI entitlement. Worker profiling still would be used as an allocation tool because funding for job search assistance and other reemployment services is likely to remain limited. Annual funding for the reemployment services component of WPRS, however, has to be permanently maintained at or above levels provided for under the American Recovery and Reinvestment Act (ARRA) of 2009. The ARRA levels were higher than the level that existed from 2001 through 2005, before the Bush administration terminated WPRS in June 2006.

Self-Employment Assistance

Self-Employment Assistance (SEA) was enacted on a temporary basis with solid preliminary empirical research from the interim evaluation report on the Massachusetts SEA Experiment (Benus et al. 1992). The SEA program follows the successful Massachusetts experiment design, which provided periodic self-employment payments, rather than the unsuccessful Washington State experiment design, which provided lump-sum payments. Uncertainty remained, however, about how the Massachusetts net impact and benefit-cost analyses would turn out. The final evaluation (Benus et al. 1995) provided strong research findings that the Massachusetts SEA Experiment was cost-effective, providing a sound basis for making SEA legislation permanent in 1998.

Self-Employment Assistance is a small but effective program in a small number of states. While similar programs serve considerably more workers in other major industrial nations, it is not clear that the SEA program will expand in the United States. The program will remain small unless a reliable source of entrepreneurial counseling and training is found to provide to workers participating in the SEA program. States with SEA programs frequently have no steady source of entrepreneurial counseling and training.

The Department of Labor currently has two entrepreneurship programs—1) the SEA program and 2) Workforce Investment Act (WIA) entrepreneurial training. Historically, only small numbers of workers have been interested in starting their own businesses. The department could help workers create their own jobs and jobs for other workers who are hired by new small firms. The WIA entrepreneurial training program has failed because of the strange way in which it assesses program performance: the department searches for owner-operators of successful unincorporated microenterprises established by WIA trainees among those entering wage and salary employment in the UI wage records. Not surprisingly, these owner-operators can never be found by searching the UI wage records. Entrepreneurial training should be assessed by conducting surveys to determine if trainees become self-employed. The department should increase funding for WIA entrepreneurial training as well as create a partnership with the Small Business Administration so that department programs can work with the Small Business Development Centers—which provide entrepreneurial counseling and training—at the state and local level.

Targeted Reemployment Bonuses

Four reemployment bonus experiments were conducted. The first experiment was conducted in the state of Illinois, and its results were hailed by economists when the results were published in the September 1987 *American Economic Review* (Spiegelman and Woodbury 1987). Reemployment bonuses received widespread support from many economists in 1987 but doubt grew as further research was conducted. Confidence by researchers had diminished sharply by 1994 when the Clinton administration proposed reemployment bonuses as part of the Reemployment Act of 1994.

The Clinton reemployment bonus proposal used the worker profiling targeting mechanism that was already being used by the WPRS system. The proposal consisted of a low-value bonus equal to four times the UI weekly benefit amount, or about $1,000. The combination of worker profiling and a low-value bonus made reemployment bonuses more cost-effective, but research findings did not demonstrate its effectiveness.

In 2003, reemployment bonuses were proposed again by the Bush administration as a component of the Personal Reemployment Accounts (PRA) initiative. Unfortunately, the final design of PRAs was flawed and was not based on the research findings; e.g., the reemployment bonuses were too large and were paid out too early. Political rather than research considerations had a strong influence on the final PRA design. Fortunately, that PRA design was not made a permanent component of federal law.

Stronger findings about targeting low-value bonuses only became available when a simulation analysis using the worker profiling mechanism was applied to the Washington State and Pennsylvania reemployment bonus experiment data (O'Leary, Decker, and Wandner 2005). This analysis suggested that limited offers of reemployment bonuses to dislocated UI claimants could be a cost-effective policy option. A reemployment bonus using this program design should be enacted.

Targeted Reemployment Services

A variety of approaches to job transition assistance (or reemployment services) have been shown to be cost-effective. They include 1) comprehensive job search assistance (discussed above and not considered here); 2) the public labor exchange function; and 3) administration of the work test—i.e., enforcing work search requirements.

Jacobson and Petta (2000) found the public labor exchange to be cost-effective. Public labor exchanges administered by the state workforce agencies also have been shown to be more cost-effective than providing these services either privately or by public agencies other than the state Wagner-Peyser Act agencies. The department commissioned an evaluation to determine whether public, merit-staff labor exchanges administered by the state workforce agencies were more cost-effective than providing the services through private providers or public agencies other than the state workforce agencies. The evaluation findings indicated that the state workforce agencies performed far better than the private or public demonstration states (Jacobson et al. 2004). The evaluation findings should have resulted in retaining state labor exchange service providers and discontinuing the temporary demonstrations. The Bush administration elected, instead, to suppress the evaluation and recommend the elimination of the public employment service that provides labor exchange services. The department should reestablish the United States Employment Service, provide more funding for Employment Service–funded reemployment services, and terminate the temporary demonstrations.

Eligibility reviews of UI claimants to determine if they continue to be eligible for participation in the UI program are cost-effective. A variety of other work search measures are also cost-effective. Work search measures are particularly effective in speeding the return to work when combined with the provision of reemployment services (O'Leary 2006). The department should expand eligibility reviews in their current form of Reemployment and Eligibility Assessments and coordinate them with the provision of ES-provided reemployment services and training.

Targeted Longer-Term Training

Generally, education and training programs are more cost-effective when they are either targeted longer-term classroom training or work-based learning programs, including on-the-job training and apprenticeship. Jacobson, LaLonde, and Sullivan (2002) examine the impact on dislocated workers who enrolled in community college courses. The study identifies "high return" classes that improved the annual earnings of participants. Participants experienced high economic returns from taking and completing courses that provided technical academic and vocational skills—including courses in health, engineering, math, and science. The study's findings suggest that workers can greatly improve their economic returns to training by taking courses concentrated in the high-return classes. Other analyses also have shown that long-term education and training are key to having employment and earnings gains (USDOL 1995b).

PROGRAMS THAT DO NOT WORK OR ARE UNPROVEN

The Bush administration proposed a number of workforce development legislative initiatives, none of which were enacted into federal law. Most of these proposals either flew in the face of research findings or were proposed without first being tested.

Workforce Development Program Consolidation

The Bush administration's proposed approach of consolidating and block-granting employment and training programs was a bad idea. Specifically, it would have done three things: 1) eliminated the Employment Service (ES), 2) combined the WIA programs into a single program, and 3) block-granted the remaining consolidated program. None of these ideas would have worked separately, and they certainly would not have worked in combination.

First, eliminating the ES would have been contrary to a wide body of research. The ES is a highly cost-effective provider of inexpensive public labor exchange and other reemployment services. It has been shown to be more cost-effective than labor exchange services provided in three demonstration states (Jacobson and Petta 2000; Jacobson et al. 2004). The conclusion from evaluations of the ES is that it is cost-effective and should be retained. Similar program evaluations of other services provided by the ES—conducting UI eligibility reviews and providing reemployment services—also have proven them to be cost-effective (O'Leary 2006).

The logic of the Bush administration's WIA consolidation proposal depended on ignoring or suppressing studies that showed substantial state demand for public employment service programs. Each year states show their support of the ES by committing their own state funds to augment Wagner-Peyser Act grants to states. States also have committed a substantial portion of funds from the 2002 Reed Act distribution to supplementing Wagner-Peyser Act grants that they receive each year: 25 states spent $438 million on ES administration (CESER 2004). A study of rural One-Stops has shown the key role played by the ES in rural areas, where few other agencies join the ES in affiliated One-Stops (Dunham et al. 2005).

The public employment service provides the vast majority of reemployment services under the WPRS system (Dickinson et al. 1999). Thus, the ES is key to the effectiveness of the WPRS system. Since comprehensive job search assistance provided through the WPRS system has been proven to be highly cost-effective, the reemployment services grants to states provided under WPRS, which were discontinued by the Bush administration in June 2006, should be continued at or above ARRA levels.

Second, evaluations of the WIA Adult and Dislocated Worker programs also show that the programs are effective. The findings warrant keeping these two programs as separate categorical programs. Instead, the results were either ignored or suppressed (Barnow and King 2005; Hollenbeck et al. 2005).

Finally, block grants—the method of providing federal employment services that was principally endorsed by the Bush administration—have tended to be a subterfuge for cutting and eliminating programs. The history of block grants reveals that their funding tends to be cut shortly after they are put in place. The programs that they support inevitably become less viable as funding levels are ratcheted down (GAO 1995).

Personal Reemployment Accounts

Personal Reemployment Accounts were a bad idea. The PRAs' design combined training vouchers and reemployment bonuses. While training vouchers and reemployment bonuses can be effective if implemented separately, combining them should have been done with care. The Bush administration botched combining a reemployment bonus with a training voucher.

The Bush administration proposed PRA legislation in 2003. The legislative design ignored past research, combining a training grant that was not generous enough with a reemployment bonus grant that was too generous. The design had other flaws as well. I managed to obtain approval to have two analyses of PRAs done; these were conducted by O'Leary and Eberts (2004) and Decker and Perez-Johnson (2004). The studies pointed out the numerous program flaws and indicated that PRAs would not work. Nonetheless, the department proceeded both with a PRA legislative proposal and a PRA demonstration project. The legislation did not pass, and the demonstration did not work (Kirby et al. 2008).

Career Advancement Accounts

In 2006, the Bush administration proposed Career Advancement Accounts (CAAs), a component of President Bush's larger "Ownership Society" initiative. Since this was a big new initiative without new funding, the administration carved most of the funding for CAAs out of WIA programs. The money for CAAs would have been made available to workers through training accounts that each worker would "own." CAAs were training vouchers offered in the amount of $3,000 for one year and would have been available in the same amount for a second year. The department recommended offering CAAs over the Internet, since the proposed administrative funding for the program was minuscule.

Career Advancement Accounts would have required closing most of the One-Stop Career Centers. CAAs would have received 75 percent of the state workforce development grants—both WIA and Wagner-Peyser Act state grants—and an additional 3 percent of these grants would have been made available for CAA administration. The remaining 22 percent would not have been enough to keep many One-Stops open, since state funding levels would have been reduced to barely over one-fifth of their former levels. If CAAs had been enacted, a massive closure of the One-Stops would have occurred.

The CAA proposal ignored and misread, perhaps purposefully, the research findings on training. The marketing of CAAs broadcast that they were following the "free choice" model for training vouchers, and that this model did not require any counseling, suggesting that having training vouchers on demand was a viable model. In fact, the Individual Training Account Experiment process evaluation found that, under the free choice voucher model, unemployed workers actually received a significant amount of counseling—an average of five hours—before they were offered a training voucher (McConnell et al. 2006). The CAA proposal also ignored evaluations showing the limited effectiveness of short-term, untargeted, inexpensive public job training. Finally, the CAA proposal did not propose a rational mechanism for allocating funds for the training vouchers despite the fact that the demand for training vouchers would have greatly exceeded the federal funding.

Wage Supplements

Over the past 25 years, wage supplements (sometimes known as "wage insurance") have been proposed mostly by Brookings Institution staff as an income transfer to respond to the wage loss of experienced dislocated workers (Baily, Burtless, and Litan 1993; Brainard 2007;

Burtless 2007; Burtless et al. 1998; Lawrence et al. 1984; Lawrence and Litan 1986). Wage supplement proposals provide temporary, partial wage supplementation to dislocated workers who lose their jobs due to either a domestic or an international dislocation. Under most proposals, affected workers usually receive up to half of their lost wages based on their predislocation wage, usually for a period of up to two years. The maximum annual supplementation is usually between $5,000 and $10,000 per year.

Wage supplements have generally been proposed as a complement to UI, not as a substitute. Under these proposals, the UI program would continue to protect workers from wage loss while they remain unemployed, while wage supplements would continue to protect workers from wage loss after they become reemployed. In both cases, the UI and wage supplement programs represent partial, temporary wage replacement.

The Alternative Trade Adjustment Assistance (ATAA) program is a small wage supplement program that has been part of the Trade Adjustment Assistance (TAA) programs since 2002. The ATAA program has been very small, and it has not been evaluated.

However, a random assignment experiment tested wage supplements in Canada in the 1990s. The results were not conclusive, and the design of the program was not applicable to the United States because of Canada's very different institutional environment (Bloom et al. 1999). It is not clear whether wage supplements would work in the United States, and, if so, what would be their optimal design. Before the United States expands wage supplements, the supplements should be tested using rigorous experimental methods to determine how American workers would respond behaviorally to wage supplement offers.

Untargeted, Short-Term Training

Research findings suggest that short-term, low-cost training is cost-effective for adult women, but generally not for anyone else. There is little evidence that it works for adult men or for dislocated workers. Short-term training seems to be particularly ineffective for youth. These research findings derive from the U.S. experience, but they have been replicated in the other industrial nations (LaLonde 1995; Martin and Grubb 2001; USDOL 1995b, pp. 58–59).

Training tends to be more cost-effective when it is long-term and targeted to high-return courses. Nevertheless, most department-sponsored training has concentrated on short-term training that is not necessarily targeted to high-return course work. Training must be rethought and tested through a variety of demonstration projects. Based on current research, it appears that training is likely to be more effective if it is provided more intensively over a longer period of time. Such training is not likely to be viable unless it provides stipends to workers that allow trainees to complete training. Alternatives to classroom training with stipends are programs that allow workers to earn a living while they are trained. The most promising options are expanded apprenticeship and on-the-job training.

IMPROVING EXISTING PROGRAMS

A great deal could be done to improve existing employment programs. Some programs have not been implemented as intended. Other programs are underfunded or need new participation incentives. Still others need to find more effective and efficient designs.

Worker Profiling and Reemployment Services

WPRS consists of two components: 1) a statistical worker profiling model and 2) a menu of reemployment services. While efforts to retain, improve, and update worker profiling models continued in the 2000s, the provision of a reemployment services component was neglected and then abandoned. Unfortunately, WPRS systems cannot function properly without the widespread availability of reemployment services. "Reemployment services" became a prohibited phrase at the Employment and Training Administration (ETA) for much of the Bush administration. Policy emphasis focused solely on training, to the neglect of all employment services. Indeed, the special funding for WPRS in the form of Reemployment Services Grants was terminated in June 2006.

Restoring the WPRS system to functionality requires reinvigorated support for the provision of reemployment services and the institutions that provide them. The primary funding for reemployment services should be provided to the ES in the form of permanently reestablished Reemployment Services Grants to the states.

Self-Employment Assistance

Self-Employment Assistance currently is available in seven states. Where it exists, the program is small—mainly because of the limited funding for entrepreneurial training. The SEA program is mistakenly seen as a UI program because its authorizing legislation is contained in the UI section of the Social Security Act. The program is more accurately viewed as a workforce development program under which workers can create a job for themselves and, possibly, for other workers.

No stable source of funding for entrepreneurial counseling and training exists in most states. Funding for training should be provided by the Workforce Investment Act and Small Business Administration (SBA) programs. The department should work with the SBA to gain the cooperation of the SBA's microenterprise program to provide counseling and training to SEA participants. The department should also ensure that its WIA Dislocated Worker Program participates in SEA.

Work Sharing

The current work sharing program suffers from two problems. These problems have potential solutions. First, the department has interpreted the 1992 federal legislation as technically deficient because it did not explicitly give the department the ability to expand the scope of work sharing beyond the five provisions specified in the federal statute. This issue can be addressed either by a federal statutory amendment or by a more expansive interpretation of the law by the secretary. The department also should provide the states with technical assistance and encourage states to adopt and use the work sharing programs, especially in recessionary times.

Second, the federal government should encourage businesses to use work sharing, particularly during recessions, by providing incentives for firms to participate. The federal government could greatly increase participation if the cost of work sharing benefits were borne by the Federal Unemployment Tax Act (FUTA)–governed account—instead of by the individual state accounts—in the Unemployment Trust Fund. Firms also would be freed from paying the cost of work sharing (i.e., benefits would not be charged to employers' UI accounts), and work sharing would be treated as if it were a part of the extended benefit program rather than the basic regular UI programs. The change is warranted for work sharing programs, particularly during recessionary periods.

Job Training

Public training programs in the United States have relied on short-term training, which generally does not work. While short-term training helps to employ adult women, it has not worked well for men and youth. It is time to shift attention to longer-term training for some, particularly making use of community colleges and four-year colleges.

Nonetheless, a large-scale effort should be taken to determine how public job training can be improved and expanded. There is a lack of information about what works. A great deal of additional research must be conducted before the most cost-effective forms of training emerge and a consensus develops about what works. The key to finding more cost-effective training programs is conducting a series of large-scale demonstrations and evaluations of various approaches to training. Given that much public job training is general, untargeted, and short-term, these program characteristics should be reexamined and variations should be tested. Demonstrations should examine particular types of training (e.g., on-the-job training, apprenticeship, customized, classroom), targeting of training (e.g., high-return training courses, training by type of provider), and longer-term and more concentrated training.

TARGETING EMPLOYMENT SERVICES

Targeting employment services to those workers who can most benefit from them is important both as an allocation tool and as a way to increase the cost-effectiveness of employment services. The recent acute shortage of funding for employment services calls out for a more rational method of allocating services among the many individuals who seek services from the workforce development One-Stop centers.

Targeting is also a key tool for increasing the cost-effectiveness of reemployment services in general. Targeting in the form of worker profiling has been developed for use in operating the WPRS system as well as the SEA programs. Worker profiling also would be available for use by a reemployment bonus program if federal legislation were enacted to permit the operation of such a program.

Targeting has been shown to make various treatments more cost-effective, including comprehensive job search assistance, self-employment assistance, and reemployment bonuses. More recently, targeting methods have been used for a number of programs such as Temporary Assistance for Needy Families (TANF), welfare-to-work, and training and education programs (Eberts, O'Leary, and Wandner 2002). Better uses of targeting methods can improve the effectiveness of existing programs. Targeting also should be considered for use by other employment and training programs.

Targeting can be applied more comprehensively to provide a broad array of employment services, including job matching, provision of labor market information, and selection of cost-effective employment services. The Frontline Decision Support System (FDSS) was tested as a demonstration in Georgia to provide decision support to unemployed workers in the provision of reemployment services. The FDSS incorporated a comprehensive approach to targeting reemployment services for workforce development programs at local One-Stops. The FDSS systematically helped dislocated workers return to work by matching them with job openings, by helping them search for work, and by referring them to targeted, cost-effective reemployment services (Eberts and O'Leary 2002). The public workforce system requires a substantial increase in funding. Targeting is not a substitute for more funding, but it can make the limited funds more cost-effective.

FUNDING

The responsibilities of the workforce development system have greatly expanded since the mid-1990s. The implementation of One-Stop Career Centers provided for the availability of core services to all workers whether they were unemployed, employed, or not participating in the labor force. The demand for reemployment services also has grown as the problem of worker dislocation has spread. Researchers and policymakers have increasingly understood that American workers must improve their skills to compete in a global economy. Yet new programs, such as WPRS, and new systems, such as the One-Stop Career Centers, have been created but have not been reasonably funded. Moreover, while federal funding has declined in monetary terms, it has declined even more sharply in real terms. (See Table 6.1.) To provide the services to American workers that Congress has deemed critical, the federal workforce system must have a sustained increase in funding.

THE NEED FOR MORE RESEARCH

A book on the impact of research on employment and training policy cannot possibly end without a call for more rigorous research and evaluation. After a period of profound neglect, research on getting America's workers back to work is especially needed. The new research should be applied research that aims at helping to improve American human resources. Once again, public policymakers should pay attention to the research findings.

As Bill Brock told me, the success of the U.S. economy depends upon its workers, and the federal government must do a great deal more to improve human development, including education, training, and transition assistance.[1] Training and transition assistance come, in part, from USDOL-funded programs, and these programs must be updated and improved. Research, demonstrations, and evaluations can ensure that the states and localities administering these programs have the information about what works and what does not. For program administration to be effective, however, the federal government must release the research results, provide technical assistance, encourage states to carefully consider the research findings, and then make use of the findings to guide its own public policy and programs.

The research capacity of the ETA was sharply reduced during the Bush administration. Secretary Chao, Assistant Secretary DeRocco, and her deputy, Mason Bishop, systematically starved a structure that had been built over half a century. It will not be easy to revive and reinvigorate it. But it needs to be done.

Research needs to be conducted to better understand workforce development programs: how they work, whom they serve, and what the short- and long-term impacts of the programs are on individuals and their families.

Employment programs will work better if they are guided by evaluations that are conducted frequently and at regular intervals, e.g., every five years, using administrative data and quasiexperimental methods. Random assignment evaluations should be used, but only for large, nonentitlement programs, such as the WIA and Job Corps programs. Smaller programs should have more modest evaluations and should use more modest methods (Balducchi and Wandner 2009).

Demonstrations should be widely used to look for new, modified, and improved programs, and they should be used for the major populations that are served by the department and other federal agencies, including disadvantaged adults and youth, dislocated workers, and UI recipients. Large demonstration projects should use random assignment methods so that the findings are convincing when they identify cost-effective treatments. Some demonstrations that are needed include the following: wage supplements; employment bonuses for low-wage workers; various types of training (by training type, training duration, and types of training courses); and employment and retention services for former TANF recipients, prisoners reentering the labor force, and other low-wage workers.

Other, more qualitative research is needed as well. Since training is provided by many federal and state agencies other than those sponsored by the USDOL (Mikelson and Nightingale 2005), the relationship of these training programs to department-sponsored programs should be studied closely. The department should pay particular attention to customized training, which is funded by an offset against state UI taxes in some states (Duscha and Graves 1999, 2007). Research is also needed on the close relationship between job training and education programs, as well as on institutions such as community colleges, which provide both education and workforce training in one place.

The central message of this book is that employment, unemployment, and training programs are too important to be the product of weak data, poor analysis, and callous marketing. Research and analysis should be carefully designed and used to determine what works and what does not. This analysis should be the basis for federal and state policy. Policy should follow good research—and, one hopes, good policy is good politics.

The Department of Labor should provide the major funding for employment and training research. The department should provide technical assistance to the states for the twin purposes of 1) assuring that they have the best information for use in designing, implementing, and refining programs that will help all workers have an opportunity to achieve the American Dream, and 2) serving American workers and their employers, who are, after all, the key to the economic success of the U.S. economy.

The Great Recession has presented many public policy challenges to the United States, particularly given the prospects of a weak and slow job recovery. Workforce public policy will be particularly critical during a period of labor market weakness. Workforce policy must be guided by solid research and evaluation, and new research and evaluations should be conducted to help shape public policy in the years to come.

Note

1. William Brock, telephone interview with the author, October 24, 2008.

References

AARP. 2009. "Saving Jobs in a Recession: How Work-Sharing Can Help." Presented by the AARP Public Policy Institute and the AARP Office of International Affairs at an AARP Solutions Forum, held in Washington, DC, December 11, 2009. http://assets.aarp.org/rgcenter/ppi/econ-sec/transcript_forum_091211.pdf (accessed May 26, 2010).

Abraham, Katharine G., and Susan N. Houseman. 1993. *Job Security in America: Lessons from Germany.* Washington, DC: Brookings Institution.

———. 1994a. "Labor Adjustment under Different Institutional Structures: A Case Study of Germany and the United States." Upjohn Institute Working Paper 94–26. Kalamazoo, MI: W.E. Upjohn Institute for Employment Research.

———. 1994b. "Does Employment Protection Inhibit Labor Market Flexibility? Lessons from Germany, France, and Belgium." In *Social Protection versus Economic Flexibility: Is There a Trade-Off?* Rebecca M. Blank, ed. Chicago: University of Chicago Press, pp. 59–94.

Advisory Council on Unemployment Compensation. 1995. *Unemployment Insurance in the United States: Benefits, Financing, Coverage.* Washington, DC: Advisory Council on Unemployment Compensation.

Almandsmith, Sherry, Lorena Ortiz Adams, and Han Bos. 2006. *Evaluation of the "Strengthening the Connections between Unemployment Insurance and the One-Stop Delivery Systems" Demonstration Project in Wisconsin: Final Report.* ETA Occasional Paper 2006-11. Washington, DC: U.S. Department of Labor, Employment and Training Administration.

Altmeyer, Arthur J. 1966. *The Formative Years of Social Security: A Chronicle of Social Security Legislation and Administration, 1934–1954.* Madison, WI: University of Wisconsin Press.

Anderson, Patricia, Walter Corson, and Paul Decker. 1991. *The New Jersey Unemployment Insurance Reemployment Demonstration Project: Follow-Up Report.* Unemployment Insurance Occasional Paper 91-1. Washington, DC: U.S. Department of Labor, Employment and Training Administration.

Auer, Peter, Umit Efendioğlu, and Janine Leschke. 2005. *Active Labour Market Policies around the World: Coping with the Consequences of Globalism.* Geneva: International Labour Office.

Austermann, V. Christine, Robert L. Crosslin, and David W. Stevens. 1975. *Can the Unemployment Insurance Service Improve the Employment Prospects of Claimants? The St. Louis Service to Claimants Program: An Evaluation.* Columbia, MO: University of Missouri, Economics Department, Human Resources Research Program.

Baily, Martin Neil, Gary Burtless, and Robert E. Litan. 1993. *Growth with Equity: Economic Policymaking for the Next Century*. Washington, DC: Brookings Institution.

Balducchi, David E., ed. 1996. *Worker Profiling and Reemployment Services (WPRS) Systems: National WPRS Colloquium, June 1996: Selected Papers and Materials*. Washington, DC: U.S. Department of Labor, Employment and Training Administration.

Balducchi, David E., Randall W. Eberts, and Christopher J. O'Leary, eds. 2004. *Labor Exchange Policy in the United States*. Kalamazoo, MI: W.E. Upjohn Institute for Employment Research.

Balducchi, David E., Terry R. Johnson, and R. Mark Gritz. 1997. "The Role of the Employment Service." In *Unemployment Insurance in the United States: Analysis of Policy Issues*, Christopher J. O'Leary and Stephen A. Wandner, eds. Kalamazoo, MI: W.E. Upjohn Institute for Employment Research, pp. 457–503.

Balducchi, David E., and Alison J. Pasternak. 2001. "One-Stop Statecraft: Restructuring Workforce Development Programs in the United States." In *Labour Market Policies and the Public Employment Service: Lessons from Recent Experience and Directions for the Future*. OECD Proceedings from the Prague Conference. Paris: Organisation for Economic Co-operation and Development, pp. 141–168.

———. 2004. "Federal-State Relations in Labor Exchange Policy." In *Labor Exchange Policy in the United States*, David E. Balducchi, Randall W. Eberts, and Christopher J. O'Leary, eds. Kalamazoo, MI: W.E. Upjohn Institute for Employment Research, pp. 33–71.

Balducchi, David E., and Stephen A. Wandner. 2008. "Work Sharing Policy: Power Sharing and Stalemate in American Federalism." *Publius: The Journal of Federalism* 38(1): 111–136.

———. 2009. "Managing Applied Research in Federal Employment Policy." *Journal of Policy Analysis and Management* 28(1): 166–168.

Barnow, Burt S. 2000. "Vouchers for Federal Targeted Training Programs." In *Vouchers and the Provision of Public Services*, C. Eugene Steuerle, Van Doorn Ooms, George Peterson, and Robert D. Reischauer, eds. Washington, DC: Brookings Institution Press, pp. 224–250.

Barnow, Burt S., and Christopher T. King, eds. 2000. *Improving the Odds: Increasing the Effectiveness of Publicly Funded Training*. Washington, DC: Urban Institute Press.

Barnow, Burt S., and Christopher T. King. 2005. *The Workforce Investment Act in Eight States*. ETA Occasional Paper 2005-01. Washington, DC: U.S. Department of Labor, Employment and Training Administration.

Barnow, Burt S., and John Trutko. 1999. "Vouchers under JTPA: Lessons for

Implementation of the Workforce Investment Act." Unpublished paper prepared for the U.S. Department of Labor. Arlington, VA: James Bell Associates.

Benus, Jacob M., Terry R. Johnson, Michelle Wood, Neelima Grover, and Theodore Shen. 1995. *Self-Employment Programs: A New Reemployment Strategy*. Final Report on the UI Self-Employment Demonstration. Unemployment Insurance Occasional Paper 95-4. Washington, DC: U.S. Department of Labor, Employment and Training Administration, Unemployment Insurance Service.

Benus, Jacob, Sheena McConnell, Jeanne Bellotti, Theodore Shen, Kenneth Fortson, and Daver Kahvecioglu. 2008. *Growing America through Entrepreneurship: Findings from the Evaluation of Project GATE*. Columbia, MD: IMPAQ International.

Benus, Jacob, Eileen Poe-Yamagata, Ying Wang, and Etan Blass. 2008. *Reemployment Eligibility Assessment (REA) Study: FY 2005 Initiative*. Final Report. ETA Occasional Paper 2008-02. Washington, DC: U.S. Department of Labor, Employment and Training Administration.

Benus, Jacob M., Michelle L. Wood, Chris J. Napierala, and Terry R. Johnson. 1992. "Massachusetts Unemployment Insurance Self-Employment Demonstration: Interim Report to Congress." In *Self Employment Programs for Unemployed Workers*, Stephen A. Wandner, ed. Unemployment Insurance Occasional Paper 92-2. Washington, DC: U.S. Department of Labor, Employment and Training Administration, pp. 167–236.

Berlin, Gordon L. 2007. "Experimentation and Social Welfare Policymaking in the United States." Adapted from a speech given at the conference "Lancement du Grenelle de l'insertion: Les rencontres de l'experimentation sociale," held in Grenoble, France, November 23–24. http://www.mdrc.org/publications/467/presentation.pdf (accessed October 1, 2009).

Best, Fred. 1981. *Work Sharing: Issues, Policy Options, and Prospects*. Kalamazoo, MI: W.E. Upjohn Institute for Employment Research.

———. 1988. *Reducing Workweeks to Prevent Layoffs: The Economic and Social Impacts of Unemployment Insurance–Supported Work Sharing*. Philadelphia: Temple University Press.

Black, Dan A., Jeffrey A. Smith, Mark C. Berger, and Brett J. Noel. 2003. "Is the Threat of Reemployment Services More Effective than the Services Themselves?" Evidence from Random Assignment in the UI System." *American Economic Review* 93(4): 1313–1327.

Black, Dan A., Jeffrey A. Smith, Miana Plesca, and Suzanne Shannon. 2003. *Profiling UI Claimants to Allocate Reemployment Services: Evidence and Recommendations for States*. ETA Occasional Paper 2003-02. Washington, DC: U.S. Department of Labor, Employment and Training Administration.

Bloom, Howard S. 1990. *Back to Work: Testing Reemployment Services for*

Dislocated Workers. Kalamazoo, MI: W.E. Upjohn Institute for Employment Research.

Bloom, Howard S., and Jane D. Kulik. 1996. *Evaluation of the Worker Adjustment Demonstration: Final Report*. Cambridge, MA: Abt Associates.

Bloom, Howard S., Larry L. Orr, Stephen H. Bell, George Cave, Fred Doolittle, Winston Lin, and Johannes M. Bos. 1997. "The Benefits and Costs of JTPA Title II-A Programs: Key Findings from the National Job Training Partnership Act Study." *Journal of Human Resources* 32(3): 549–576.

Bloom, Howard, Saul Schwartz, Susanna Lui-Gurr, and Suk-Won Lee. 1999. *Testing a Reemployment Incentive for Displaced Workers: The Earnings Supplement Project*. Draft Report. Ottawa: Social Research and Demonstration Corporation.

Brainard, Lael. 2007. "Statement of Dr. Lael Brainard, Vice President and Director, Global Economy and Development, the Brookings Institution, Washington, DC." U.S. Congress. Joint Economic Committee. *Meeting the Challenge of Income Instability*. 110th Cong., 1st sess., pp. 13–15. http:// ftp.resource.org/gpo.gov/hearings/110s/34852.wais.pdf (accessed February 12, 2010).

Buhl, William C. 1989. "Transforming Leadership in a Political Environment: A Case Study of William Brock at the Department of Labor." PhD diss., University of California at Los Angeles.

Bureau of Labor Statistics (BLS). 1997. *Unemployment Insurance Recipients 1993*. Washington, DC: Bureau of Labor Statistics.

———. 2008. *Job Openings and Labor Force Turnover*. Washington, DC: Bureau of Labor Statistics.

Burtless, Gary. 1995. "The Case for Randomized Field Trials in Economic and Policy Research." *Journal of Economic Perspectives* 9(2): 63–84.

———. 2007. "Income Supports for Workers and Their Families: Earnings Supplements and Health Insurance." In *Reshaping the American Workforce in a Changing Economy*, Harry J. Holzer and Demetra Smith Nightingale, eds. Washington, DC: Urban Institute, pp. 239–271.

Burtless, Gary, Robert Z. Lawrence, Robert E. Litan, and Robert J. Shapiro. 1998. *Globaphobia: Confronting Fears about Open Trade*. Washington, DC: Brookings Institution Press.

Cadrain, Diane. 2002. "State Programs Offer Alternative to Layoffs." News release, April 29. Washington, DC: Stateline.org. http://www.stateline.org/ live/ViewPage.action?siteNodeId=136&languageId=1&contentId=14794 (accessed April 28, 2010).

CareerOneStop. 2010. *America's Service Locator*. Washington, DC: CareerOneStop. http://www.servicelocator.org (accessed January 12, 2010).

Center for Employment Security Education and Research (CESER). 2004.

Unemployment Insurance: Assessment of the Impact of the 2002 Reed Act Distribution. Final Report: Qualitative and Quantitative Analysis. ETA Occasional Paper 2004-11, released in 2008. Washington, DC: Center for Employment Security Education and Research.

Clinton, Bill. 1993. "Statement by the President Announces Unemployment Insurance Extension." News release, February 8. Washington, DC: White House, Office of the Press Secretary.

———. 2004. *My Life.* New York: Alfred A. Knopf.

Clinton, Bill, and Al Gore. 1992. *Putting People First: How We Can All Change America.* New York: Times Books.

Congressional Budget Office (CBO). 1993. *Displaced Workers: Trends in the 1980s and Implications for the Future.* A CBO Study. Washington, DC: Congressional Budget Office.

Cook, Robert F., Anthony Brinsko, and Alexandra G. Tan. 1995. "Short-Time Compensation: A Literature Review." In *Background Papers* of the Advisory Council on Unemployment Compensation. Vol. 2. Washington, DC: Advisory Council on Unemployment Compensation, pp. R1–R25.

Corson, Walter, and Paul T. Decker. 1996. "Using the Unemployment Insurance System to Target Services to Dislocated Workers." In *Background Papers* of the Advisory Council on Unemployment Compensation. Vol. 3. Washington, DC: U.S. Department of Labor.

Corson, Walter, Paul T. Decker, Sherri Miller Dunstan, and Anne R. Gordon. 1989. *The New Jersey Unemployment Insurance Reemployment Demonstration Project: Final Evaluation Report.* Unemployment Insurance Occasional Paper 89-3. Washington, DC: U.S. Department of Labor, Employment and Training Administration.

Corson, Walter, Paul Decker, Shari Miller Dunstan, and Stuart Kerachsky. 1991. *Pennsylvania Reemployment Bonus Demonstration: Final Report.* Unemployment Insurance Occasional Paper 92-1. Washington, DC: U.S. Department of Labor, Employment and Training Administration.

Corson, Walter, and Mark Dynarski. 1990. *A Study of Unemployment Insurance Recipients and Exhaustees: Findings from a National Survey.* Unemployment Insurance Occasional Paper 90-3. Washington, DC: U.S. Department of Labor, Employment and Training Administration, Unemployment Insurance Service.

Corson, Walter, and Joshua Haimson. 1996. *The New Jersey Unemployment Insurance Reemployment Demonstration Project: Six-Year Follow-Up and Summary Report.* 2d ed., rev. Unemployment Insurance Occasional Paper 96-2. Washington, DC: U.S. Department of Labor, Employment and Training Administration.

Corson, Walter, David Long, and Walter Nicholson. 1985. *Evaluation of the*

Charleston Claimant Placement and Work Test Demonstration. Unemployment Insurance Occasional Paper 85-2. Washington, DC: U.S. Department of Labor, Employment and Training Administration.

Corson, Walter, Sharon Long, and Rebecca A. Maynard. 1985. *An Impact Evaluation of the Buffalo Dislocated Worker Demonstration Program*. Princeton, NJ: Mathematica Policy Research.

Council of Economic Advisers (CEA). 2003. *Economic Report of the President, Transmitted to the Congress, February 2003*. Washington, DC: Government Printing Office.

Crimaldi, Laura. 2009. "Employers' Demand for WorkSharing Benefits to Jump." *Boston Herald*, January 11. http://www.bostonherald.com/news/regional/view.bg?articleid=1144498 (accessed January 29, 2010).

D'Amico, Ronald, Gardner Carrick, Kate Dunham, Jennifer Henderson-Frakes, Deborah Kogan, Vinz Koller, Melissa Mack, Micheline Magnotta, Jeffrey Salzman, Dan Weissbein, and Andrew Wiegand. 2004. *The Workforce Investment Act after Five Years: Results from the National Evaluation of the Implementation of WIA*. ETA Occasional Paper 2004-05. Washington, DC: U.S. Department of Labor, Employment and Training Administration, Office of Policy Development, Evaluation, and Research.

D'Amico, Ronald, Deborah Kogan, Suzanne Kreutzer, Andrew Wiegand, Alberta Baker, Gardner Carrick, and Carole McCarthy. 2001. *A Report on Early State and Local Progress towards WIA Implementation*. Final Interim Report. Research and Evaluation Monograph Series 01-I. Washington, DC: U.S. Department of Labor, Employment and Training Administration.

D'Amico, Ronald, and Jeffrey Salzman. 2005. *An Evaluation of the Individual Training Account/Eligible Training Provider Demonstration*. ETA Occasional Paper 2005-02. Washington, DC: U.S. Department of Labor, Employment and Training Administration.

Davidson, Carl, and Stephen A. Woodbury. 1990. "The Displacement Effect of Reemployment Bonus Programs." Upjohn Institute Working Paper 90-02. Kalamazoo, MI: W.E. Upjohn Institute for Employment Research.

———. 1991. "Effects of a Reemployment Bonus under Differing Benefit Entitlements, or, Why the Illinois Experiment Worked." Unpublished manuscript, Michigan State University, Lansing; and W.E. Upjohn Institute for Employment Research, Kalamazoo, MI.

———. 1993. "The Displacement Effects of Reemployment Bonus Programs." *Journal of Labor Economics* 11(4): 575–605.

Decker, Paul T. 1994. "The Impact of Reemployment Bonuses on Insured Unemployment in the New Jersey and Illinois Reemployment Bonus Experiments." *Journal of Human Resources* 29(3): 718–741.

———. 1997. "Work Incentives and Disincentives." In *Unemployment Insur-*

ance in the United States: Analysis of Policy Issues, Christopher J. O'Leary and Stephen A. Wandner, eds. Kalamazoo, MI: W.E. Upjohn Institute for Employment Research, pp. 285–320.

Decker, Paul T., and Christopher J. O'Leary. 1992. *An Analysis of Pooled Evidence from the Pennsylvania and Washington Reemployment Bonus Demonstrations.* Unemployment Insurance Occasional Paper 92-7. Washington, DC: U.S. Department of Labor.

———. 1995. "Evaluating Pooled Evidence from the Reemployment Bonus Experiments." *Journal of Human Resources* 30(3): 534–550.

Decker, Paul T., Robert B. Olsen, Lance Freeman, and Daniel H. Klepinger. 2000. *Assisting Unemployment Insurance Claimants: The Long-Term Impacts of the Job Search Assistance Demonstration.* Office of Workforce Security Occasional Paper 2000-02. Washington, DC: U.S. Department of Labor, Employment and Training Administration.

Decker, Paul T., and Irma L. Perez-Johnson. 2004. *What Can We Expect under Personal Reemployment Accounts? Predictions and Procedures.* ETA Occasional Paper 2004-04. Washington, DC: U.S. Department of Labor.

Dickinson, Katherine P., Paul T. Decker, Suzanne D. Kreutzer, and Richard W. West. 1999. *Evaluation of Worker Profiling and Reemployment Services: Final Report.* Research and Evaluation Report 99-D. Washington, DC: U.S. Department of Labor, Employment and Training Administration.

Dickinson, Katherine P., Suzanne D. Kreutzer, and Paul T. Decker. 1997. *Evaluation of Worker Profiling and Reemployment Services Systems.* Report to Congress. Menlo Park, CA: Social Policy Research Associates.

Dolton, Peter, and Donal O'Neill. 1996. "Unemployment Duration and the Restart Effect: Some Experimental Evidence." *Economic Journal* 106(2): 387–400.

———. 2002. "The Long-Run Effects of Unemployment Monitoring and Work-Search Programs: Experimental Evidence from the United Kingdom." *Journal of Labor Economics* 20(2): 381–403.

Donahue, John D. 2008. "The Unaccustomed Inventiveness of the Labor Department." In *Innovations in Government: Research, Recognition and Replication*, Sandford Borins, ed. Washington, DC: Brookings Institution Press, pp. 93–112.

Dunham, Kate, Annelies Goger, Jennifer Henderson-Frakes, and Nichole Tucker. 2005. *Workforce Development in Rural Areas: Changes in Access, Service Delivery, and Partnerships.* ETA Occasional Paper 2005-07, released 2008. Washington, DC: U.S. Department of Labor, Employment and Training Administration.

Duscha, Steve, and Wanda Lee Graves. 1999. *State Financed and Customized Training Programs.* Research and Evaluation Report Series 99-E. Washington, DC: U.S. Department of Labor, Employment and Training Administration, Office of Policy and Research.

———. 2007. *The Employer as the Client: State-Financed Customized Training 2006.* ETA Occasional Paper 2007-14. Washington, DC: U.S. Department of Labor, Employment and Training Administration.

Eberts, Randall W., and Christopher J. O'Leary. 2002. "A Frontline Decision Support System for One-Stop Centers." In *Targeting Employment Services*, Randall W. Eberts, Christopher J. O'Leary, and Stephen A. Wandner, eds. Kalamazoo, MI: W.E. Upjohn Institute for Employment Research, pp. 337–380.

———. 2004. "A Frontline Decision Support System for Georgia Career Centers." In *A Compilation of Selected Papers from the Employment and Training Administration's 2003 Biennial Research Conference,* Joshua Riley, Aquila Branch, Stephen A. Wandner, and Wayne Gordon, eds. Washington, DC: U.S. Department of Labor, Employment and Training Administration, pp. 80–129.

Eberts, Randall W., Christopher J. O'Leary, and Stephen A. Wandner, eds. 2002. *Targeting Employment Services*. Kalamazoo, MI: W.E. Upjohn Institute for Employment Research.

Eichhorst, Werner, and Klaus F. Zimmermann. 2007. "And Then There Were Four . . . How Many (and Which) Measures of Active Labour Market Policy Do We Still Need?" CEPR Discussion Paper 6246. London: Centre for Economic Policy Research.

Ekos Research Associates. 1993. *Work Sharing Evaluation: Technical Report.* Ottawa: Employment and Immigration Canada.

Electronic Recruiting News. 2007. "Of Note." Mill Valley, CA: interbiznet. http://www.interbiznet.com/ern/archives/07411.html (accessed December 7, 2009).

Employment and Immigration Canada. 1984. *Evaluation of the Work Sharing Program.* Ottawa: Employment and Immigration Canada.

Employment Development Department (EDD). 1982. *California Shared Work Unemployment Insurance Evaluation.* Sacramento: State of California, Employment Development Department.

Emsellem, Maurice, Jessica Goldberg, Rick McHugh, Wendell Primus, Rebecca Smith, and Jeffrey Wenger. 2002. *Failing the Unemployed: A State by State Examination of Unemployment Insurance Systems.* Washington, DC: Economic Policy Institute and Center on Budget and Policy Priorities; New York: National Employment Law Project.

European Commission. 2005. *Working Together for Growth and Jobs: Integrated Guidelines for Growth and Jobs, 2005–2008.* Luxembourg: Office for Official Publications of the European Communities.

————. 2006. *European Social Statistics: Labour Market Policy Expenditures and Participants: Data 2004.* Luxembourg: Office for Official Publications of the European Communities.

————. 2007. *Toward Common Principles of Flexicurity: More and Better Jobs through Flexibility and Security.* Luxembourg: Office for Official Publications of the European Communities.

————. 2009. *Employment in Europe 2009.* Brussels: European Commission, Directorate-General for Employment, Social Affairs, and Equal Opportunities.

European Employment Observatory Review. 2005. "Germany: Self-Employment Programmes for Unemployed People." *European Employment Observatory Review* 2005(Spring): 47–52.

Farber, Henry S. 1997. "The Changing Face of Job Loss in the United States, 1981–1995." Industrial Relations Section Working Paper 382. Princeton, NJ: Princeton University.

————. 2005. "What Do We Know about Job Loss in the United States? Evidence from the Displaced Workers Survey, 1984–2004." Industrial Relations Section Working Paper 498. Princeton, NJ: Princeton University.

Federal Register. 2000. "Workforce Investment Act: Final Rules." *Federal Register* 65(156): 49249-49464.

————. 2006. "Workforce Investment Act Amendments; Proposed Rule." *Federal Register* 71(244): 76558–76569.

4President.org. 1992. *Bill Clinton for President 1992 Campaign Brochures.* Shoreview, MN: 4President.org. http://www.4president.org/brochures/billclinton1992brochure.htm (accessed October 29, 2009).

Frauenheim, Ed. 2007a. "Rivals Bid to Replace America's Job Bank." *Workforce Management*, April 9. http://www.workforce.com/section//00/article/24/84/59.html (accessed May 26, 2010).

————. 2007b. "A Rocky Road to Shuttering of America's Job Bank." *Workforce Management*, June. http://www.workforce.com/section/06/feature/24/94/21/249423_printer.html (accessed May 26, 2010).

————. 2007c. "Bank Withdrawal: The Closure of America's Job Bank." *Workforce Management* 86(13): 32–34, 36. http://www.workforce.com/section/06/feature/24/99/21/index.html (accessed May 26, 2010).

Frölich, Markus. 2006. *Statistical Treatment Choice: An Application to Active Labour Market Programmes.* IZA Discussion Paper 2187. Berlin: Institute for the Study of Labor.

General Accounting Office (GAO). 1995. *Block Grants: Characteristics, Experience, and Lessons Learned.* Report to the Chairman, Committee on Economic and Educational Opportunities, House of Representatives. GAO/HEHS-95-74. Washington, DC: General Accounting Office.

Gore, Al. 1993. *From Red Tape to Results: Creating a Government That Works*

Better and Costs Less. Report of the National Performance Review. Washington, DC: Office of the Vice President.

Government Accountability Office (GAO). 2007. *Unemployment Insurance: More Guidance and Evaluation of Worker-Profiling Initiative Could Help Improve State Efforts.* Report to Congressional Requesters. GAO-07-680. Washington, DC: Government Accountability Office.

Greenberg, David, and Mark Shroder. 2004. *The Digest of Social Experiments.* 3rd ed. Washington, DC: Urban Institute Press.

Greenhouse, Steven. 2009. "Work-Sharing May Help Companies Avoid Layoffs." *New York Times*, June 16, B:1. http://www.nytimes.com/2009/06/16/business/economy/16workshare.html (accessed July 27, 2010).

Groshen, Erica L., and Simon Potter. 2003. "Has Structural Change Contributed to a Jobless Recovery?" *Current Issues in Economics and Finance* 9(8): 1–7.

Haber, William, and Daniel H. Kruger. 1964. *The Role of the United States Employment Service in a Changing Economy.* Kalamazoo, MI: W.E. Upjohn Institute for Employment Research.

Hamermesh, Daniel S. 1977. *Jobless Pay and the Economy.* Baltimore: Johns Hopkins University Press.

Hawkins, Evelyn K., Suzanne D. Kreutzer, Katherine P. Dickinson, Paul T. Decker, and Walter S. Corson. 1996. *Evaluation of Worker Profiling and Reemployment Services Systems: Interim Report.* UI Occasional Paper 96-1. Washington, DC: U.S. Department of Labor, Employment and Training Administration.

Heckman, James J., Robert J. LaLonde, and Jeffrey A. Smith. 1999. "The Economics and Econometrics of Active Labor Market Programs." In *Handbook of Labor Economics*, Orley C. Ashenfelter and David Card, eds. Vol. 3A. Amsterdam: Elsevier, pp. 1865–2097.

Heckman, James J., Rebecca Roselius, and Jeffrey A. Smith. 1994. "U.S. Education and Training Policy: A Reevaluation of the Underlying Assumptions behind the 'New Consensus.'" In *Labor Markets, Employment Policy, and Job Creation*, Lewis C. Solomon and Alec R. Levenson, eds. The Milken Institute Series in Economics and Education. Boulder, CO: Westview Press.

Helwig, Ryan T. 2001. "Worker Displacement in a Strong Labor Market." *Monthly Labor Review* 124(6): 13–28.

———. 2004. "Worker Displacement in 1999–2000." *Monthly Labor Review* 127(6): 54–68. http://www.bls.gov/opub/mlr/2004/06/art4full.pdf (accessed October 5, 2009).

Henle, Peter. 1976. *Work Sharing as an Alternative to Layoffs.* Washington, DC: Congressional Research Service, Library of Congress.

Hess, Ryan. 2004. "ETA Picks 7 States for PRA Demo." *Employment and Training Reporter*, November 8, pp. 168–169.

————. 2005. "PRA Demo Launches Planned This Month in Selected Areas." *Employment and Training Reporter*, March 7, pp. 391–393.

————. 2008. "ETA Dusts Off Reed Act Paper." *Employment and Training Reporter* 40(1977): 14.

Hipple, Steven. 1999. "Worker Displacement in the Mid-1990s." *Monthly Labor Review* 122(7): 15–32.

Hollenbeck, Kevin M., and Wei-Jang Huang. 2006. "Net Impact and Benefit-Cost Estimates of the Workforce Development System in Washington State." Upjohn Institute Technical Report TR06–20. Kalamazoo, MI: W.E. Upjohn Institute for Employment Research.

————. 2008. *Workforce Program Performance Indicators for the Commonwealth of Virginia*. Upjohn Institute Technical Report 08-024. Kalamazoo, MI: W.E. Upjohn Institute for Employment Research.

Hollenbeck, Kevin M., Daniel Schroeder, Christopher T. King, and Wei-Jang Huang. 2005. *Net Impact Estimates for Services Provided through the Workforce Investment Act*. Report prepared as part of the Administrative Data Research and Evaluation Project for the U.S. Department of Labor, completed in October 2005. ETA Occasional Paper 2005-06, released August 15, 2008. Washington, DC: U.S. Department of Labor, Employment and Training Administration, Office of Policy and Research. http://wdr.doleta.gov/research/keyword.cfm?fuseaction=dsp_resultDetails&pub_id=2367&mp=y (accessed March 331, 2010).

Holtz-Eakin, Douglas. 2004. "Statement of Douglas Holtz-Eakin, Director of the Congressional Budget Office." U.S. Congress. House of Representatives. Committee on Rules. Subcommittee on Legislative and Budget Process. *Reforming the Federal Budget Process*, 108th Cong., 2d sess., pp. 1–13.

House Education and Workforce Committee. 2005. *Fact Sheet: Worker Recovery Act (H.R. 3976): Giving Gulf Coast Workers Greater Choice and More Control of Their Job Search*. Washington, DC: House Education and Workforce Committee.

Human Resources and Skills Development Canada (HRSDC). 2005. *Summative Evaluation of Work Sharing while Learning and Increased Referrals to Training*. Ottawa: HRSDC, Strategic Policy and Planning Branch. http://www.hrsdc.gc.ca/eng/cs/sp/hrsd/evaluation/reports/SP-AH-665-04-05/page00.shtml (accessed April 28, 2010).

International Labour Organization. 1990. *The Promotion of Self-Employment*. 77th Session of the International Labor Conference. Geneva: International Labor Organization.

Ittner, Linda. 1984. "The Federal Response to Short-Time Compensation." In *Short-Time Compensation: A Formula for Work Sharing*, Ramelle MaCoy and Martin J. Morand, eds. New York: Pergamon Press, pp. 120–135.

Jacobson, Louis, Robert LaLonde, and Daniel Sullivan. 2002. "Measures of Program Performance and the Training Choices of Displaced Workers." In *Targeting Employment Services*, Randall W. Eberts, Christopher J. O'Leary, and Stephen A. Wandner, eds. Kalamazoo, MI: W.E. Upjohn Institute for Employment Research, pp. 187–214.

Jacobson, Louis, and Ian Petta. 2000. *Measuring the Effect of Public Labor Exchange (PLX) Referrals and Placements in Washington and Oregon.* Office of Workforce Security Occasional Paper 2000-06. Washington, DC: U.S. Department of Labor, Employment and Training Administration. http://wdr.doleta.gov/owsdrr/00-6/00-6.pdf (accessed December 4, 2009).

Jacobson, Louis, Ian Petta, Amy Shimshak, and Regina Yudd. 2004. *Evaluation of Labor Exchange Services in a One-Stop Delivery System Environment.* Final Report. ETA Occasional Paper 2004-09, released in September 2008. Washington, DC: U.S. Department of Labor, Employment and Training Administration. http://wdr.doleta.gov/research/FullText_Documents/Evaluation%20of%20Labor%20Exchange%20in%20One-Stop%20Delivery%20System%20-%20Final%20Report.pdf (accessed April 27, 2010).

Jenks, Stephen S., Lois MacGillivray, and Karen Needels. 2006. *Youth Offender Demonstration Project Evaluation, Final Report.* ETA Occasional Paper 2006-06. Washington, DC: U.S. Department of Labor.

Jensen, Tomas. 1995. *Short-Time Compensation in Germany and the United States—a Comparison.* San Francisco: New Ways to Work.

Johnson, Terry R. 1996. "Reemployment Service Strategies for Dislocated Workers: Lessons Learned from Research." In *Worker Profiling and Reemployment Services (WPRS) Systems: National WPRS Colloquium, June 1996: Selected Papers and Materials.* Washington, DC: U.S. Department of Labor, Employment and Training Administration, pp. 201–209.

Johnson, Terry R., Katherine P. Dickinson, and Richard W. West. 1985. "An Evaluation of the Impact of ES Referrals on Applicant Earnings." *Journal of Human Resources* 20(1): 117–137.

Johnson, Terry R., Katherine P. Dickinson, Richard W. West, Susan E. McNicoll, Jennifer M. Pfiester, Alex L. Stagner, and Betty J. Harris. 1983. *A National Evaluation of the Impact of the United States Employment Service.* A Report to the U.S. Department of Labor. Menlo Park, CA: SRI International.

Johnson, Terry R., and Daniel H. Klepinger. 1991. *Evaluation of the Impacts of the Washington Alternative Work Search Experiment.* Unemployment Insurance Occasional Paper 91-4. Washington, DC: U.S. Department of Labor, Employment and Training Administration.

————. 1994. "Experimental Evidence on Unemployment Insurance Work Search Policies." *Journal of Human Resources* 29(3): 695–717.

Johnson, Terry R., and Janice J. Leonard. 1992. "Washington Self-Employment and Enterprise Development (SEED) Demonstration: Interim Report." In *Self Employment Programs for Unemployed Workers*, Stephen A. Wandner, ed. Unemployment Insurance Occasional Paper 92-2. Washington, DC: U.S. Department of Labor, Employment and Training Administration, pp. 40–166. http://www.ows.doleta.gov/dmstree/op/op92/op_02-92 .pdf (accessed January 14, 2010).

Johnston, William B., and Arnold E. Packer. 1987. *Workforce 2000: Work and Workers for the Twenty-First Century*. Indianapolis, IN: Hudson Institute.

Katz, Arnold. 1991. "Length of Joblessness and the Employment Service with Special Reference to Philadelphia and Pittsburgh, Pennsylvania, 1979–1987." In *The Potential Effectiveness of the Employment Service in Serving Dislocated Workers under EDWAA: Evidence from the 1980s*, Carol J. Romero, Donald Cox, and Arnold Katz, eds. Research Report 91-02. Washington, DC: National Commission for Employment Policy, pp. 6–48.

Katz, Lawrence F. 1985. "Worker Mobility and Unemployment." PhD diss., Massachusetts Institute of Technology, Cambridge, MA.

Katz, Lawrence F., and Bruce D. Meyer. 1990. "Unemployment Insurance, Recall Expectations, and Unemployment Outcomes." *Quarterly Journal of Economics* 105(4): 973–1002.

Keith, Robert. 2007. *Federal Budget Process Reform in the 110th Congress: A Brief Overview*. CRS Report for Congress. Order Code RL33818. Washington, DC: Congressional Research Service.

Kerachsky, Stuart, Walter Nicholson, Edward Cavin, and Alan Hershey. 1986. *An Evaluation of Short-Time Compensation Programs*. UI Occasional Paper 86-4. Washington, DC: U.S. Department of Labor, Employment and Training Administration, Unemployment Insurance Service.

King, Christopher T. 2004. "The Effectiveness of Publicly Financed Training in the United States: Implications for WIA and Related Programs." In *Job Training Policy in the United States*, Chistopher O'Leary, Robert A. Straits, and Stephen A. Wandner, eds. Kalamazoo, MI: W.E. Upjohn Institute for Employment Research, pp. 57–100.

Kirby, Gretchen, Margaret Sullivan, Elizabeth Potamites, Jackie Kauff, Elizabeth Clary, and Charles McGlew. 2008. *Responses to Personal Reemployment Accounts (PRAs): Findings from Seven Demonstration Sites: Final Evaluation Report (Draft)*. Washington, DC: Mathematica Policy Research.

Klepinger, Daniel H., Terry R. Johnson, and Jutta M. Joesch. 2002. "Effects of Unemployment Insurance Work-Search Requirements: The Maryland Experiment." *Industrial and Labor Relations Review* 56(1): 3–22.

Klepinger, Daniel H., Terry R. Johnson, Jutta M. Joesch, and Jacob M. Benus. 1998. *Evaluation of the Maryland Unemployment Insurance Work Search Demonstration: Final Report*. Unemployment Insurance Occasional Paper 98-2. Washington, DC: U.S. Department of Labor, Employment and Training Administration.

Kletzer, Lori G. 1998. "Job Displacement." *Journal of Economic Perspectives* 12(1): 115–136.

Knaup, Amy E. 2005. "Survival and Longevity in the Business Employment Dynamics Data." *Monthly Labor Review* 128(5): 50–56.

Krueger, Alan B. 2008. "The Best Way to Help the Unemployed." *New York Times*, October 20. http://economix.blogs.nytimes.com/2008/10/20/the-best-way-to-help-the-unemployed/ (accessed December 7, 2009).

Kulik, Jane, D. Alton Smith, and Ernst W. Stromsdorfer. 1984. *The Downriver Community Conference Economic Readjustment Program: Final Evaluation Report*. Cambridge, MA: Abt Associates.

LaLonde, Robert J. 1986. "Evaluating the Econometric Evaluations of Training Programs with Experimental Data." *American Economic Review* 76(4): 604–620.

———. 1995. "The Promise of Public Sector–Sponsored Training Programs." *Journal of Economic Perspectives* 9(2): 149–168.

Lammers, John, and Timothy Lockwood. 1984. "The California Experiment." In *Short-Time Compensation: A Formula for Work Sharing*, Ramelle MaCoy and Martin J. Morand, eds. New York: Pergamon Press, pp. 61–81.

Lawrence, Robert Z., Lawrence B. Krause, Robert H. Meyer, and Linda Cohen. 1984. "Adjusting to Economic Change." In *Economic Choices 1984*, Alice M. Rivlin, ed. Washington, DC: Brookings Institution, pp. 119–156.

Lawrence, Robert Z., and Robert E. Litan. 1986. *Saving Free Trade: A Pragmatic Approach*. Washington, DC: Brookings Institution.

Leonhardt, David. 2008. "A Free-Market-Loving, Big-Spending, Fiscally Conservative Wealth Distributionist." *New York Times Magazine*, August 24, pp. 28–35, 52, 54.

Lerman, Robert, and C. Eugene Steuerle. 2000. "Structured Choice versus Fragmented Choice: Bundling of Vouchers." In *Vouchers and the Provision of Public Services*, C. Eugene Steuerle, Van Doorne Ooms, George Peterson, and Robert D. Reischauer, eds. Washington, DC: Brookings Institution Press, pp. 471–502.

Levine, Linda, and Ann Lordeman. 2005. *Personal Reemployment Accounts: Results from Bonus Experiments*. Washington, DC: Congressional Research Service.

Levitan, Sar A., and Richard S. Belous. 1977. *Shorter Hours, Shorter Weeks:*

Spreading the Work to Reduce Unemployment. Baltimore: Johns Hopkins University Press.

Lordeman, Ann. 2003. *Workforce Investment Act of 1998 (WIA): Reauthorization of Title I Job Training Programs in the 108th Congress*. CRS Report for Congress RS21484. Washington, DC: Congressional Research Service, Library of Congress.

———. 2005. *The Workforce Investment Act of 1998 (WIA): Reauthorization of Job Training Programs in the 109th Congress*. CRS Report for Congress RL32778. Washington, DC: Congressional Research Service, Library of Congress.

Lordeman, Ann, and Linda Levine. 2007. *The President's Demand-Driven Workforce Development Initiatives*. CRS Report for Congress RL33811. Washington, DC: Congressional Research Service.

MaCoy, Ramelle, and Martin J. Morand. 1984. *Short-Time Compensation: A Formula for Work Sharing*. New York: Pergamon Press.

MaCurdy, Thomas, James Pearce, and Richard Kihlthau. 2004. "An Alternative to Layoffs: Work Sharing Unemployment Insurance." *California Policy Review* (August): 1–11.

Mangum, Garth L. 1973. "MDTA: A Decade of Achievement." In *Manpower Policy: Perspectives and Prospects*, Seymour L. Wolfbein, ed. Papers on the Occasion of the Tenth Anniversary of the Manpower Development and Training Act of 1962. Philadelphia: Temple University Press, pp. 41–64.

Marshall, Will, and Martin Schram. 1993. *Mandate for Change*. New York: Berkley Books.

Martin, John P., and David Grubb. 2001. "What Works and for Whom: A Review of OECD Countries' Experiences with Active Labour Market Policies." *Swedish Economic Policy Review* 8(2): 9–56.

McConnell, Sheena, Elizabeth Stuart, Kenneth Fortson, Paul Decker, Irma Perez-Johnson, Barbara Harris, and Jeffrey Salzman. 2006. *Managing Customers' Training Choices: Findings from the Individual Training Account Experiment*. Final Report. Princeton, NJ: Mathematica Policy Research.

McVicar, Duncan. 2008. "Job Search Monitoring Intensity, Unemployment Exit, and Job Entry: Quasi-Experimental Evidence from the UK." *Labour Economics* 15(2008): 1451–1468.

Messenger, Jon C. 2009. *Work Sharing: A Strategy to Preserve Jobs during the Global Jobs Crisis*. Travail Policy Brief 1. Geneva: International Labour Organization.

Messenger, Jon C., Carolyn Peterson-Vaccaro, and Wayne Vroman. 2002. "Profiling in Self-Employment Assistance Programs." In *Targeting Employment Services*, Randall W. Eberts, Christopher J. O'Leary, and Stephen A. Wandner, eds. Kalamazoo, MI: W.E. Upjohn Institute for Employment Research, pp. 113–153.

Meyer, Bruce D. 1988. "Implications of the Illinois Reemployment Bonus Experiments for Theories of Unemployment and Policy Design." NBER Working Paper 2783. Cambridge, MA: National Bureau of Economic Research.

———. 1991. "What Have We Learned from the Illinois Reemployment Bonus Experiment?" *Journal of Labor Economics* 14(1): 26–51

———. 1992. "Policy Lessons from the U.S. Unemployment Insurance Experiments." NBER Working Paper 4197. Cambridge, MA: National Bureau of Economic Research.

———. 1995. "Lessons from the U.S. Unemployment Insurance Experiments." *Journal of Economic Literature* 33(1): 91–131.

———. 1996. "What Have We Learned from the Illinois Reemployment Bonus Experiment?" *Journal of Labor Economics* 14(1): 26–51.

Mikelson, Kelly S., and Demetra Smith Nightingale. 2005. *Expenditures on Public and Private Job Skills Training in the United States*. Washington, DC: Urban Institute.

———. 2006. *Estimating Public and Private Expenditures on Occupational Training in the United States*. ETA Occasional Paper 2006-01. Washington, DC: U.S. Department of Labor, Employment and Training Administration.

Miller, Cynthia, Johannes M. Bos, Kristin E. Porter, Fannie M. Tseng, and Yasuyo Abe. 2006. *The Challenge of Repeating Success in a Changing World: Final Report on the Center for Employment Training Replication Sites*. ETA Occasional Paper 2006-04. Washington, DC: U.S. Department of Labor, Employment and Training Administration.

Mooney, Chris. 2005. *The Republican War on Science*. New York: Basic Books.

Morand, Martin J. 1990. "Unemployment Insurance and Short-Time Compensation." In *Unemployment Insurance: The Second Half-Century*, W. Lee Hansen and James F. Byers, eds. Madison, WI: University of Wisconsin Press, pp. 302–354.

Mueser, Peter R., and Deanna L. Sharpe. 2006. *Anatomy of Two One-Stops: Camdenton, Missouri, and Columbia, Missouri*. ETA Occasional Paper 2006-08. Washington, DC: U.S. Department of Labor, Employment and Training Administration.

Nathan, Richard P., and Robinson G. Hollister Jr. 2008. "Point/Counterpoint: The Role of Random Assignment in Social Policy Research." *Journal of Policy Analysis and Management* 27(2): 401–415.

National Association of State Workforce Agencies (NASWA). 2008. *Workforce

ATM. Washington, DC: National Association of State Workforce Agencies. http://www.workforceatm.org (accessed January 12, 2010).

Naughton, Blake Alan, and Ann Lordeman. 2007. *The Workforce Investment Act of 1998 (WIA): Reauthorization of Job Training Programs in the 109th Congress*. CRS Report RL32778. Washington, DC: Congressional Research Service.

Needels, Karen, Walter Corson, and Michelle Van Noy. 2002. *Evaluation of the Significant Improvement Demonstration Grants for the Provision of Reemployment Services for UI Claimants*. ETA Occasional Paper 2002–09. Washington, DC: U.S. Department of Labor, Employment and Training Administration.

Nickisch, Curt. 2008. *"WorkSharing" to Avoid Layoffs*. Boston: WBUR.org. http://www.wbur.org/2008/08/07/worksharing-to-avoid-layoffs (accessed April 28, 2010).

Office of Inspector General (OIG). 2007. *High Growth Job Training Initiative: Decisions for Noncompetitive Awards Not Adequately Justified*. Report 02-08-201-03-390. Washington, DC: U.S. Department of Labor, Office of Inspector General. http://www.oig.dol.gov/public/reports/oa/2008/02-08 -201-03-390.pdf (accessed January 6, 2010).

O'Leary, Christopher J. 2006. "State UI Job Search Rules and Reemployment Services." *Monthly Labor Review* 129(6): 27–37.

O'Leary, Christopher J., Paul T. Decker, and Stephen A. Wandner. 1998. "Reemployment Bonuses and Profiling." Upjohn Institute Working Paper 98-51. Kalamazoo, MI: W.E. Upjohn Institute for Employment Research.

———. 2005. "Cost-Effectiveness of Targeted Reemployment Bonuses." *Journal of Human Resources* 40(1): 270–279.

O'Leary, Christopher J., and Randall W. Eberts. 2004. *Personal Reemployment Accounts: Simulations for Planning Implementation*. ETA Occasional Paper 2004-08. Washington, DC: U.S. Department of Labor.

O'Leary, Christopher J., and Kenneth J. Kline. 2008. *UI as a Safety Net for Former TANF Recipients*. Final Report. Washington, DC: U.S. Department of Health and Human Services, Assistant Secretary for Planning and Evaluation. http://aspe.hhs.gov/hsp/08/UI-TANF/index.htm (accessed November 11, 2009).

O'Leary, Christopher J., Robert G. Spiegelman, and Kenneth J. Kline. 1995. "Do Bonus Offers Shorten Unemployment Insurance Spells? Results from the Washington Experiment." *Journal of Policy Analysis and Management* 14(2): 245–269.

O'Leary, Christopher J., Robert A. Straits, and Stephen A. Wandner, eds. 2004. *Job Training Policy in the United States*. Kalamazoo, MI: W.E. Upjohn Institute for Employment Research.

O'Leary, Christopher J., and Stephen A. Wandner. 1997. "Summing Up: Achievements, Problems, and Prospects." In *Unemployment Insurance in the United States: Analysis of Policy Issues*, Christopher J. O'Leary and Stephen A. Wandner, eds. Kalamazoo, MI: W.E. Upjohn Institute for Employment Research, pp. 669–722.

———. 2005. "Do Job Search Rules and Reemployment Services Reduce Insured Unemployment?" Upjohn Institute Working Paper 05-112. Kalamazoo, MI: W.E. Upjohn Institute for Employment Research.

Organisation for Economic Co-operation and Development (OECD). 1995. *Self-Employment Programmes for the Unemployed: Papers and Proceedings from a Joint U.S. Department of Labor/OECD International Conference*. Paris: Organisation for Economic Co-operation and Development.

———. 1998. *Early Identification of Jobseekers at Risk of Long-Term Unemployment: The Role of Profiling*. OECD Proceedings. Paris: Organisation for Economic Co-operation and Development.

Orr, Larry L., Howard S. Bloom, Stephen H. Bell, Fred Doolittle, Winston Lin, and George Cave. 1996. *Does Training for the Disadvantaged Work? Evidence from the National JTPA Study*. Washington, DC: Urban Institute Press.

Orr, Larry L., Stephen A. Wandner, David Lah, and Jacob M. Benus. 1994. "The Use of Evaluation Results in Employment and Training Policy: Two Case Studies." Paper presented at the sixteenth annual research conference of the Association for Public Policy Analysis and Management, held in Chicago, October 26–29.

Osborne, David, and Ted Gaebler. 1992. *Reinventing Government: How the Entrepreneurial Spirit Is Transforming the Public Sector*. Reading, MA: Addison-Wesley Publishing.

O'Shea, Daniel, and Christopher T. King. 2001. "The Workforce Investment Act of 1998: Restructuring Workforce Development Initiatives in States and Localities." Rockefeller Report 12. Albany, NY: State University of New York, Nelson A. Rockefeller Institute of Government.

Perez-Johnson, Irma, Sheena McConnell, Paul Decker, Jeanne Bellotti, Jeffrey Salzman, and Jessica Pearlman. 2004. *The Effects of Customer Choice: First Findings from the Individual Training Account Experiment*. Final Interim Report. ETA Occasional Paper 2005-03. Washington, DC: U.S. Department of Labor, Employment and Training Administration.

Plastrik, Peter. 1994. *Reinventing the Federal Unemployment and Training System: Helping Millions of American Workers Secure New Jobs*. PPI Policy Report 19. Washington, DC: Progressive Policy Institute.

Platt, Robert. 1956. "Layoff, Recall, and Work Sharing Procedures." *Monthly Labor Review* 79(12): 1385–1393.

Public Policy Associates (PPA). 1999. *Dislocated Worker Program Report: Findings from the Career Management Account Demonstration.* Washington, DC: U.S. Department of Labor, Employment and Training Administration.

Reed, Gary, and Ray Uhalde. 1994. "Reemployment Act of 1994: Projected Costs and Participation." Unpublished manuscript. U.S. Department of Labor, Washington, DC.

Reich, Robert B. 1992. *The Work of Nations: Preparing Ourselves for 21st Century Capitalism.* New York: Alfred A. Knopf.

———. 1993. "Statement by Secretary Robert Reich." USDL-93-48. News release, February 8. Washington, DC: U.S. Department of Labor, Office of the Secretary.

———. 1996. "Remarks." In *Worker Profiling and Reemployment Services (WPRS) Systems: National WPRS Colloquium, June 1996: Selected Papers and Materials*, David E. Balducchi, ed. Washington, DC: U.S. Department of Labor, Employment and Training Administration, pp. 7–9.

———. 1997. *Locked in the Cabinet.* New York: Alfred A. Knopf.

Reich, Robert B., and John D. Donahue. 1985. *New Deals: The Chrysler Revival and the American System.* New York: Times Books.

Ridley, Neil. 2009. *Work Sharing—An Alternative to Layoffs for Tough Times.* Washington, DC: Center for Law and Social Policy.

Ridley, Neil, and William A. Tracy. 2004. "State and Local Labor Exchange Services." In *Labor Exchange Policy in the United States*, David E. Balducchi, Randall W. Eberts, and Christopher J. O'Leary, eds. Kalamazoo, MI: W.E. Upjohn Institute for Employment Research, pp. 73–99.

Robins, Philip K., and Robert G. Spiegelman, eds. 2001. *Reemployment Bonuses in the Unemployment Insurance System: Evidence from Three Field Experiments.* Kalamazoo, MI: W.E. Upjohn Institute for Employment Research.

Ross, Doug. 1993. "Enterprise Economics on the Front Lines: Empowering Firms and Workers to Win." In *Mandate for Change*, Will Marshall and Martin Schram, eds. New York: Berkley Books, pp. 51–80.

Rudolph, Helmut, and Regina Konle-Seidl. 2005. *Profiling for Better Services: Report on the European Profiling Seminar, Nuremberg, January 12–14, 2005.* Nuremberg, Germany: Institute for Employment Research.

Sass, Steven A., and Alicia H. Munnell. 2006. *Social Security and the Stock Market: How the Pursuit of Market Magic Shapes the System.* Kalamazoo, MI: W.E. Upjohn Institute for Employment Research.

Schirm, Allen, Elizabeth Stuart, and Allison McKie. 2006. *The Quantum Opportunity Program Demonstration: Final Impacts.* ETA Occasional Paper 2007-05. Washington, DC: U.S. Department of Labor, Employment and Training Administration.

Schroeder, Patricia. 1984. Foreword to *Short-Time Compensation: A Formula for Work Sharing*, Ramelle MaCoy and Martin J. Morand, eds. New York: Pergamon Press, pp. ix–xi.

Scott, Douglas. 1992. "Self-Employment Programs for the Unemployed: An Analysis of Program Evaluation and Operations Research in Europe and North America." In *Self Employment Programs for Unemployed Workers*, Stephen A. Wandner, ed. Unemployment Insurance Occasional Paper 92-2. Washington, DC: U.S. Department of Labor, Employment and Training Administration, pp. 237–260.

Shelton, Alison M. 2009. *Compensated Work Sharing Arrangements (Short-Time Compensation) as an Alternative to Layoffs*. Washington, DC: Congressional Budget Office.

Small Business Administration (SBA). 2008. *The Small Business Economy: A Report to the President*. Washington, DC: Small Business Administration, Office of Advocacy.

Smith, Andy. 2008. "State Program Helps Companies Stem Layoffs." *Providence Journal*, May 27. http://www.projo.com/business/content/JO _WORKSHARE_05-25-08_R1A6RV2_v22.1246c0a.html (accessed April 28, 2010).

Smole, David P. 2004. "Labor Exchange Performance Measurement." In *Labor Exchange Policy in the United States*, David E. Balducchi, Randall W. Eberts, and Christopher J. O'Leary, eds. Kalamazoo, MI: W.E. Upjohn Institute for Employment Research, pp. 101–133.

Social Policy Research Associates (SPRA). 2004. *The Workforce Investment Act after Five Years: Results from the National Evaluation of the Implementation of WIA*. ETA Occasional Paper 2004-05. Washington, DC: U.S. Department of Labor, Employment and Training Administration, Office of Policy Development, Evaluation, and Research.

Spiegelman, Robert G., Christopher J. O'Leary, and Kenneth J. Kline. 1992. *The Washington Reemployment Bonus Experiment: Final Report*. Unemployment Insurance Occasional Paper 92-6. Washington, DC: U.S. Department of Labor, Employment and Training Administration.

Spiegelman, Robert G., and Stephen A. Woodbury. 1987. *The Illinois Unemployment Insurance Incentive Experiments*. Final Report to the Illinois Department of Employment Security. Kalamazoo, MI: W.E. Upjohn Institute for Employment Research.

Stack, Treva, and David Stevens. 2006. *Anatomy of a One-Stop: Baltimore City Eastside Career Center*. ETA Occasional Paper 2006-07. Washington, DC: U.S. Department of Labor, Employment and Training Administration.

Staghoj, Jonas, Michael Svarer, and Michael Rosholm. 2007. *A Statistical Pro-

gramme Assignment Model. IZA Discussion Paper 3165. Bonn, Germany: Institute for the Study of Labor.

State of the Union Letter. 2006. "Letter from President Bush to the American People." Washington, DC: White House.

State of the Union Press Release. 2006. "State of the Union: American Competitiveness Initiative." Washington, DC: White House.

Stephanopoulos, George. 1999. *All Too Human: A Political Education.* Boston: Little, Brown and Company.

Steuerle, C. Eugene. 2000. "Common Issues for Voucher Programs." In *Vouchers and the Provision of Public Services,* by C. Eugene Steuerle, Van Doorn Ooms, George Peterson, and Robert D. Reischauer, eds. Washington, DC: Brookings Institution Press, pp. 3–39.

Steuerle, C. Eugene, Van Doorn Ooms, George Peterson, and Robert D. Reischauer, eds. 2000. *Vouchers and the Provision of Public Services.* Washington, DC: Brookings Institution Press.

Stevens, David W. 1974. *Assisted Job Search for the Insured Unemployed.* Kalamazoo, MI: W.E. Upjohn Institute for Employment Research.

Stiglitz, Joseph E., Peter R. Orszag, and Jonathan M. Orszag. 2000. *The Role of Government in a Digital Age.* Washington, DC: Computer and Communications Industry Association.

St. Louis, Robert. 1984. "Arizona, Motorola, and STC." In *Short-Time Compensation: A Formula for Work Sharing,* Ramelle MaCoy and Martin J. Morand, eds. New York: Pergamon Press, pp. 82–94.

Sullivan, William F. Jr., Lester Coffey, Lisa Kolovich, Charles W. McGlew, Douglas Sanford, and Richard Sullivan. 2007. *Worker Profiling and Reemployment Services Evaluation of State Worker Profiling Models: Final Report.* Washington, DC: U.S. Department of Labor, Employment and Training Administration, Office of Workforce Security.

Sweeney, John E. 1995. *New York Self-Employment Program Shows Encouraging Initial Results.* Washington, DC: National Association of State Workforce Agencies.

Technical Assistance and Training Corporation (TATC). 2001. *America's Job Bank: Outcome Study.* Prepared for the U.S. Department of Labor, Employment and Training Administration. Washington, DC: Technical Assistance and Training Corporation.

U.S. Congress. 1992. *Unemployment Compensation Extension: Conference Report.* House of Representatives. H. Report 102–650. Washington, DC: Government Printing Office.

———. 2007. "Revised Continuing Appropriations Resolution, 2007." H.J. Res. 20. 110th Cong., 1st sess., pp. 21–22.

U.S. Department of Labor (USDOL). 1973. *Manpower Report of the President*. Washington, DC: U.S. Department of Labor.

———. 1983. *Model Legislative Language to Implement a Short-Time (Work-Sharing) Compensation Program and Recommended Improvements in State Provision for Partial Unemployment Benefits*. UI Program Letter 39-83, Attachment I. Washington, DC: U.S. Department of Labor.

———. 1985. *Causes and Remedies for Displacement of Steel Workers: An Analysis of the Characteristics of Displaced Steel Workers and of Programs Designed to Assist Their Readjustment, Including a Policy Agenda Developed by the Administration*. A report submitted to Congress pursuant to a request made in the Trade and Tariff Act of 1984. Washington, DC: U.S. Department of Labor.

———. 1990. *Reemployment Services to Unemployed Workers Having Difficulty Becoming Reemployed*. UI Occasional Paper 90-2. Washington, DC: U.S. Department of Labor, Employment and Training Administration.

———. 1993. "Idea Packs a Punch: ETA Employees Plant Seed That Sprouts into Law." *Labor Exchange: The Employee Newsletter of the U.S. Department of Labor* 1993(May): 1–2.

———. 1994a. *The Workforce Security Act of 1994: A Consultation Paper*. Washington, DC: U.S. Department of Labor.

———. 1994b. *The Worker Profiling and Reemployment Services System: Legislation, Implementation Process, and Research Findings*. Unemployment Insurance Occasional Paper 94-4. Washington, DC: U.S. Department of Labor, Employment and Training Administration.

———. 1995a. "The Department of Labor's Position on Issues and Concerns Associated with the Utilization of Telephone and Other Electronic Methods in the Unemployment Insurance (UI) Program." Unemployment Insurance Program Letter 35-95. Washington, DC: U.S. Department of Labor, Employment and Training Administration.

———. 1995b. *What's Working (and what's not): A Summary of Research on the Economic Impacts of Employment and Training Programs*. Washington, DC: U.S. Department of Labor, Office of the Chief Economist.

———. 1995c. Fact Sheet: *The One-Stop Career Center System*. Washington, DC: U.S. Department of Labor, Employment and Training Administration. http://www.doleta.gov/programs/factsht/one-stop.htm (accessed December 8, 2009).

———. 1996. *U.S. Employment Service Annual Report: PY 1995 Program Report Data*. Washington, DC: U.S. Department of Labor, Employment and Training Administration.

———. 1998. *Permanent Authorization of the Self-Employment Assistance Program*. Unemployment Insurance Program Letter 11-99. Washington,

DC: U.S. Department of Labor, Employment and Training Administration.

———. 2001. *Annual Report for Wagner-Peyser Act Funded Activities, Program Year 2001.* Washington, DC: U.S. Department of Labor, Employment and Training Administration.

———. 2004. "U.S. Secretary of Labor Elaine L. Chao Announces Seven States Selected to Participate in a Test of Personal Reemployment Accounts." News release, October 29. Washington, DC: U.S. Department of Labor, Employment and Training Administration.

———. 2007. *2007 Performance and Accountability Report.* Washington, DC: U.S. Department of Labor.

———. 2008a. *UI Outlook: FY 2009 President's Budget.* Washington, DC: U.S. Department of Labor, Employment and Training Administration, Office of Workforce Security. http://www.ows.doleta.gov/unemploy/content/fy2009/home.asp#content (accessed May 27, 2010).

———. 2008b. *Comparison of State Unemployment Insurance Laws.* Washington, DC: U.S. Department of Labor, Bureau of Employment Security, Unemployment Insurance Service.

U.S. House of Representatives. 2005. "Making Appropriations for the Departments of Labor, Health and Human Services, and Education, and Related Agencies for the Fiscal Year Ending September 30, 2006, and for Other Purposes." Conference Report 109-337. U.S. Congress. House. Committee on Conference. 109th Cong., 1st sess.

Vroman, Wayne. 1991. *The Decline in Unemployment Insurance Claims Activity in the 1980s.* UI Occasional Paper 91-2. Washington, DC: U.S. Department of Labor, Employment and Training Administration.

———. 1992. "Short-Time Compensation in the U.S., Germany, and Belgium." Urban Institute working paper. Washington, DC: Urban Institute.

———. 1997. *Self Employment Assistance: Revised Report.* Report to Congress. Washington, DC: U.S. Department of Labor, Employment and Training Administration, Unemployment Insurance Service.

———. 2008. *Unemployment Insurance Benefits: 2005 CPS Supplement Results.* Columbia, MD: IMPAQ International.

Vroman, Wayne, and Stephen Woodbury. 2004. *Trend and Cycle Analysis of Unemployment Insurance and the Employment Service.* ETA Occasional Paper 2005-04. Washington, DC: U.S. Department of Labor, Employment and Training Administration.

Walsh, Stephen, Rebecca London, Deana McCanne, Karen Needels, Walter Nicholson, and Stuart Kerachsky. 1997. *Evaluation of Short-Time Compensation Programs: Final Report.* UI Occasional Paper 97-3. Washington, DC: U.S. Department of Labor, Employment and Training Administration.

Wandner, Stephen A., ed. 1994a. *Self-Employment as a Reemployment Option:*

Demonstration Results and National Legislation. Unemployment Insurance Occasional Paper 94-3. Washington, DC: U.S. Department of Labor, Employment and Training Administration, Unemployment Insurance Service.

———, ed. 1994b. *The Worker Profiling and Reemployment Services System: Legislation, Implementation Process, and Research Findings.* UI Occasional Paper 94-4. Washington, DC: U.S. Department of Labor, Employment and Training Administration.

———. 2002. "Targeting Employment Services under the Workforce Investment Act." In *Targeting Employment Services,* Randall W. Eberts, Christopher J. O'Leary, and Stephen A. Wandner, eds. Kalamazoo, MI: W.E. Upjohn Institute for Employment Research, pp. 1–25.

———. 2008. "Employment Programs for Recipients of Unemployment Insurance." *Monthly Labor Review* 131(10): 17–27.

Wandner, Stephen A., and Jon C. Messenger. 1992. "From Unemployed to Self-Employed: Self-Employment as a Reemployment Option in the United States." In *Self Employment Programs for Unemployed Workers,* Stephen A. Wandner, ed. Unemployment Insurance Occasional Paper 92-2. Washington, DC: U.S. Department of Labor, Employment and Training Administration, pp. 1–39.

———, eds. 1999. *Worker Profiling and Reemployment Services Policy Workgroup: Final Report and Recommendations.* Washington, DC: U.S. Department of Labor, Employment and Training Administration.

Wandner, Stephen A., and Thomas Stengle. 1997. "Unemployment Insurance: Measuring Who Receives It." *Monthly Labor Review* 120(7): 15–24.

Wandner, Stephen A., and Andrew Stettner. 2000. "Why Are Many Jobless Workers Not Applying for Benefits?" *Monthly Labor Review* 123(6): 21–32.

Wiessner, Frank. 2008. *A Brief Overview of Start-Up Schemes for the Unemployed: The German Case.* Nuremberg, Germany: Institute for Employment Research.

Woodbury, Stephen A., and Robert G. Spiegelman. 1987. "Bonuses to Workers and Employers to Reduce Unemployment: Randomized Trials in Illinois." *American Economic Review* 77(4): 513–530.

Woods, Jim, and Pam Frugoli. 2004. "Information, Tools, and Technology: Informing Labor Exchange Participants." In *Labor Exchange Policy in the United States,* David E. Balducchi, Randall W. Eberts, and Christopher J. O'Leary, eds. Kalamazoo, MI: W.E. Upjohn Institute for Employment Research, pp. 179–210.

The Author

Stephen A. Wandner is a Visiting Fellow at the Urban Institute. Until recently he directed strategic planning for the Employment and Training Administration of the U.S. Department of Labor in Washington, D.C. Previously he was the director of research for the ETA, and before that he held the same position with the Unemployment Insurance Service—in both cases conducting and directing research on a wide variety of labor issues. In that capacity, he conducted eight Unemployment Insurance Experiments as well as three other experiments, all dealing with dislocated workers.

Wandner is the author of many articles and an editor of three previous books for the Upjohn Institute: *Unemployment Insurance in the United States: Analysis of Policy Issues* (1997), which he coedited with Christopher J. O'Leary; *Targeting Employment Services* (2002), coedited with Randall W. Eberts and O'Leary; and *Job Training Policy in the United States* (2004), coedited with O'Leary and Robert A. Straits. He received his PhD in economics from Indiana University.

Index

The italic letters *n* and *t* following a page number indicate that the subject information of the heading is within a note or table, respectively, on that page. Double italics indicate multiple but consecutive elements.

About the Institute

The W.E. Upjohn Institute for Employment Research is a nonprofit research organization devoted to finding and promoting solutions to employment-related problems at the national, state, and local levels. It is an activity of the W.E. Upjohn Unemployment Trustee Corporation, which was established in 1932 to administer a fund set aside by Dr. W.E. Upjohn, founder of The Upjohn Company, to seek ways to counteract the loss of employment income during economic downturns.

The Institute is funded largely by income from the W.E. Upjohn Unemployment Trust, supplemented by outside grants, contracts, and sales of publications. Activities of the Institute comprise the following elements: 1) a research program conducted by a resident staff of professional social scientists; 2) a competitive grant program, which expands and complements the internal research program by providing financial support to researchers outside the Institute; 3) a publications program, which provides the major vehicle for disseminating the research of staff and grantees, as well as other selected works in the field; and 4) an Employment Management Services division, which manages most of the publicly funded employment and training programs in the local area.

The broad objectives of the Institute's research, grant, and publication programs are to 1) promote scholarship and experimentation on issues of public and private employment and unemployment policy, and 2) make knowledge and scholarship relevant and useful to policymakers in their pursuit of solutions to employment and unemployment problems.

Current areas of concentration for these programs include causes, consequences, and measures to alleviate unemployment; social insurance and income maintenance programs; compensation; workforce quality; work arrangements; family labor issues; labor-management relations; and regional economic development and local labor markets.